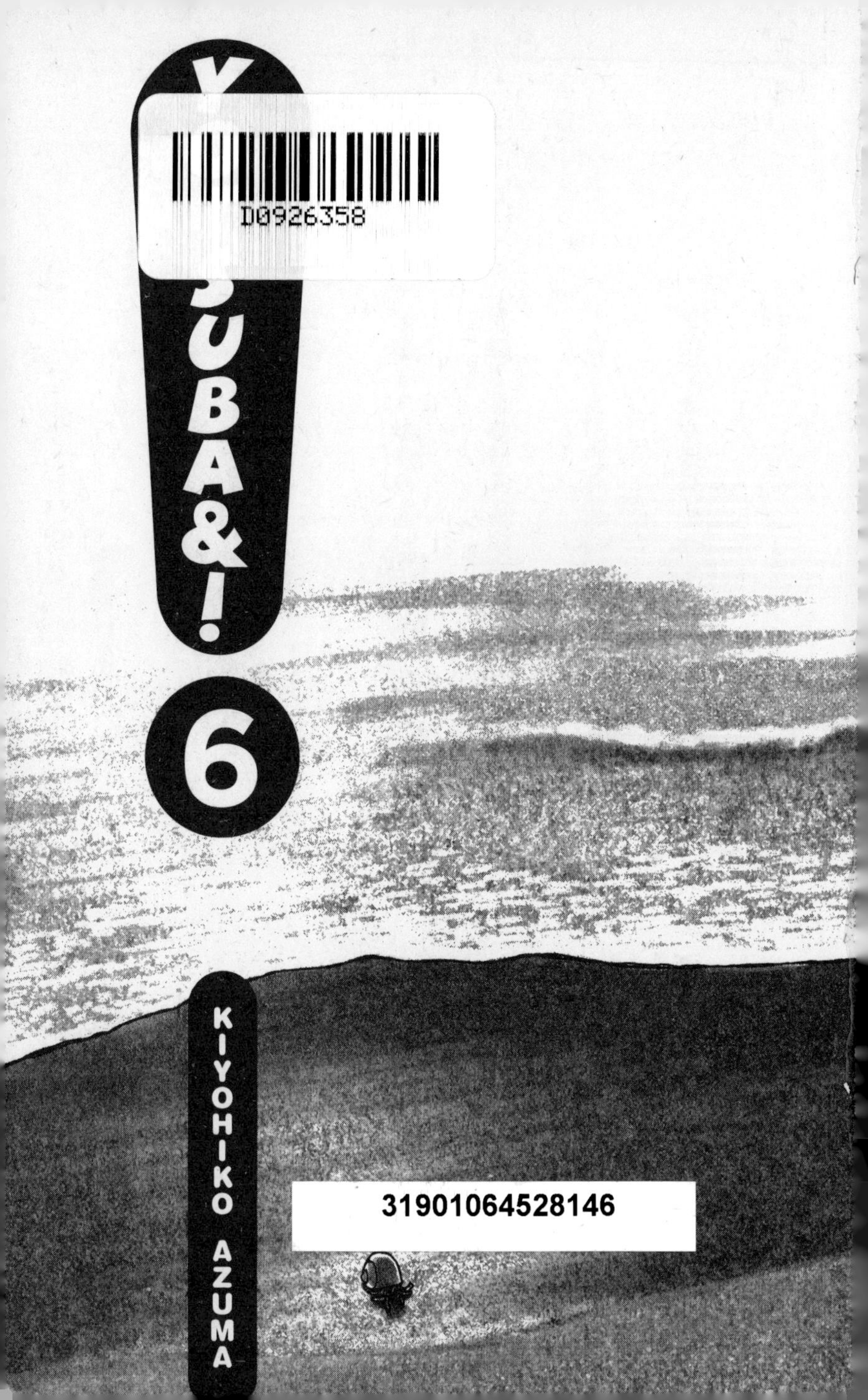
Y
SUBA&!
6
KIYOHIKO AZUMA

CONTENTS

YOTSUBA&!
KIYOHIKO AZUMA

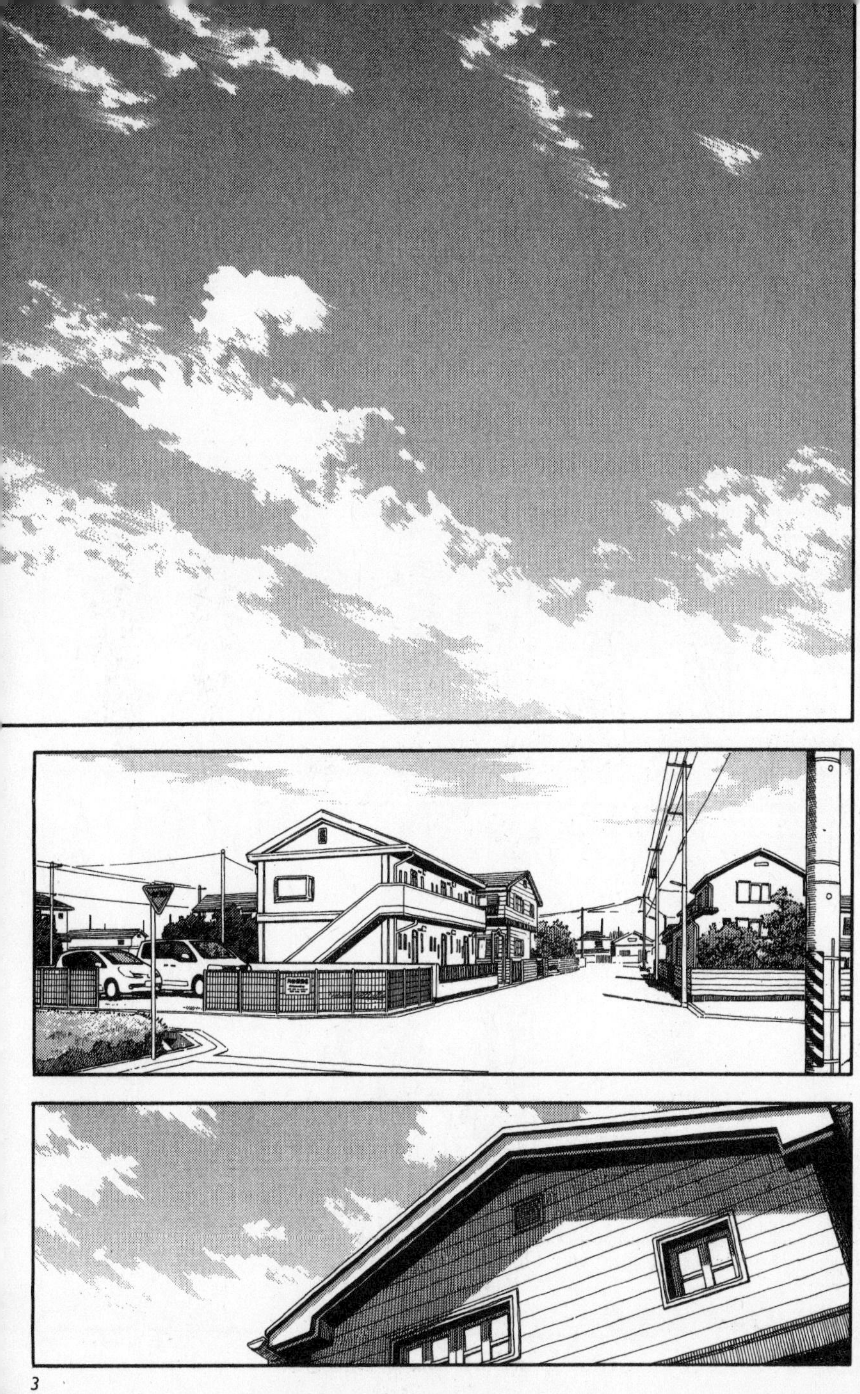

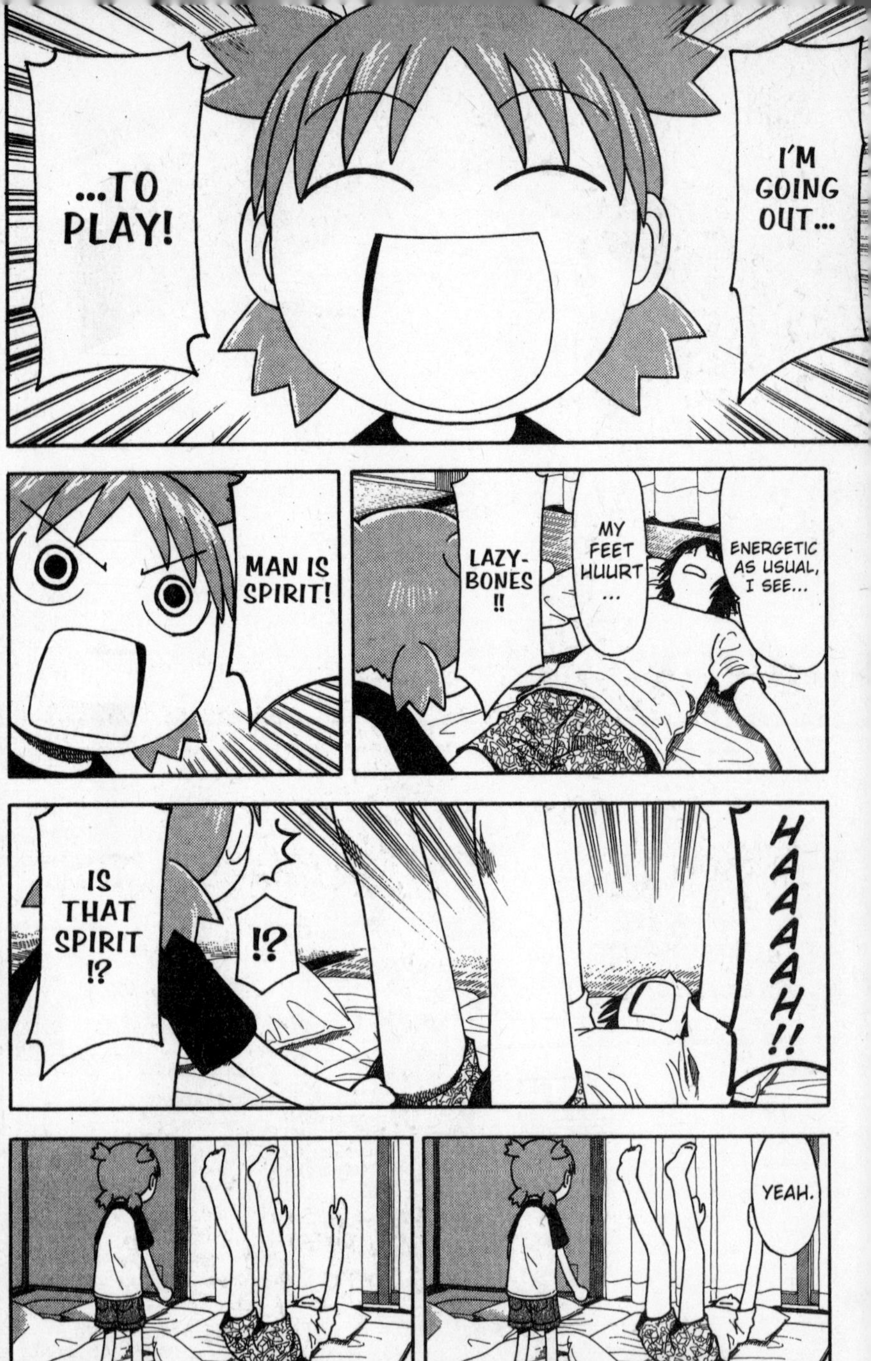
I'M GOING OUT...
...TO PLAY!
ENERGETIC AS USUAL, I SEE...
MY FEET HUURT ...
LAZY-BONES !!
MAN IS SPIRIT!
HAAAAAH!!
!?
IS THAT SPIRIT !?
YEAH.

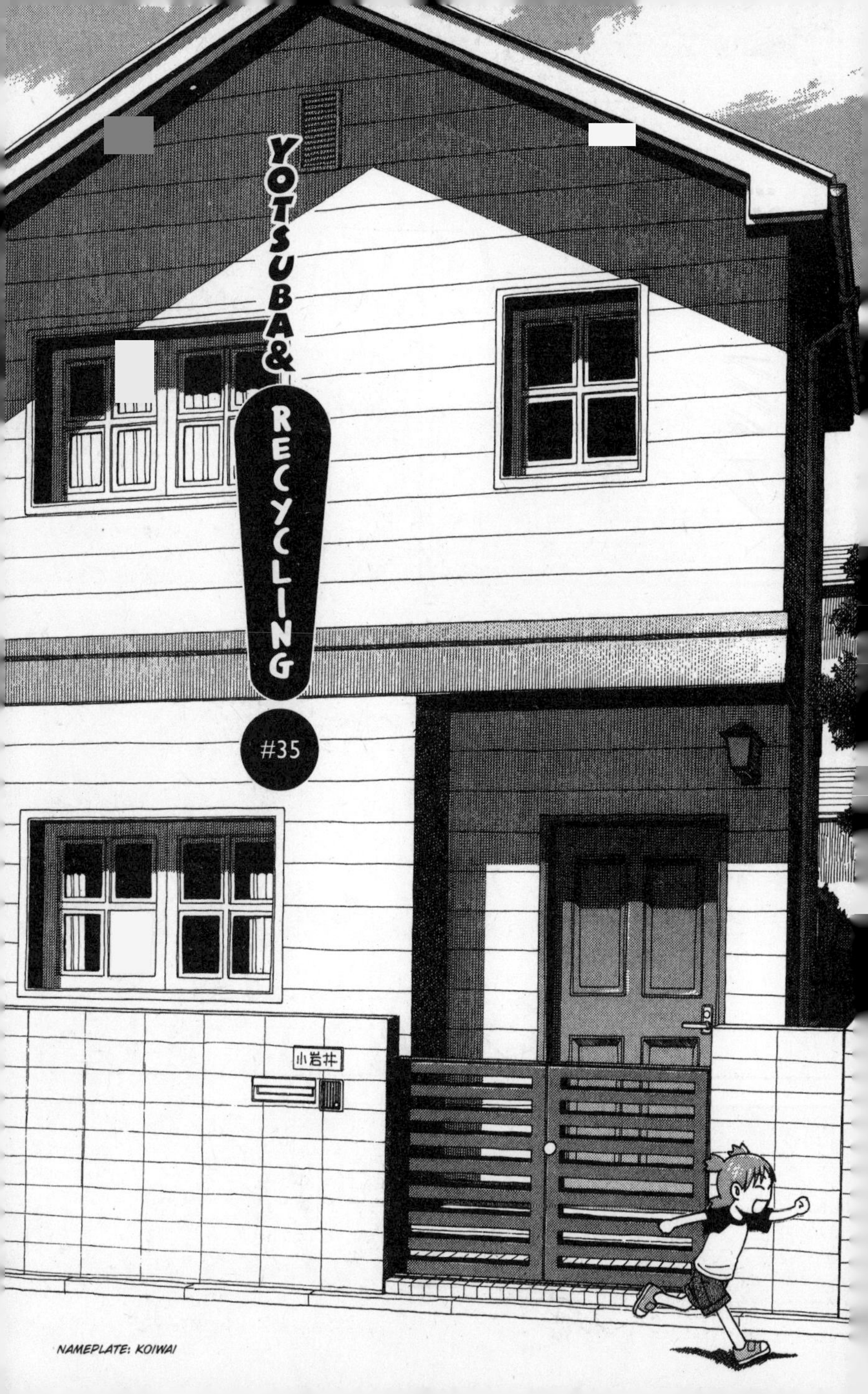
YOTSUBA&
RECYCLING
#35
小岩井
NAMEPLATE: KOIWAI

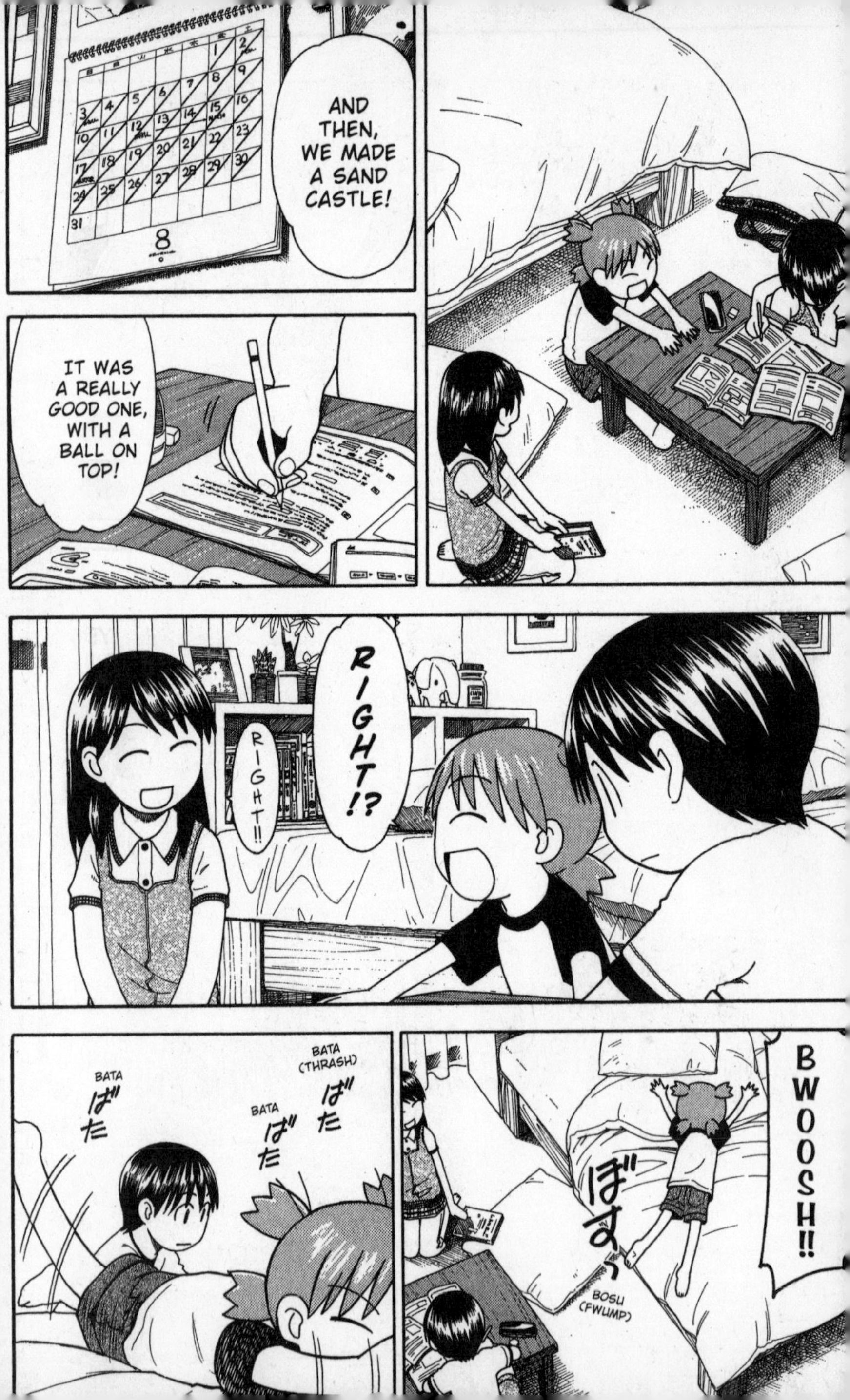
AND THEN, WE MADE A SAND CASTLE!
IT WAS A REALLY GOOD ONE, WITH A BALL ON TOP!
RIGHT!?
RIGHT!!
BWOOSH!!
ぼすっ
BOSU (FWUMP)
BATA (THRASH)
ばた
BATA
ばた
BATA
ばた

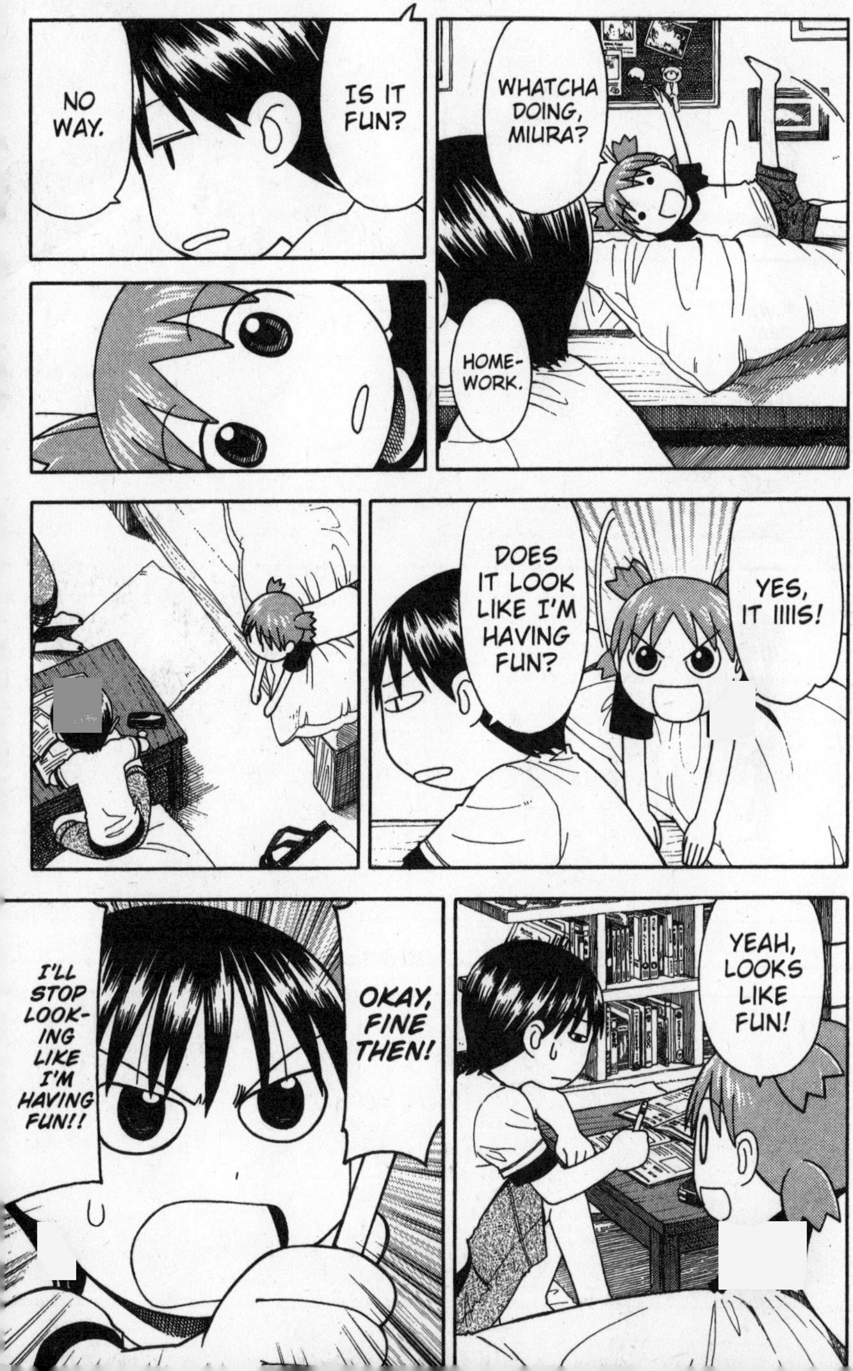
WHATCHA DOING, MIURA?
HOME-WORK.
IS IT FUN?
NO WAY.
DOES IT LOOK LIKE I'M HAVING FUN?
YES, IT IIIIS!
YEAH, LOOKS LIKE FUN!
OKAY, FINE THEN!
I'LL STOP LOOKING LIKE I'M HAVING FUN!!

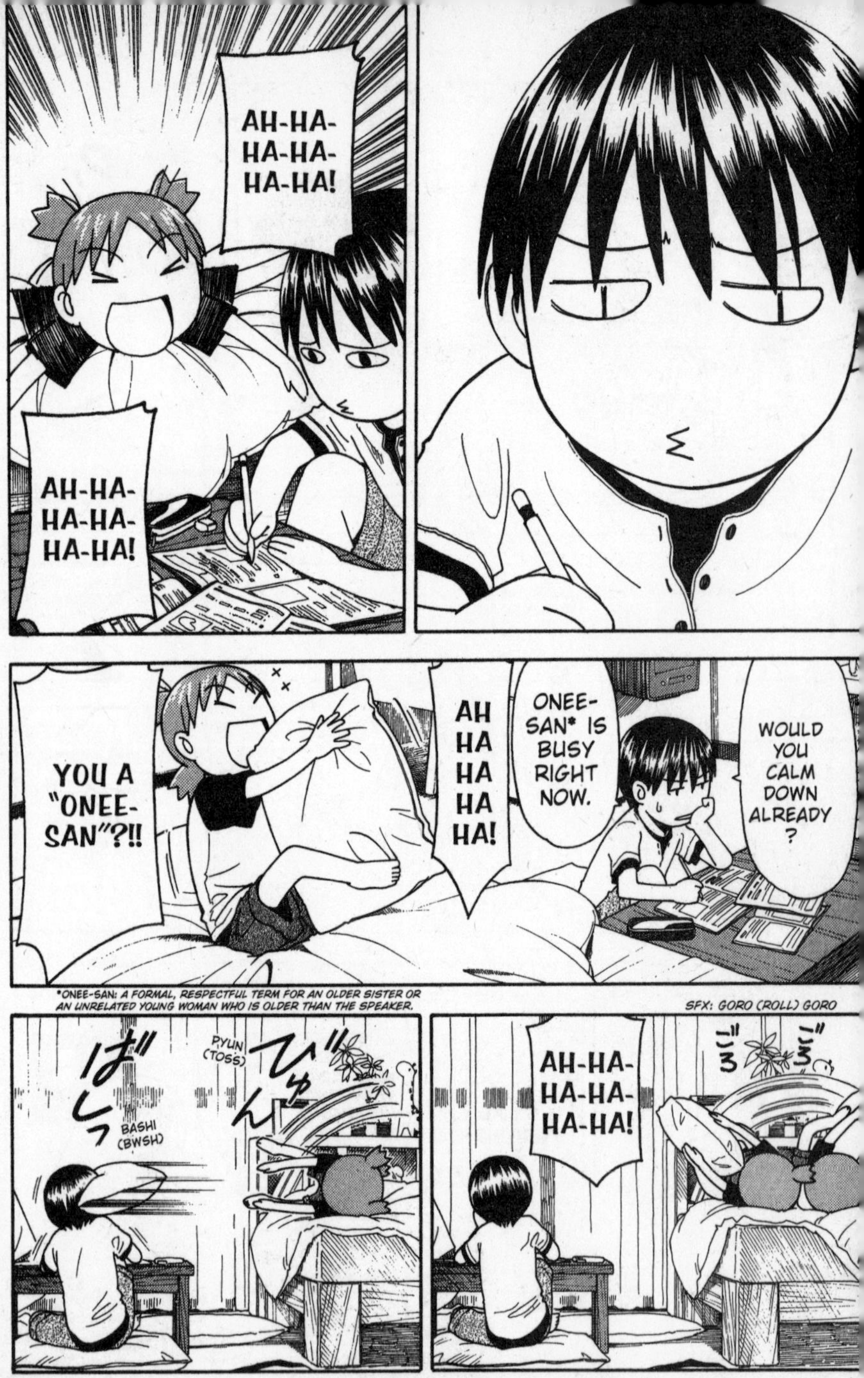
AH-HA-HA-HA-HA-HA!
AH-HA-HA-HA-HA-HA!
WOULD YOU CALM DOWN ALREADY?
ONEE-SAN* IS BUSY RIGHT NOW.
AH HA HA HA HA!
YOU A "ONEE-SAN"?!!
*ONEE-SAN: A FORMAL, RESPECTFUL TERM FOR AN OLDER SISTER OR AN UNRELATED YOUNG WOMAN WHO IS OLDER THAN THE SPEAKER.
SFX: GORO (ROLL) GORO
ごろ ごろ
AH-HA-HA-HA-HA-HA!
ひゅん
PYUN (TOSS)
ばしっ
BASHI (BWSH)

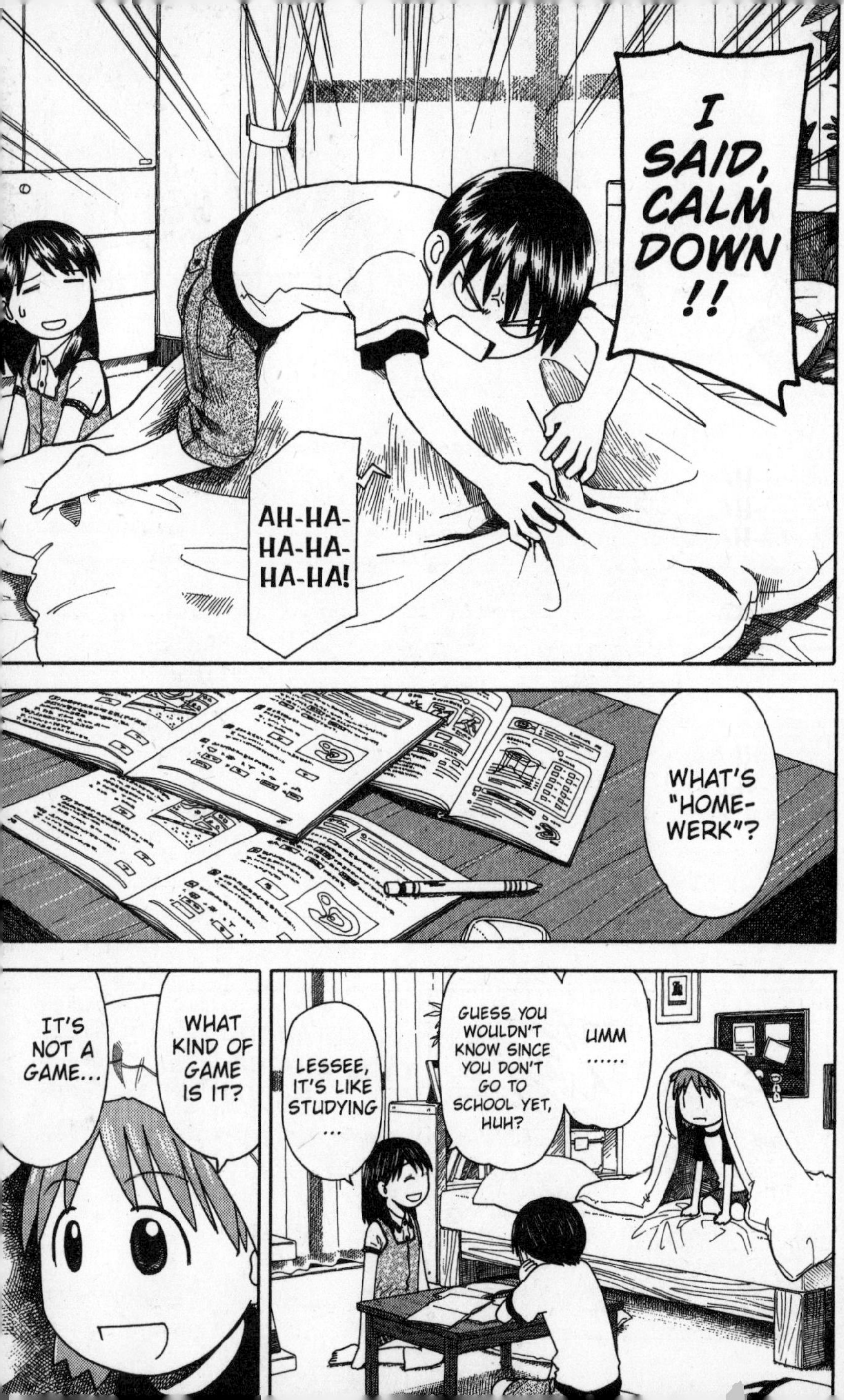
I SAID, CALM DOWN!!
AH-HA-HA-HA-HA-HA!
WHAT'S "HOME-WERK"?
UMM ......
GUESS YOU WOULDN'T KNOW SINCE YOU DON'T GO TO SCHOOL YET, HUH?
LESSEE, IT'S LIKE STUDYING ...
WHAT KIND OF GAME IS IT?
IT'S NOT A GAME...

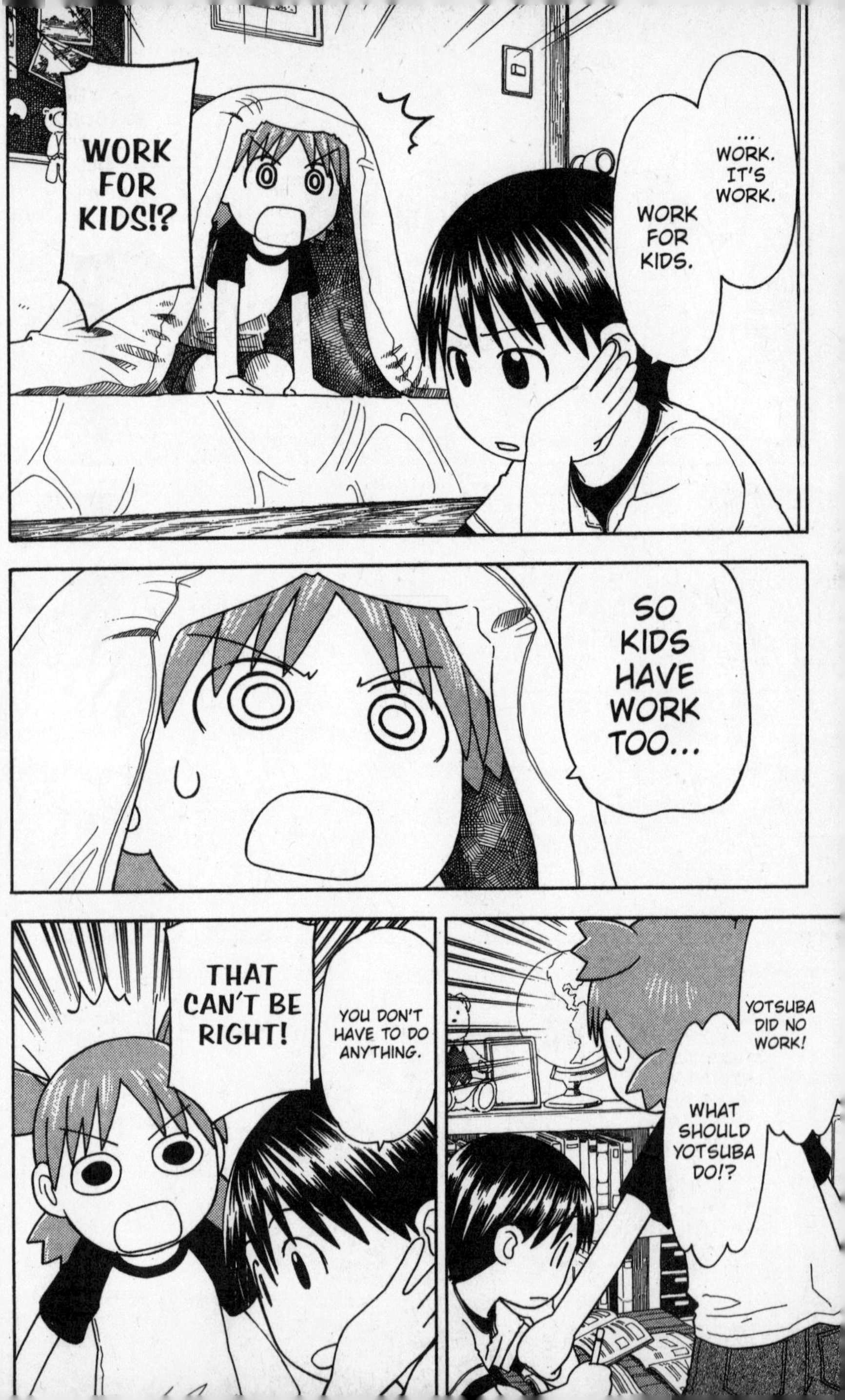
... WORK. IT'S WORK.
WORK FOR KIDS.
WORK FOR KIDS!?
SO KIDS HAVE WORK TOO...
YOTSUBA DID NO WORK!
WHAT SHOULD YOTSUBA DO!?
YOU DON'T HAVE TO DO ANYTHING.
THAT CAN'T BE RIGHT!

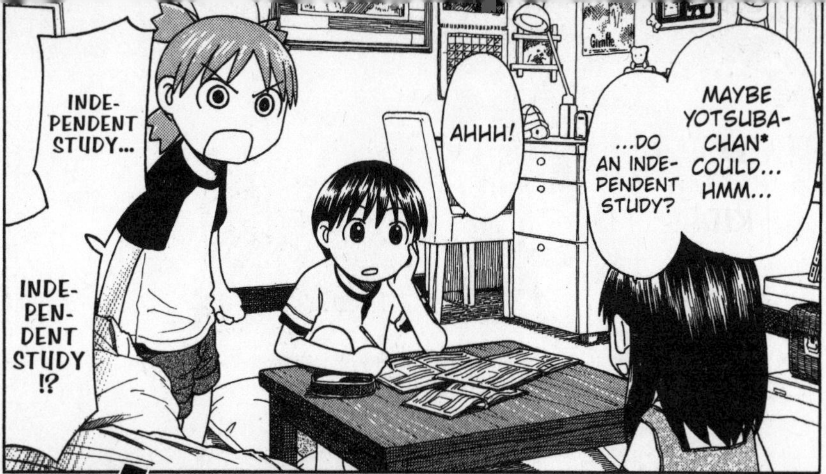
MAYBE YOTSUBA-CHAN* COULD... HMM...
...DO AN INDE-PENDENT STUDY?
AHHH!
INDE-PENDENT STUDY...
INDE-PEN-DENT STUDY !?

*-CHAN: AN INFORMAL HONORIFIC SUFFIX USED WHEN REFERRING TO CHILDREN AND YOUNG GIRLS THAT EXPRESSES FAMILIARITY.

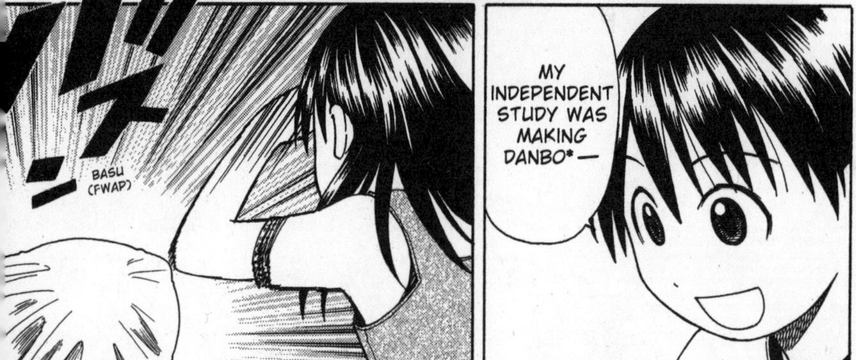
MY INDEPENDENT STUDY WAS MAKING DANBO*—
BASU (FWAP)

*DANBO: THE NAME OF MIURA'S CARDBOARD ROBOT IS FROM AN ABBREVIATION OF THE JAPANESE WORD FOR "CORRUGATED CARDBOARD." READ VOLUME 5, CHAPTER 28 TO FIND OUT MORE!

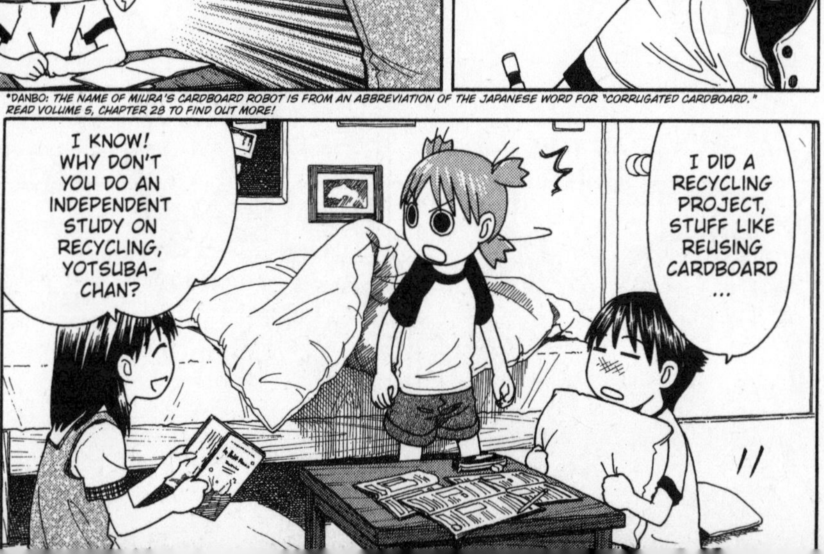
I DID A RECYCLING PROJECT, STUFF LIKE REUSING CARDBOARD ...
I KNOW! WHY DON'T YOU DO AN INDEPENDENT STUDY ON RECYCLING, YOTSUBA-CHAN?

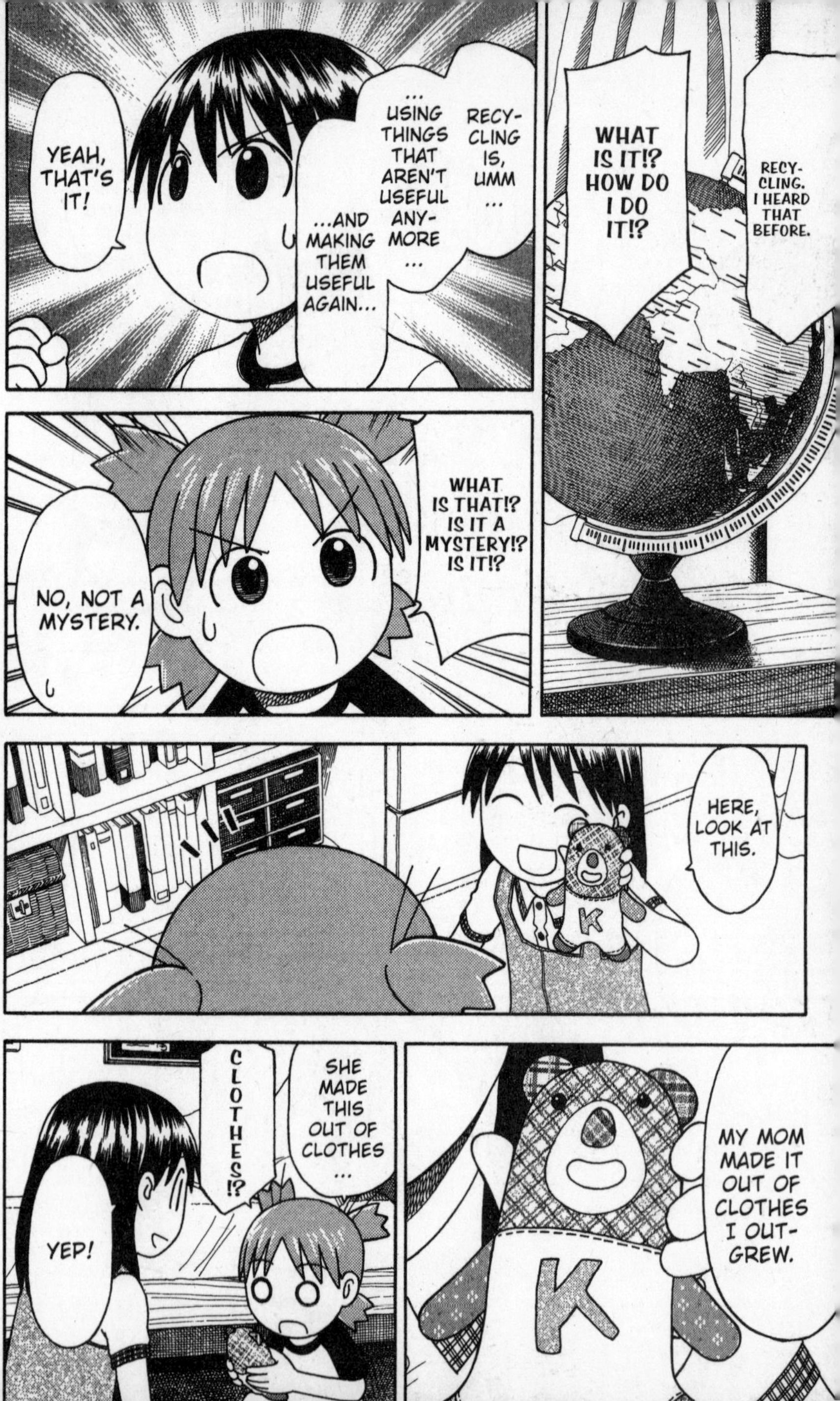
RECY-CLING. I HEARD THAT BEFORE.
WHAT IS IT!? HOW DO I DO IT!?
RECY-CLING IS, UMM ...
... USING THINGS THAT AREN'T USEFUL ANY-MORE ...
...AND MAKING THEM USEFUL AGAIN...
YEAH, THAT'S IT!
WHAT IS THAT!? IS IT A MYSTERY!? IS IT!?
NO, NOT A MYSTERY.
HERE, LOOK AT THIS.
MY MOM MADE IT OUT OF CLOTHES I OUT-GREW.
SHE MADE THIS OUT OF CLOTHES ...
CLOTHES!?
YEP!

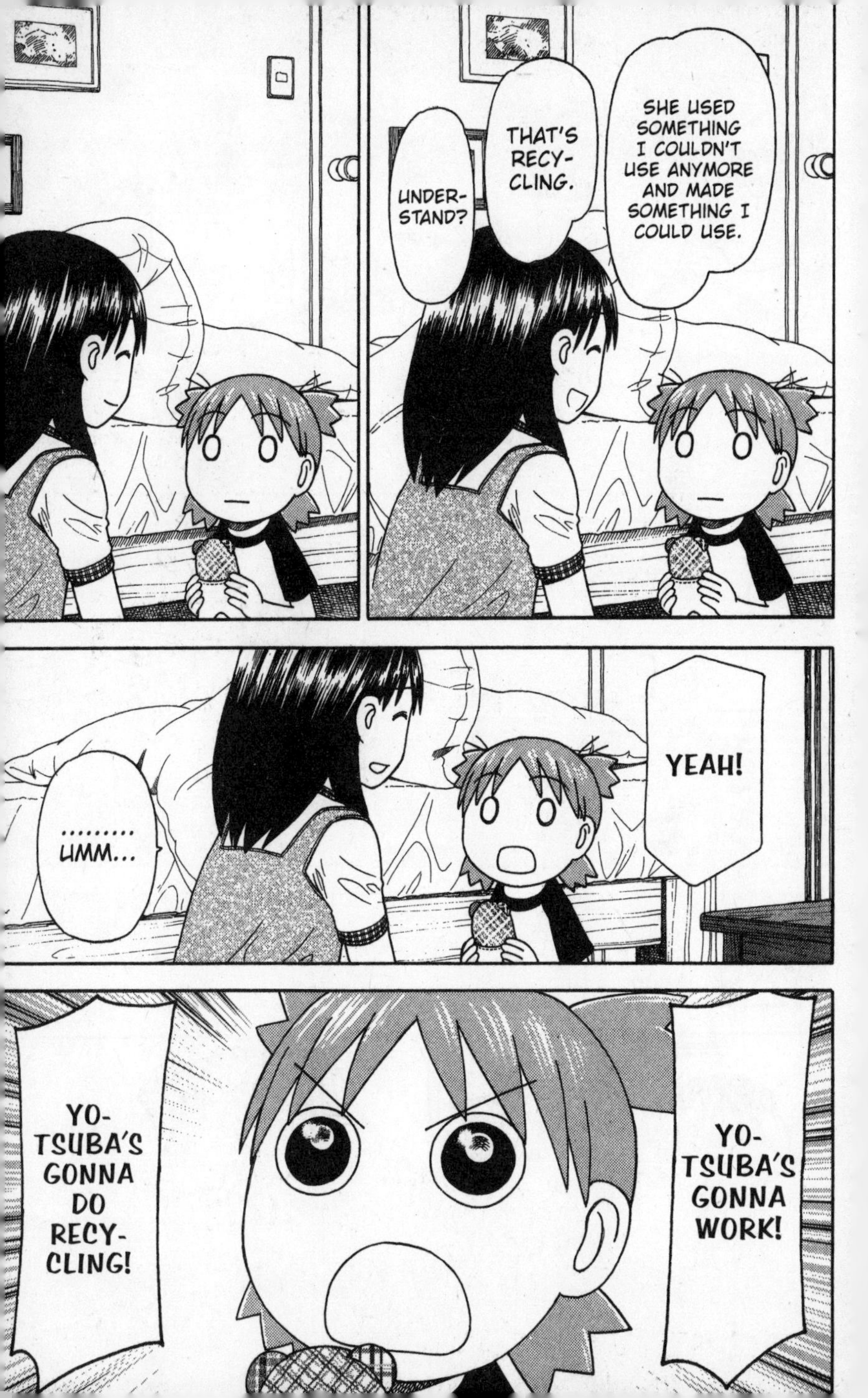
SHE USED SOMETHING I COULDN'T USE ANYMORE AND MADE SOMETHING I COULD USE.
THAT'S RECY-CLING.
UNDER-STAND?
YEAH!
.... UMM...
YO-TSUBA'S GONNA WORK!
YO-TSUBA'S GONNA DO RECY-CLING!

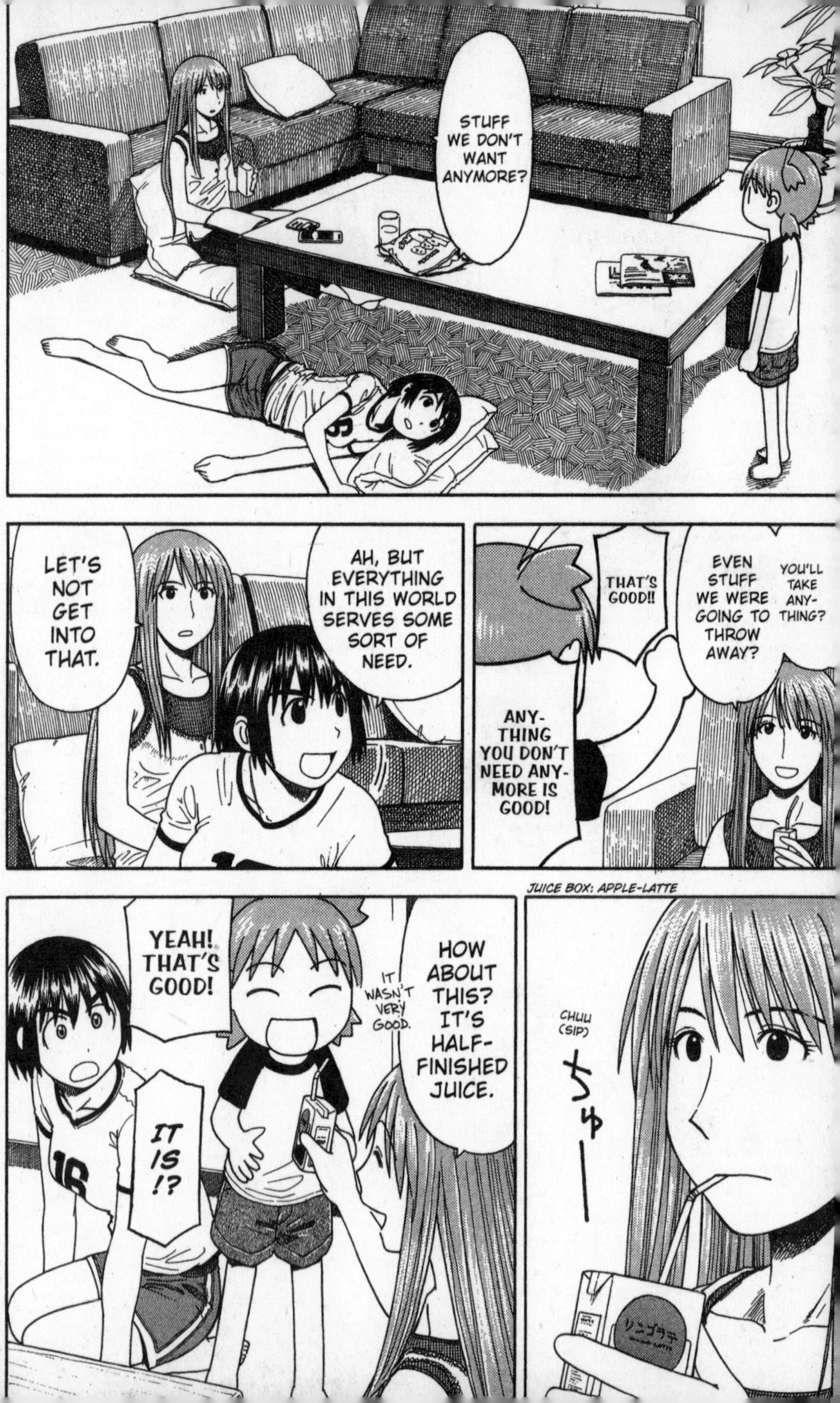
STUFF WE DON'T WANT ANYMORE?
YOU'LL TAKE ANY-THING?
EVEN STUFF WE WERE GOING TO THROW AWAY?
THAT'S GOOD!!
ANY-THING YOU DON'T NEED ANY-MORE IS GOOD!
AH, BUT EVERYTHING IN THIS WORLD SERVES SOME SORT OF NEED.
LET'S NOT GET INTO THAT.
JUICE BOX: APPLE-LATTE
CHUU (SIP)
ちゅー
HOW ABOUT THIS? IT'S HALF-FINISHED JUICE.
IT WASN'T VERY GOOD.
YEAH! THAT'S GOOD!
IT IS!?

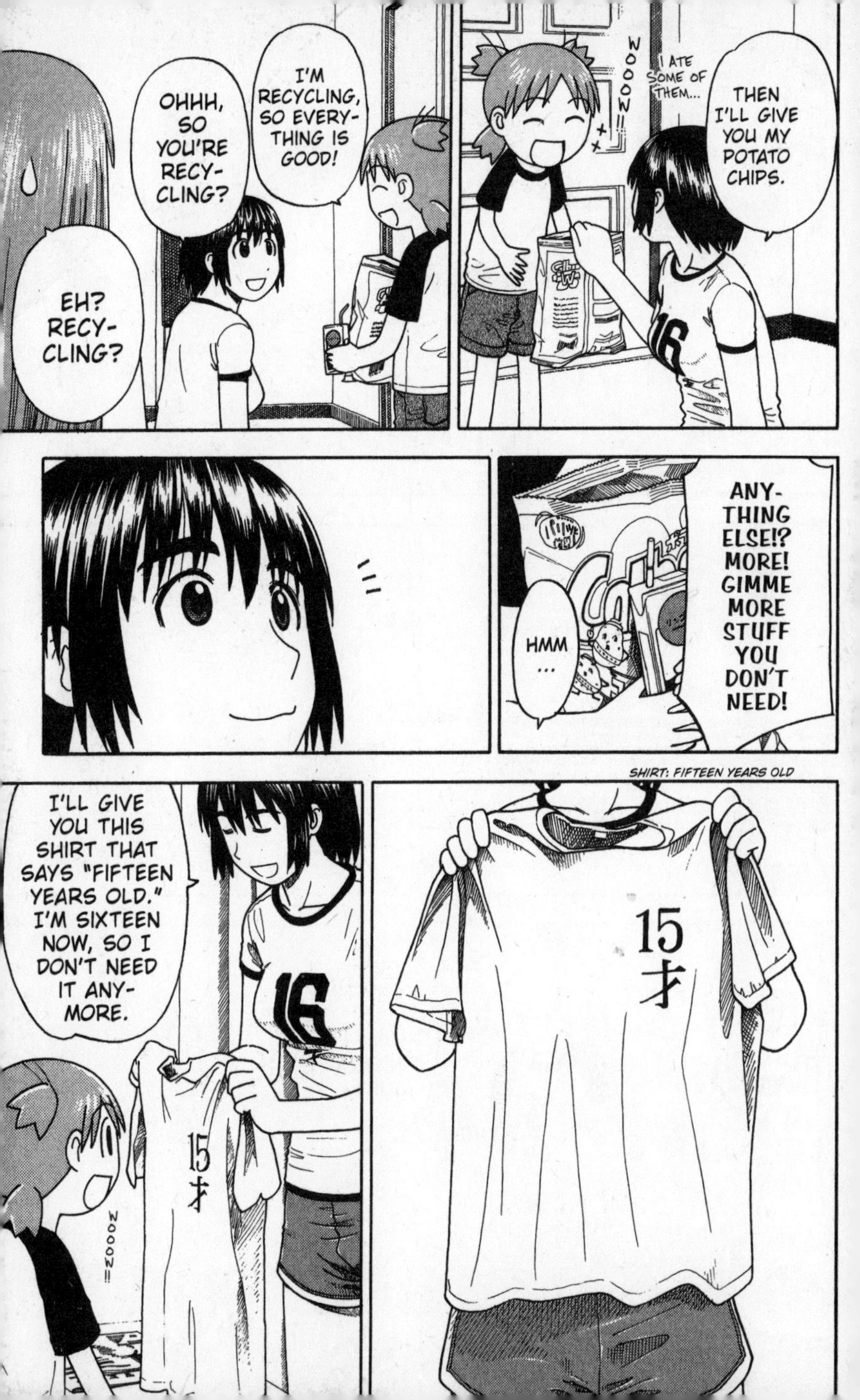
THEN I'LL GIVE YOU MY POTATO CHIPS.
I ATE SOME OF THEM...
WOOOW!!
I'M RECYCLING, SO EVERY-THING IS GOOD!
OHHH, SO YOU'RE RECY-CLING?
EH? RECY-CLING?
ANY-THING ELSE!? MORE! GIMME MORE STUFF YOU DON'T NEED!
HMM ...
SHIRT: FIFTEEN YEARS OLD
I'LL GIVE YOU THIS SHIRT THAT SAYS "FIFTEEN YEARS OLD." I'M SIXTEEN NOW, SO I DON'T NEED IT ANY-MORE.
WOOOOW!!

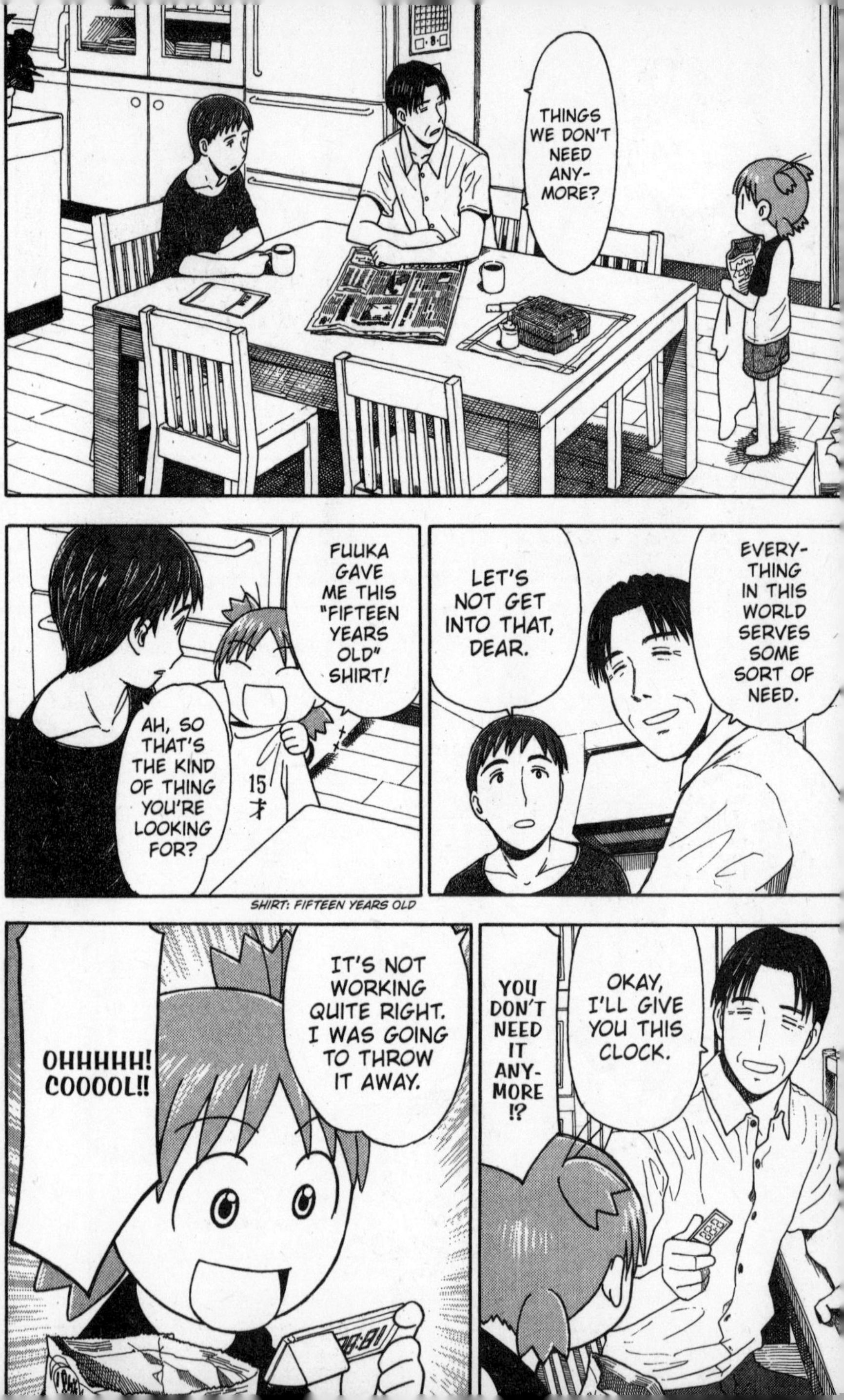
THINGS WE DON'T NEED ANYMORE?
EVERYTHING IN THIS WORLD SERVES SOME SORT OF NEED.
LET'S NOT GET INTO THAT, DEAR.
FUUKA GAVE ME THIS "FIFTEEN YEARS OLD" SHIRT!
AH, SO THAT'S THE KIND OF THING YOU'RE LOOKING FOR?
15才
SHIRT: FIFTEEN YEARS OLD
OKAY, I'LL GIVE YOU THIS CLOCK.
YOU DON'T NEED IT ANYMORE!?
IT'S NOT WORKING QUITE RIGHT. I WAS GOING TO THROW IT AWAY.
OHHHHH! COOOOL!!

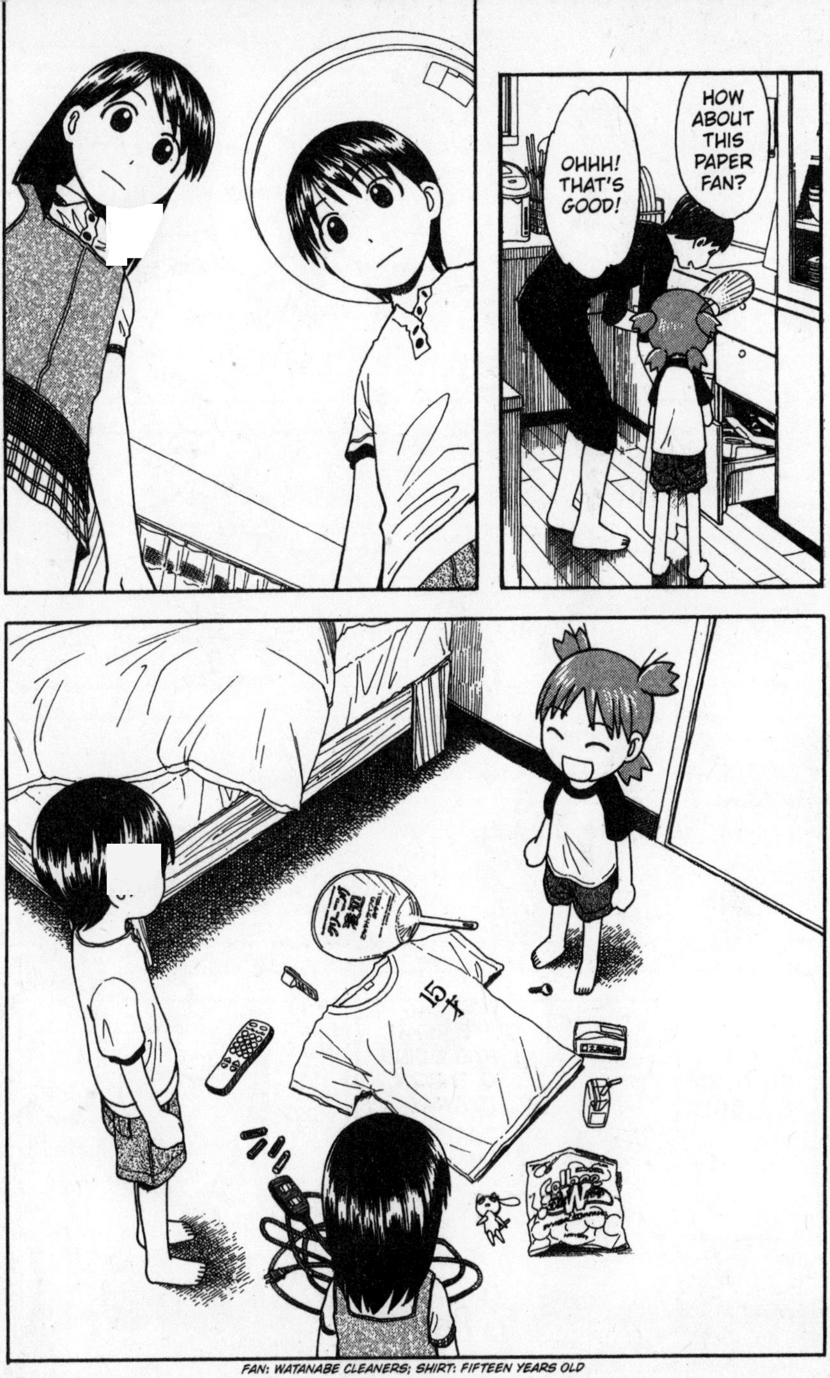
HOW ABOUT THIS PAPER FAN?
OHHH! THAT'S GOOD!

FAN: WATANABE CLEANERS; SHIRT: FIFTEEN YEARS OLD

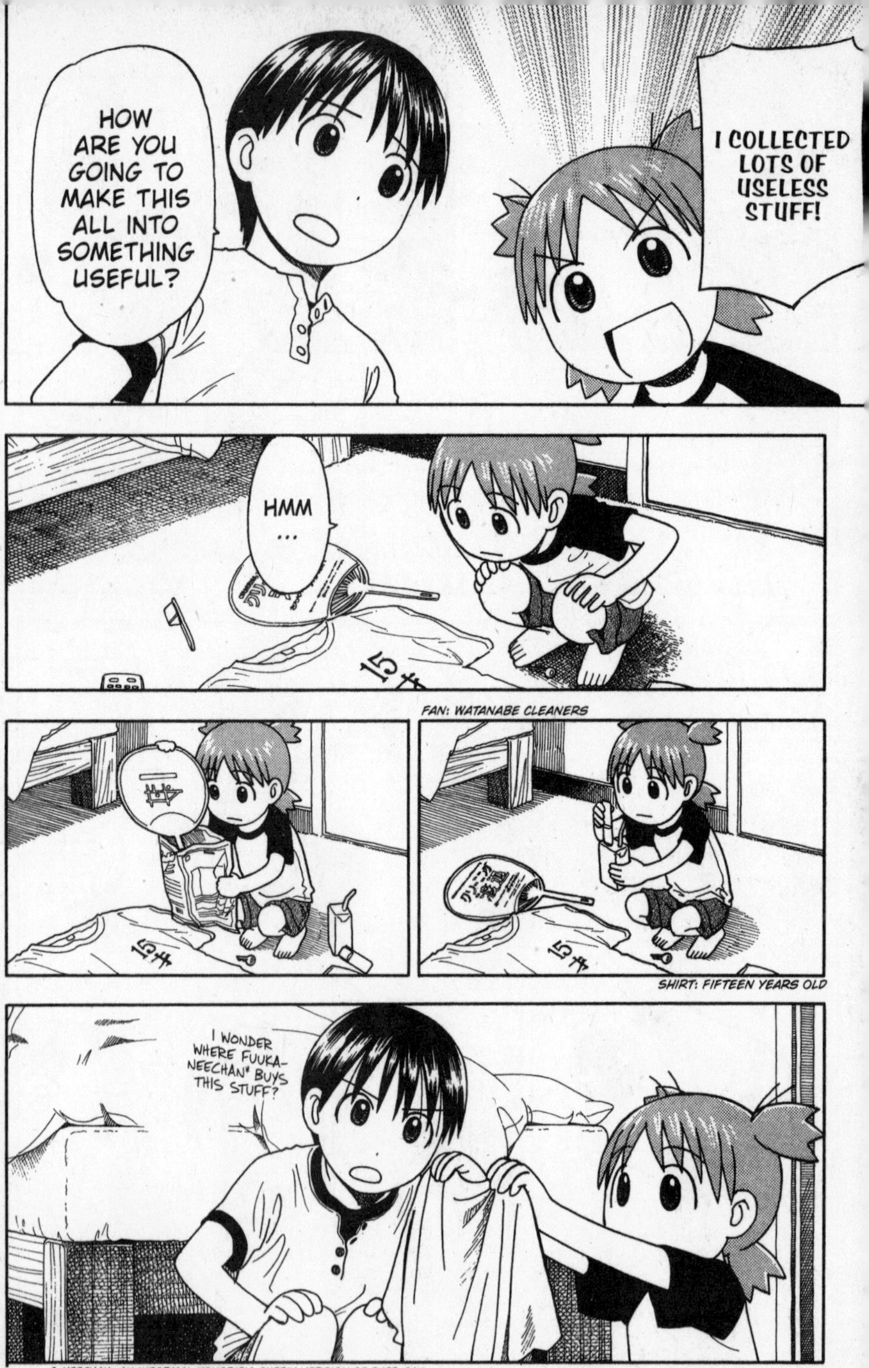
I COLLECTED LOTS OF USELESS STUFF!
HOW ARE YOU GOING TO MAKE THIS ALL INTO SOMETHING USEFUL?
HMM ...
FAN: WATANABE CLEANERS
SHIRT: FIFTEEN YEARS OLD
I WONDER WHERE FUUKA-NEECHAN* BUYS THIS STUFF?

*-NEECHAN: *AN INFORMAL HONORIFIC SUFFIX VERSION OF ONEE-SAN.*

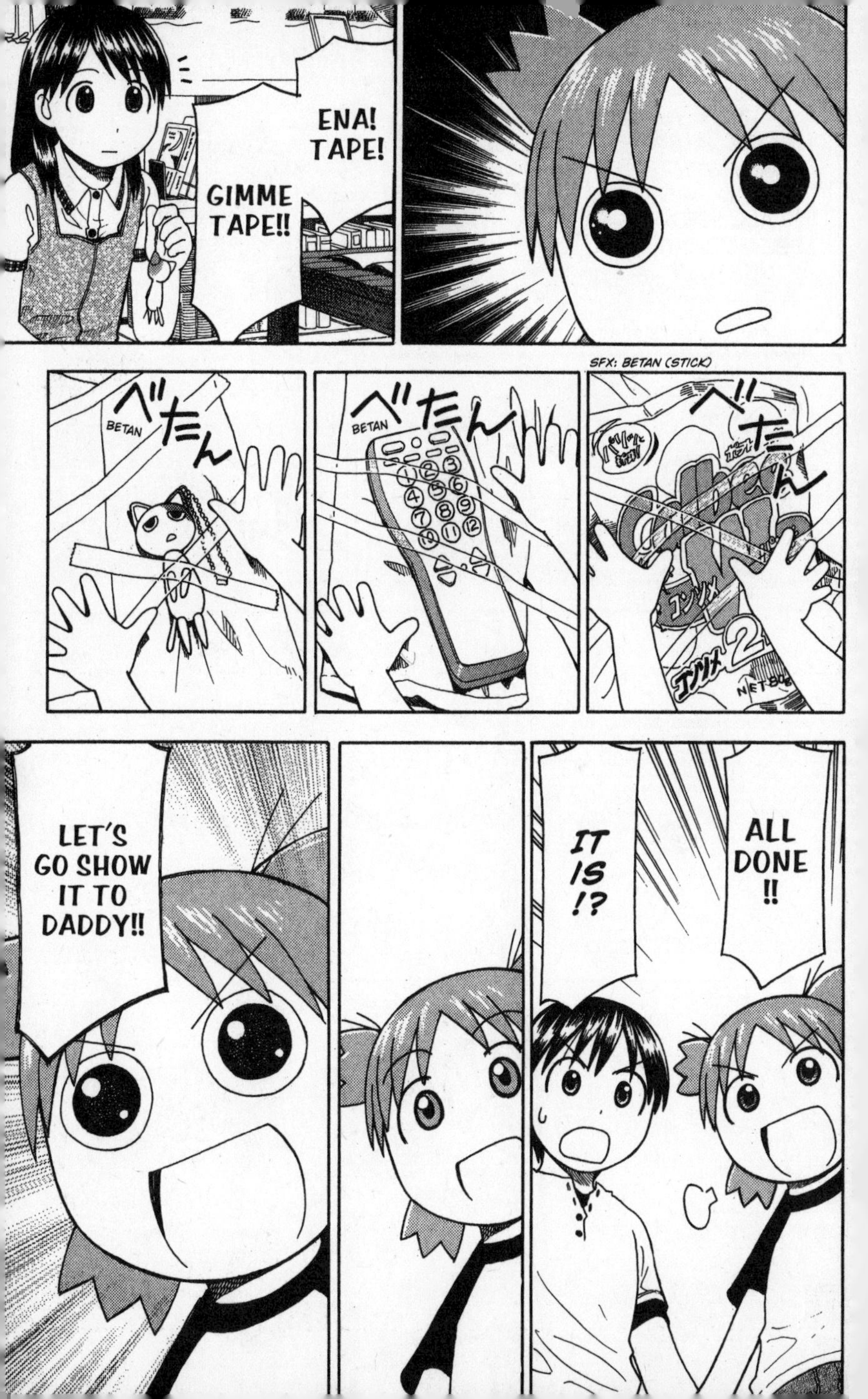
ENA! TAPE!
GIMME TAPE!!
SFX: BETAN (STICK)
べたん
べたん
BETAN
べたん
BETAN
ALL DONE!!
IT IS!?
LET'S GO SHOW IT TO DADDY!!

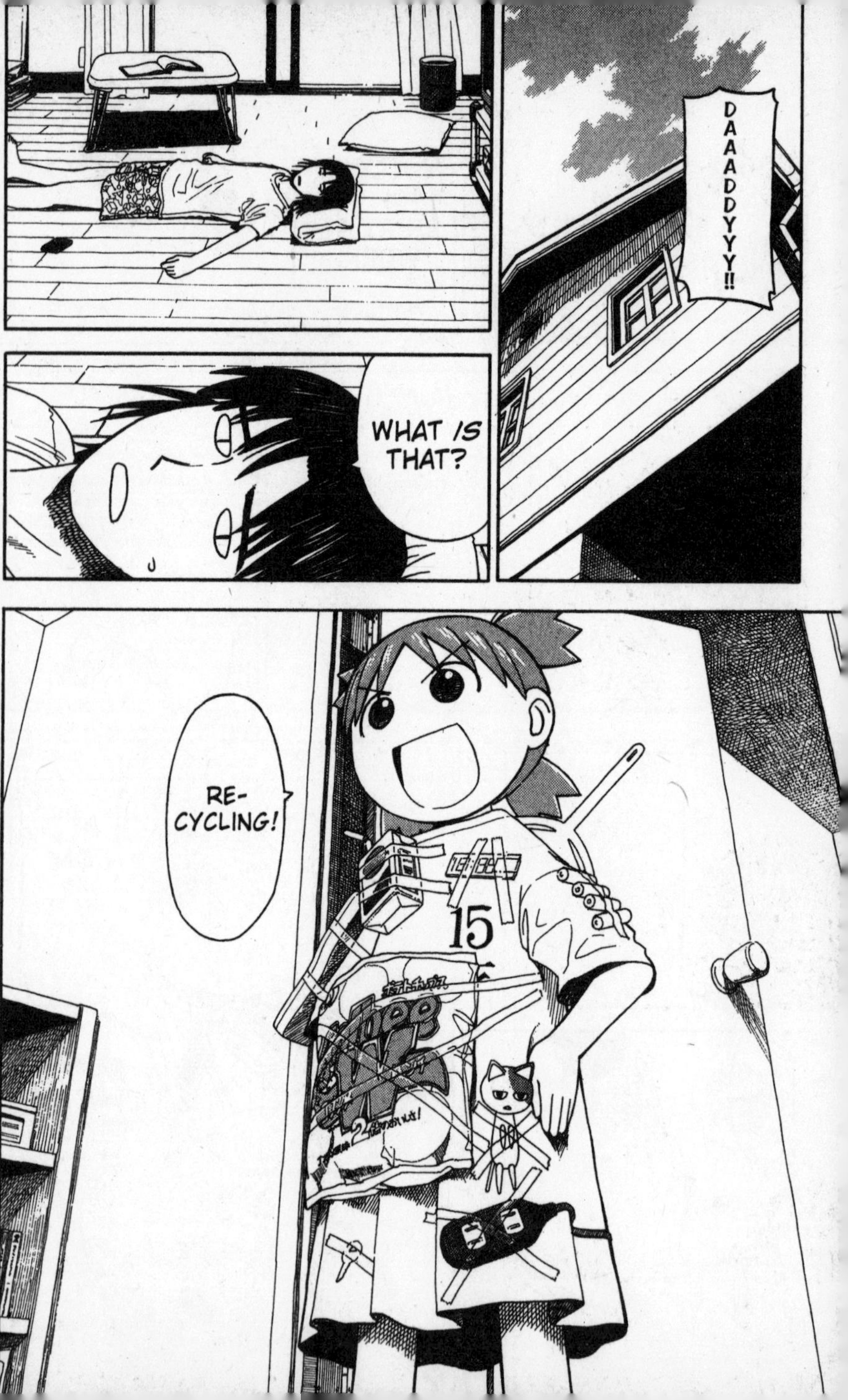
DAAAADDYYY!!
WHAT IS THAT?
RE-CYCLING!

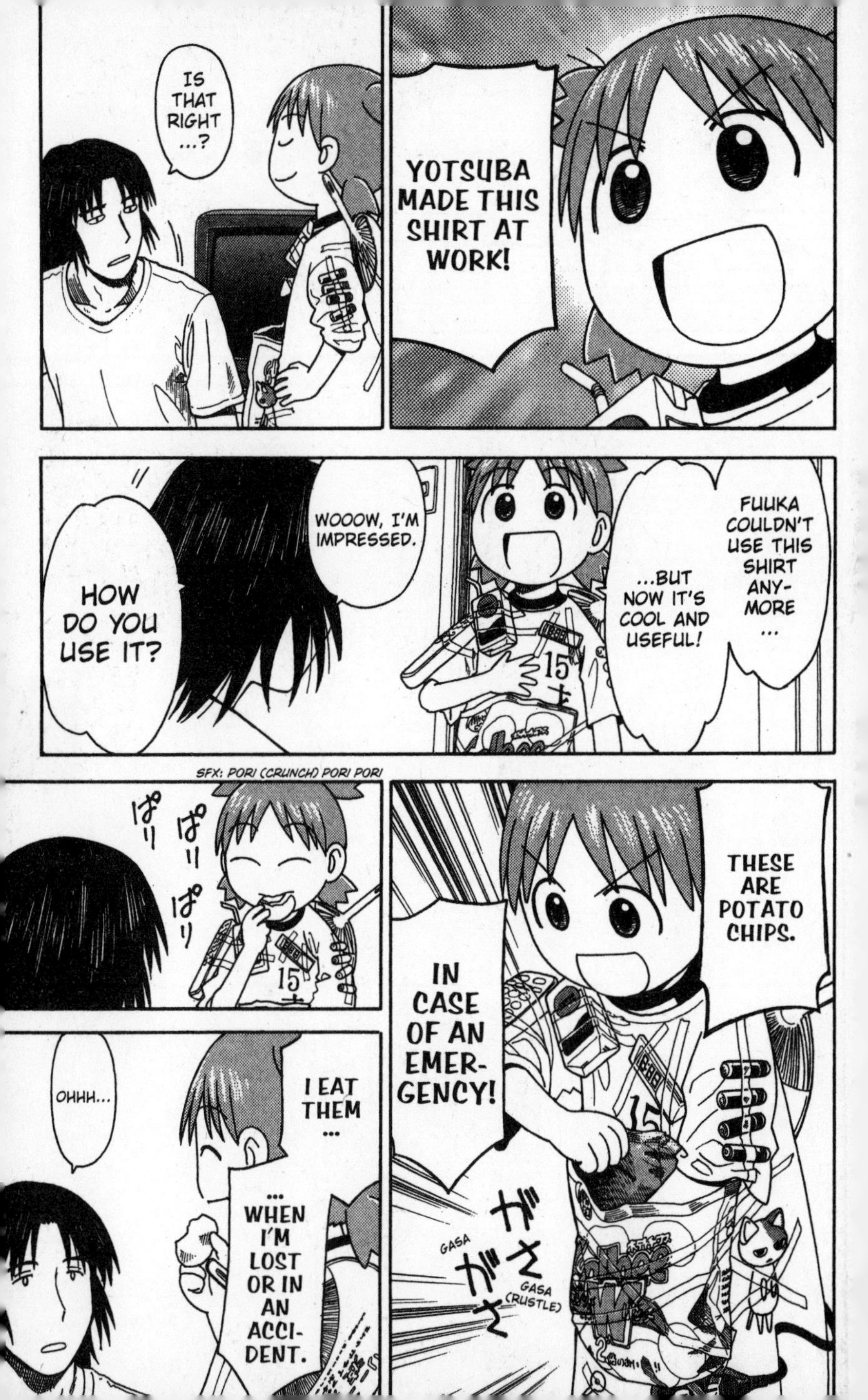
YOTSUBA MADE THIS SHIRT AT WORK!
IS THAT RIGHT ...?
FUUKA COULDN'T USE THIS SHIRT ANYMORE ...
...BUT NOW IT'S COOL AND USEFUL!
WOOOW, I'M IMPRESSED.
HOW DO YOU USE IT?
THESE ARE POTATO CHIPS.
IN CASE OF AN EMERGENCY!
がさ
GASA
がさ
GASA (RUSTLE)
SFX: PORI (CRUNCH) PORI PORI
ぱり ぱり ぱり
I EAT THEM ...
... WHEN I'M LOST OR IN AN ACCIDENT.
OHHH...

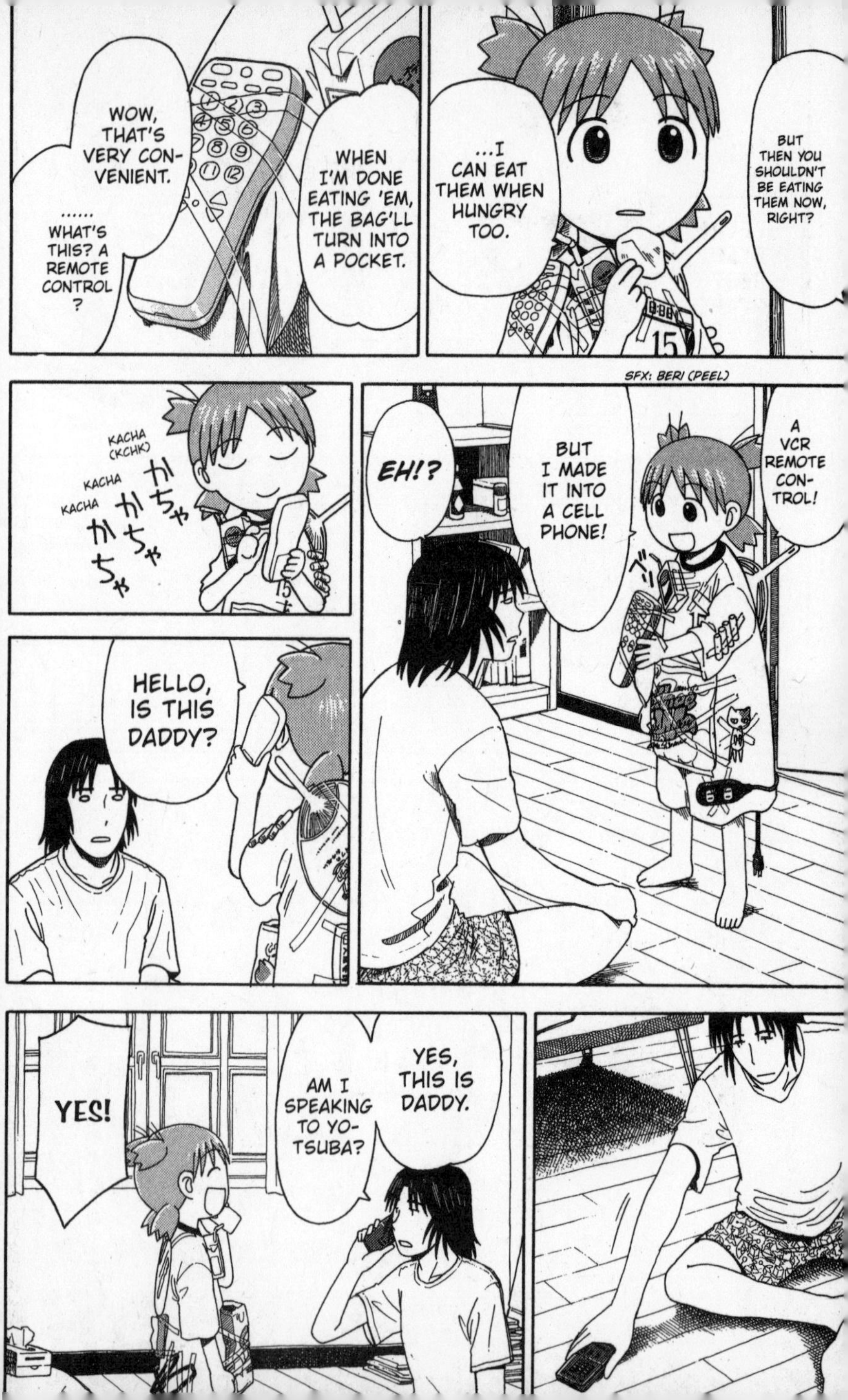
BUT THEN YOU SHOULDN'T BE EATING THEM NOW, RIGHT?
...I CAN EAT THEM WHEN HUNGRY TOO.
WHEN I'M DONE EATING 'EM, THE BAG'LL TURN INTO A POCKET.
WOW, THAT'S VERY CON-VENIENT.
...... WHAT'S THIS? A REMOTE CONTROL?
SFX: BERI (PEEL)
A VCR REMOTE CON-TROL!
BUT I MADE IT INTO A CELL PHONE!
EH!?
KACHA (KCHK)
KACHA
KACHA
かちゃ
かちゃ
かちゃ
HELLO, IS THIS DADDY?
YES, THIS IS DADDY.
AM I SPEAKING TO YO-TSUBA?
YES!

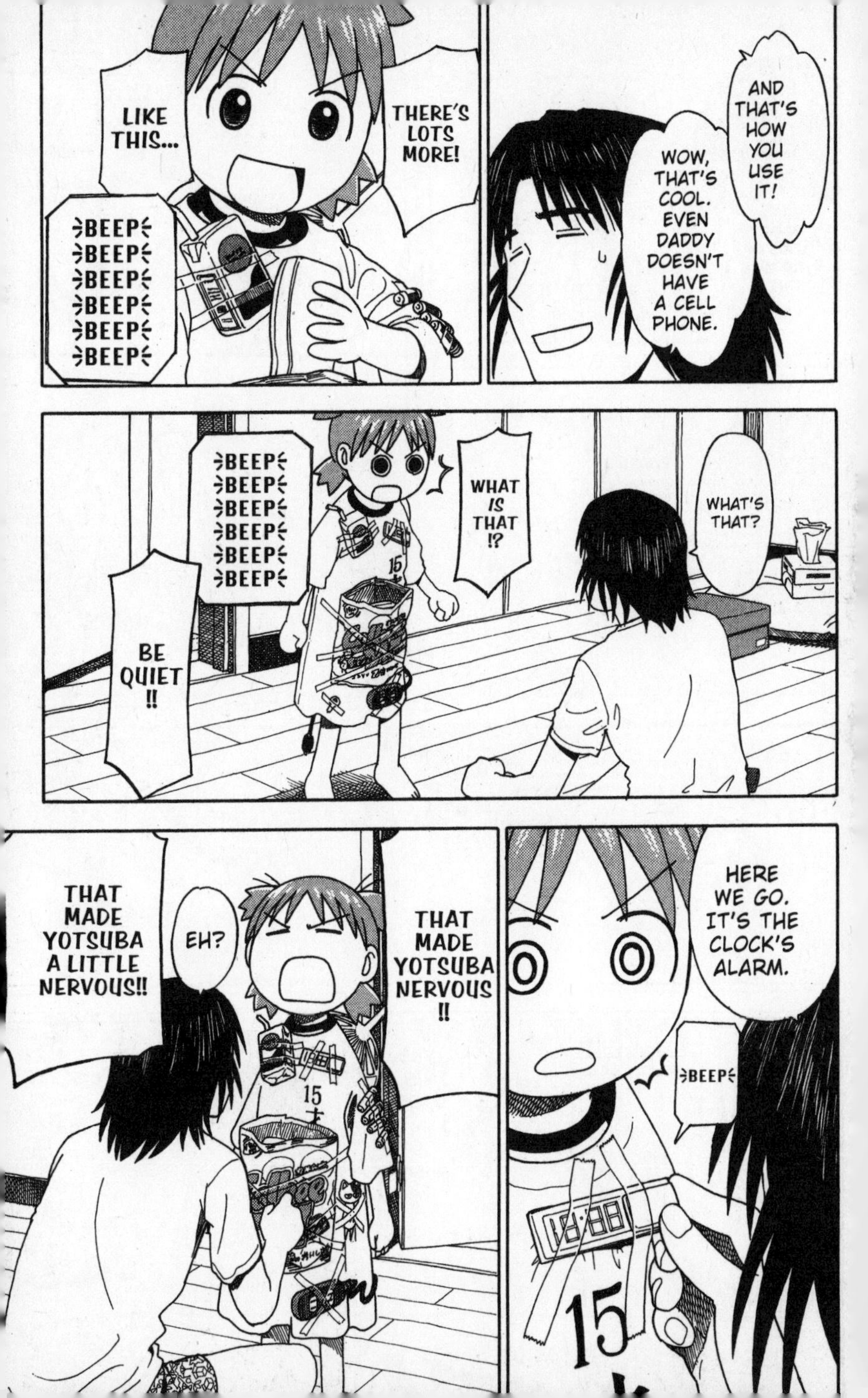
AND THAT'S HOW YOU USE IT!
WOW, THAT'S COOL. EVEN DADDY DOESN'T HAVE A CELL PHONE.
THERE'S LOTS MORE!
LIKE THIS...
BEEP BEEP BEEP BEEP BEEP BEEP
WHAT'S THAT?
WHAT IS THAT !?
BEEP BEEP BEEP BEEP BEEP BEEP
BE QUIET !!
HERE WE GO. IT'S THE CLOCK'S ALARM.
BEEP
THAT MADE YOTSUBA NERVOUS !!
EH?
THAT MADE YOTSUBA A LITTLE NERVOUS!!

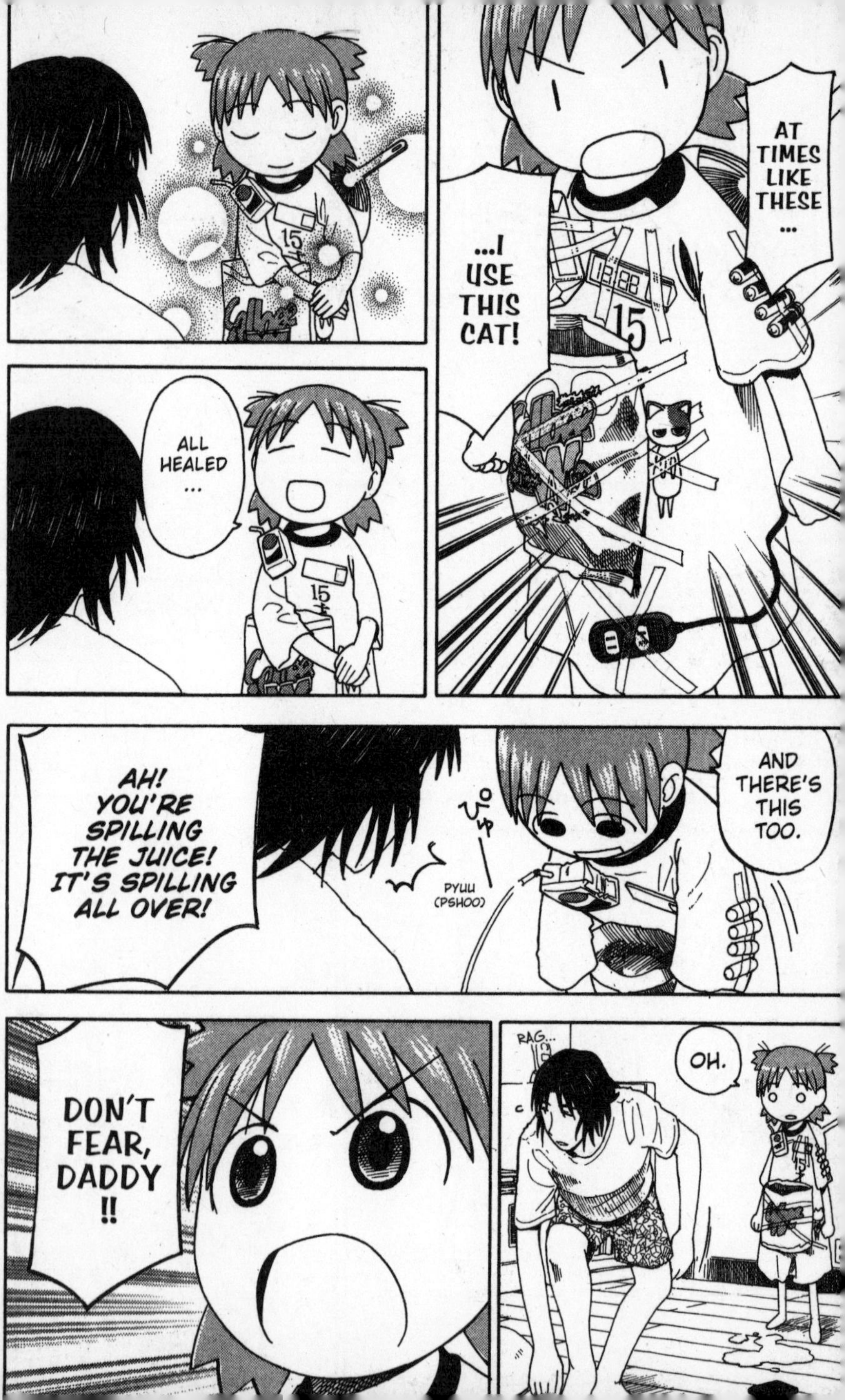
AT TIMES LIKE THESE ...
...I USE THIS CAT!
ALL HEALED ...
AND THERE'S THIS TOO.
ぴゅ
PYUU (PSHOO)
AH! YOU'RE SPILLING THE JUICE! IT'S SPILLING ALL OVER!
OH.
RAG...
DON'T FEAR, DADDY !!

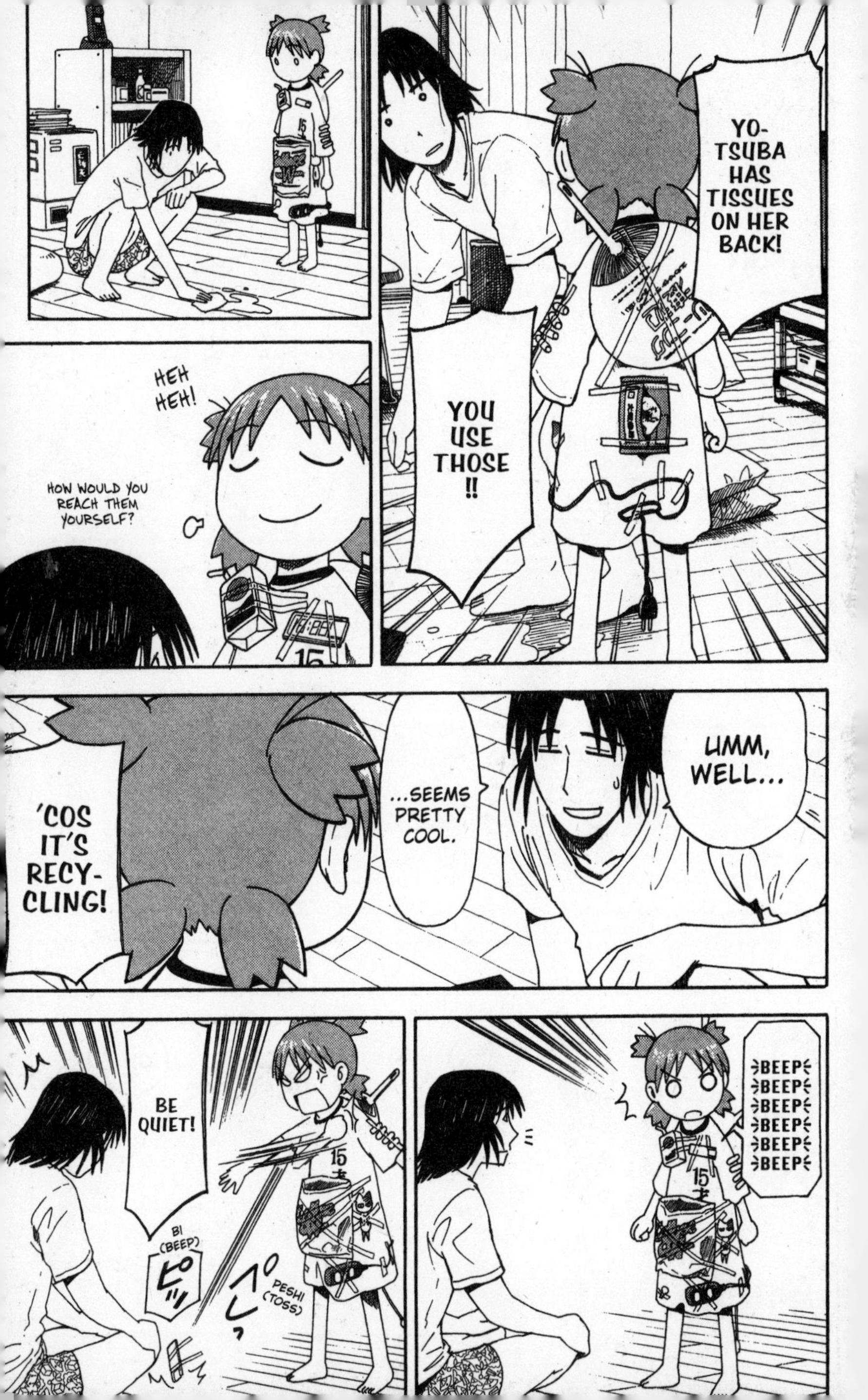
YO-TSUBA HAS TISSUES ON HER BACK!
YOU USE THOSE !!
HEH HEH!
HOW WOULD YOU REACH THEM YOURSELF?
UMM, WELL...
...SEEMS PRETTY COOL.
'COS IT'S RECY-CLING!
BEEP BEEP BEEP BEEP BEEP BEEP
BE QUIET!
BI (BEEP)
ピッ
PESHI (TOSS)

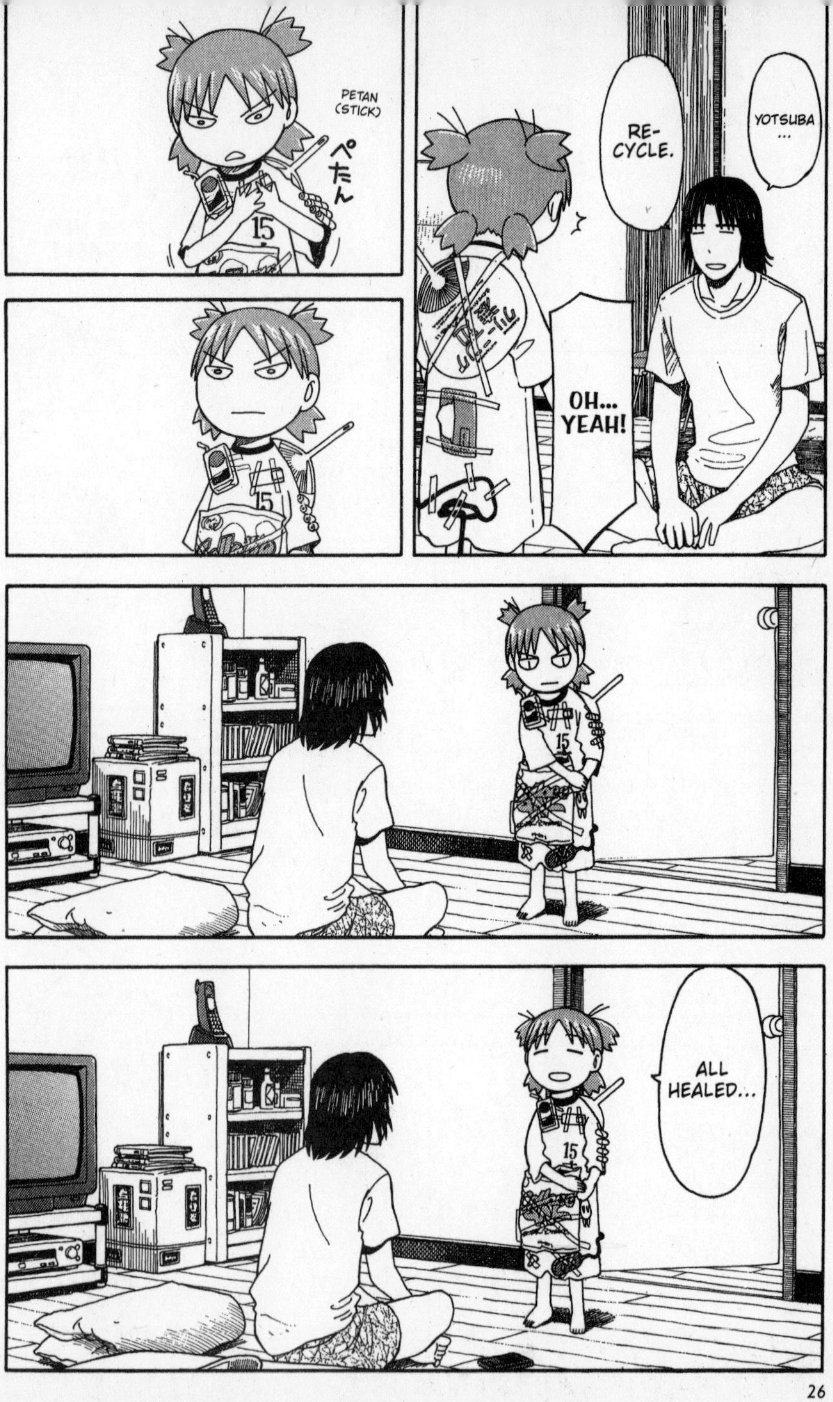
YOTSUBA ...
RE-CYCLE.
OH... YEAH!
ぺたん
PETAN (STICK)
ALL HEALED...

YOTSUBA&!

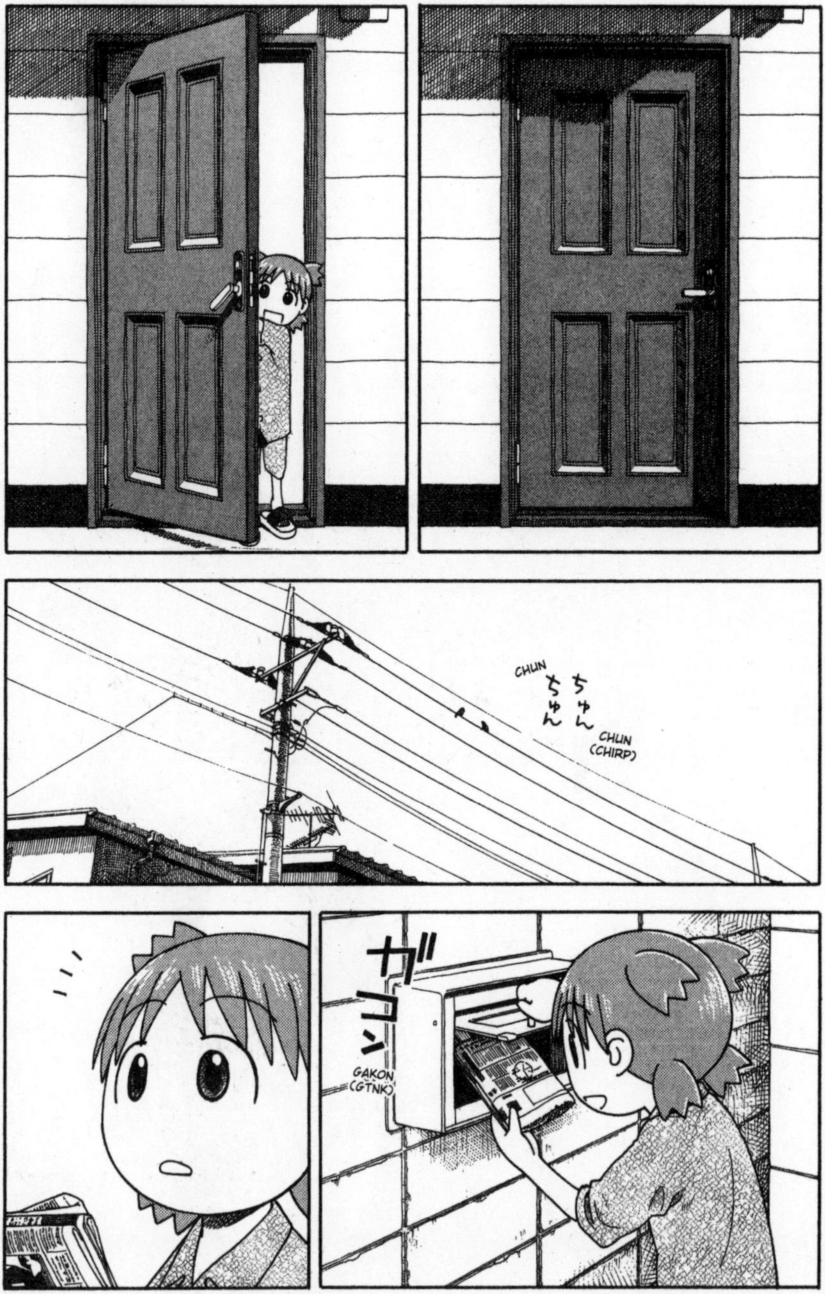
ちゅん
CHUN
ちゅん
CHUN
(CHIRP)
ガコン
GAKON
(GTNK)

YOTSUBA&BICYCLES

#36

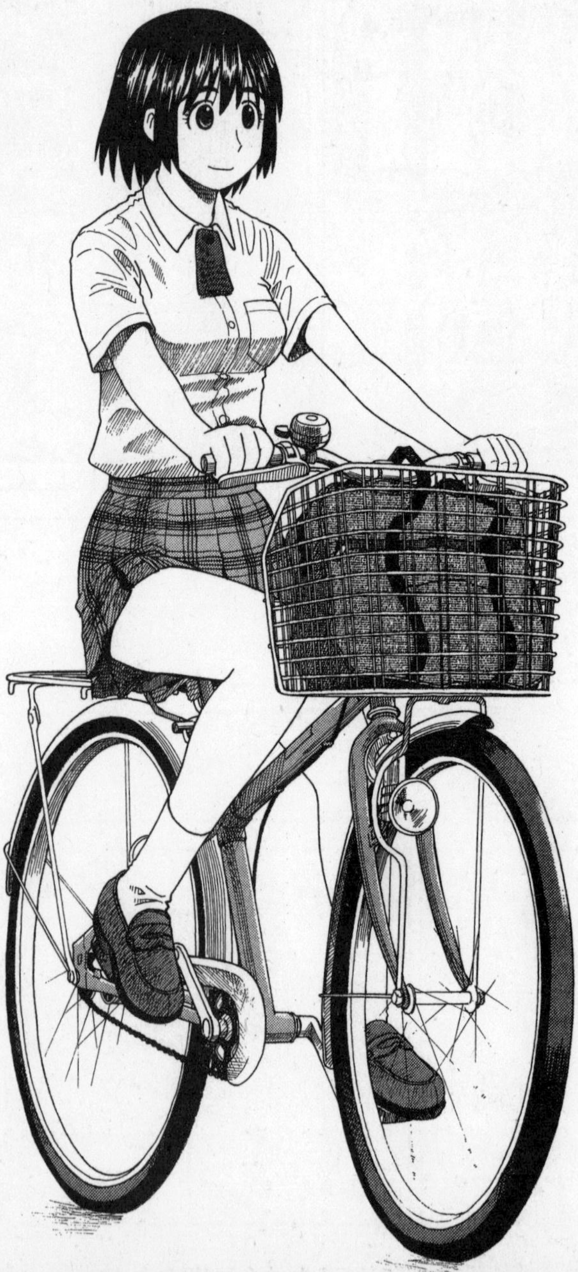

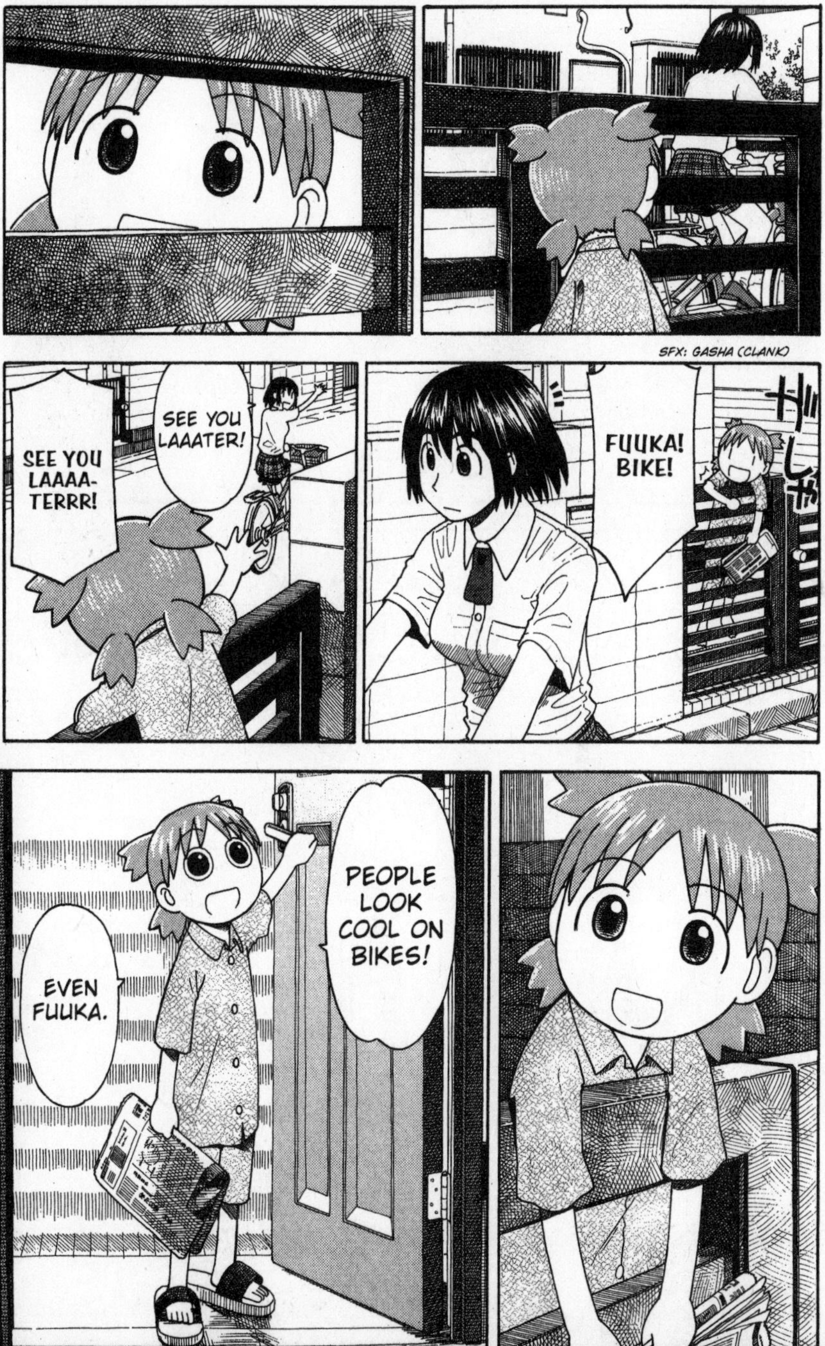
SFX: GASHA (CLANK)
FUUKA! BIKE!
SEE YOU LAAATER!
SEE YOU LAAAA-TERRR!
PEOPLE LOOK COOL ON BIKES!
EVEN FUUKA.

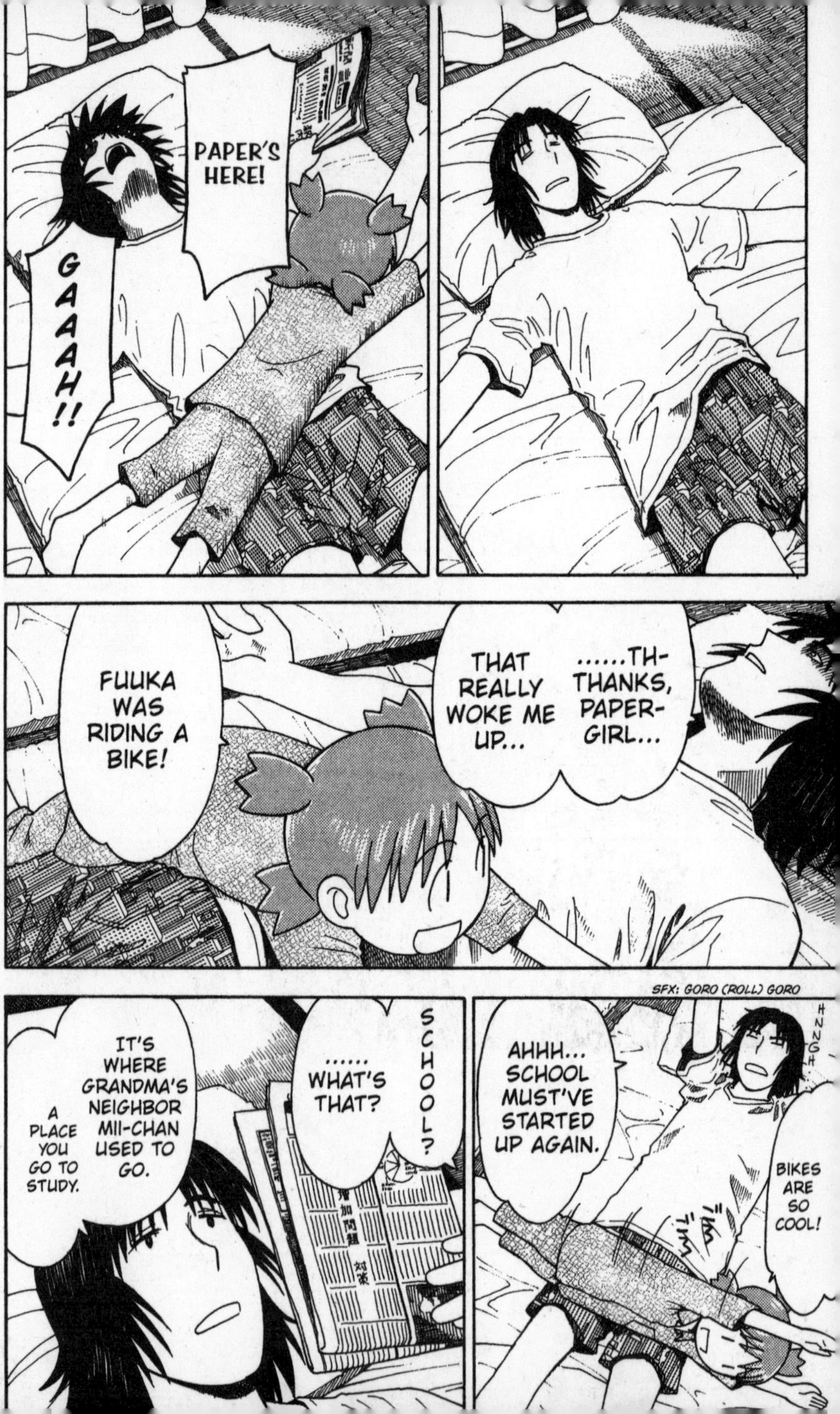
PAPER'S HERE!
GAAAAH!!
......TH-THANKS, PAPER-GIRL...
THAT REALLY WOKE ME UP...
FUUKA WAS RIDING A BIKE!
SFX: GORO (ROLL) GORO
HNNGH
AHHH... SCHOOL MUST'VE STARTED UP AGAIN.
BIKES ARE SO COOL!
SCHOOL?
......WHAT'S THAT?
IT'S WHERE GRANDMA'S NEIGHBOR MII-CHAN USED TO GO.
A PLACE YOU GO TO STUDY.

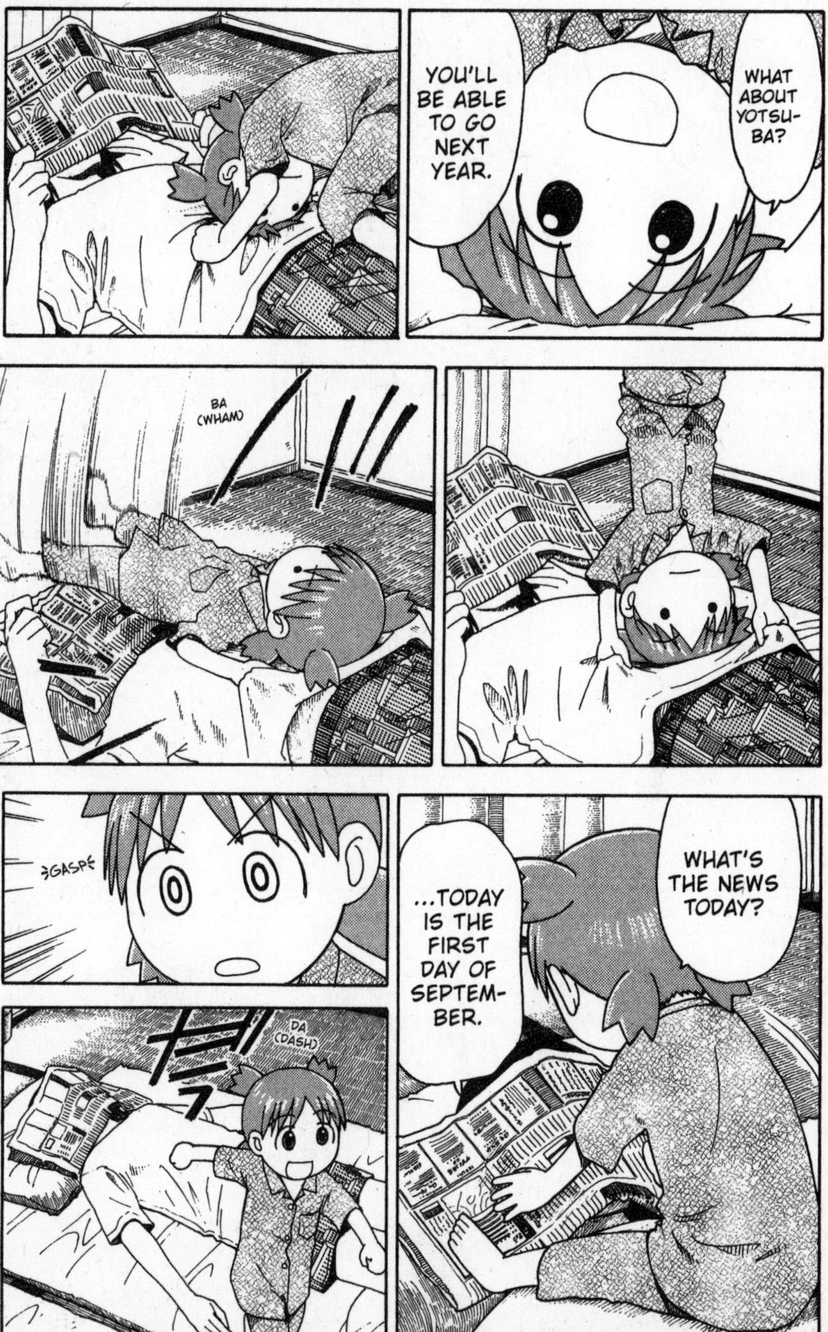
WHAT ABOUT YOTSUBA?
YOU'LL BE ABLE TO GO NEXT YEAR.
BA (WHAM)
WHAT'S THE NEWS TODAY?
...TODAY IS THE FIRST DAY OF SEPTEMBER.
GASP
DA (DASH)

へ"リ"リ"

BERIRI
(RIIIIP)

jambo

flower jambo

ひ"リ"リ"

BIRIII
(RIIIIP)

DA
(DASH)

ダ"ダ"

ダ"

DA

DA

ひ"リ"

BII
(RIIIIP)

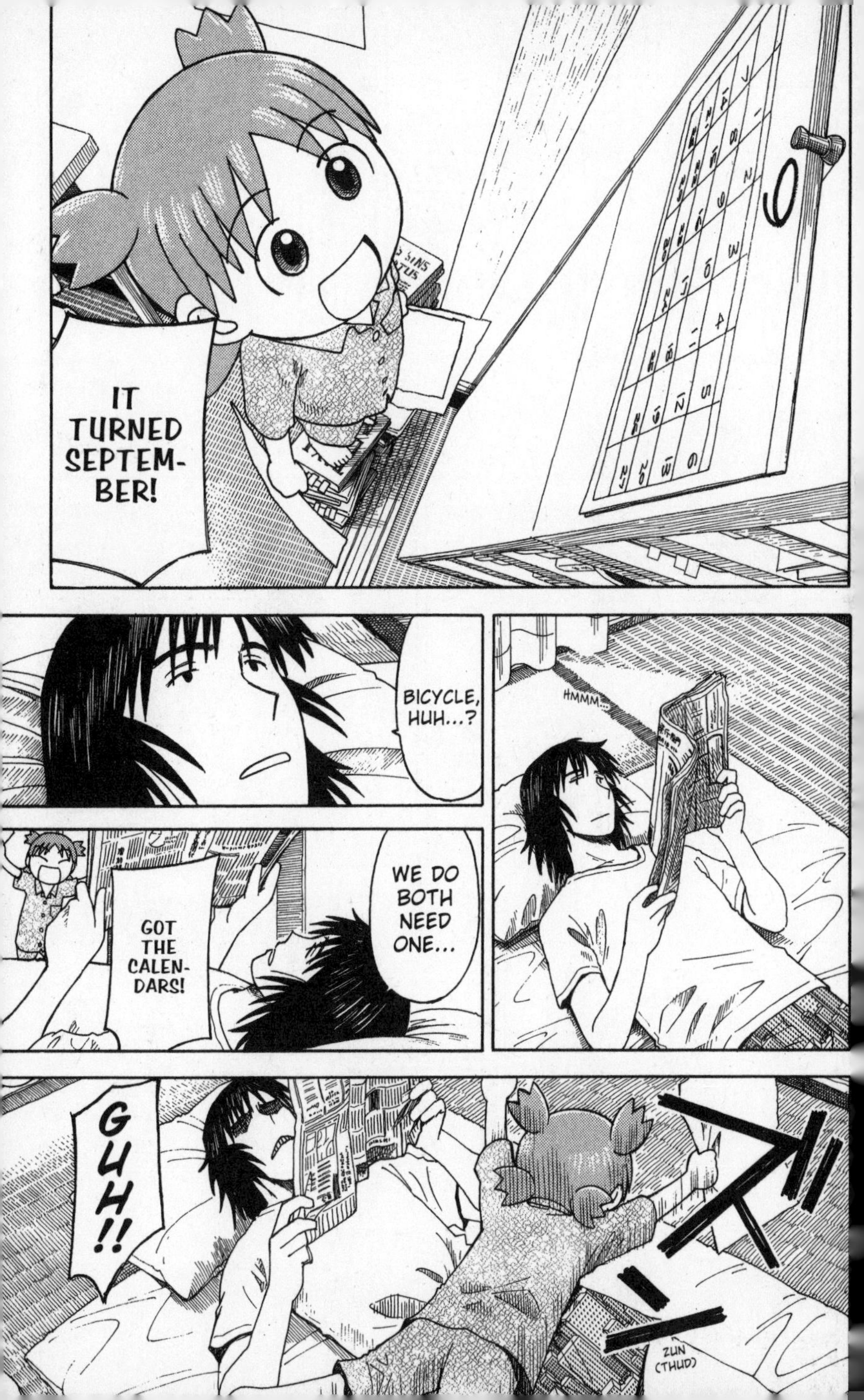
IT TURNED SEPTEMBER!
HMMM...
BICYCLE, HUH...?
WE DO BOTH NEED ONE...
GOT THE CALENDARS!
ZUN (THUD)
GUH!!

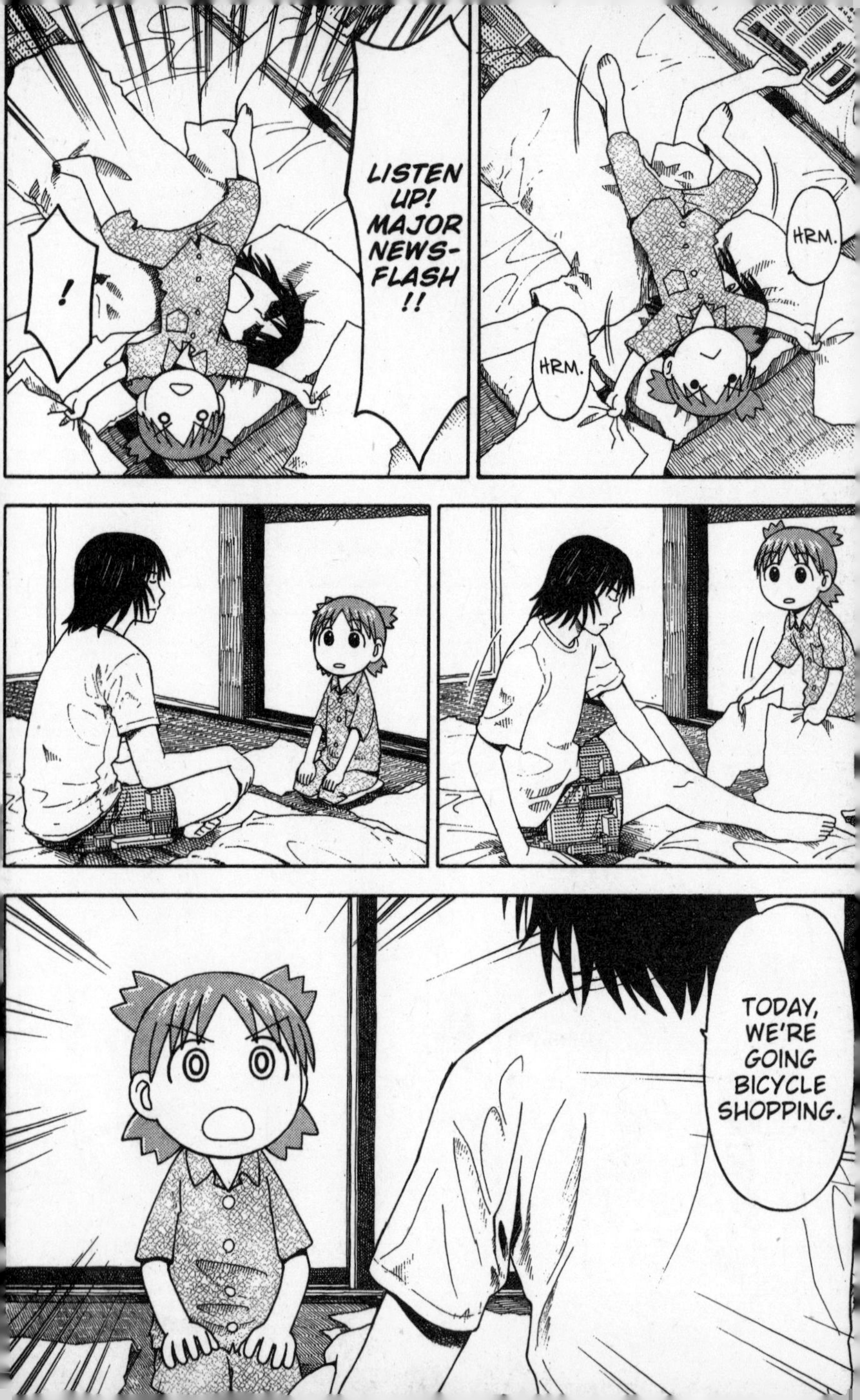
HRM.
HRM.
LISTEN UP! MAJOR NEWS-FLASH!!
!
TODAY, WE'RE GOING BICYCLE SHOPPING.

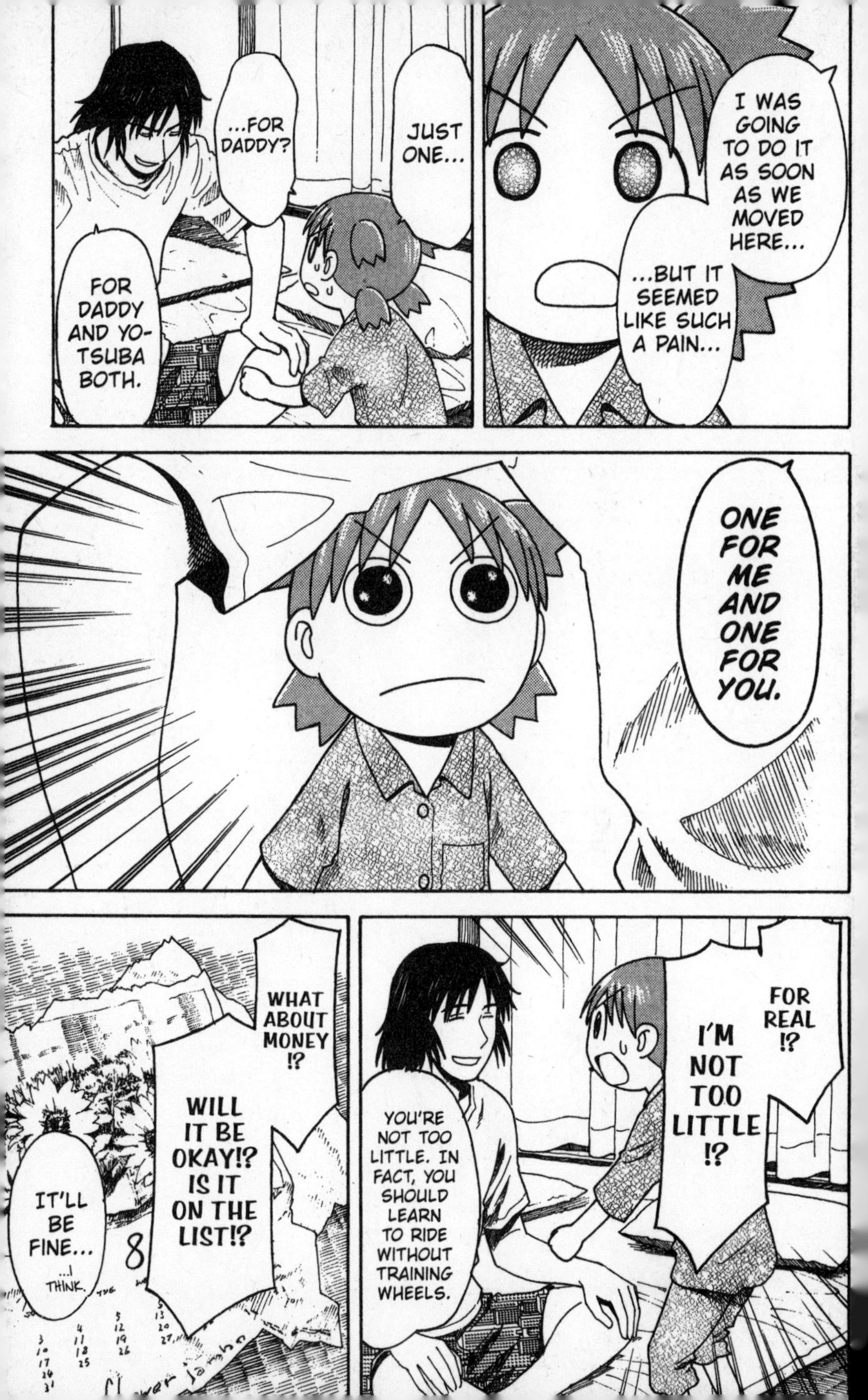
I WAS GOING TO DO IT AS SOON AS WE MOVED HERE...
...BUT IT SEEMED LIKE SUCH A PAIN...
JUST ONE...
...FOR DADDY?
FOR DADDY AND YOTSUBA BOTH.
ONE FOR ME AND ONE FOR YOU.
FOR REAL!?
I'M NOT TOO LITTLE!?
YOU'RE NOT TOO LITTLE. IN FACT, YOU SHOULD LEARN TO RIDE WITHOUT TRAINING WHEELS.
WHAT ABOUT MONEY!?
WILL IT BE OKAY!? IS IT ON THE LIST!?
IT'LL BE FINE... ...I THINK.

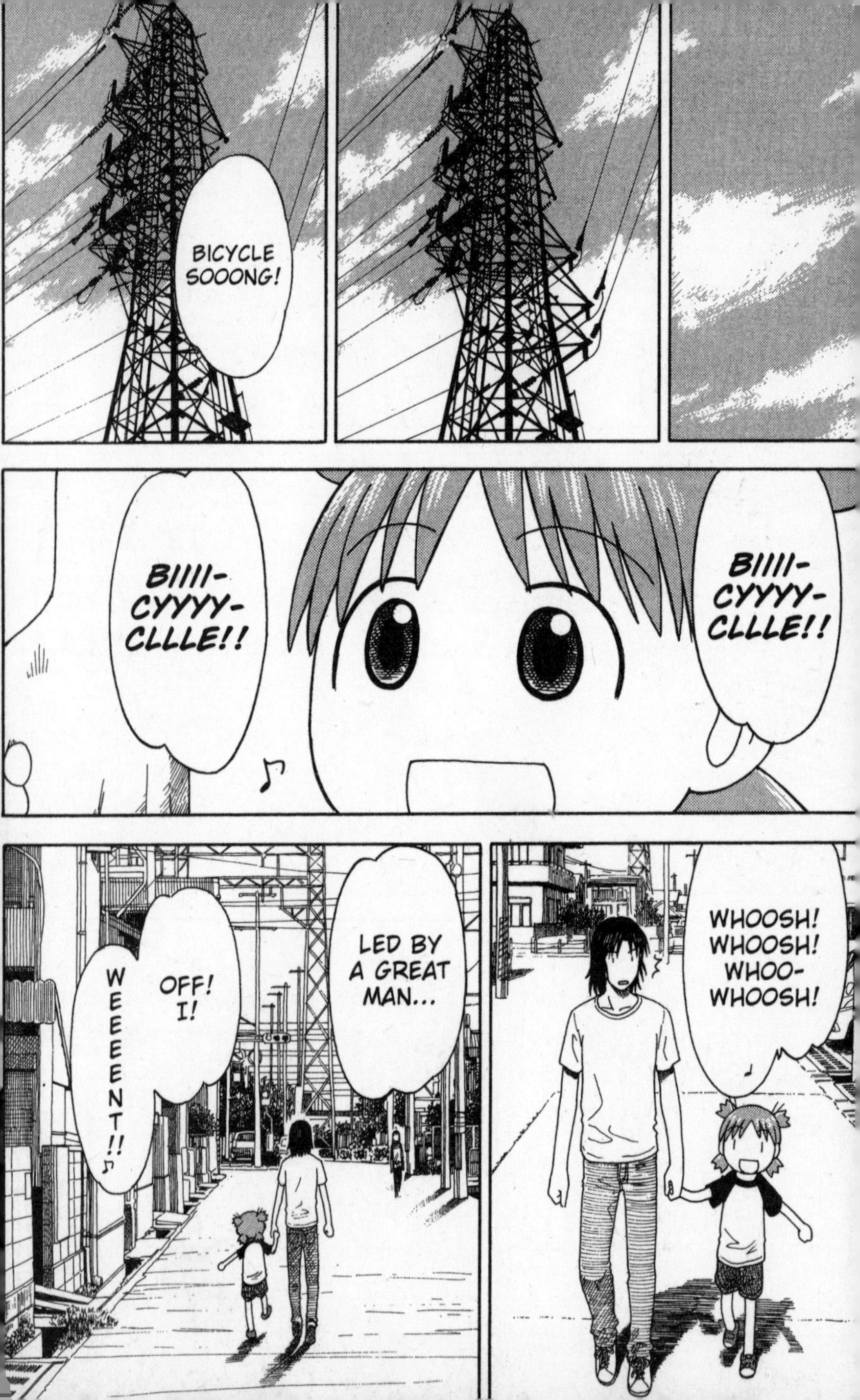
BICYCLE SOOONG!
BIIII-CYYYY-CLLLE!!
BIIII-CYYYY-CLLLE!!
WHOOSH! WHOOSH! WHOO-WHOOSH!
LED BY A GREAT MAN...
OFF! I! WEEEEENT!!

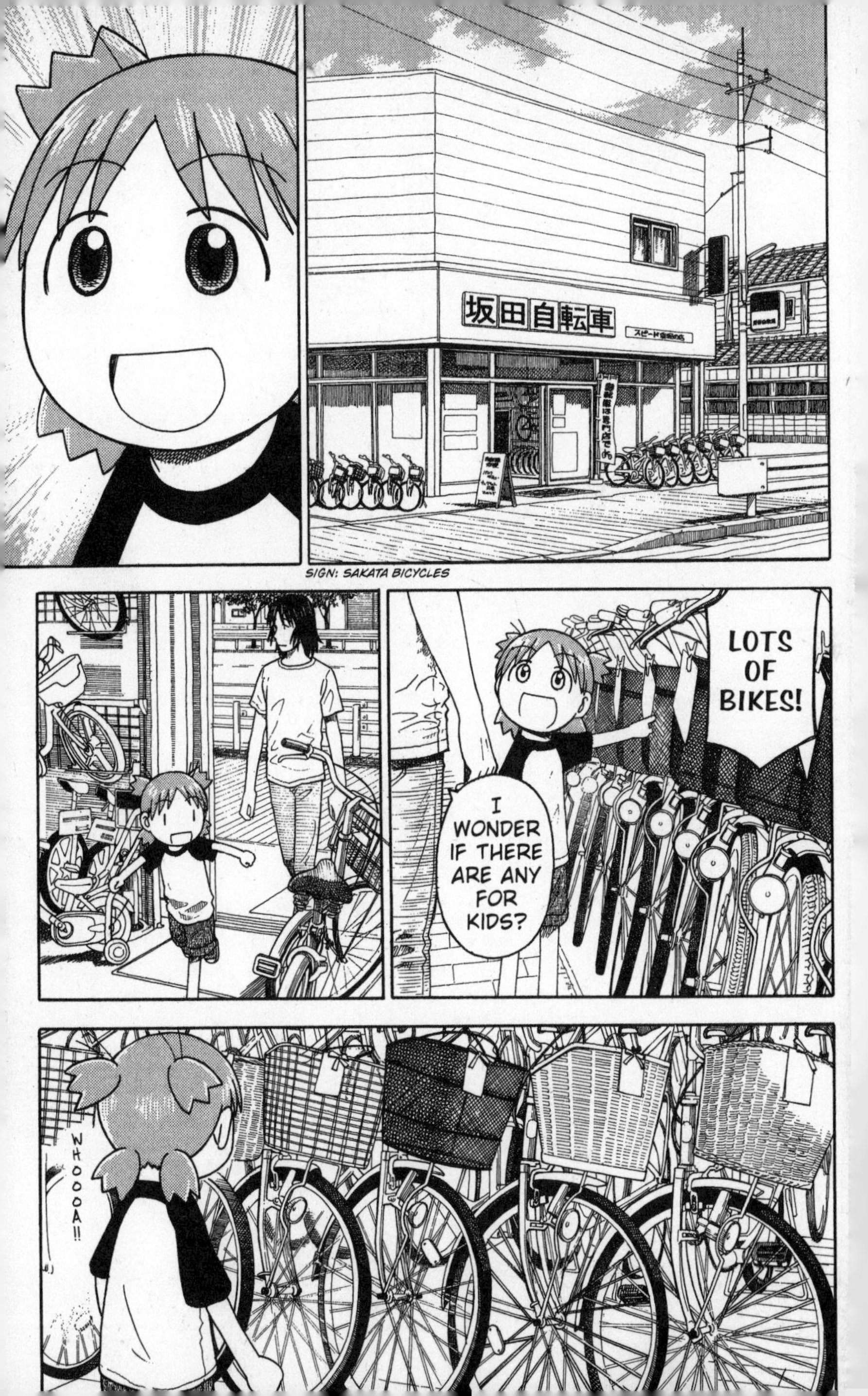
坂田自転車
SIGN: SAKATA BICYCLES
LOTS OF BIKES!
I WONDER IF THERE ARE ANY FOR KIDS?
WHOOOA!!

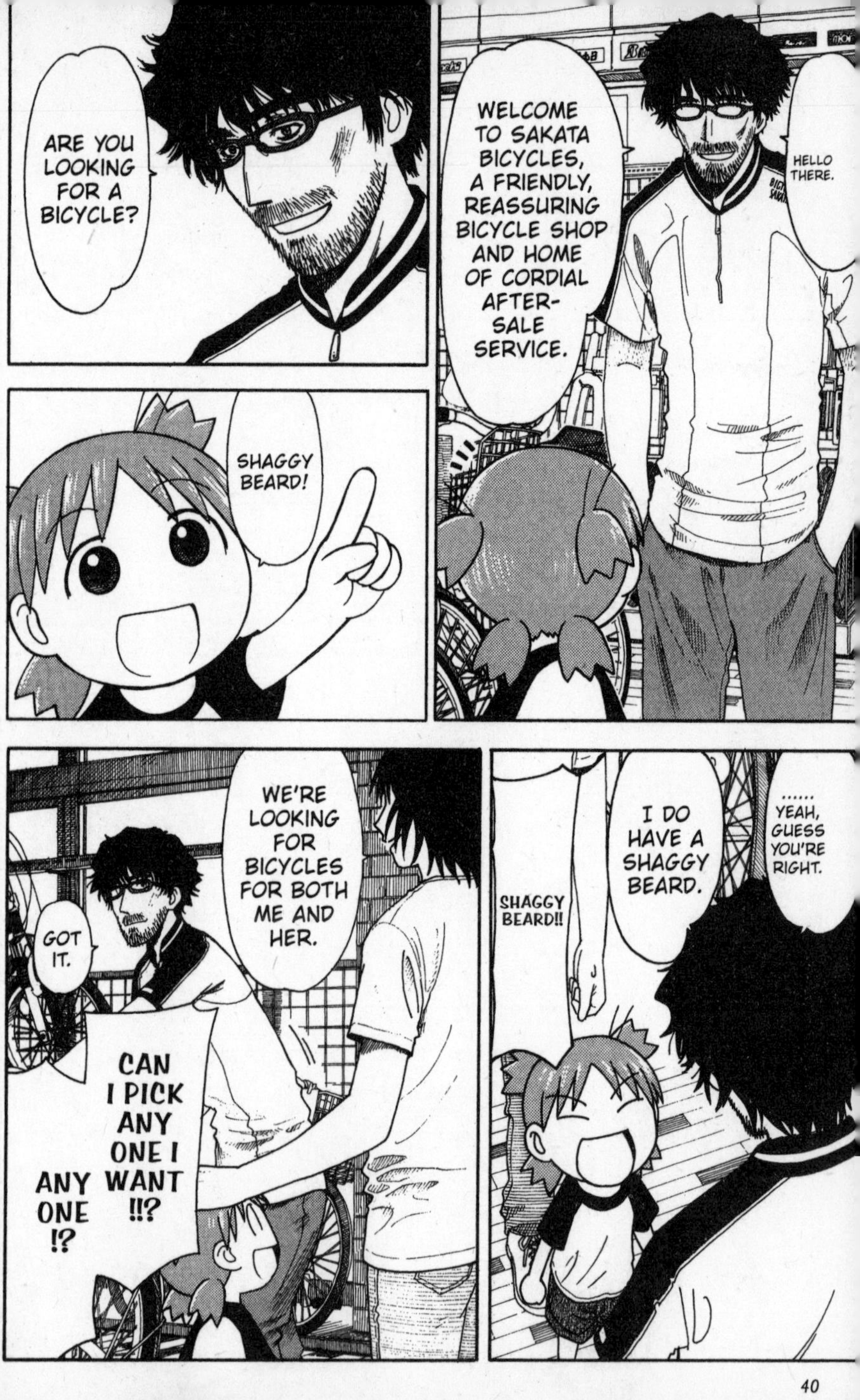
HELLO THERE.
WELCOME TO SAKATA BICYCLES, A FRIENDLY, REASSURING BICYCLE SHOP AND HOME OF CORDIAL AFTER-SALE SERVICE.
ARE YOU LOOKING FOR A BICYCLE?
SHAGGY BEARD!
...... YEAH, GUESS YOU'RE RIGHT.
I DO HAVE A SHAGGY BEARD.
SHAGGY BEARD!!
WE'RE LOOKING FOR BICYCLES FOR BOTH ME AND HER.
GOT IT.
CAN I PICK ANY ONE I WANT !!?
ANY ONE !?

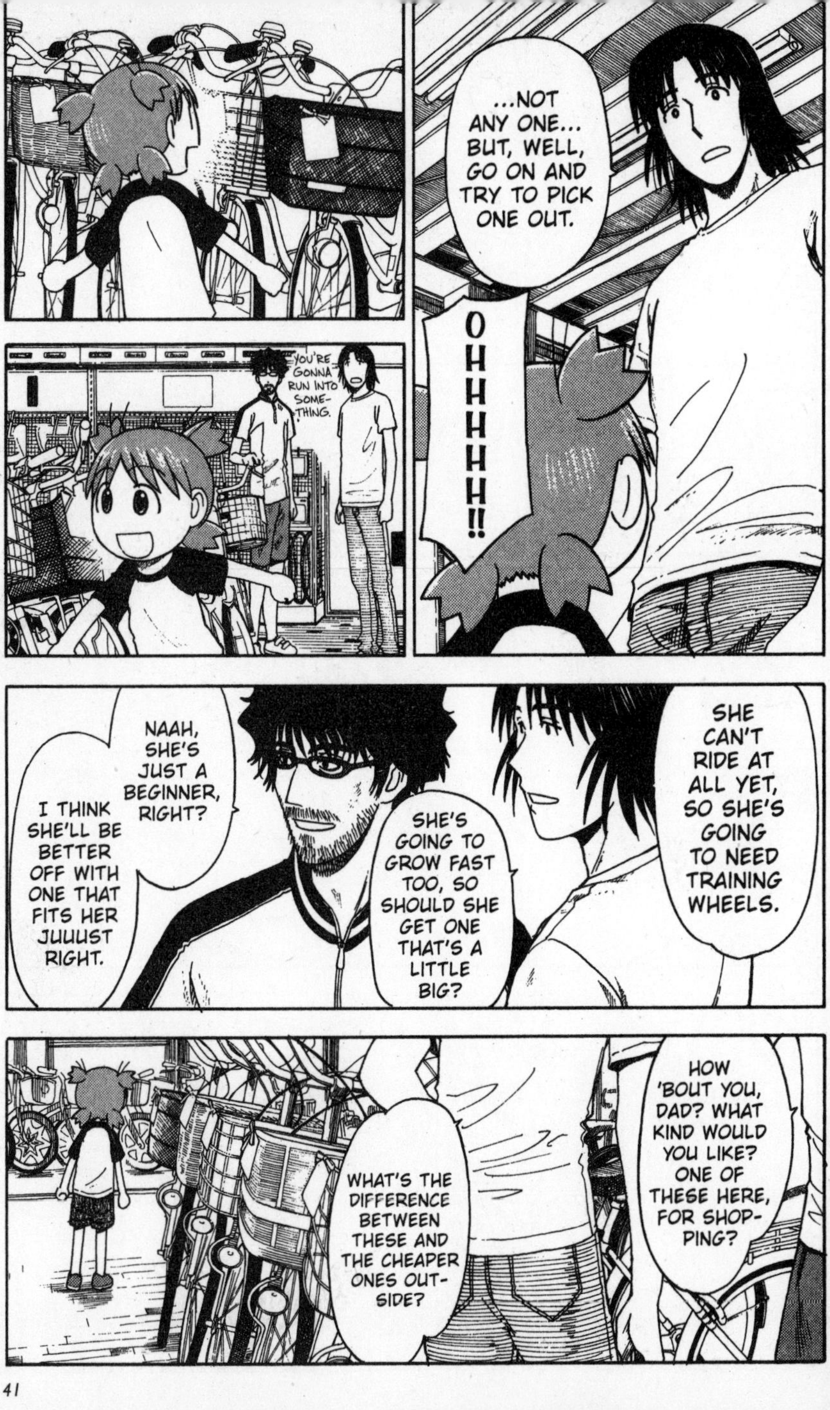
...NOT ANY ONE... BUT, WELL, GO ON AND TRY TO PICK ONE OUT.
OHHHHHH!!
YOU'RE GONNA RUN INTO SOME-THING.
SHE CAN'T RIDE AT ALL YET, SO SHE'S GOING TO NEED TRAINING WHEELS.
SHE'S GOING TO GROW FAST TOO, SO SHOULD SHE GET ONE THAT'S A LITTLE BIG?
NAAH, SHE'S JUST A BEGINNER, RIGHT?
I THINK SHE'LL BE BETTER OFF WITH ONE THAT FITS HER JUUUST RIGHT.
HOW 'BOUT YOU, DAD? WHAT KIND WOULD YOU LIKE? ONE OF THESE HERE, FOR SHOP-PING?
WHAT'S THE DIFFERENCE BETWEEN THESE AND THE CHEAPER ONES OUT-SIDE?

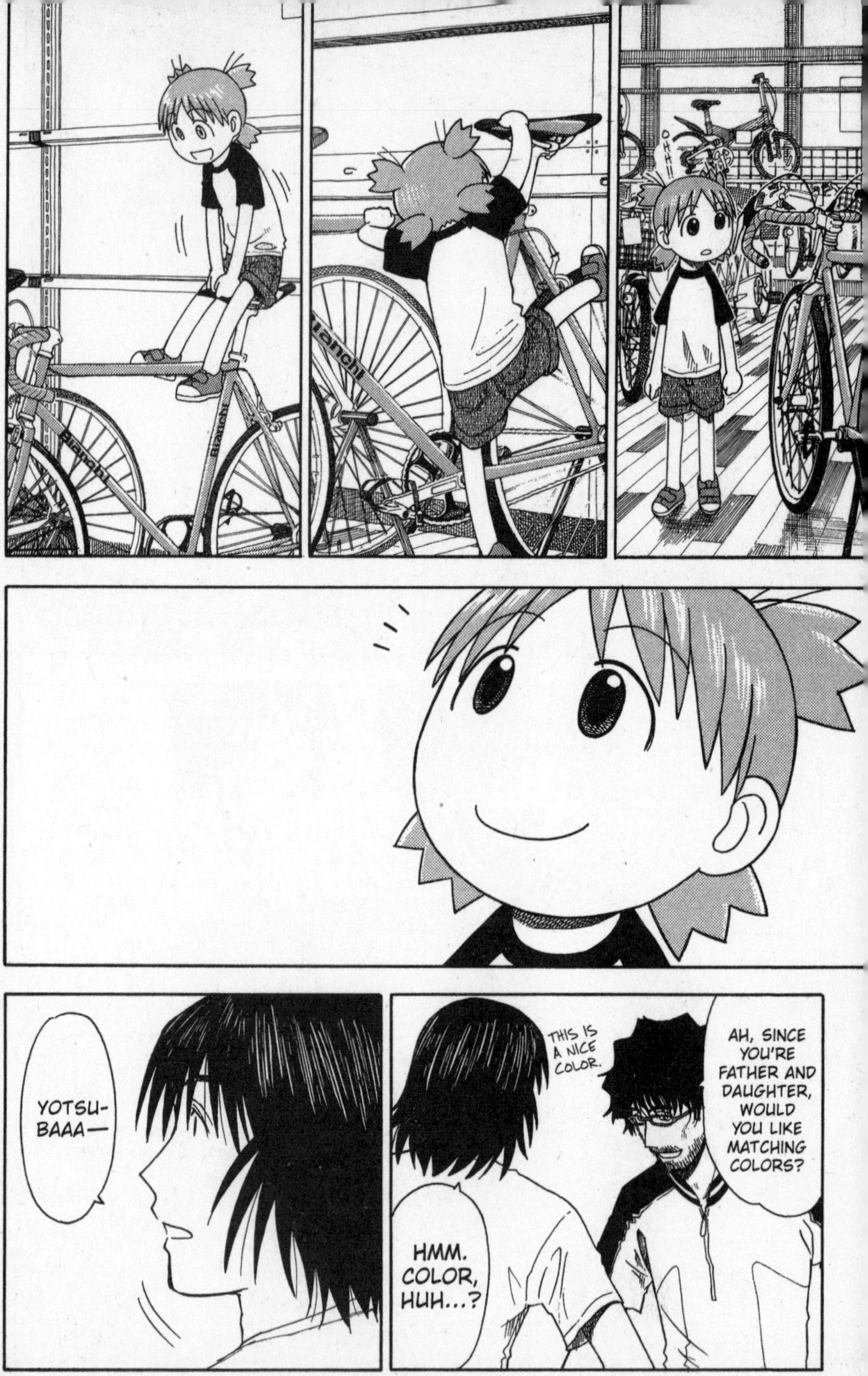
OHH!!
AH, SINCE YOU'RE FATHER AND DAUGHTER, WOULD YOU LIKE MATCHING COLORS?
THIS IS A NICE COLOR.
HMM. COLOR, HUH...?
YOTSU-BAAA—

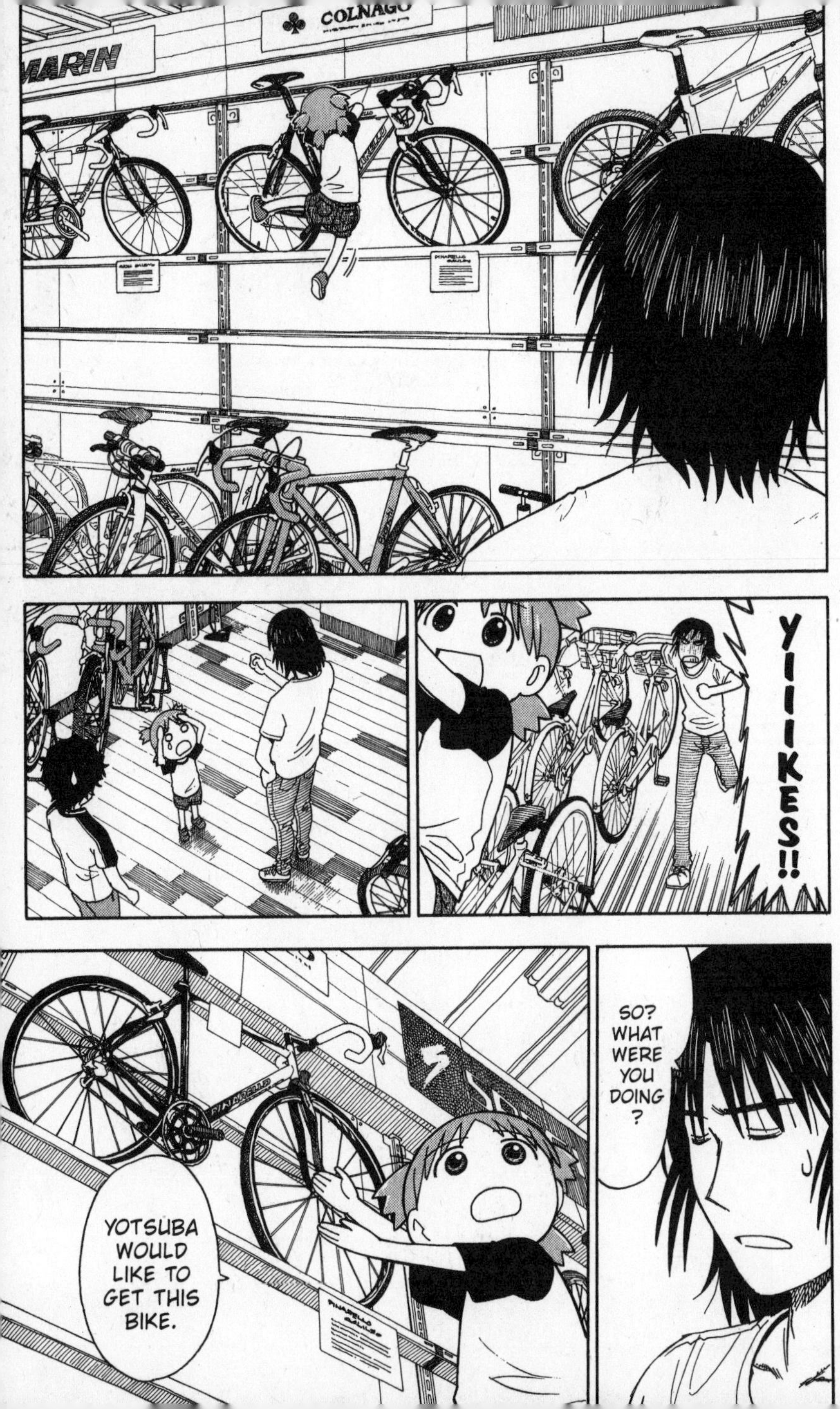
COLNAGO
MARIN
YIIIKES!!
SO? WHAT WERE YOU DOING?
YOTSUBA WOULD LIKE TO GET THIS BIKE.

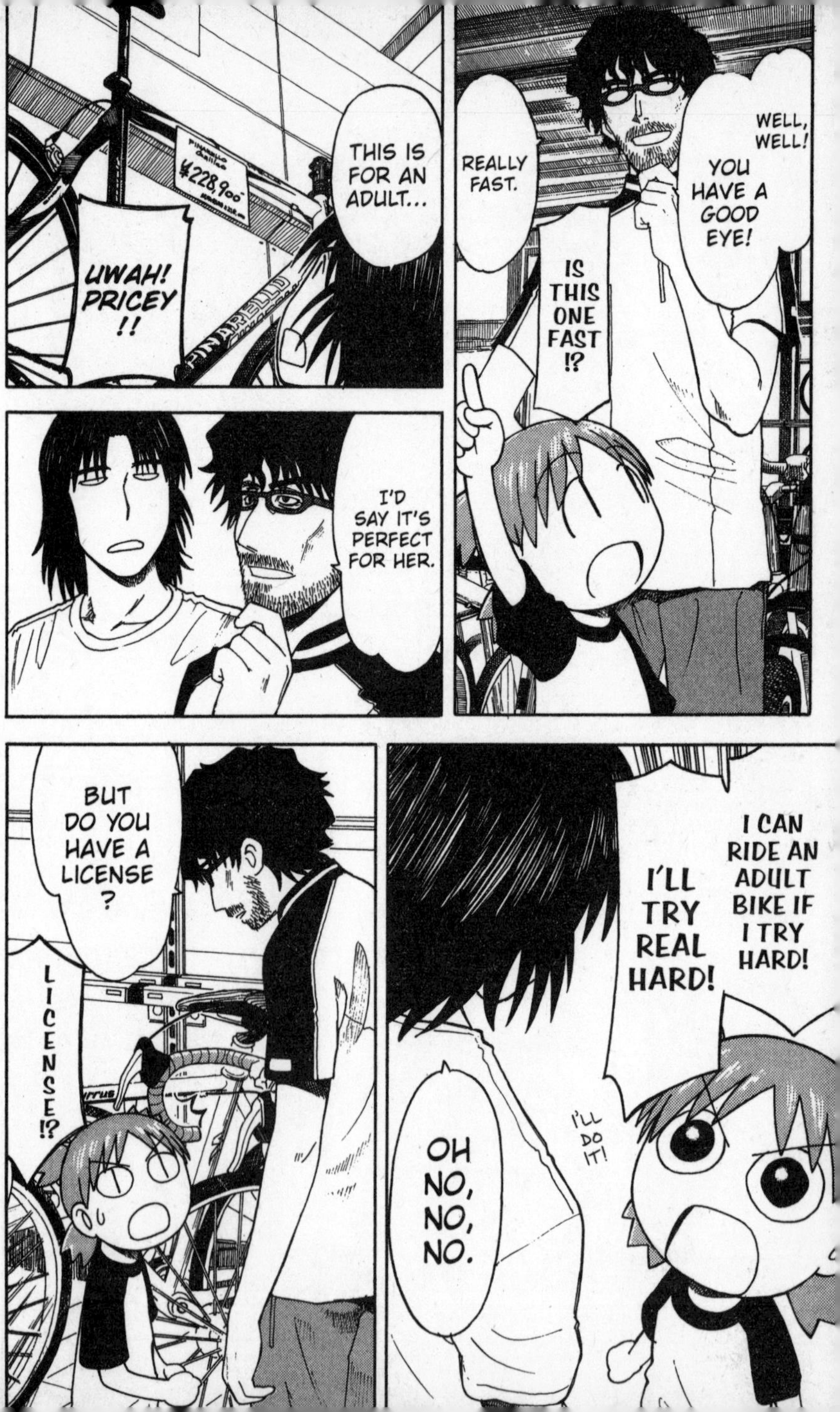
WELL, WELL!
YOU HAVE A GOOD EYE!
REALLY FAST.
IS THIS ONE FAST!?
THIS IS FOR AN ADULT...
¥228,900
UWAH! PRICEY!!
I'D SAY IT'S PERFECT FOR HER.
I CAN RIDE AN ADULT BIKE IF I TRY HARD!
I'LL TRY REAL HARD!
I'LL DO IT!
OH NO, NO, NO.
BUT DO YOU HAVE A LICENSE?
LICENSE!?

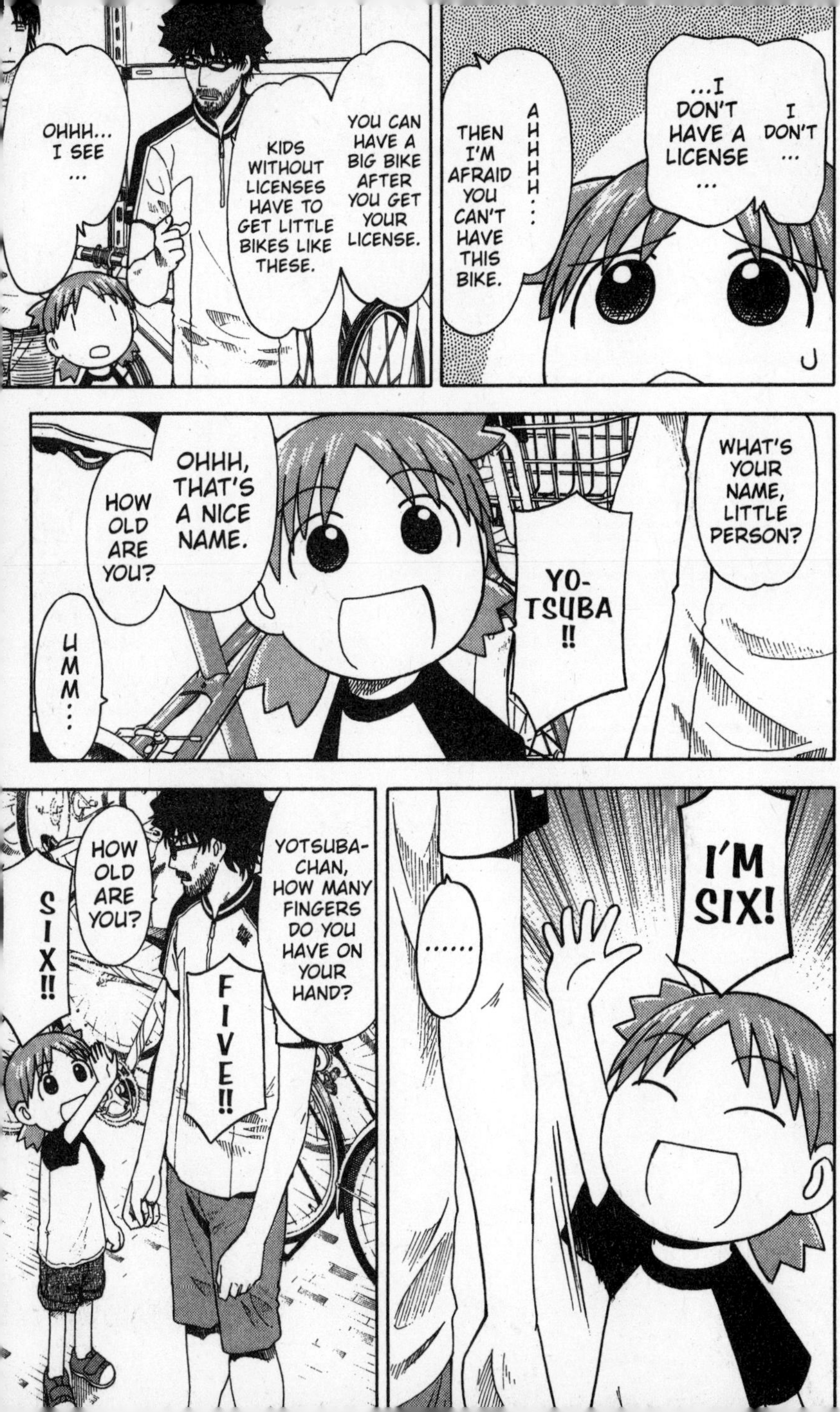
I DON'T ...
...I DON'T HAVE A LICENSE ...
AHHHHH...
THEN I'M AFRAID YOU CAN'T HAVE THIS BIKE.
YOU CAN HAVE A BIG BIKE AFTER YOU GET YOUR LICENSE.
KIDS WITHOUT LICENSES HAVE TO GET LITTLE BIKES LIKE THESE.
OHHH... I SEE ...
WHAT'S YOUR NAME, LITTLE PERSON?
YO-TSUBA!!
OHHH, THAT'S A NICE NAME.
HOW OLD ARE YOU?
UMM...
I'M SIX!
......
YOTSUBA-CHAN, HOW MANY FINGERS DO YOU HAVE ON YOUR HAND?
FIVE!!
HOW OLD ARE YOU?
SIX!!

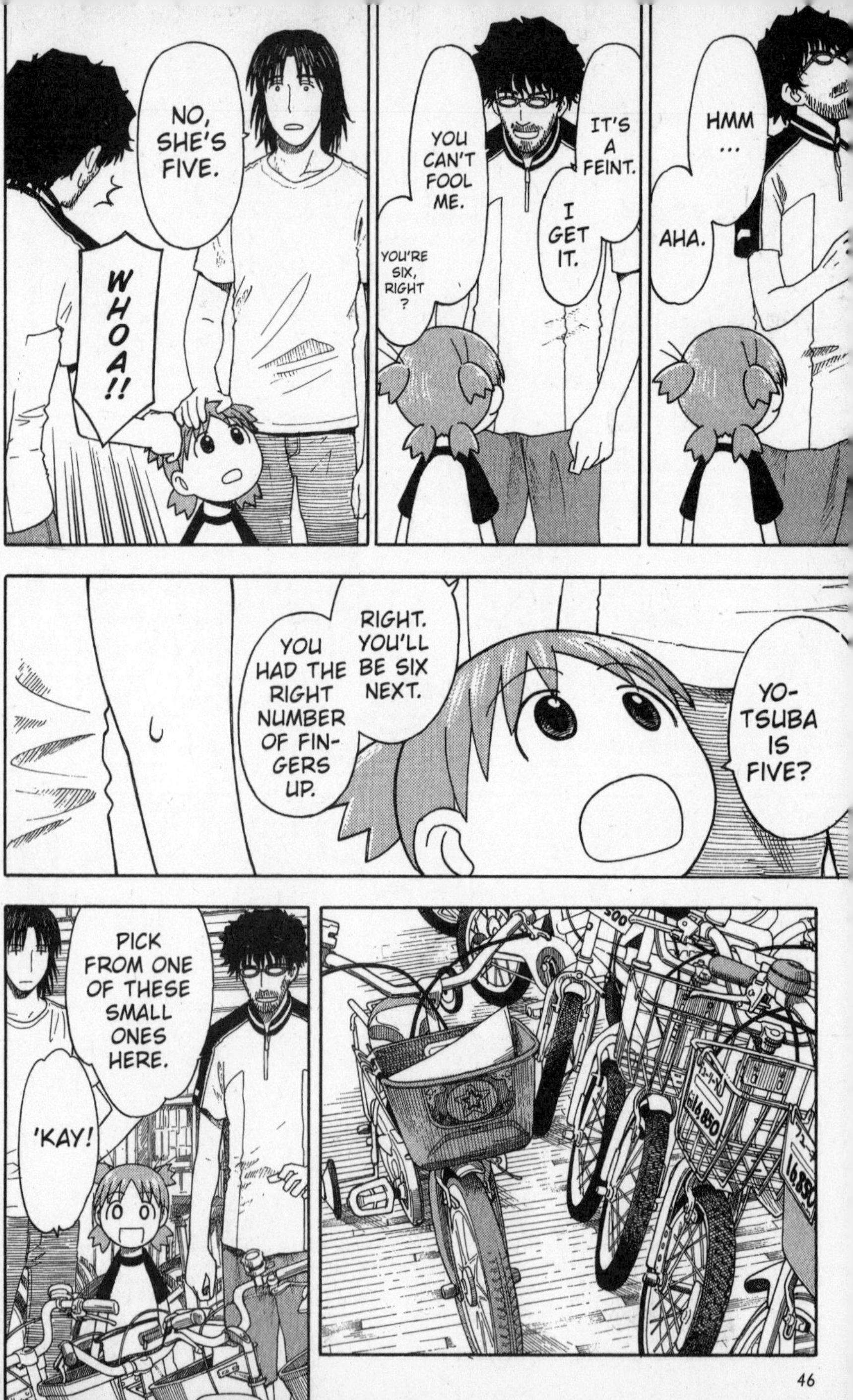
HMM ...
AHA.
IT'S A FEINT.
I GET IT.
YOU CAN'T FOOL ME.
YOU'RE SIX, RIGHT?
NO, SHE'S FIVE.
WHOA!!
YOTSUBA IS FIVE?
RIGHT. YOU'LL BE SIX NEXT.
YOU HAD THE RIGHT NUMBER OF FINGERS UP.
PICK FROM ONE OF THESE SMALL ONES HERE.
'KAY!

SFX: PON (PAT) PON

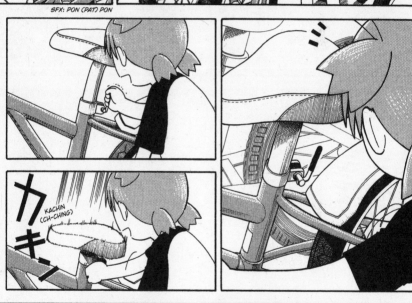

KACHIN
(CH-CHING)

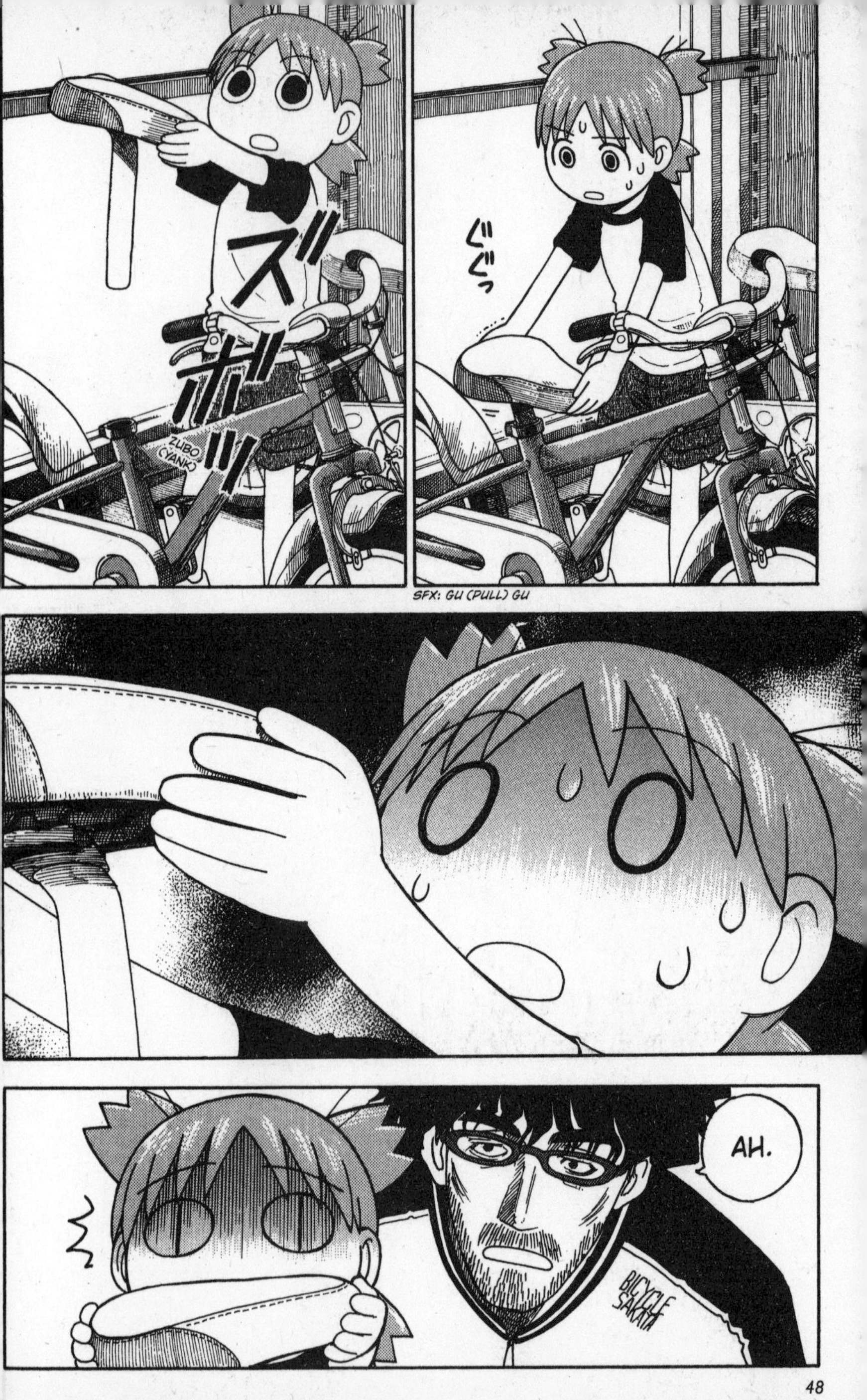
ぐぐっ
SFX: GU (PULL) GU
ズボッ
ZUBO (YANK)
AH.
BICYCLE SAKATA

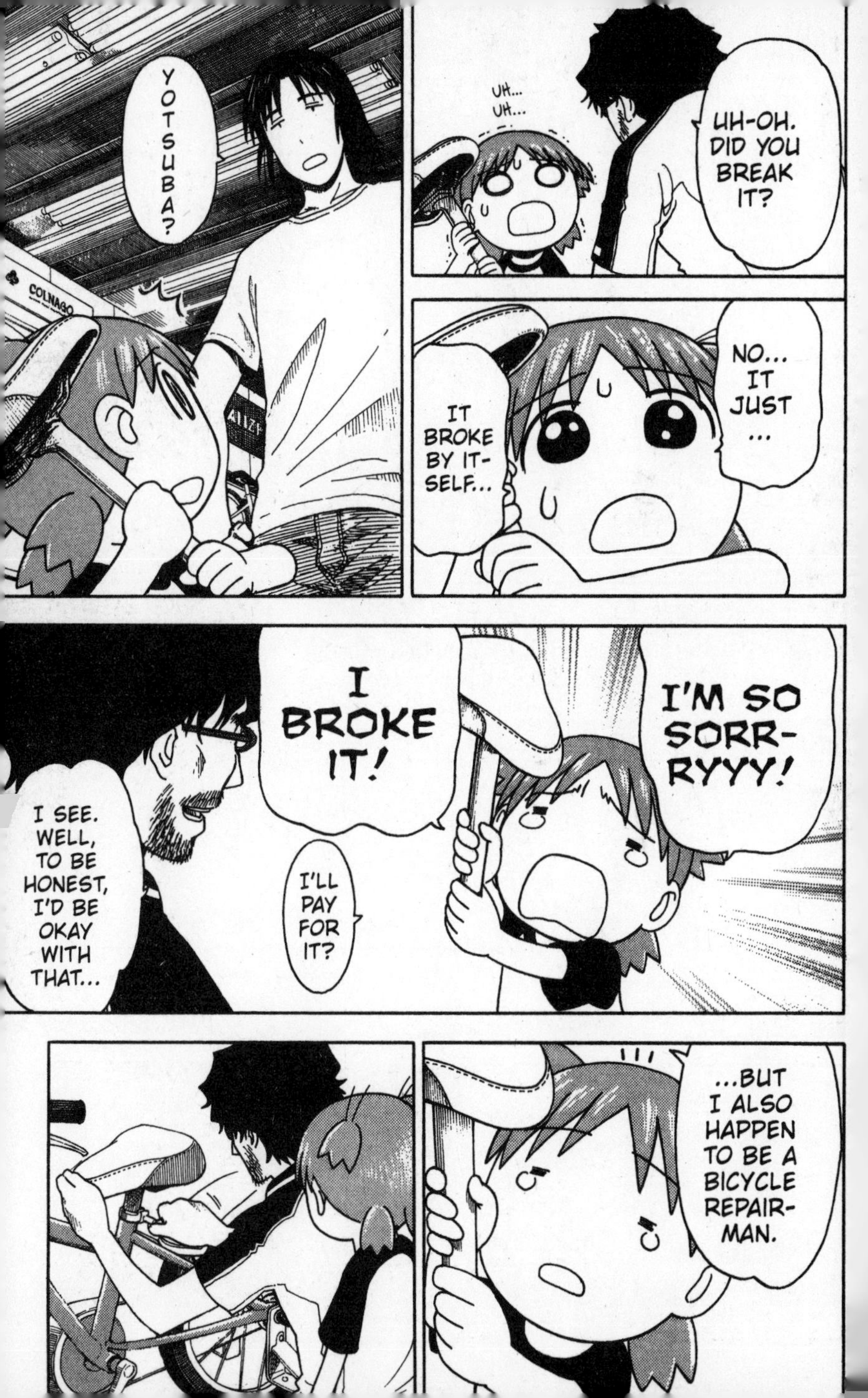
UH-OH. DID YOU BREAK IT?
UH... UH...
NO... IT JUST ...
IT BROKE BY IT-SELF...
YOTSUBA?
COLNAGO
I'M SO SORR-RYYY!
I BROKE IT!
I'LL PAY FOR IT?
I SEE. WELL, TO BE HONEST, I'D BE OKAY WITH THAT...
...BUT I ALSO HAPPEN TO BE A BICYCLE REPAIR-MAN.

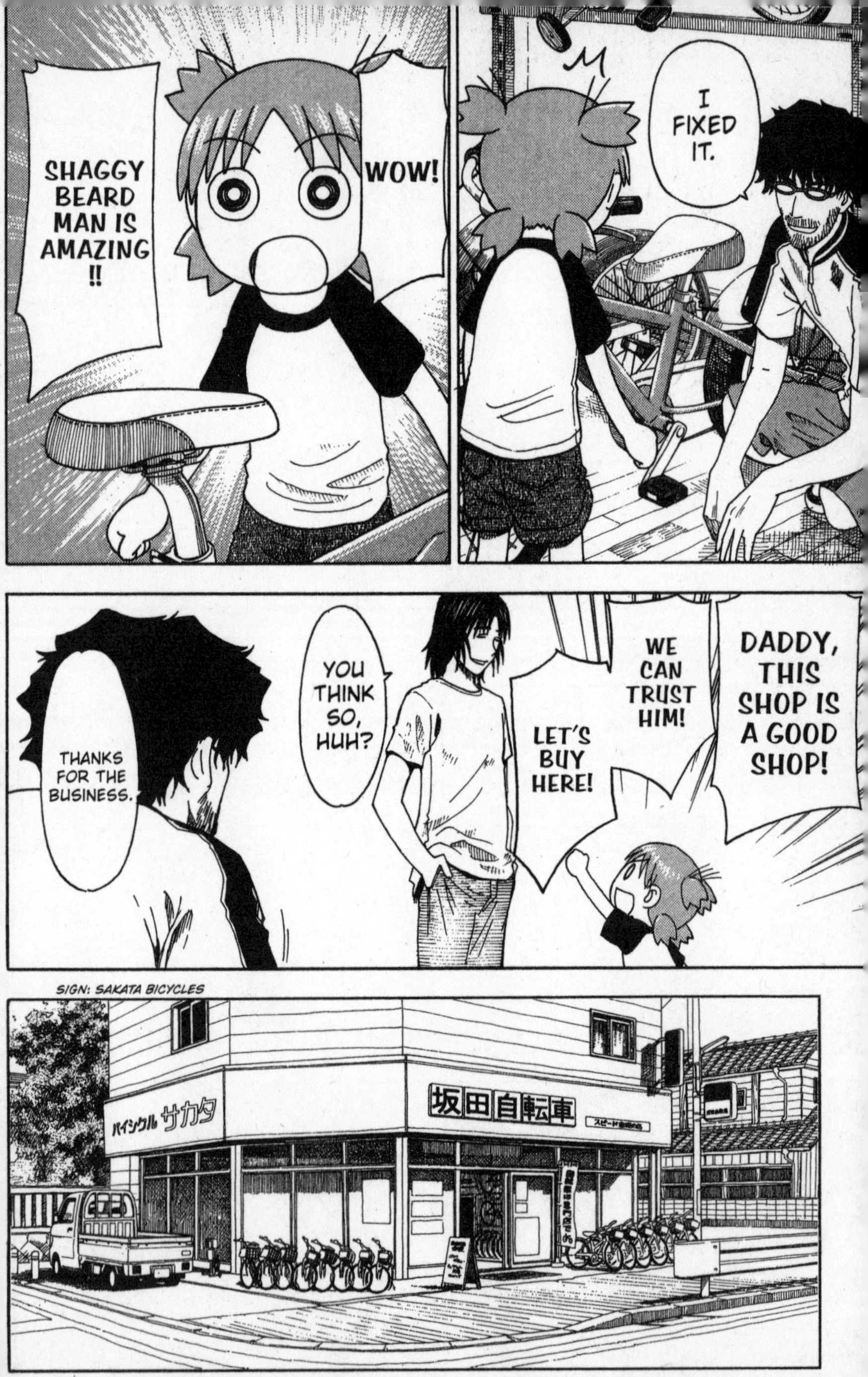

I FIXED IT.
WOW!
SHAGGY BEARD MAN IS AMAZING!!
DADDY, THIS SHOP IS A GOOD SHOP!
WE CAN TRUST HIM!
LET'S BUY HERE!
YOU THINK SO, HUH?
THANKS FOR THE BUSINESS.
SIGN: SAKATA BICYCLES
坂田自転車
バイシクル サカタ

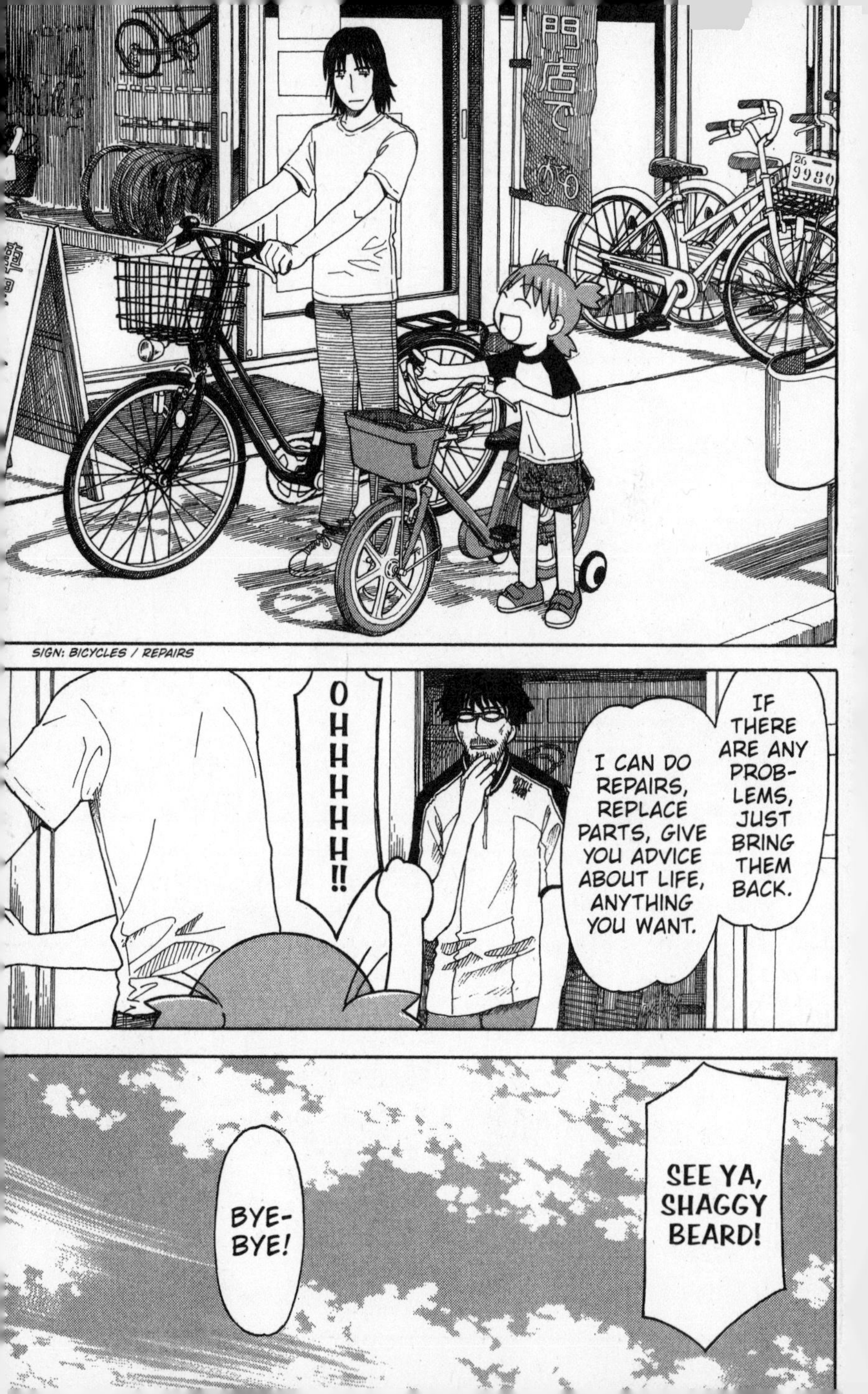
SIGN: BICYCLES / REPAIRS
IF THERE ARE ANY PROBLEMS, JUST BRING THEM BACK.
I CAN DO REPAIRS, REPLACE PARTS, GIVE YOU ADVICE ABOUT LIFE, ANYTHING YOU WANT.
OHHHHHH!!
SEE YA, SHAGGY BEARD!
BYE-BYE!

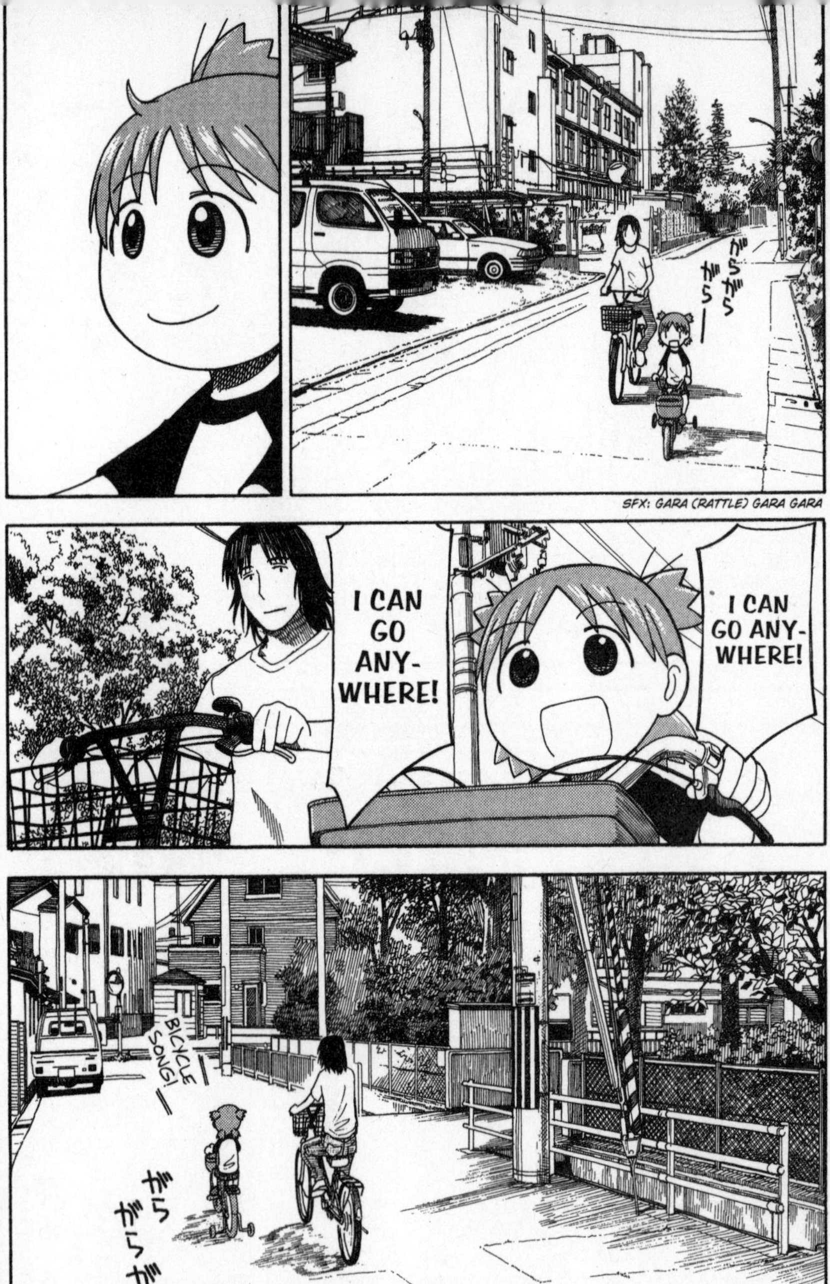
がらがらがらー
SFX: GARA (RATTLE) GARA GARA
I CAN GO ANY-WHERE!
I CAN GO ANY-WHERE!
BICYCLE SONG!
がらがらがらー
SFX: GARA GARA GARA

YOTSUBA&!

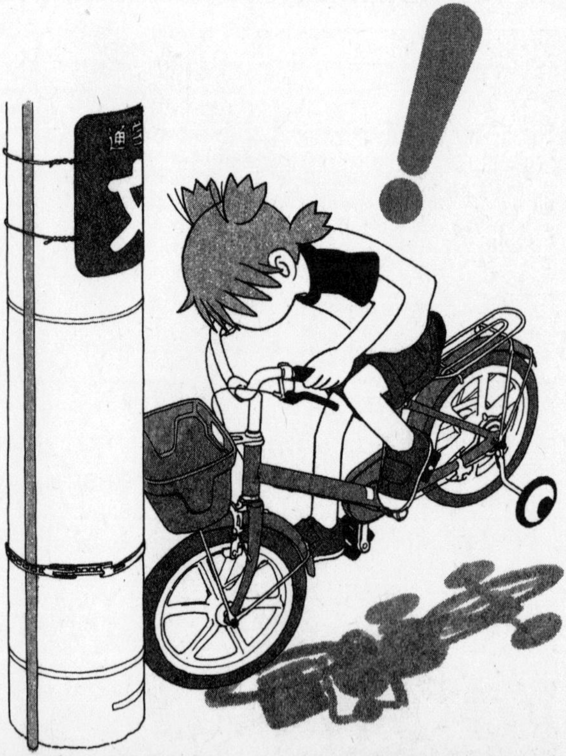
文

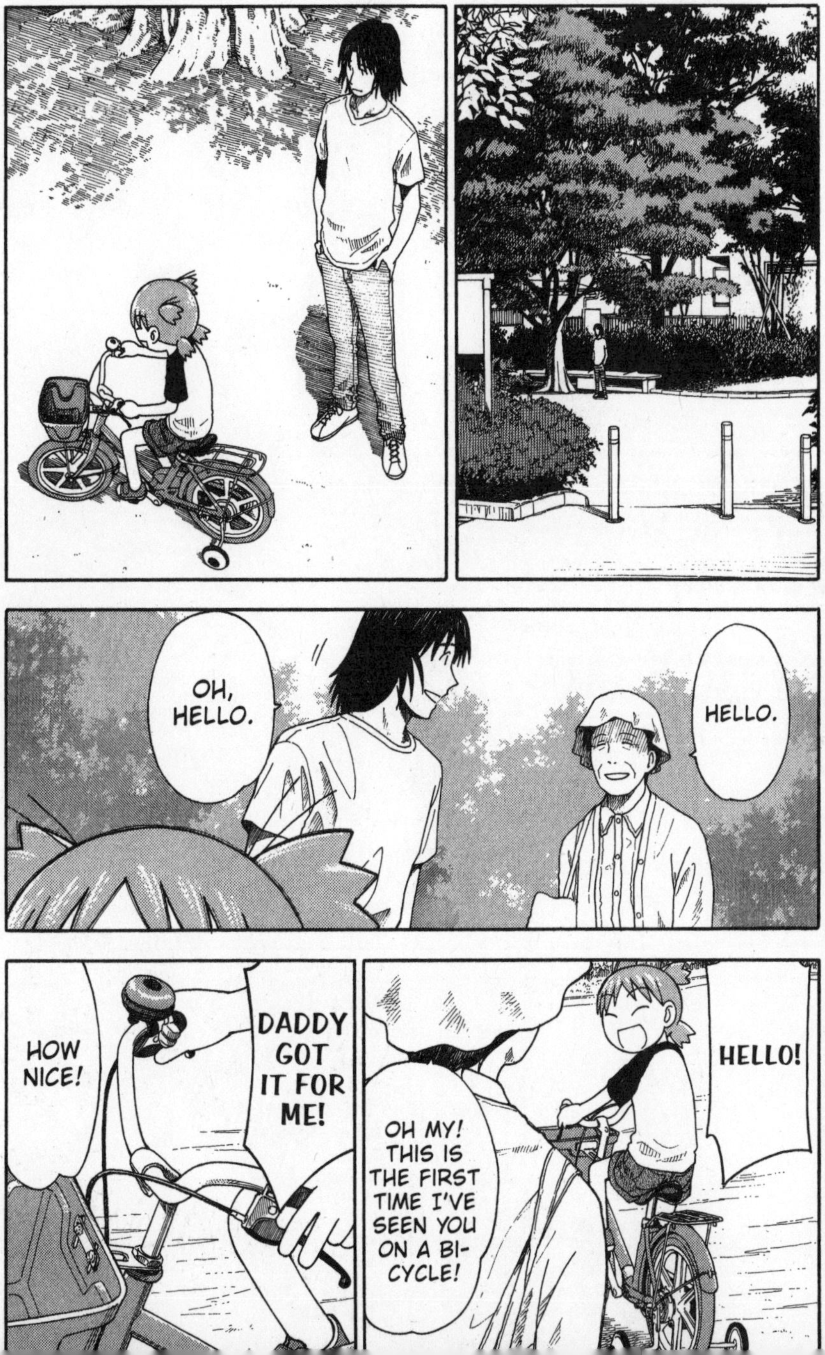
HELLO.
OH, HELLO.
HELLO!
OH MY! THIS IS THE FIRST TIME I'VE SEEN YOU ON A BI-CYCLE!
DADDY GOT IT FOR ME!
HOW NICE!

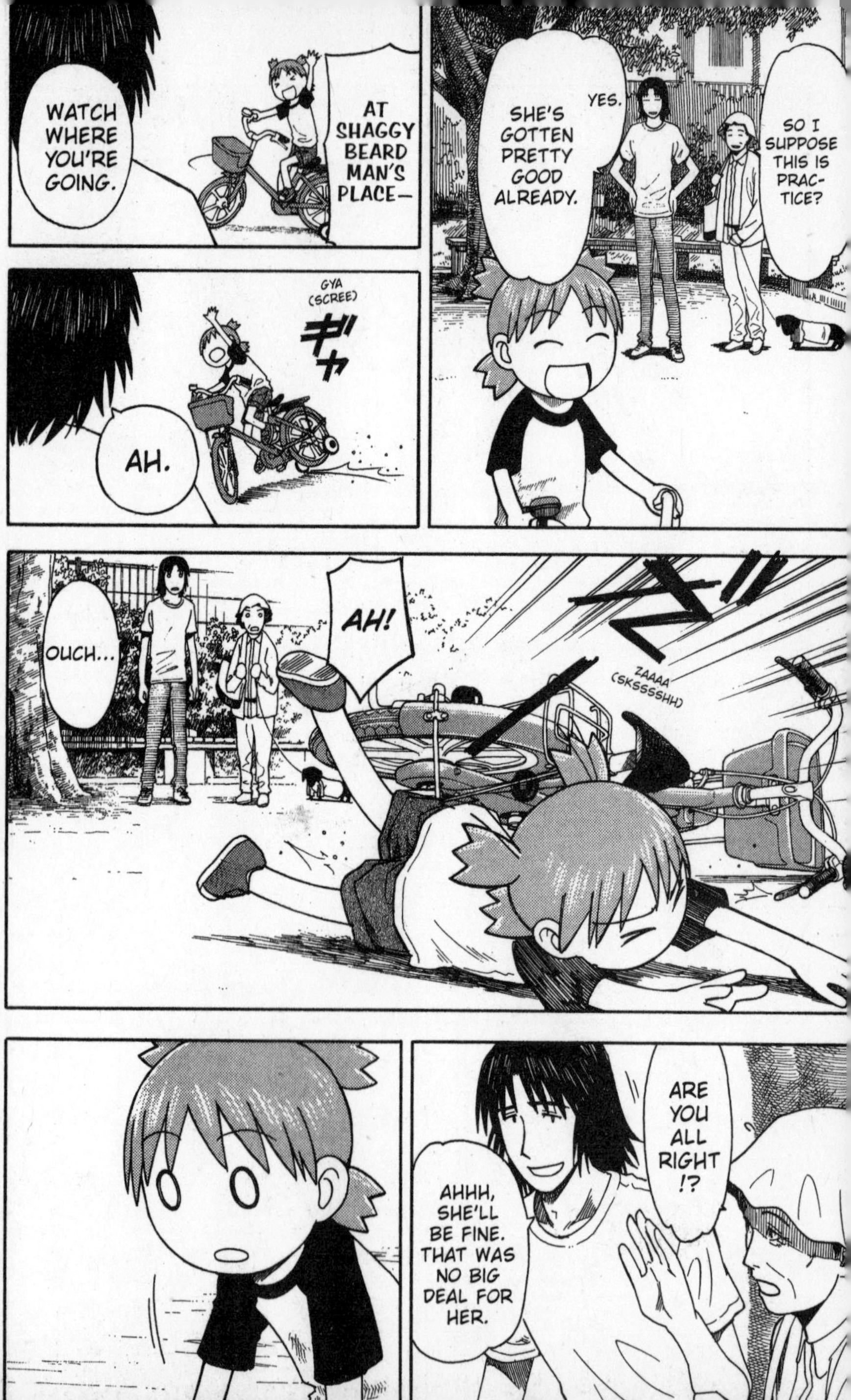
SO I SUPPOSE THIS IS PRAC-TICE?
YES.
SHE'S GOTTEN PRETTY GOOD ALREADY.
AT SHAGGY BEARD MAN'S PLACE—
WATCH WHERE YOU'RE GOING.
GYA (SCREE)
AH.
ZAAAA (SKSSSSHH)
AH!
OUCH...
ARE YOU ALL RIGHT !?
AHHH, SHE'LL BE FINE. THAT WAS NO BIG DEAL FOR HER.

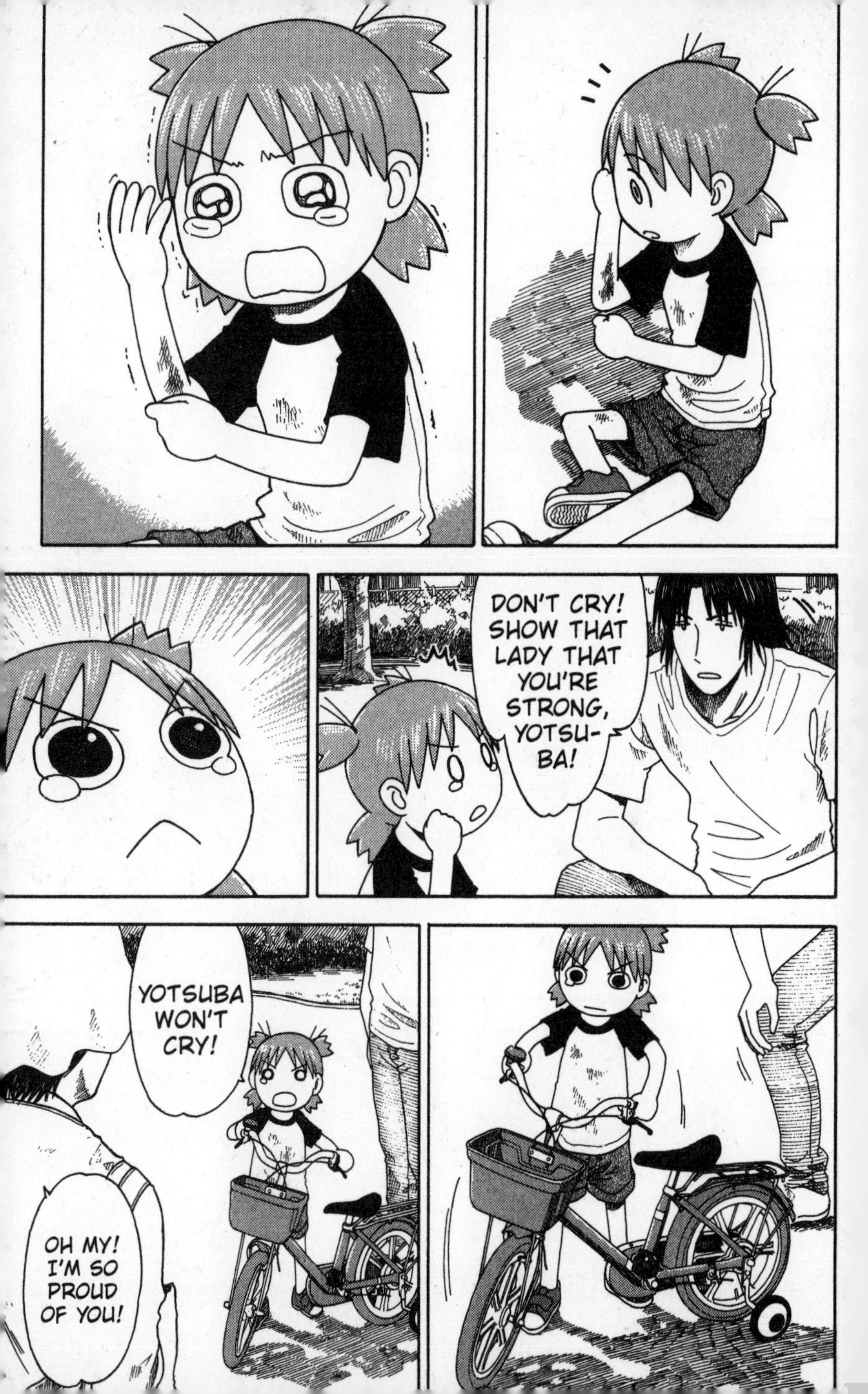
DON'T CRY! SHOW THAT LADY THAT YOU'RE STRONG, YOTSU-BA!
YOTSUBA WON'T CRY!
OH MY! I'M SO PROUD OF YOU!

YOTSUBA&

POTTERING AROUND

#37

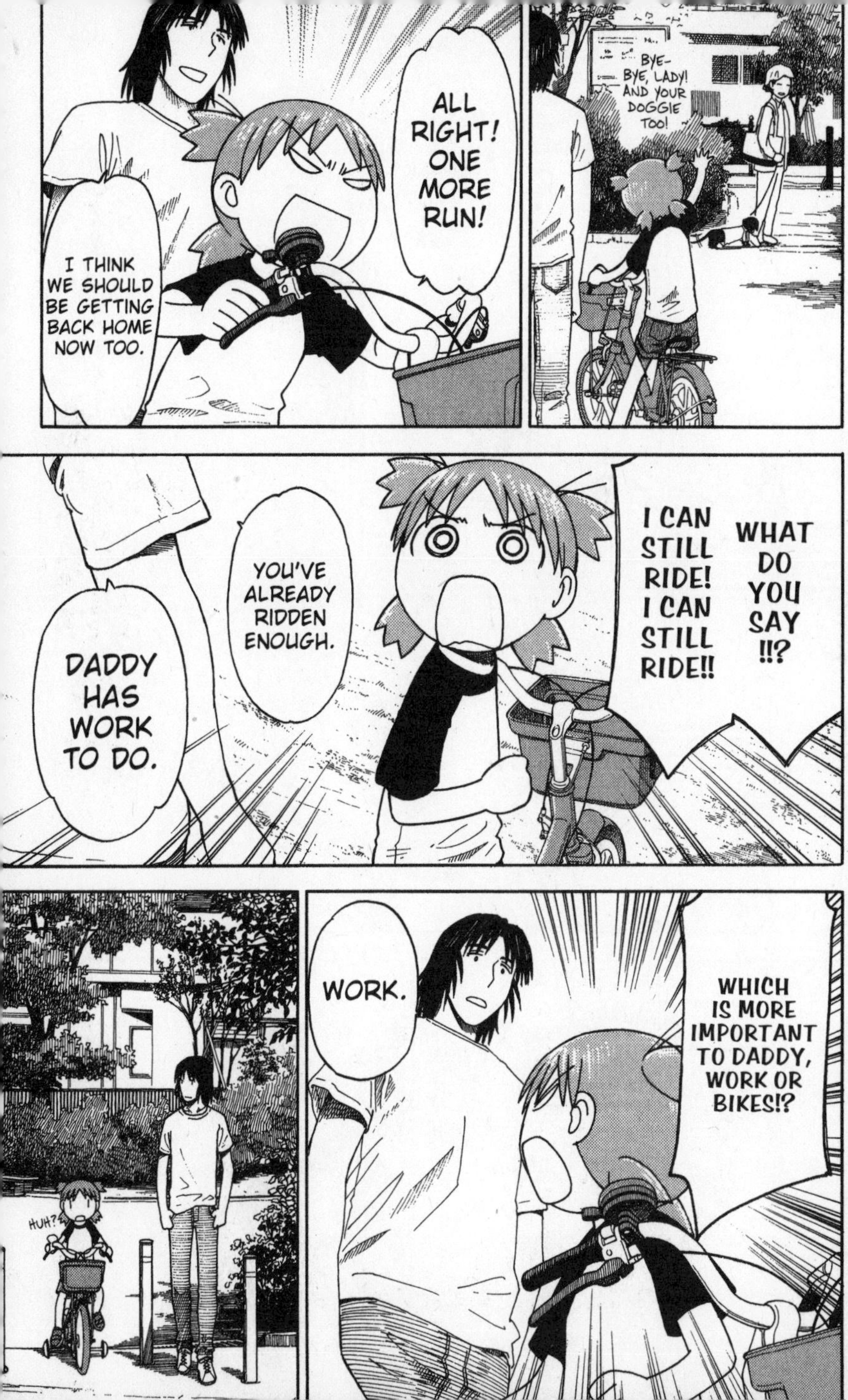
BYE-BYE, LADY! AND YOUR DOGGIE TOO!
ALL RIGHT! ONE MORE RUN!
I THINK WE SHOULD BE GETTING BACK HOME NOW TOO.
WHAT DO YOU SAY!!?
I CAN STILL RIDE! I CAN STILL RIDE!!
YOU'VE ALREADY RIDDEN ENOUGH.
DADDY HAS WORK TO DO.
WHICH IS MORE IMPORTANT TO DADDY, WORK OR BIKES!?
WORK.
HUH?

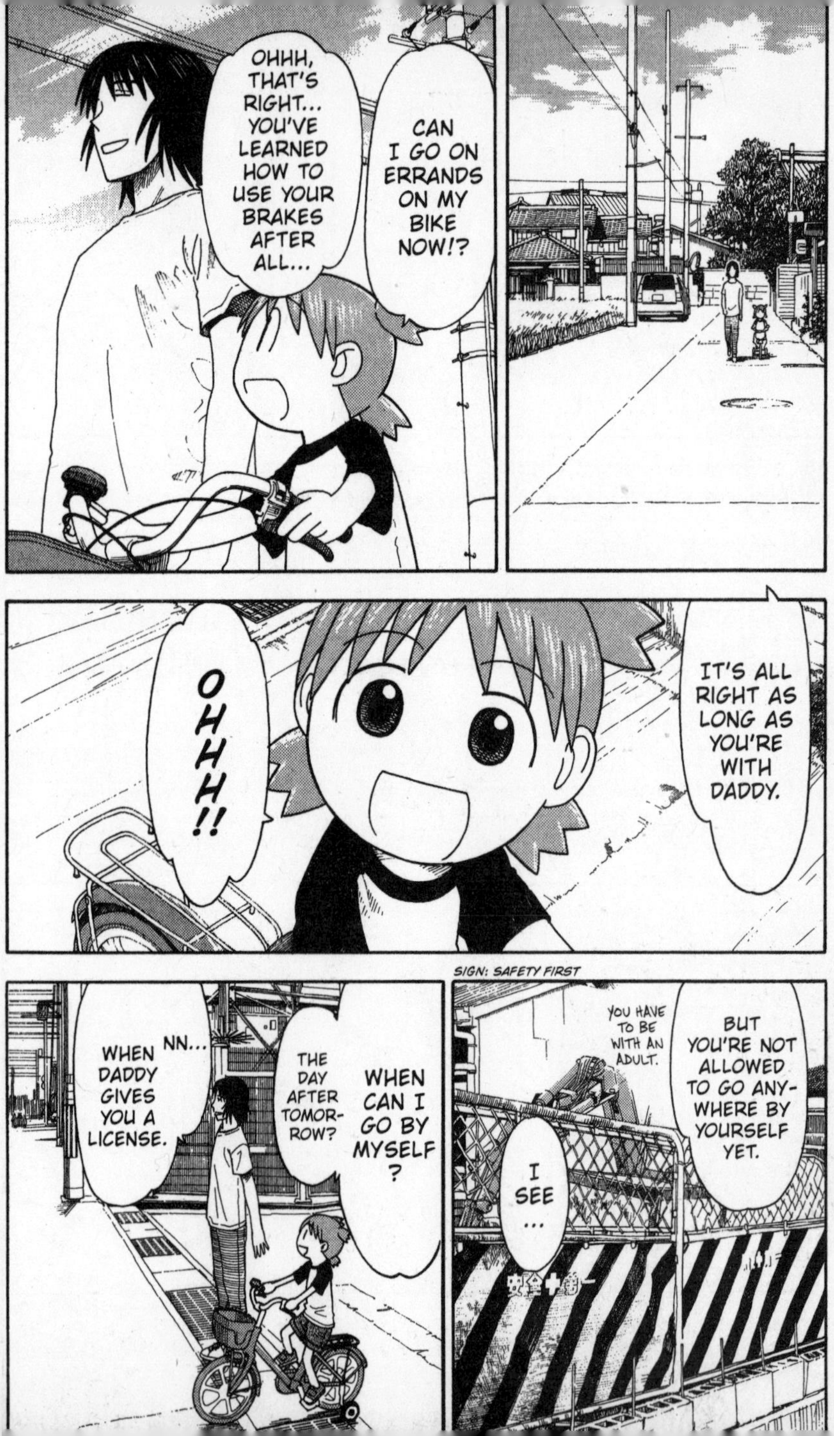
CAN I GO ON ERRANDS ON MY BIKE NOW!?
OHHH, THAT'S RIGHT... YOU'VE LEARNED HOW TO USE YOUR BRAKES AFTER ALL...
IT'S ALL RIGHT AS LONG AS YOU'RE WITH DADDY.
OHHHH!!
SIGN: SAFETY FIRST
BUT YOU'RE NOT ALLOWED TO GO ANY-WHERE BY YOURSELF YET.
YOU HAVE TO BE WITH AN ADULT.
I SEE ...
WHEN CAN I GO BY MYSELF?
THE DAY AFTER TOMOR-ROW?
NN...
WHEN DADDY GIVES YOU A LICENSE.

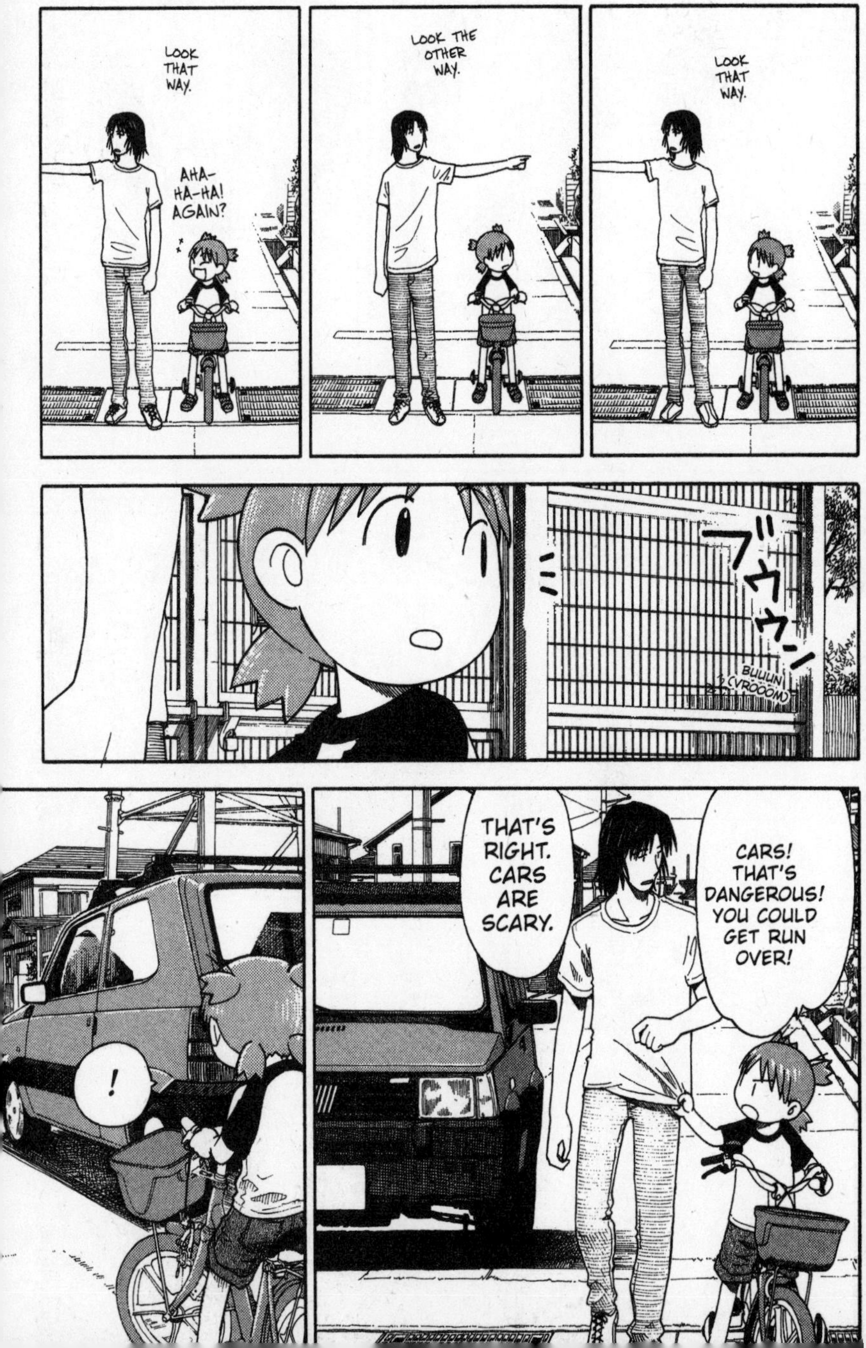
LOOK THAT WAY.
LOOK THE OTHER WAY.
LOOK THAT WAY.
AHA-HA-HA! AGAIN?
BUUUN (VROOOM)
CARS! THAT'S DANGEROUS! YOU COULD GET RUN OVER!
THAT'S RIGHT. CARS ARE SCARY.
!

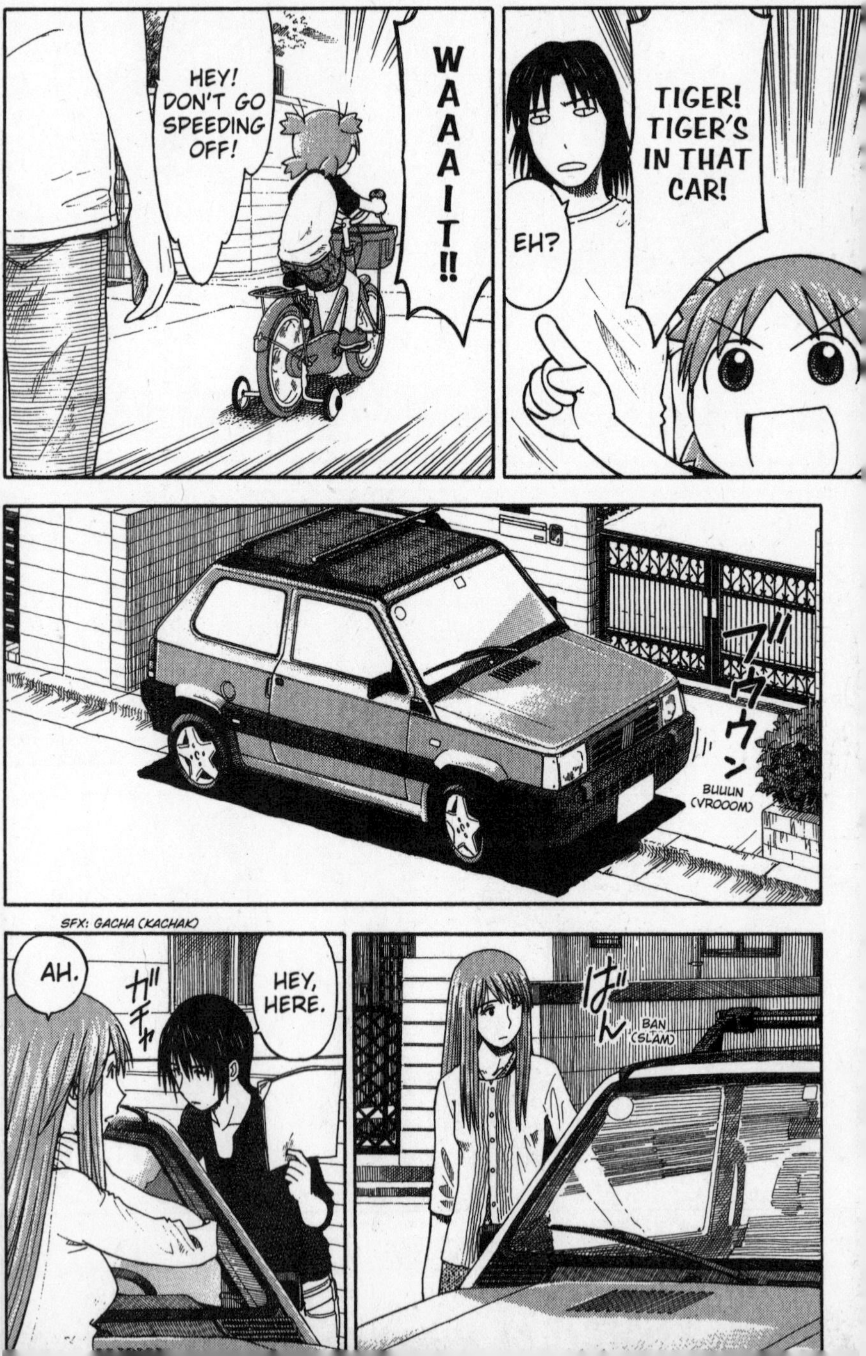
TIGER! TIGER'S IN THAT CAR!
EH?
WAAAIT!!
HEY! DON'T GO SPEEDING OFF!
BUUUN (VROOOM)
SFX: GACHA (KACHAK)
ばん
BAN (SLAM)
HEY, HERE.
ガチャ
AH.

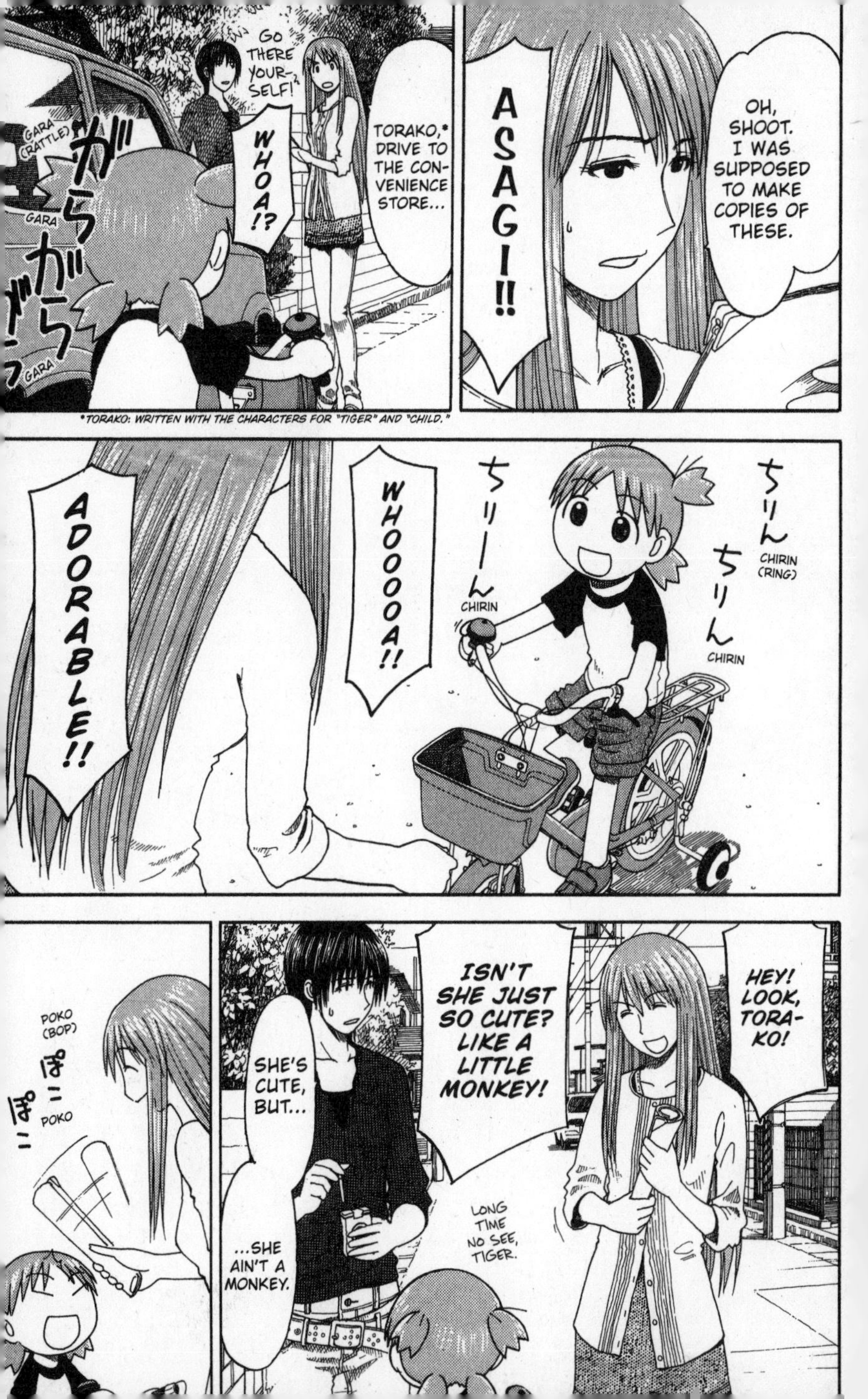
OH, SHOOT. I WAS SUPPOSED TO MAKE COPIES OF THESE.
ASAGI!!
TORAKO,* DRIVE TO THE CONVENIENCE STORE...
GO THERE YOURSELF!
WHOA!?
GARA (RATTLE)
がらがら
GARA
GARA
ちりん
CHIRIN (RING)
ちりん
CHIRIN
ちりーん
CHIRIN
WHOOOOOA!!
ADORABLE!!
HEY! LOOK, TORAKO!
ISN'T SHE JUST SO CUTE? LIKE A LITTLE MONKEY!
LONG TIME NO SEE, TIGER.
SHE'S CUTE, BUT...
...SHE AIN'T A MONKEY.
POKO (BOP)
ぽこ
ぽこ
POKO

*TORAKO: WRITTEN WITH THE CHARACTERS FOR "TIGER" AND "CHILD."

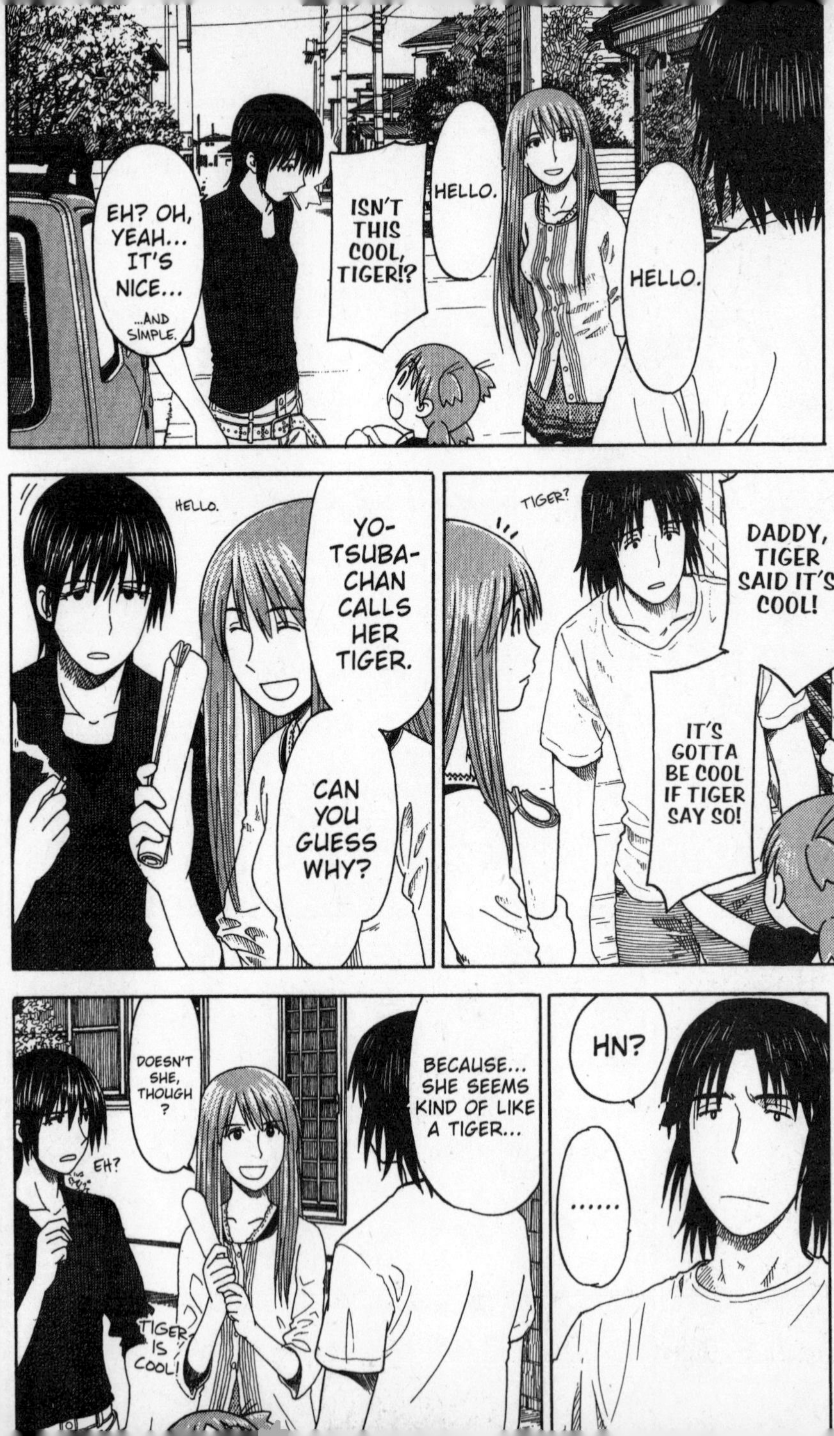
HELLO.
HELLO.
ISN'T THIS COOL, TIGER!?
EH? OH, YEAH... IT'S NICE...
...AND SIMPLE.
DADDY, TIGER SAID IT'S COOL!
IT'S GOTTA BE COOL IF TIGER SAY SO!
TIGER?
YO-TSUBA-CHAN CALLS HER TIGER.
CAN YOU GUESS WHY?
HELLO.
HN?
......
BECAUSE... SHE SEEMS KIND OF LIKE A TIGER...
DOESN'T SHE, THOUGH?
EH?
TIGER IS COOL!

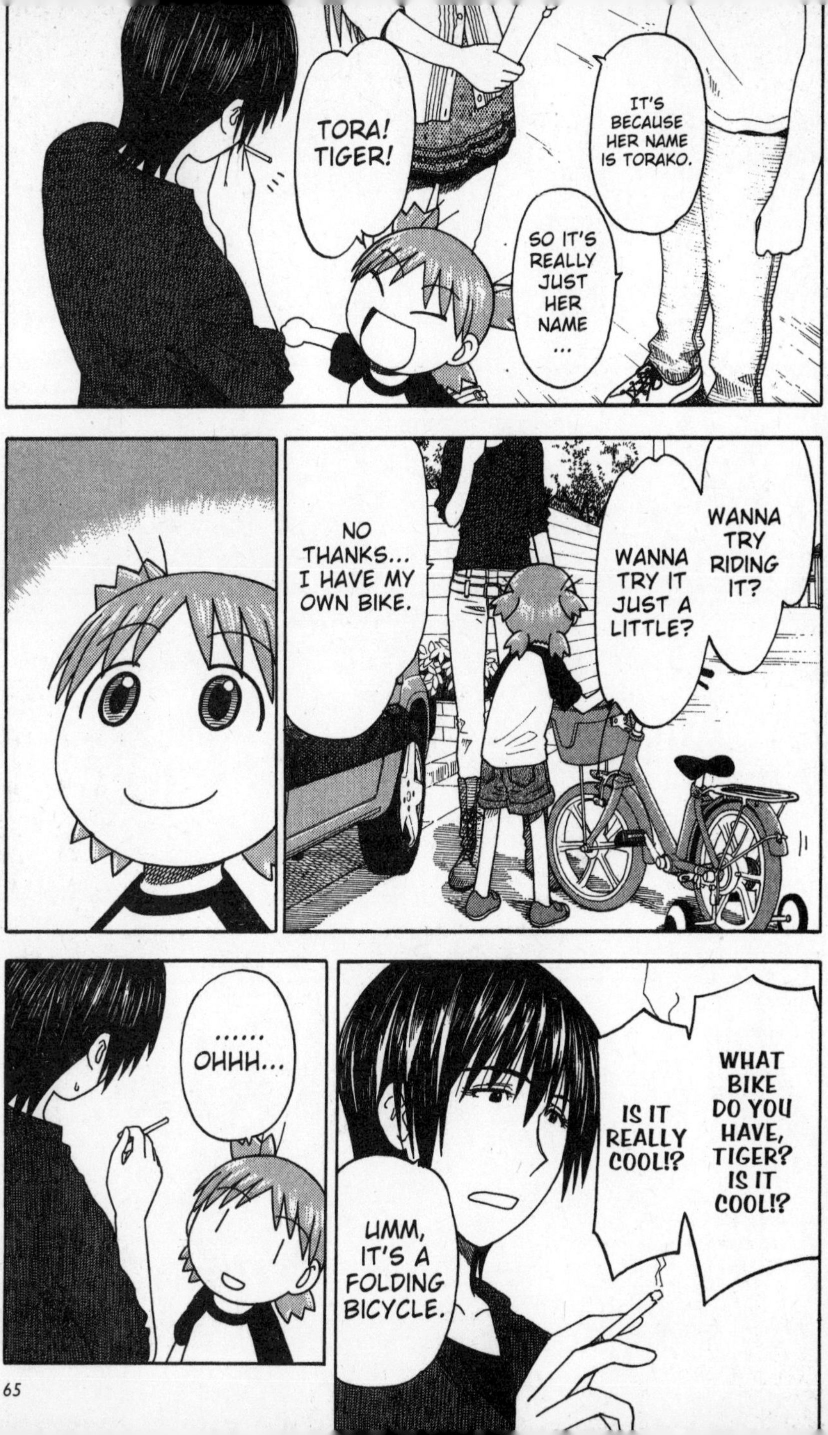
IT'S BECAUSE HER NAME IS TORAKO.
TORA! TIGER!
SO IT'S REALLY JUST HER NAME ...
WANNA TRY RIDING IT?
WANNA TRY IT JUST A LITTLE?
NO THANKS... I HAVE MY OWN BIKE.
WHAT BIKE DO YOU HAVE, TIGER? IS IT COOL!?
IS IT REALLY COOL!?
UMM, IT'S A FOLDING BICYCLE.
...... OHHH...

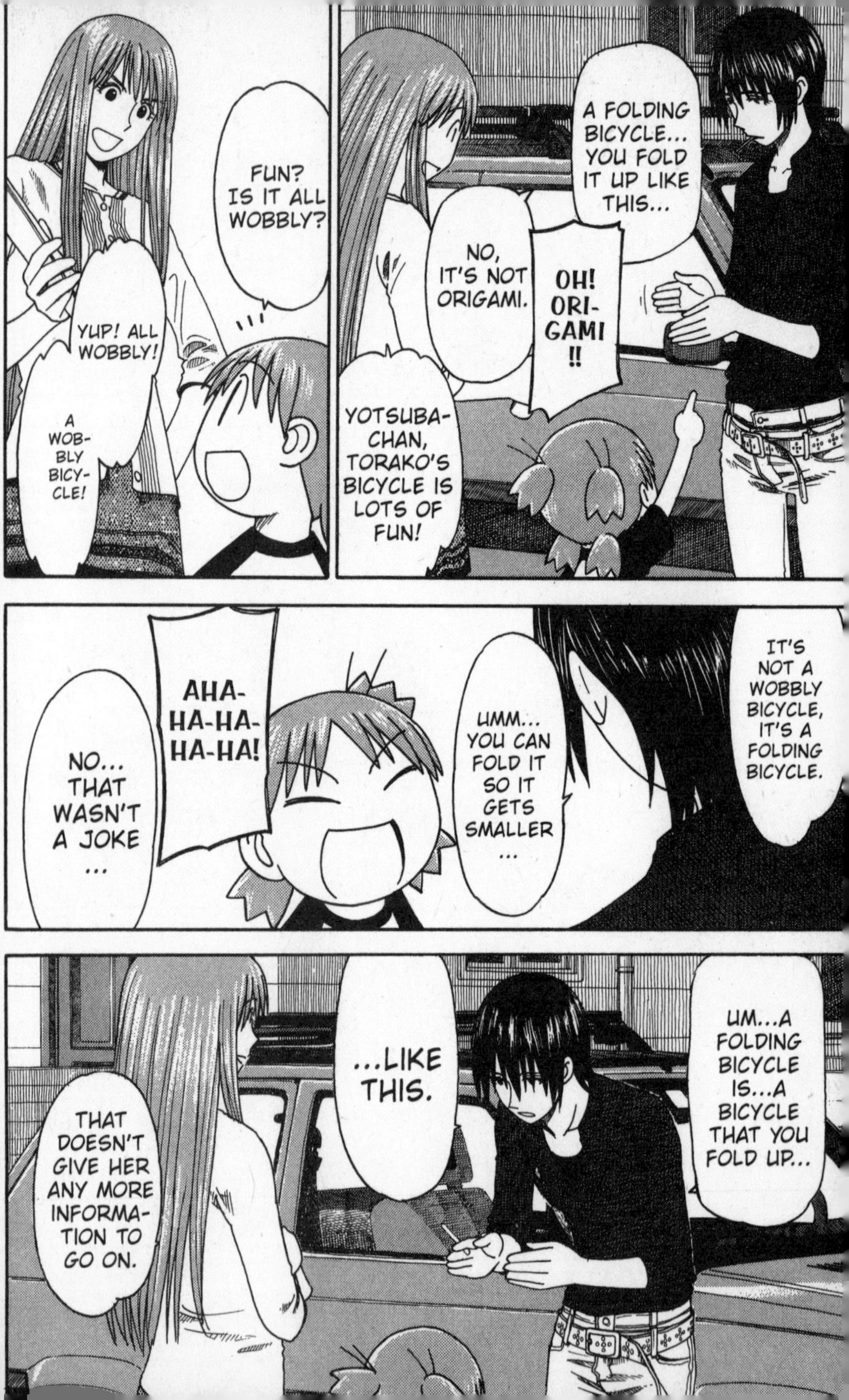
A FOLDING BICYCLE... YOU FOLD IT UP LIKE THIS...
OH! ORIGAMI !!
NO, IT'S NOT ORIGAMI.
YOTSUBA-CHAN, TORAKO'S BICYCLE IS LOTS OF FUN!
FUN? IS IT ALL WOBBLY?
YUP! ALL WOBBLY!
A WOBBLY BICYCLE!
IT'S NOT A WOBBLY BICYCLE, IT'S A FOLDING BICYCLE.
UMM... YOU CAN FOLD IT SO IT GETS SMALLER ...
AHA-HA-HA-HA-HA!
NO... THAT WASN'T A JOKE ...
UM...A FOLDING BICYCLE IS...A BICYCLE THAT YOU FOLD UP...
...LIKE THIS.
THAT DOESN'T GIVE HER ANY MORE INFORMATION TO GO ON.

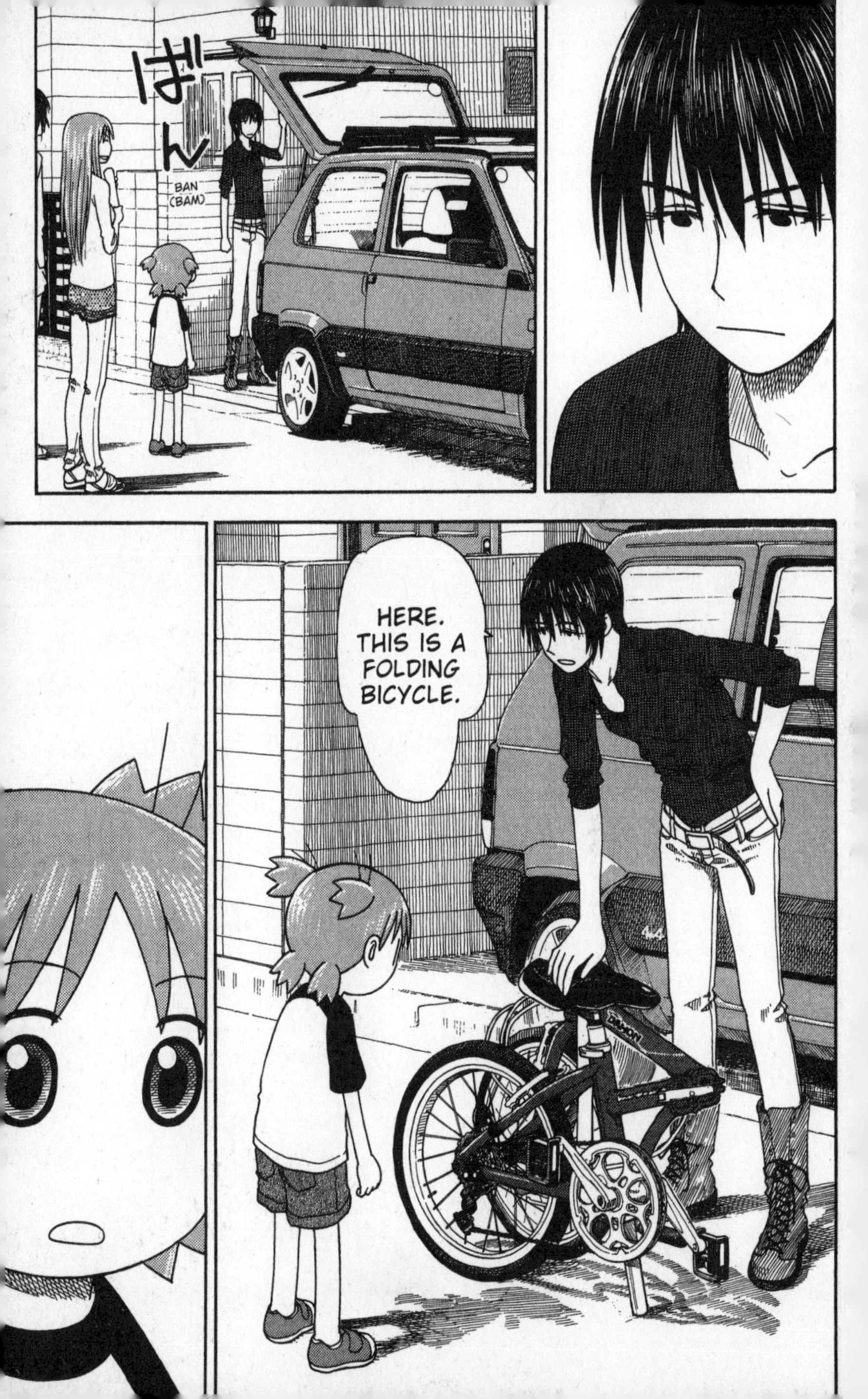
ばん
BAN (BAM)
HERE. THIS IS A FOLDING BICYCLE.

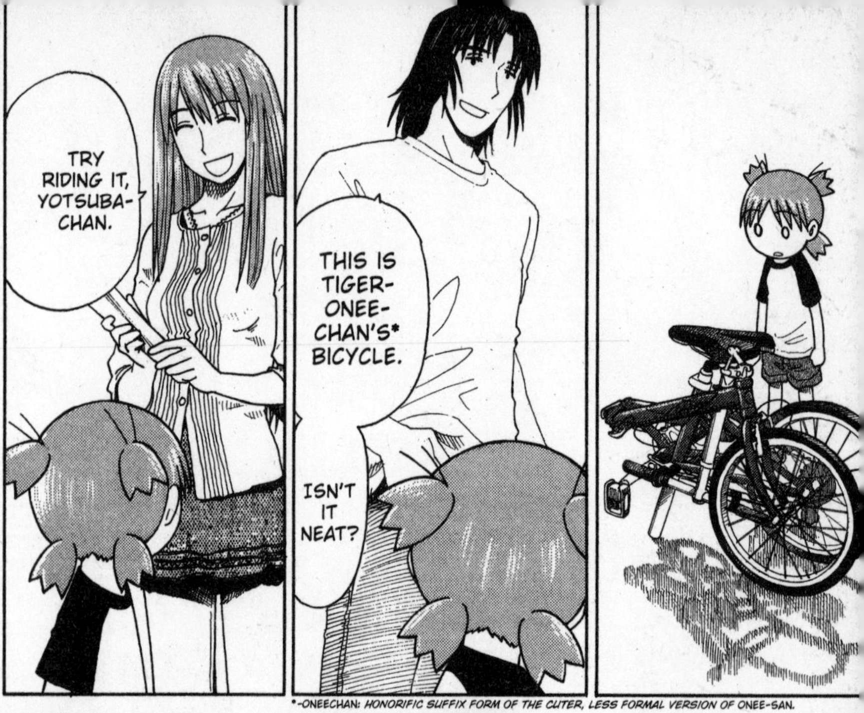
THIS IS TIGER-ONEE-CHAN'S* BICYCLE.
ISN'T IT NEAT?
TRY RIDING IT, YOTSUBA-CHAN.

*-ONEECHAN: *HONORIFIC SUFFIX FORM OF THE CUTER, LESS FORMAL VERSION OF* ONEE-SAN.

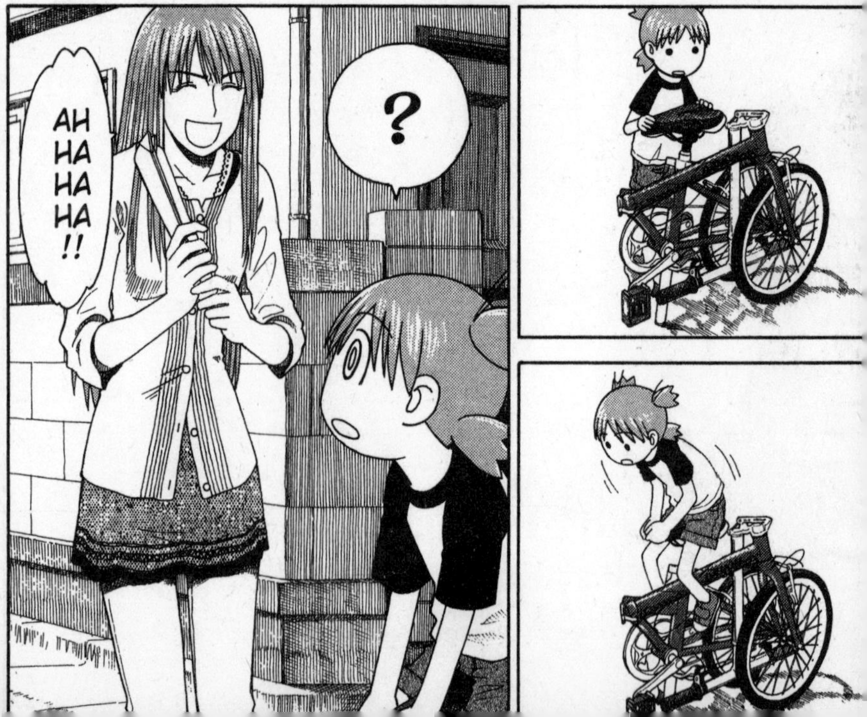
?
AH HA HA HA!!

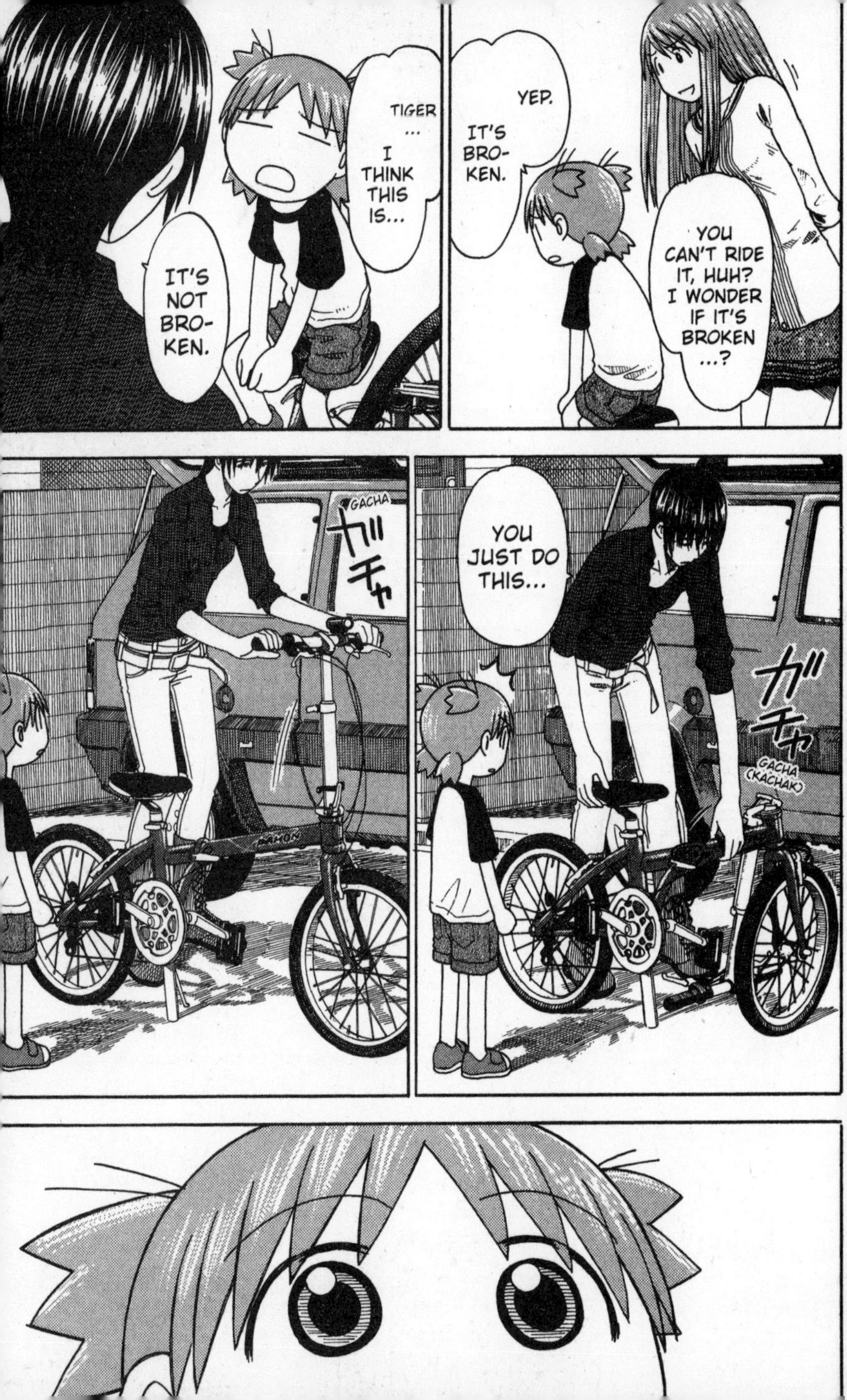
YOU CAN'T RIDE IT, HUH? I WONDER IF IT'S BROKEN ...?
YEP. IT'S BROKEN.
TIGER ... I THINK THIS IS...
IT'S NOT BROKEN.
YOU JUST DO THIS...
ガチャ
GACHA (KACHAK)
ガチャ
GACHA

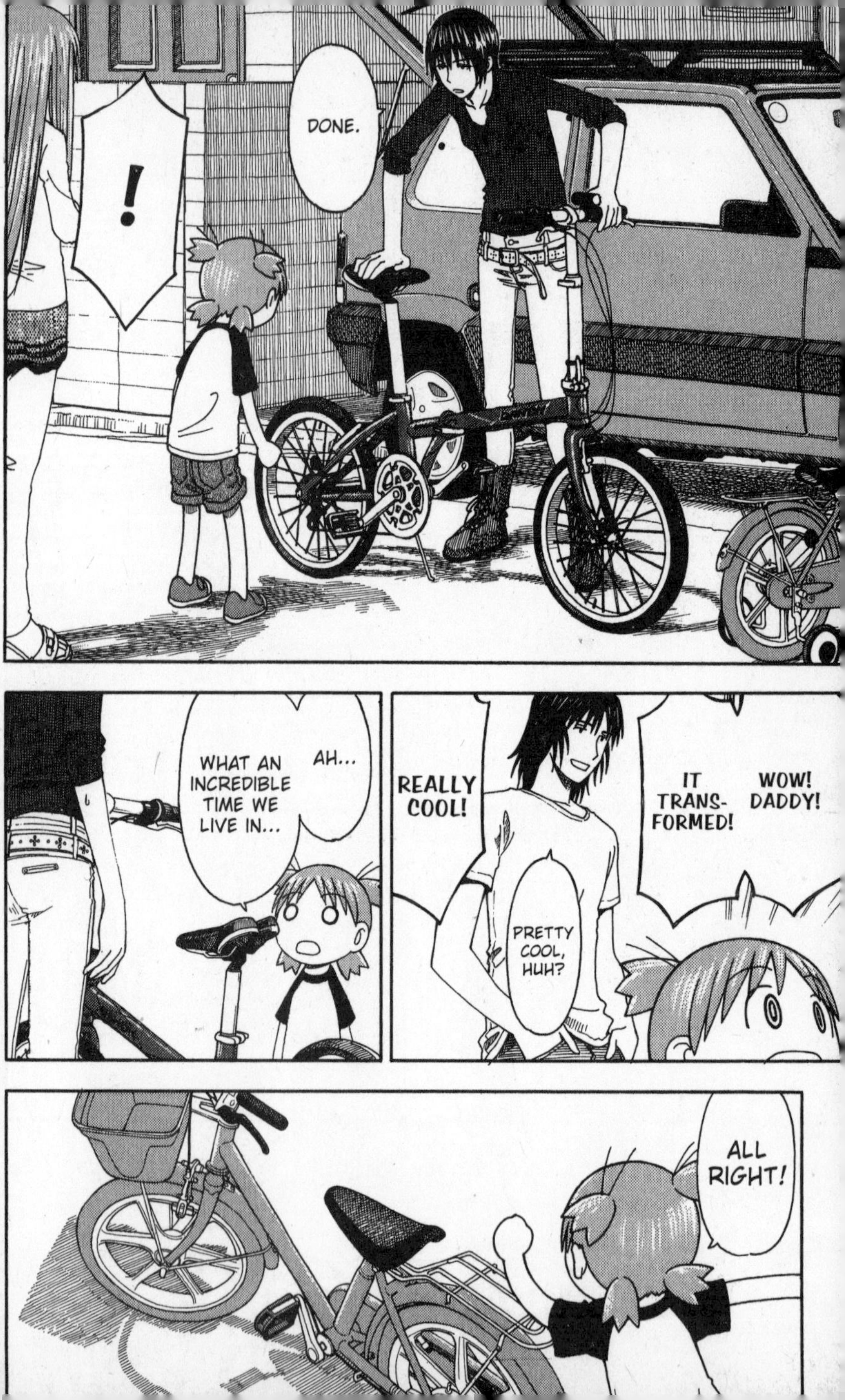
DONE.
!
WOW! DADDY!
IT TRANS-FORMED!
REALLY COOL!
PRETTY COOL, HUH?
AH...
WHAT AN INCREDIBLE TIME WE LIVE IN...
ALL RIGHT!

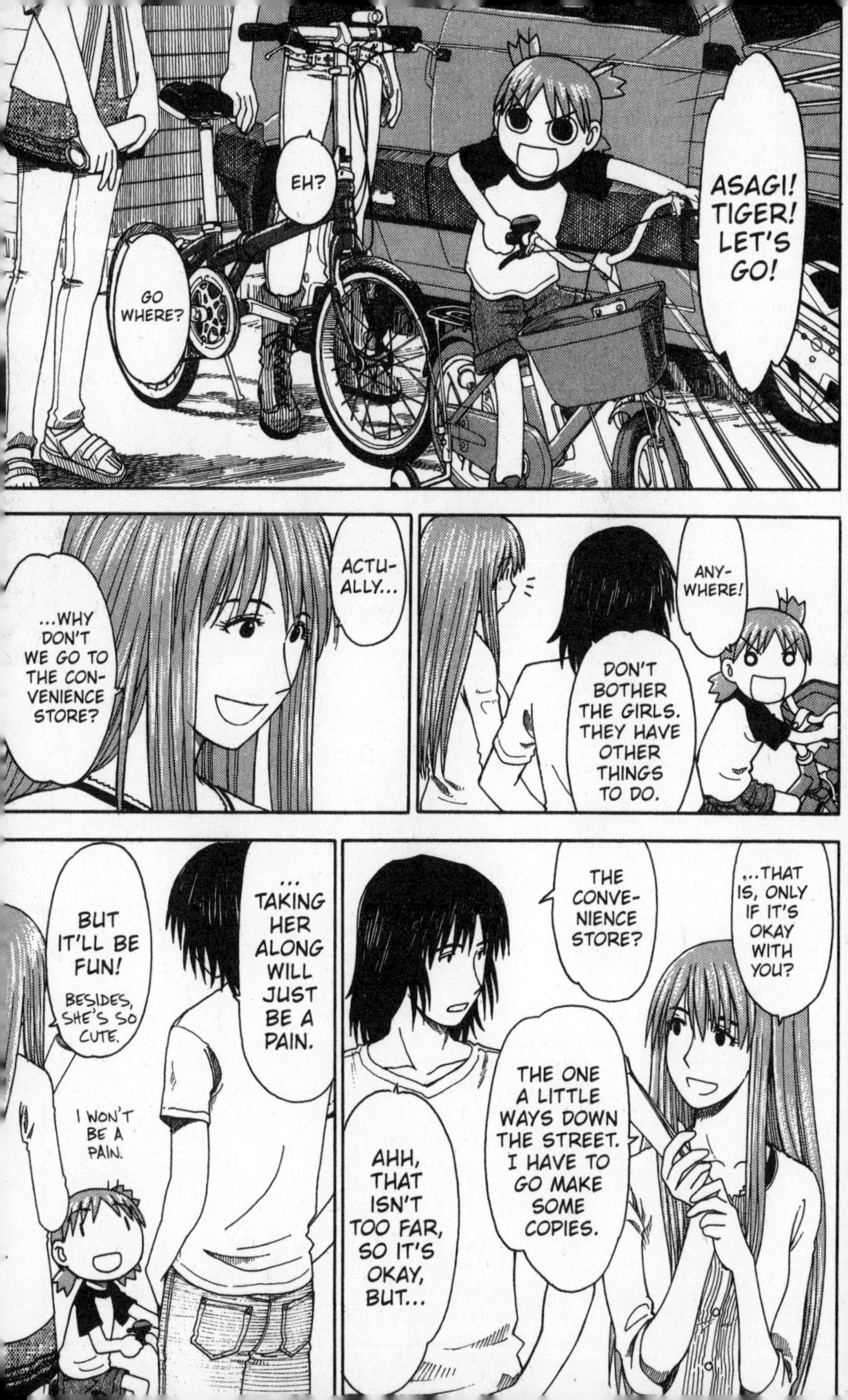
ASAGI! TIGER! LET'S GO!
EH?
GO WHERE?
ANYWHERE!
DON'T BOTHER THE GIRLS. THEY HAVE OTHER THINGS TO DO.
ACTUALLY...
...WHY DON'T WE GO TO THE CONVENIENCE STORE?
...THAT IS, ONLY IF IT'S OKAY WITH YOU?
THE CONVENIENCE STORE?
THE ONE A LITTLE WAYS DOWN THE STREET. I HAVE TO GO MAKE SOME COPIES.
AHH, THAT ISN'T TOO FAR, SO IT'S OKAY, BUT...
...TAKING HER ALONG WILL JUST BE A PAIN.
BUT IT'LL BE FUN!
BESIDES, SHE'S SO CUTE.
I WON'T BE A PAIN.

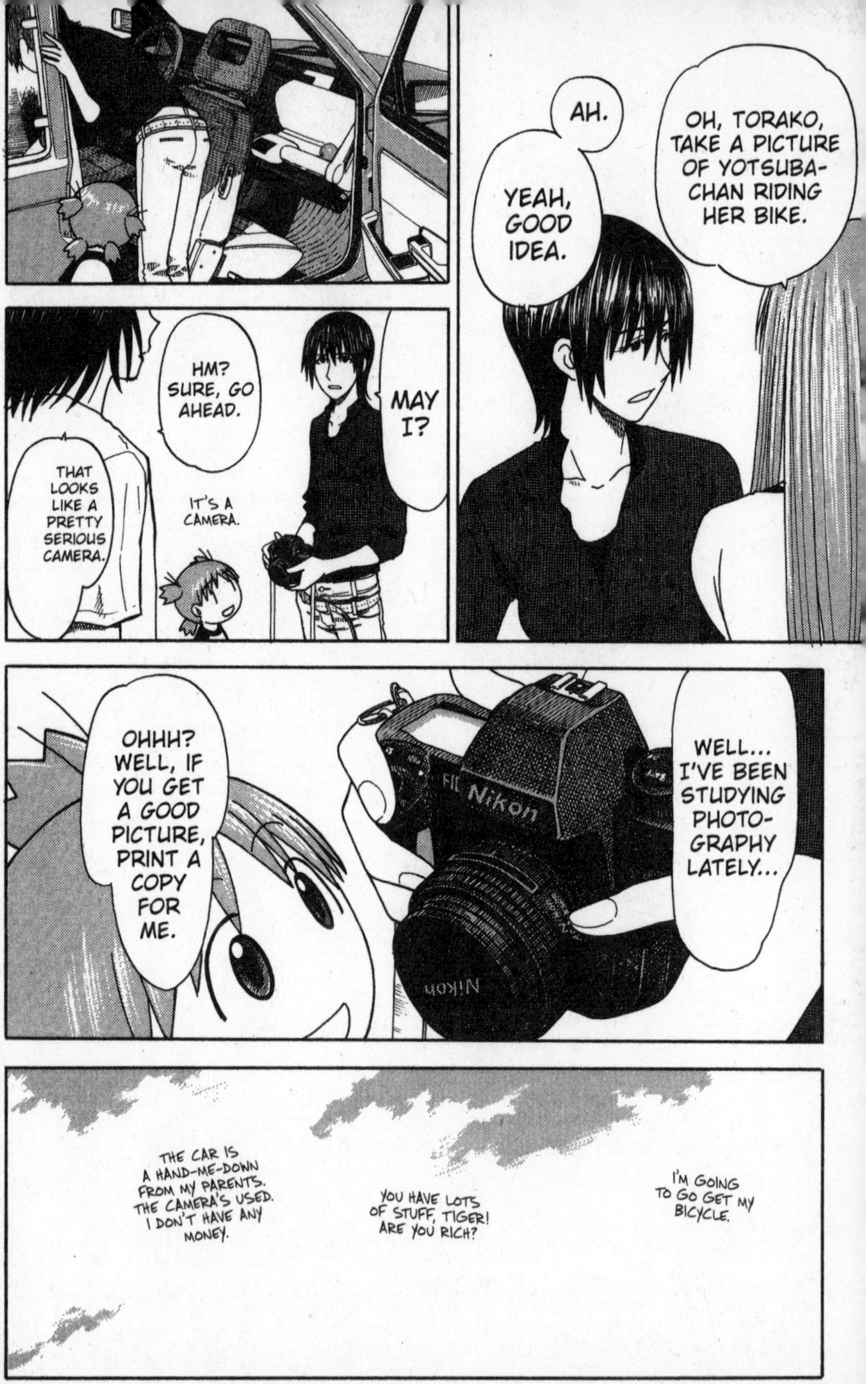
OH, TORAKO, TAKE A PICTURE OF YOTSUBA-CHAN RIDING HER BIKE.
AH.
YEAH, GOOD IDEA.
MAY I?
HM? SURE, GO AHEAD.
IT'S A CAMERA.
THAT LOOKS LIKE A PRETTY SERIOUS CAMERA.
WELL... I'VE BEEN STUDYING PHOTO-GRAPHY LATELY...
Nikon
OHHH? WELL, IF YOU GET A GOOD PICTURE, PRINT A COPY FOR ME.
I'M GOING TO GO GET MY BICYCLE.
YOU HAVE LOTS OF STUFF, TIGER! ARE YOU RICH?
THE CAR IS A HAND-ME-DOWN FROM MY PARENTS. THE CAMERA'S USED. I DON'T HAVE ANY MONEY.

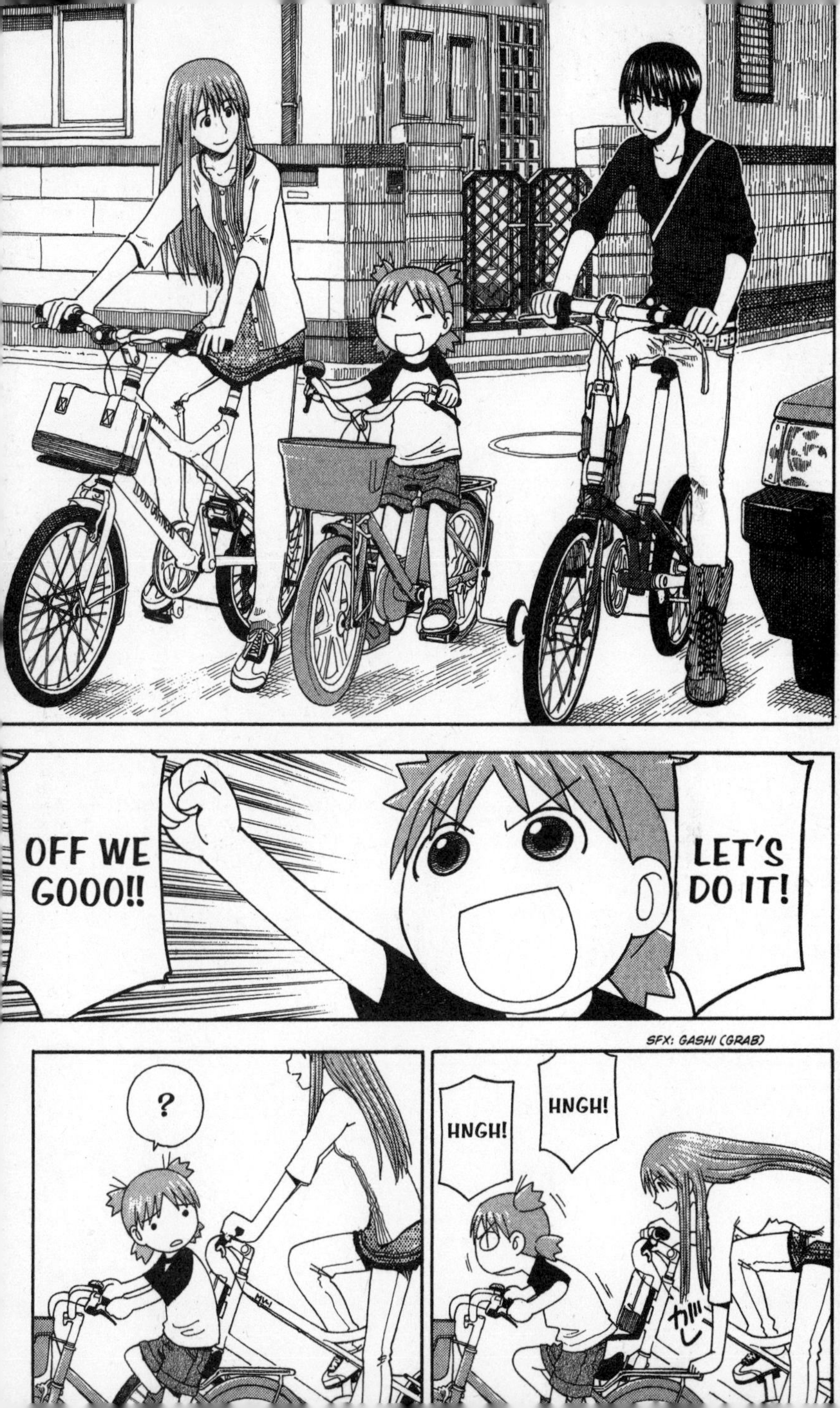
LET'S DO IT!
OFF WE GOOO!!
SFX: GASHI (GRAB)
HNGH!
HNGH!
?

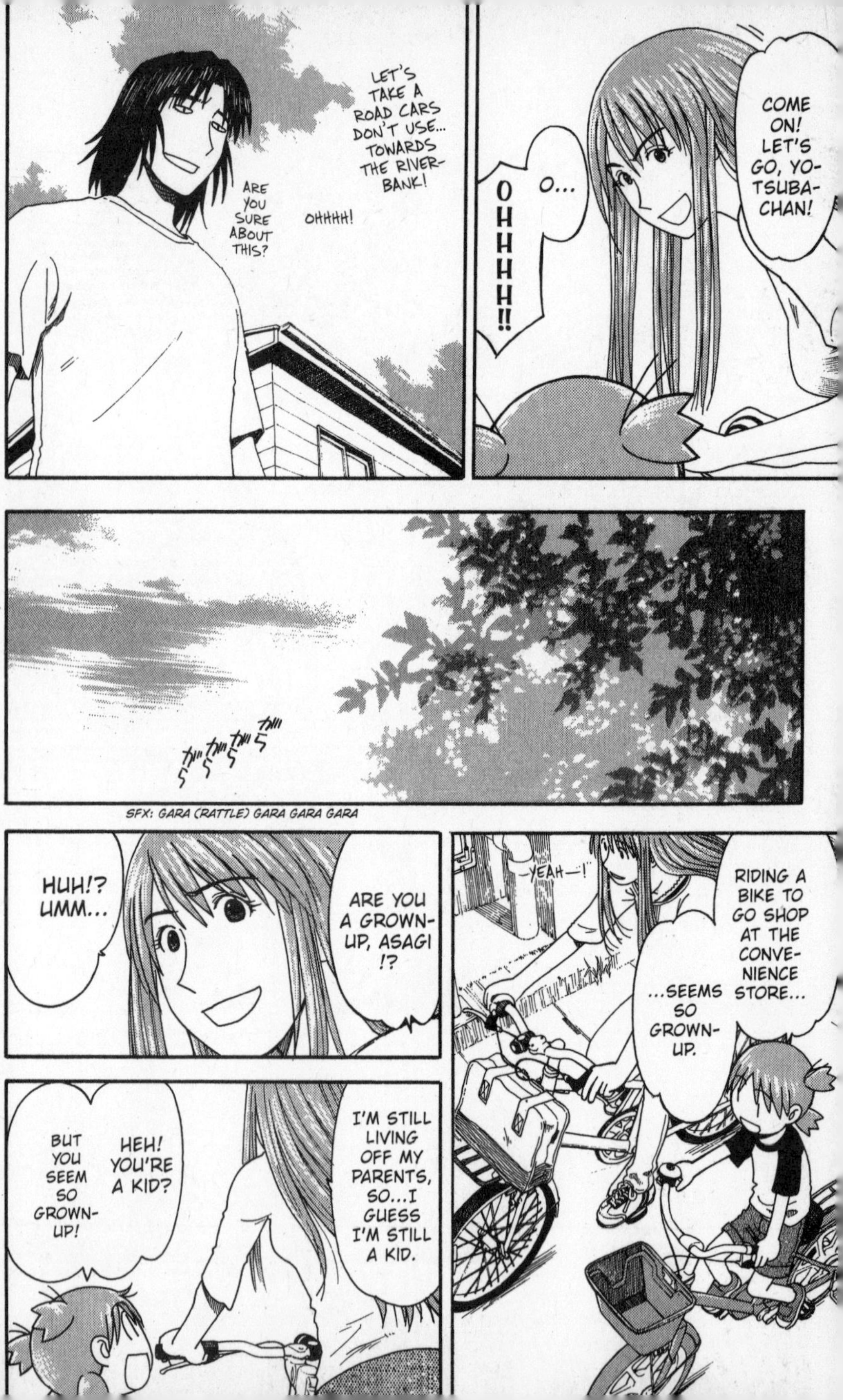
COME ON! LET'S GO, YO-TSUBA-CHAN!
O... OHHHHH!!
LET'S TAKE A ROAD CARS DON'T USE... TOWARDS THE RIVER-BANK!
OHHHH!
ARE YOU SURE ABOUT THIS?
SFX: GARA (RATTLE) GARA GARA GARA
RIDING A BIKE TO GO SHOP AT THE CONVE-NIENCE STORE...
...SEEMS SO GROWN-UP.
-YEAH-!
ARE YOU A GROWN-UP, ASAGI !?
HUH!? UMM...
I'M STILL LIVING OFF MY PARENTS, SO...I GUESS I'M STILL A KID.
HEH! YOU'RE A KID?
BUT YOU SEEM SO GROWN-UP!

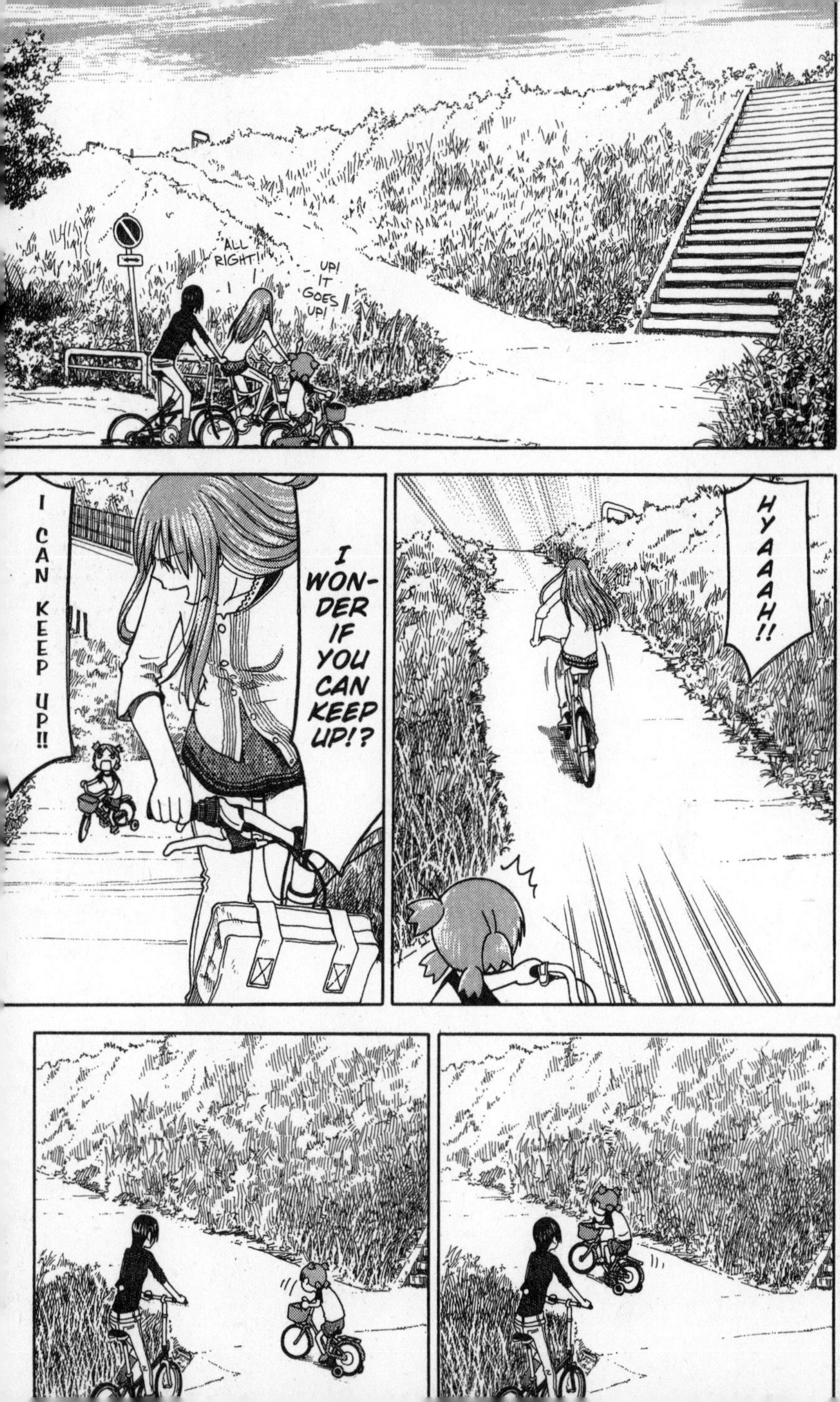

UP! IT GOES UP!
ALL RIGHT!!
HYAAAAH!!
I WONDER IF YOU CAN KEEP UP!?
I CAN KEEP UP!!

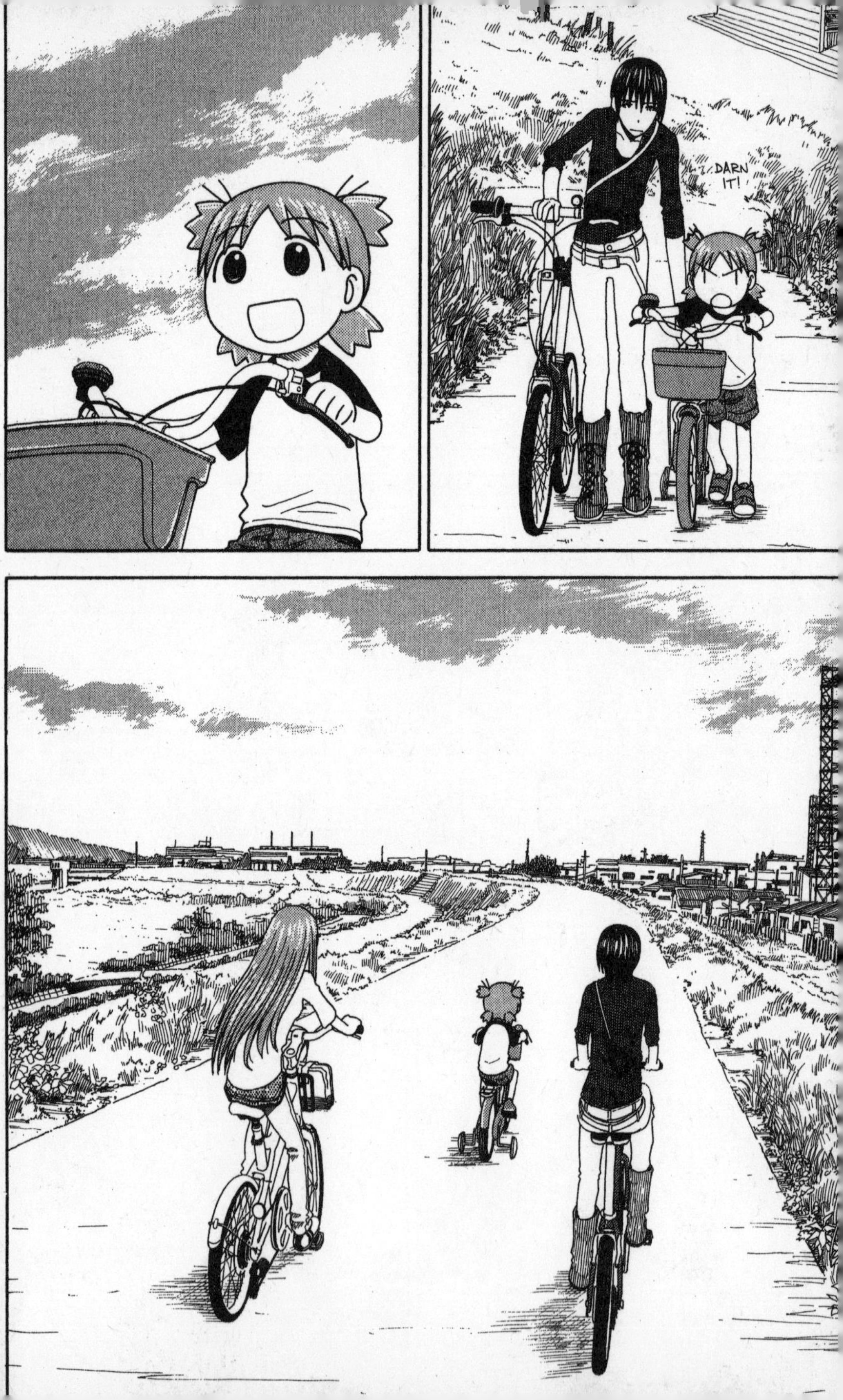
DARN IT!

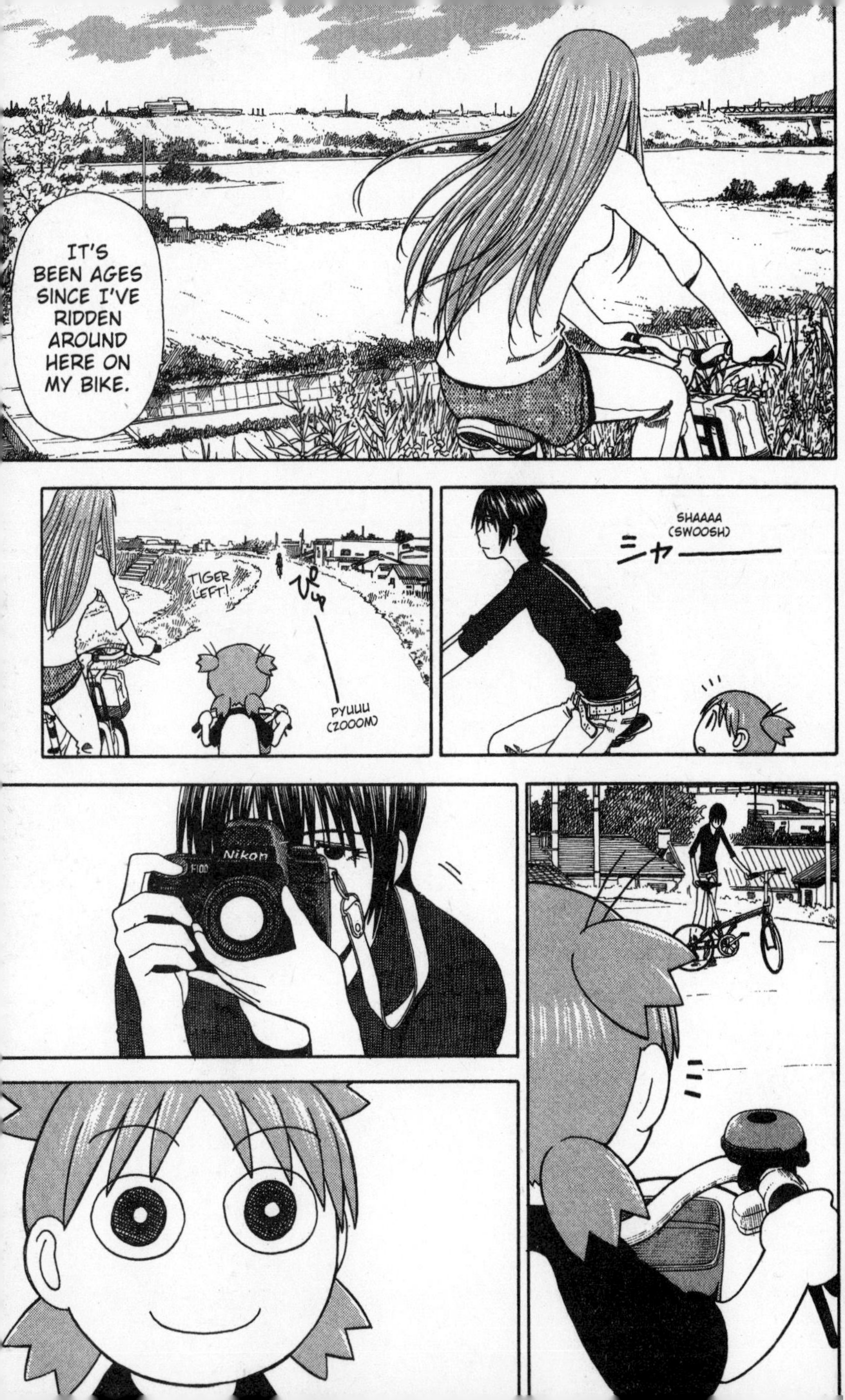
IT'S BEEN AGES SINCE I'VE RIDDEN AROUND HERE ON MY BIKE.
SHAAAA (SWOOSH)
シャー
TIGER LEFT!
PYUUU (ZOOOM)
Nikon
F100

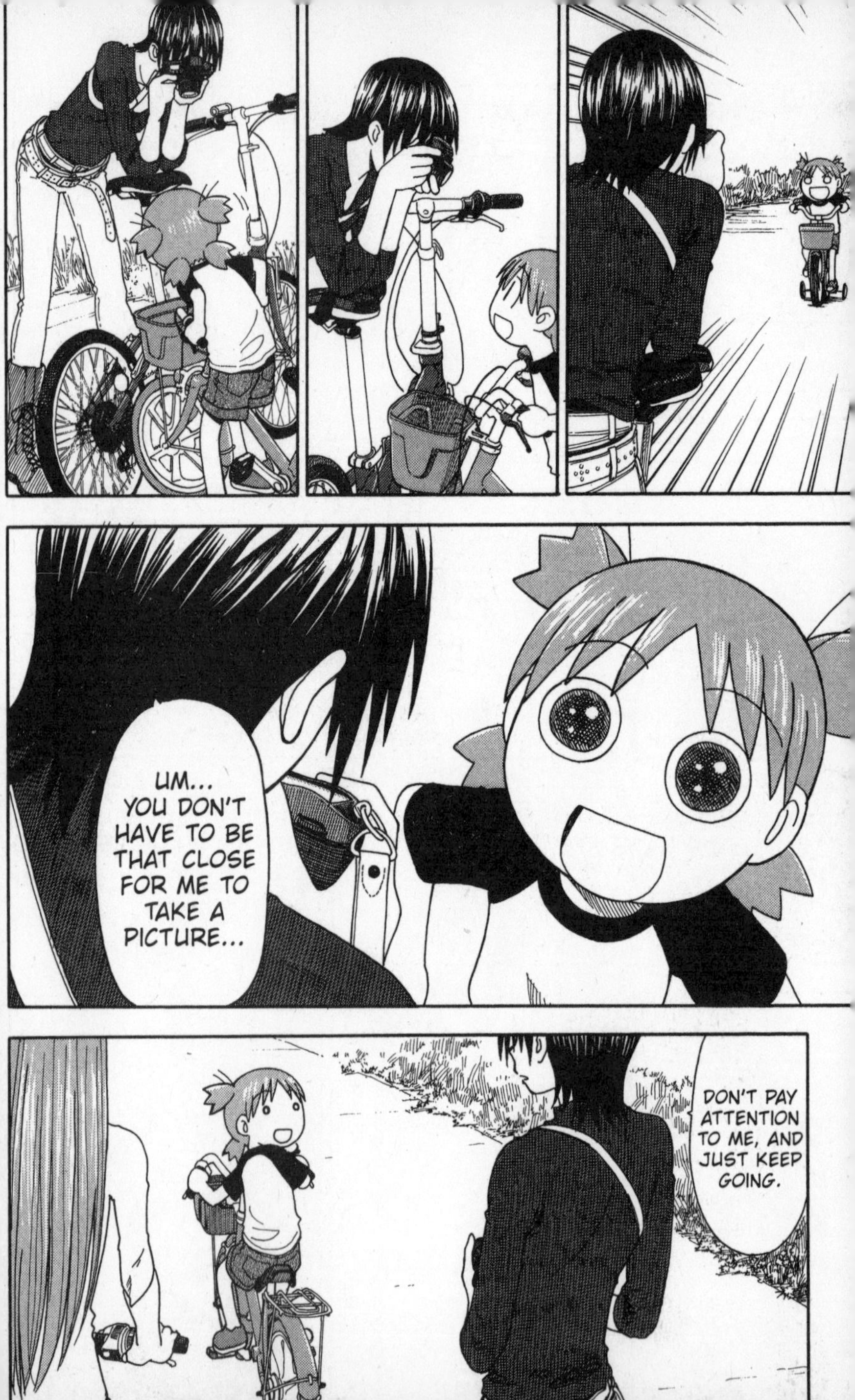
UM... YOU DON'T HAVE TO BE THAT CLOSE FOR ME TO TAKE A PICTURE...
DON'T PAY ATTENTION TO ME, AND JUST KEEP GOING.

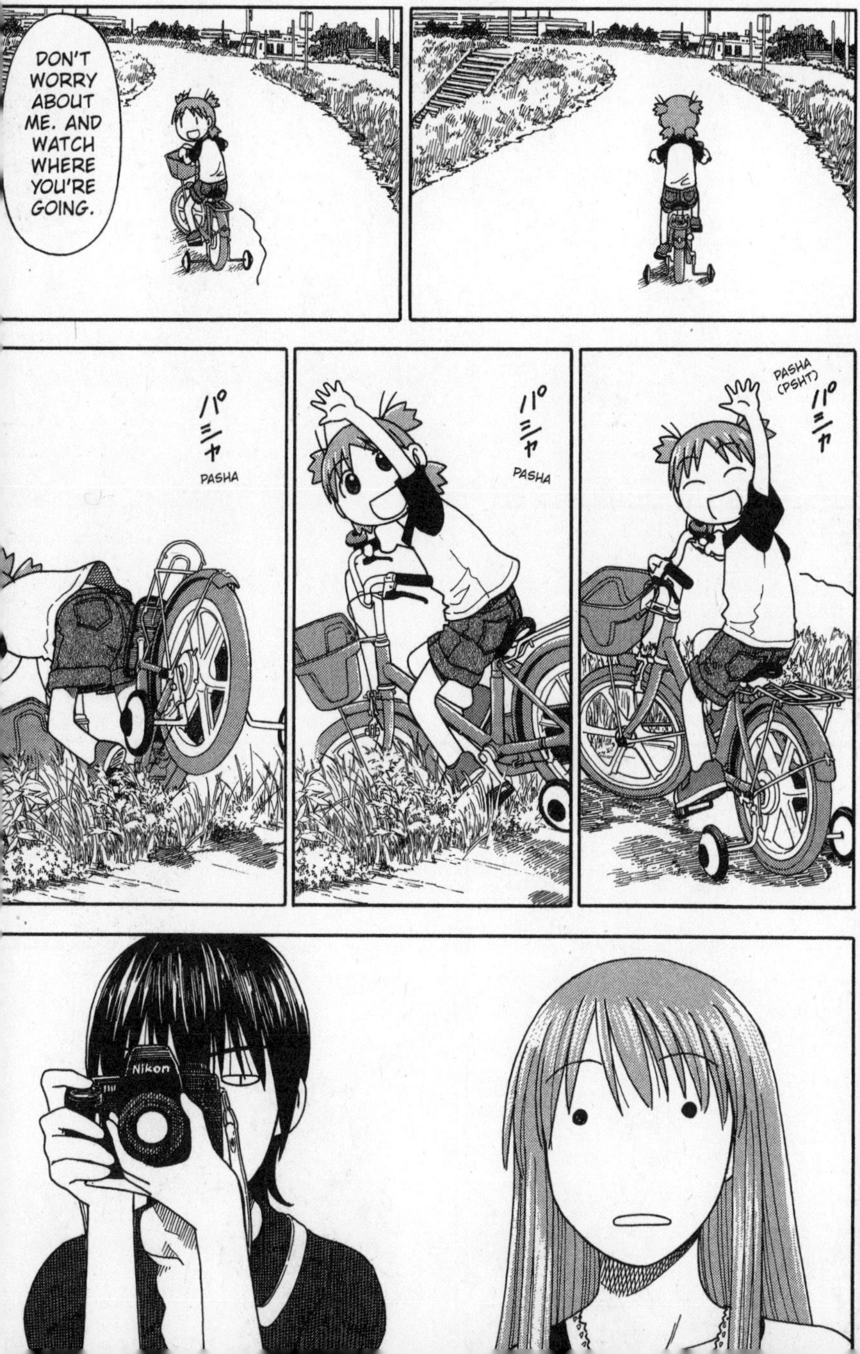
DON'T WORRY ABOUT ME. AND WATCH WHERE YOU'RE GOING.
PASHA (PSHT)
パシャ
パシャ
PASHA
パシャ
PASHA

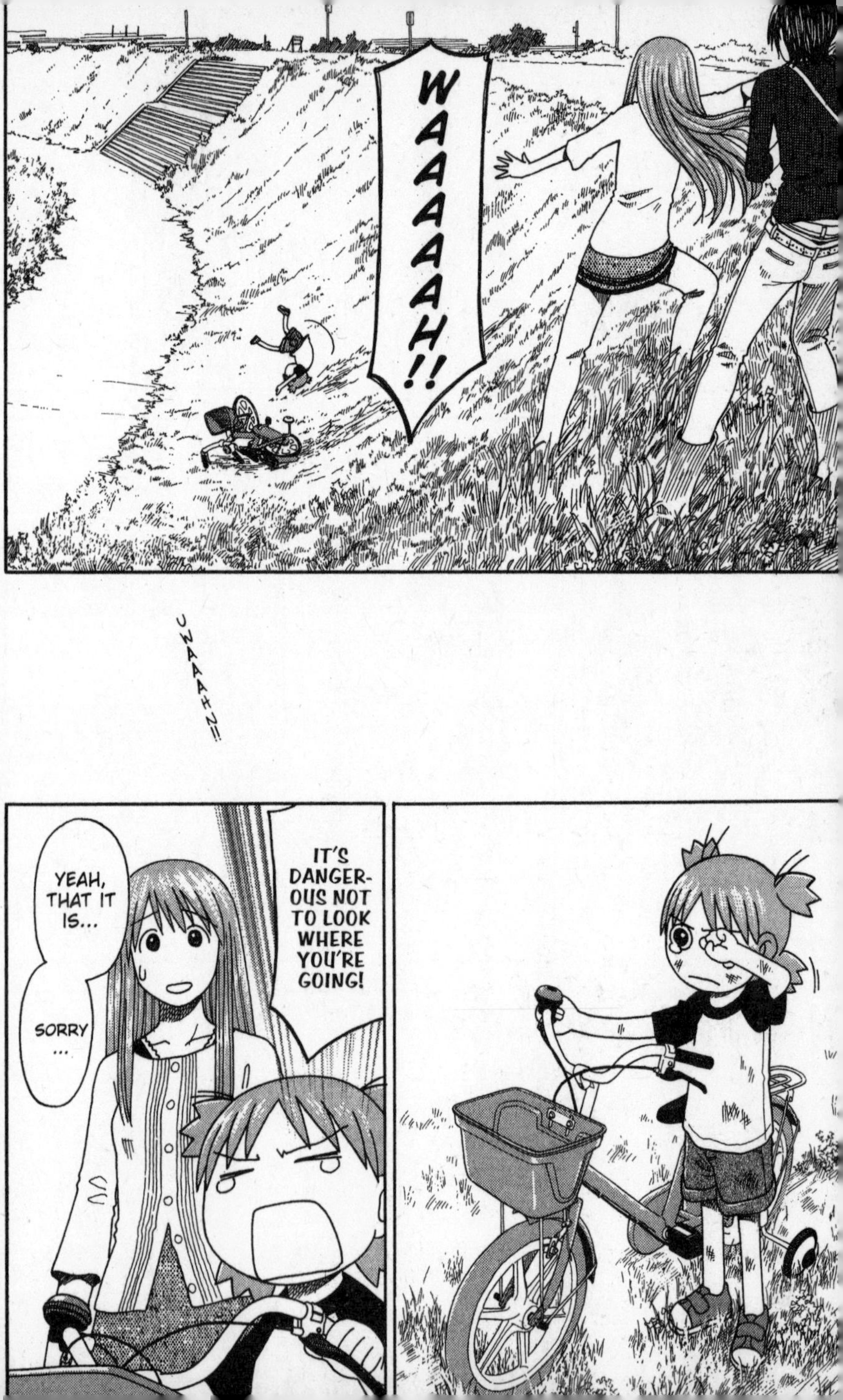

WAAAAAAH!!
UWAAAHN!!
IT'S DANGER-OUS NOT TO LOOK WHERE YOU'RE GOING!
YEAH, THAT IT IS...
SORRY...

KNOCK IT OFF.

READY!

READY TO GO?

HYAAH!

AH! LOOK OU—

HA AAH!!

ZA
(SKID)

UWAAH!!

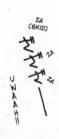

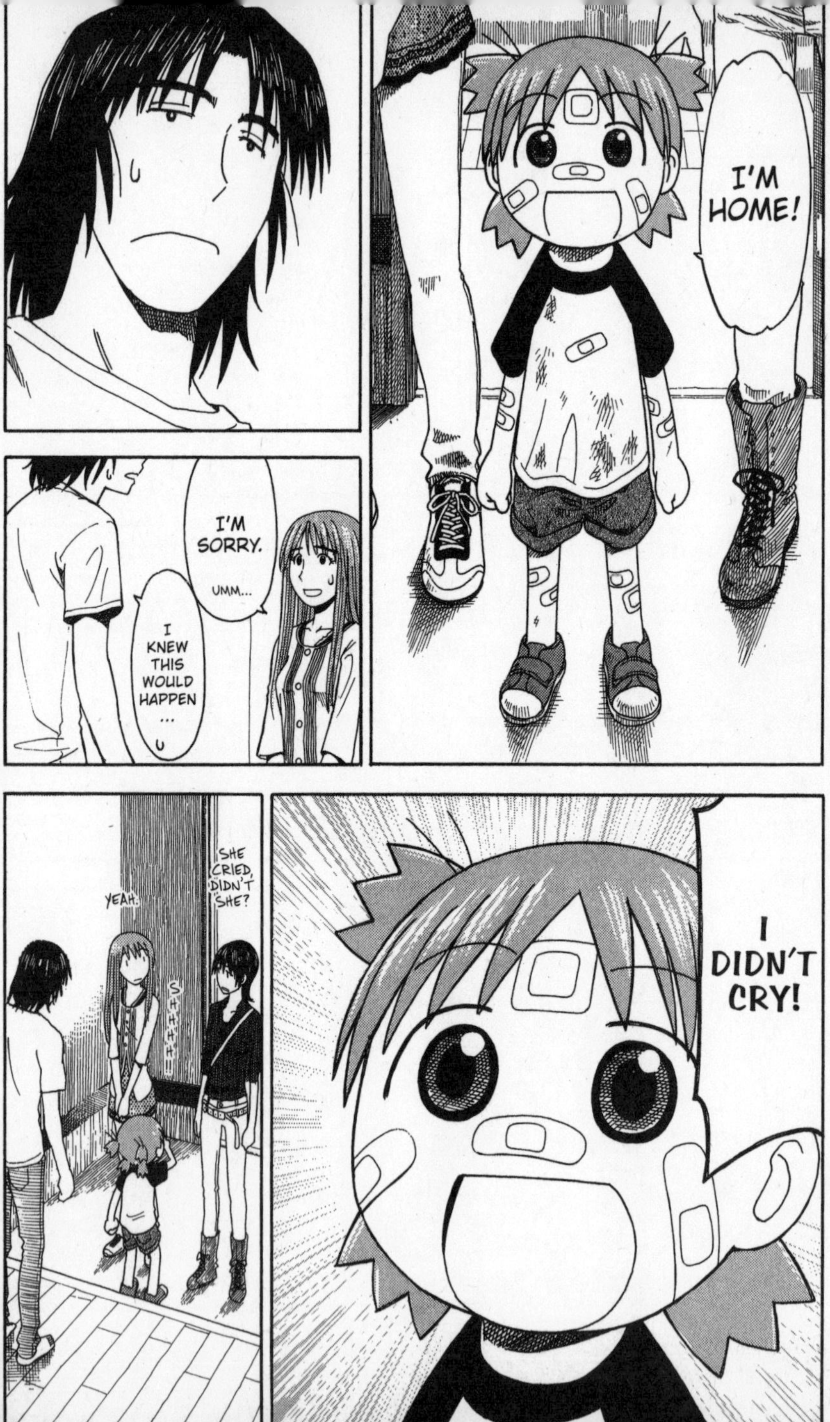
I'M HOME!
I'M SORRY.
UMM...
I KNEW THIS WOULD HAPPEN...
I DIDN'T CRY!
SHE CRIED, DIDN'T SHE?
YEAH.
SHHHH!!

YOTSUBA&!

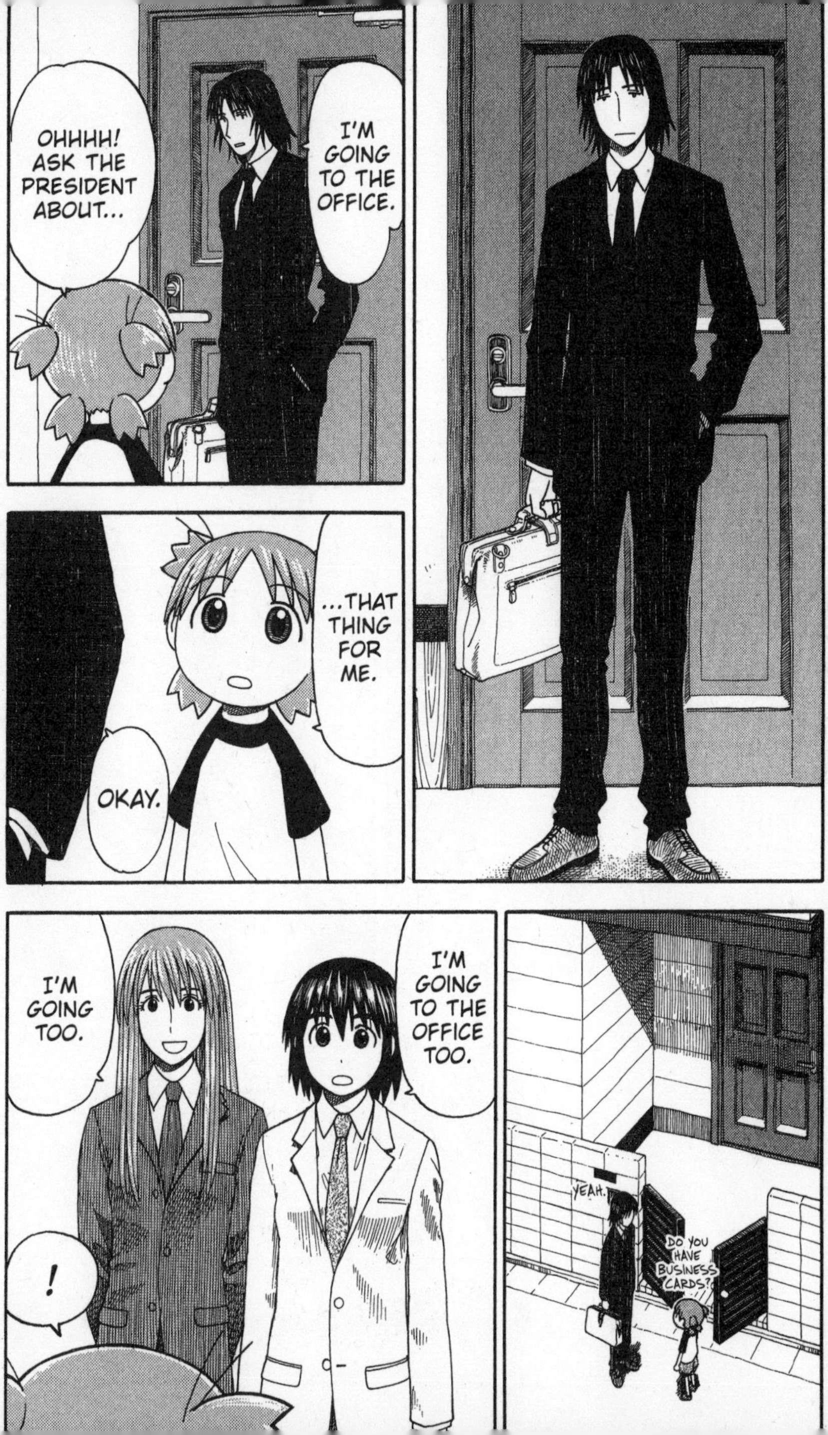
I'M GOING TO THE OFFICE.
OHHHH! ASK THE PRESIDENT ABOUT...
...THAT THING FOR ME.
OKAY.
DO YOU HAVE BUSINESS CARDS?
YEAH.
I'M GOING TO THE OFFICE TOO.
I'M GOING TOO.
!

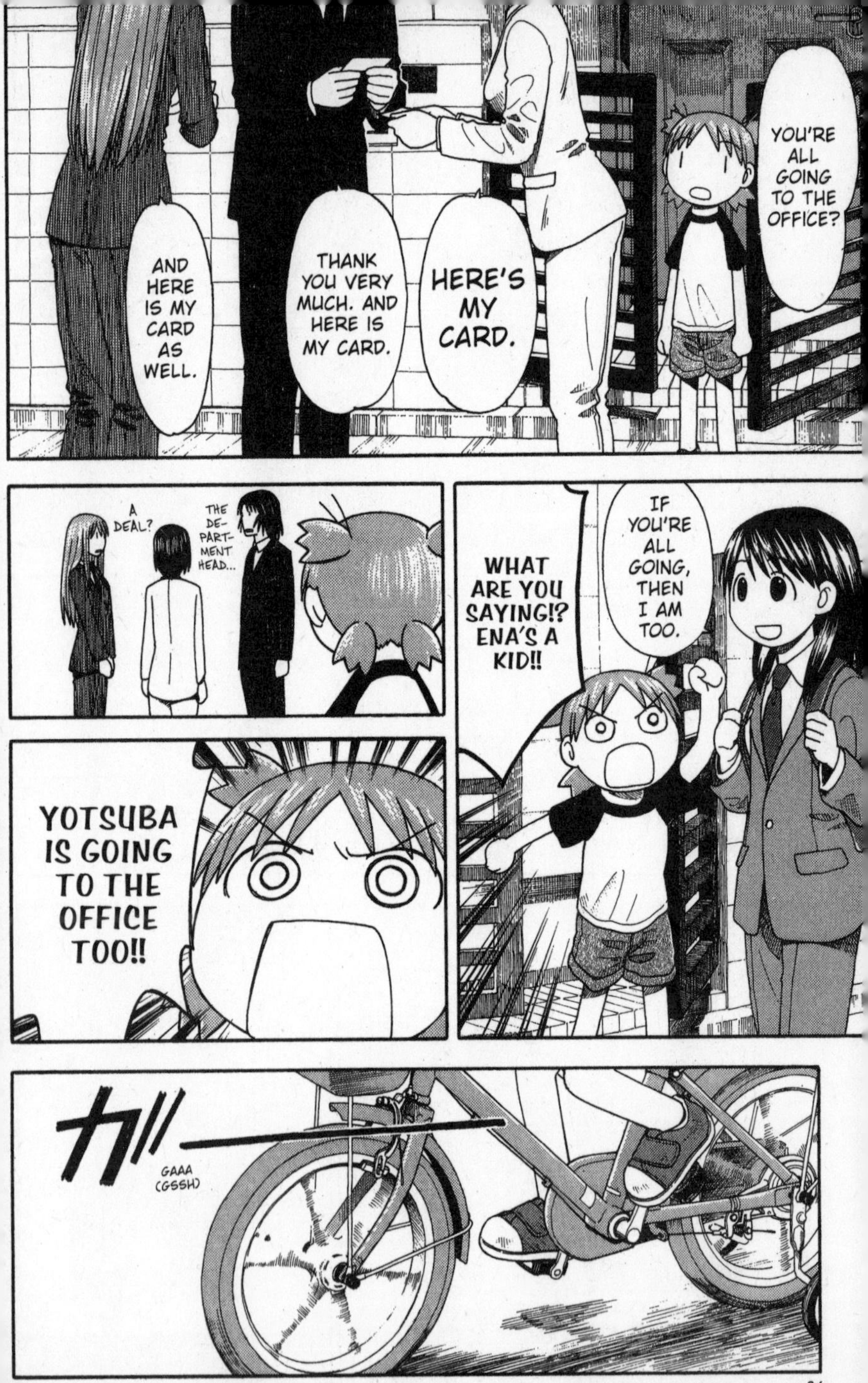
YOU'RE ALL GOING TO THE OFFICE?
HERE'S MY CARD.
THANK YOU VERY MUCH. AND HERE IS MY CARD.
AND HERE IS MY CARD AS WELL.
IF YOU'RE ALL GOING, THEN I AM TOO.
WHAT ARE YOU SAYING!? ENA'S A KID!!
THE DE-PART-MENT HEAD...
A DEAL?
YOTSUBA IS GOING TO THE OFFICE TOO!!
ガッ
GAAA (GSSH)

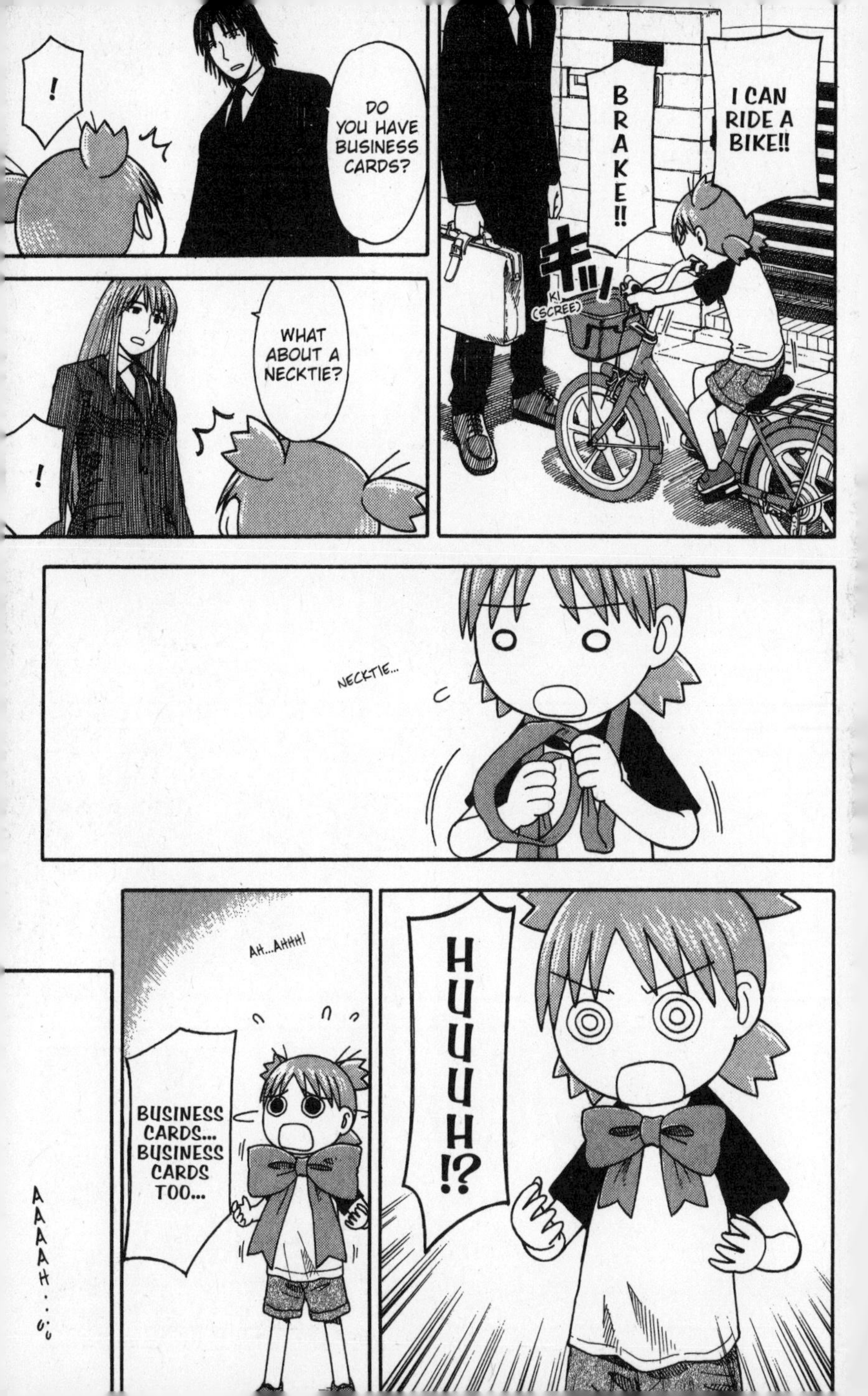
I CAN RIDE A BIKE!!
BRAKE!!
KI (SCREE)
DO YOU HAVE BUSINESS CARDS?
!
WHAT ABOUT A NECKTIE?
!
NECKTIE...
HUUUUH!?
AH...AHHH!
BUSINESS CARDS... BUSINESS CARDS TOO...
AAAAH...

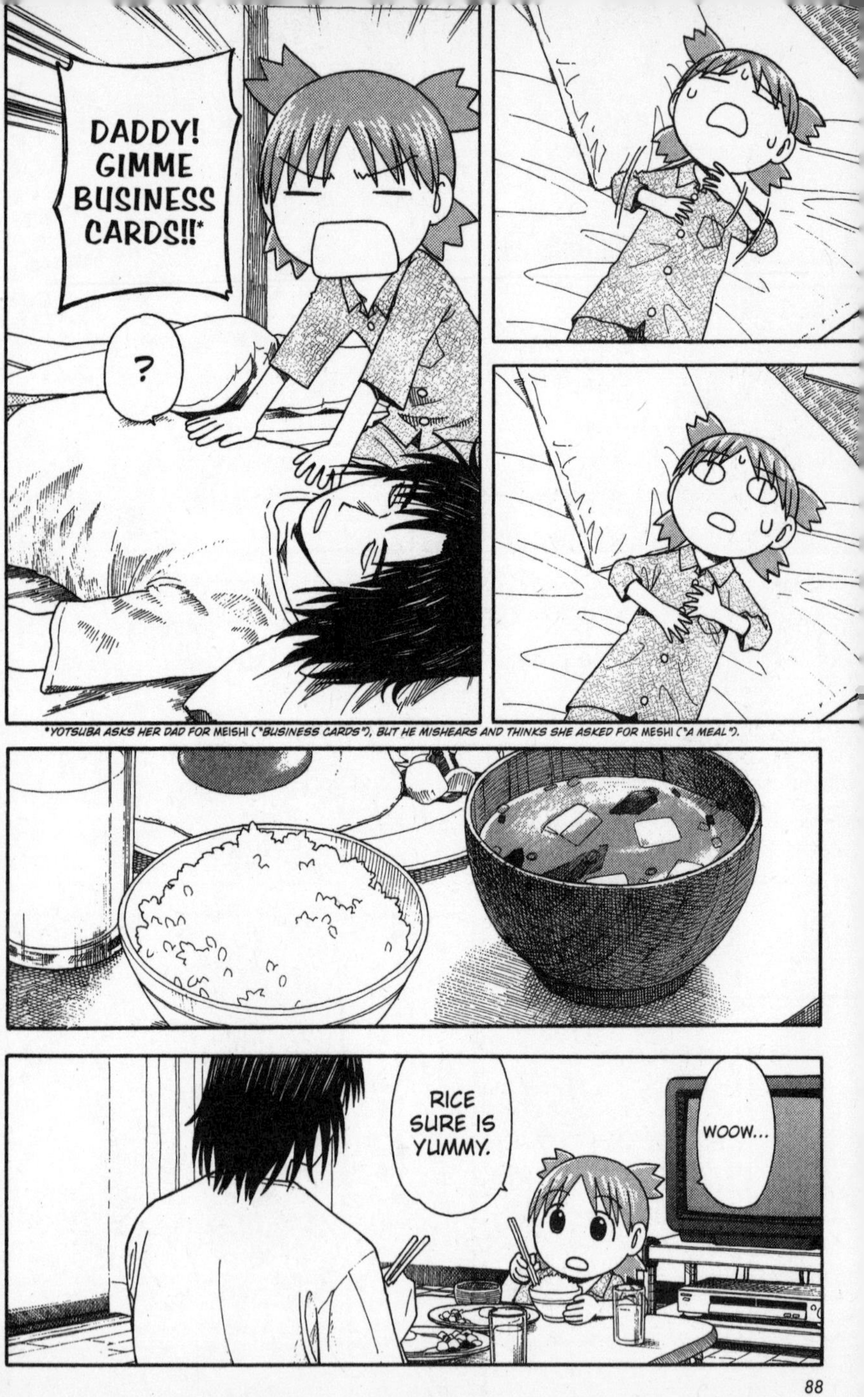
DADDY! GIMME BUSINESS CARDS!!*
?
WOOW...
RICE SURE IS YUMMY.
*YOTSUBA ASKS HER DAD FOR MEISHI ("BUSINESS CARDS"), BUT HE MISHEARS AND THINKS SHE ASKED FOR MESHI ("A MEAL").

YOTSUBA&! FRIDAY

#38

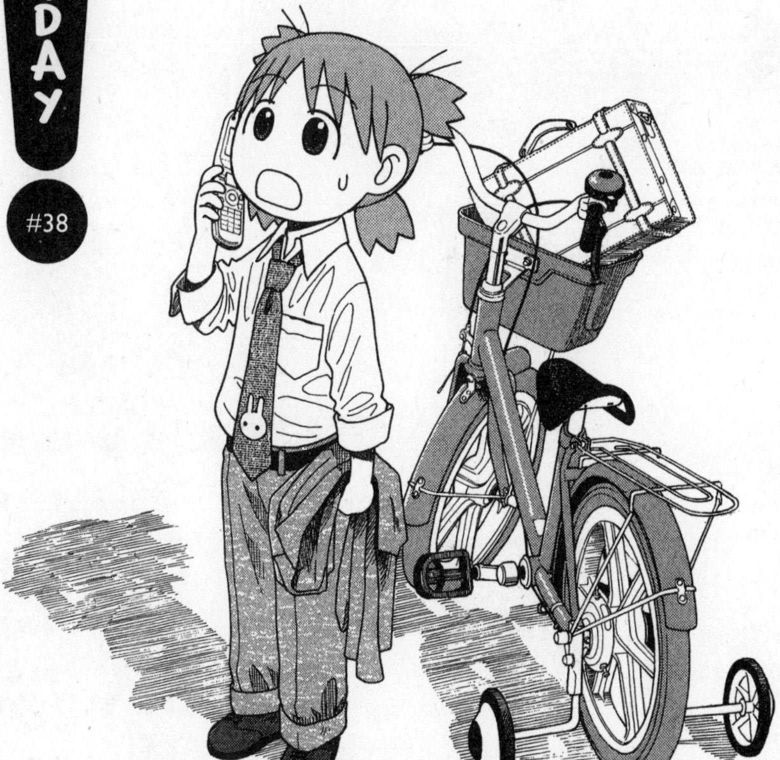

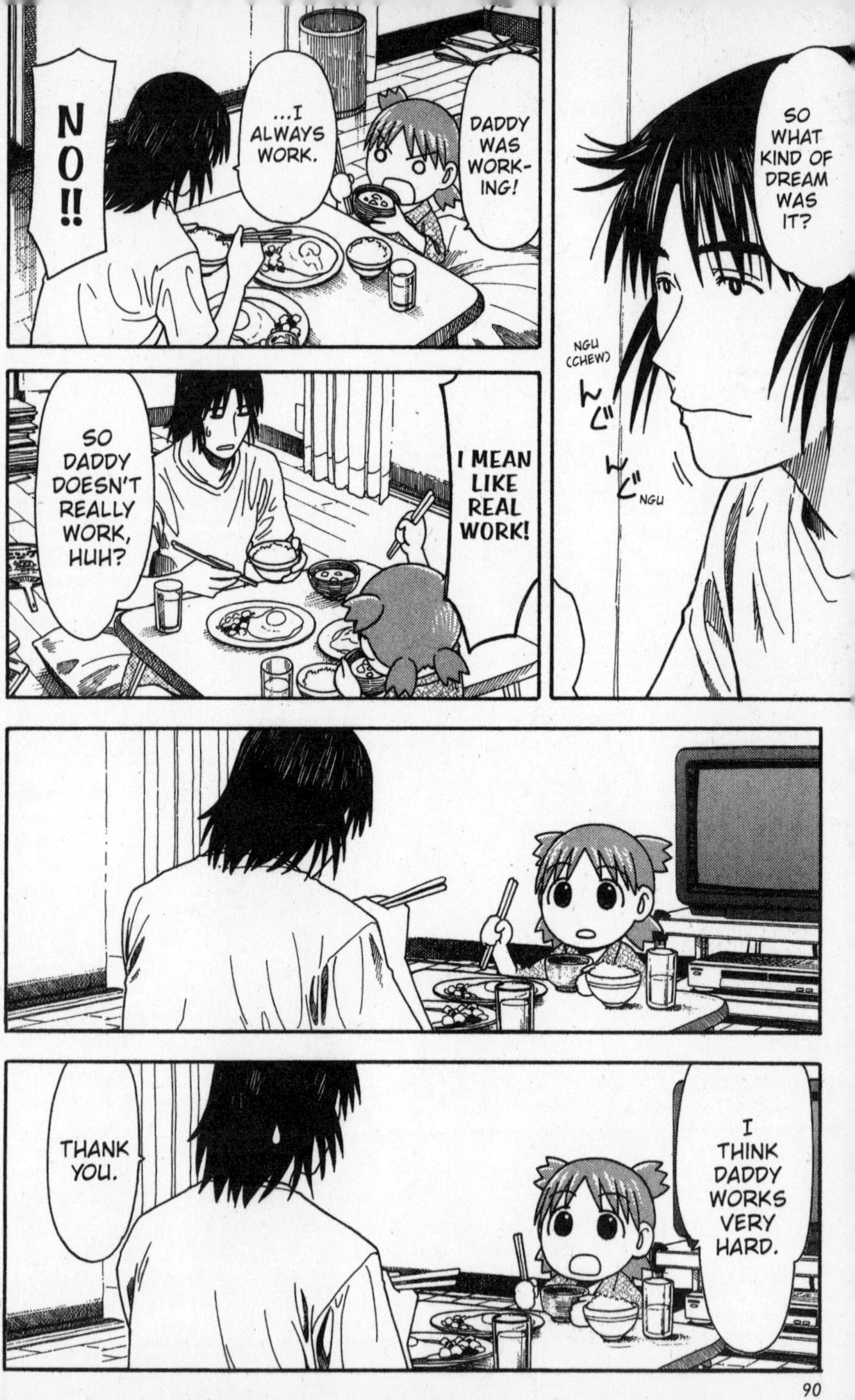
SO WHAT KIND OF DREAM WAS IT?
NGU (CHEW)
んぐ
んぐ
NGU
DADDY WAS WORK-ING!
...I ALWAYS WORK.
NO!!
I MEAN LIKE REAL WORK!
SO DADDY DOESN'T REALLY WORK, HUH?
I THINK DADDY WORKS VERY HARD.
THANK YOU.

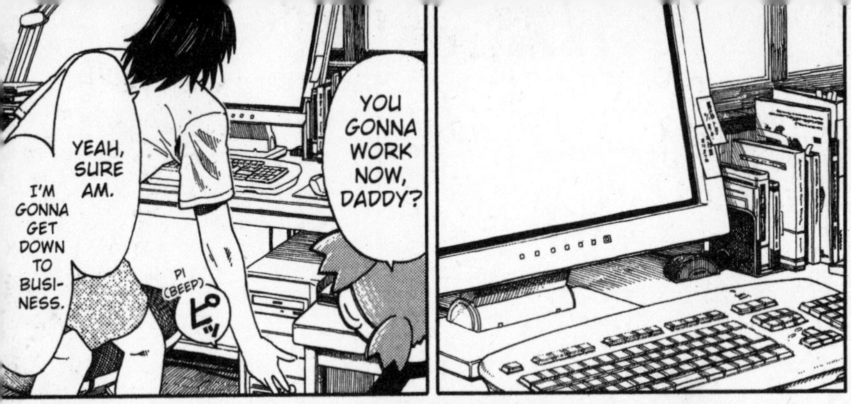
YOU GONNA WORK NOW, DADDY?
YEAH, SURE AM.
I'M GONNA GET DOWN TO BUSINESS.
PI (BEEP)
ピッ

SFX: BA (BWSH) BA BA BA

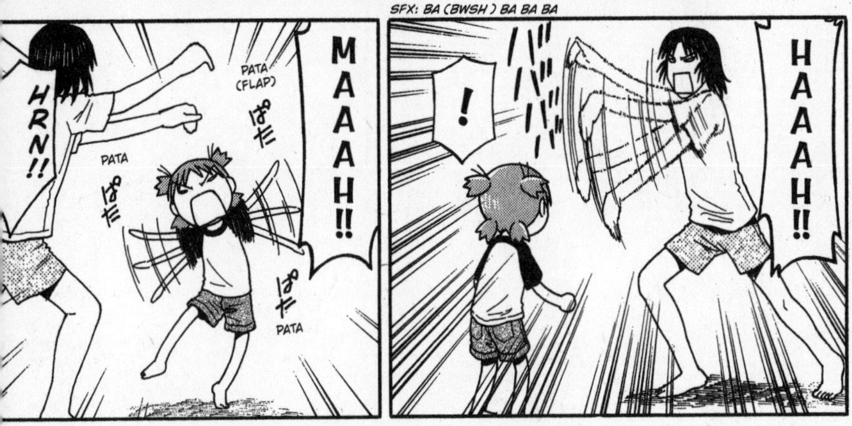
HAAAAH!!
バババ
!
MAAAAH!!
PATA (FLAP)
ぱた
PATA
ぱた
ぱた
PATA
HRN!!

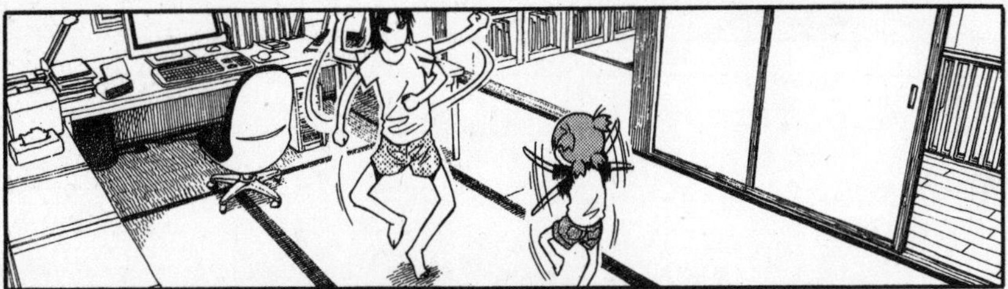

*KOIWAI ACTUALLY SAYS HE'S "COOL BIZ," A REFERENCE TO A JAPANESE GOVERNMENT INITIATIVE IN 2005 INTENDED TO HELP REDUCE ELECTRICITY USAGE IN OFFICES BY ADVISING WORKERS TO DRESS IN LIGHT AND BREATHABLE CLOTHES.

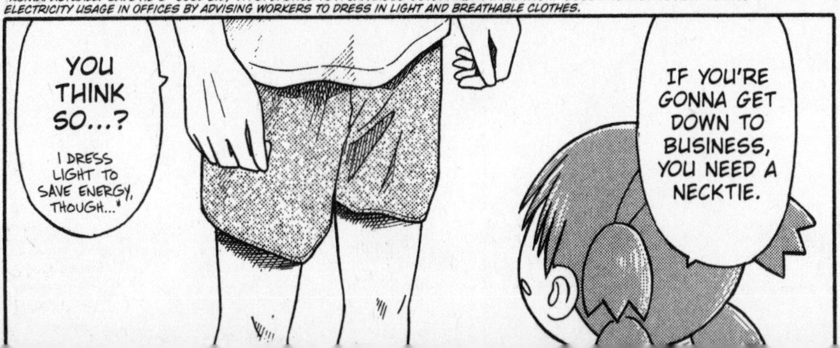
IF YOU'RE GONNA GET DOWN TO BUSINESS, YOU NEED A NECKTIE.
YOU THINK SO...?
I DRESS LIGHT TO SAVE ENERGY, THOUGH...*

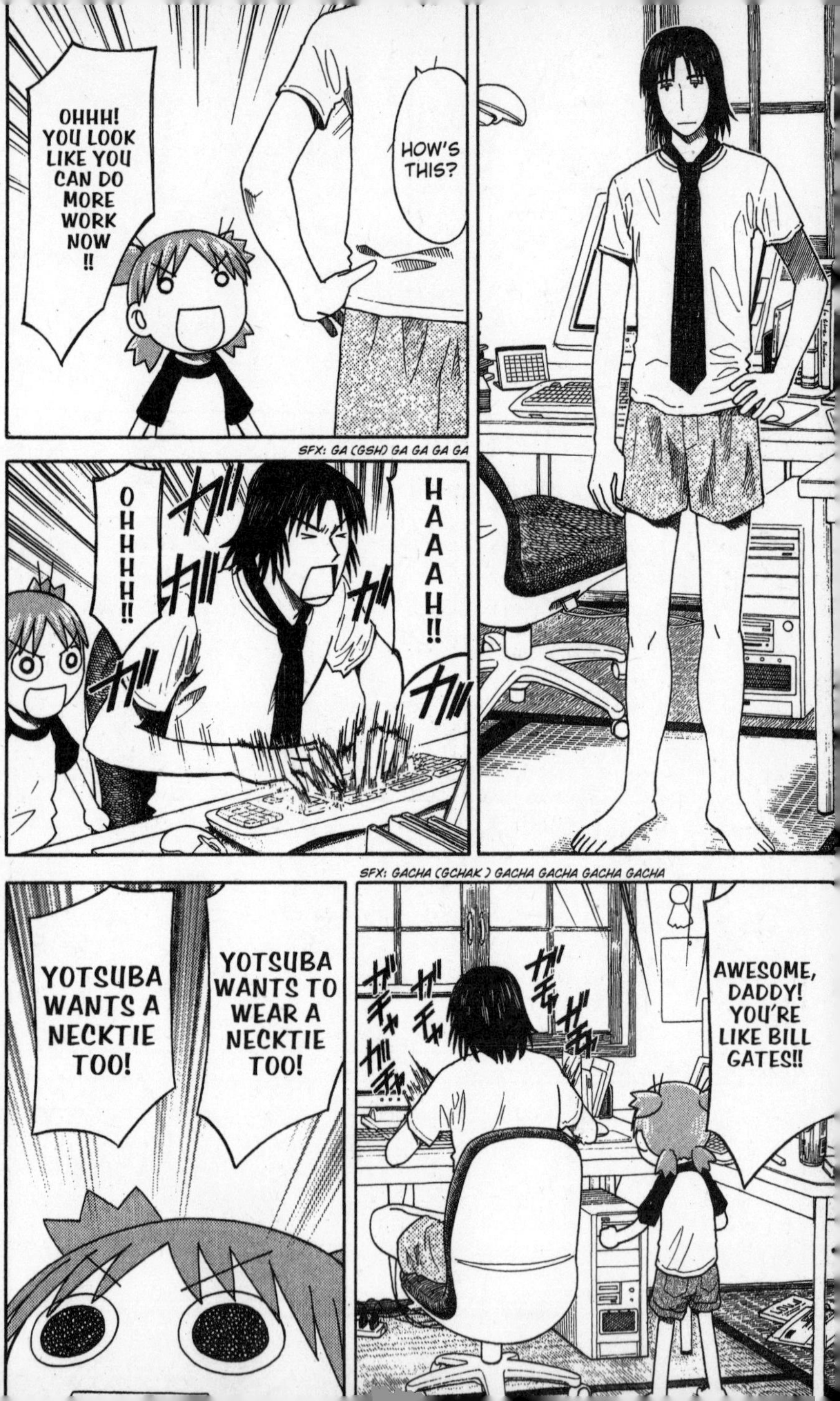
HOW'S THIS?
OHHH! YOU LOOK LIKE YOU CAN DO MORE WORK NOW!!
SFX: GA (GSH) GA GA GA GA
HAAAAH!!
OHHHHH!!
SFX: GACHA (GCHAK) GACHA GACHA GACHA GACHA
AWESOME, DADDY! YOU'RE LIKE BILL GATES!!
YOTSUBA WANTS TO WEAR A NECKTIE TOO!
YOTSUBA WANTS A NECKTIE TOO!

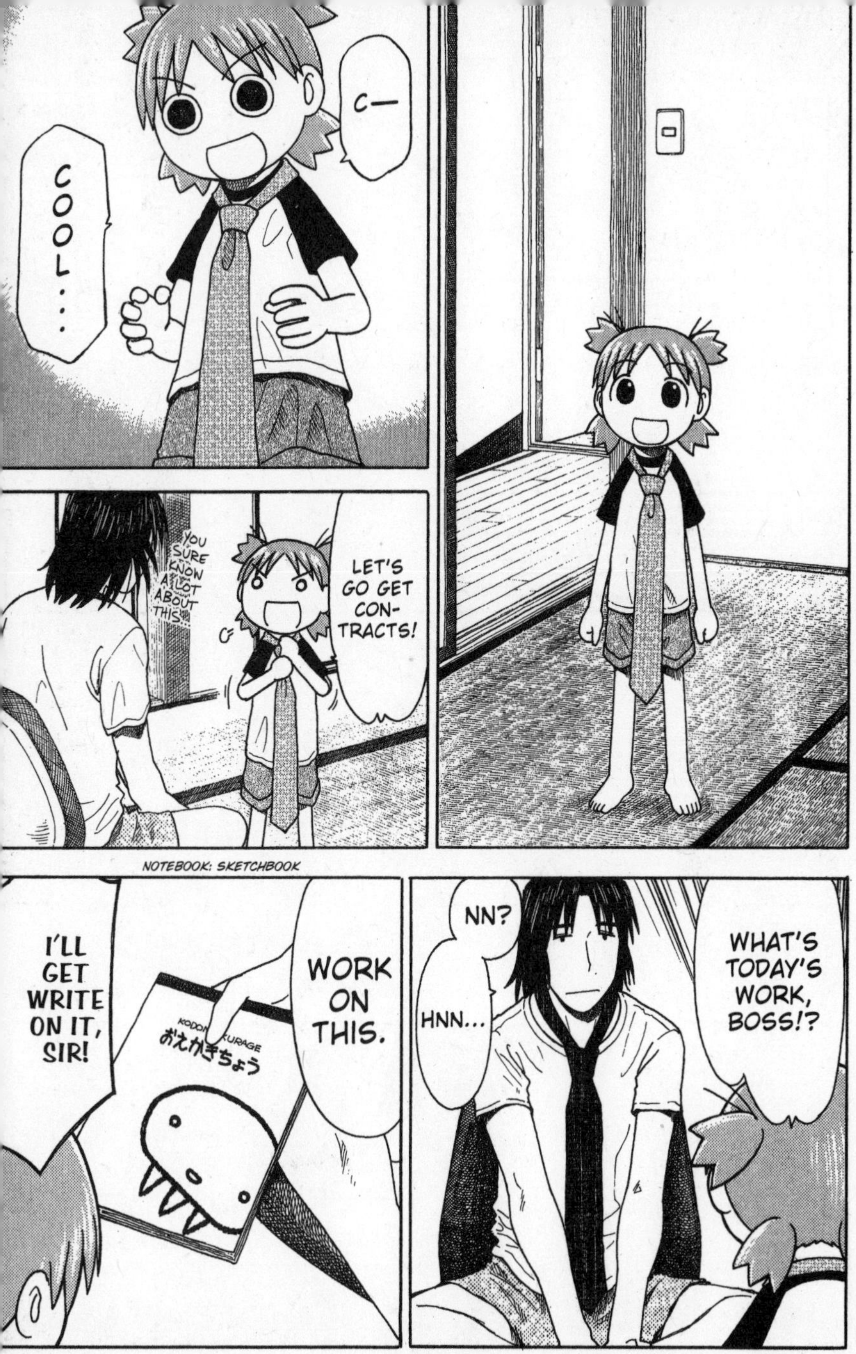
C—
COOL...
LET'S GO GET CONTRACTS!
YOU SURE KNOW A LOT ABOUT THIS.
NOTEBOOK: SKETCHBOOK
WHAT'S TODAY'S WORK, BOSS!?
NN?
HNN...
WORK ON THIS.
おえかきちょう
I'LL GET WRITE ON IT, SIR!

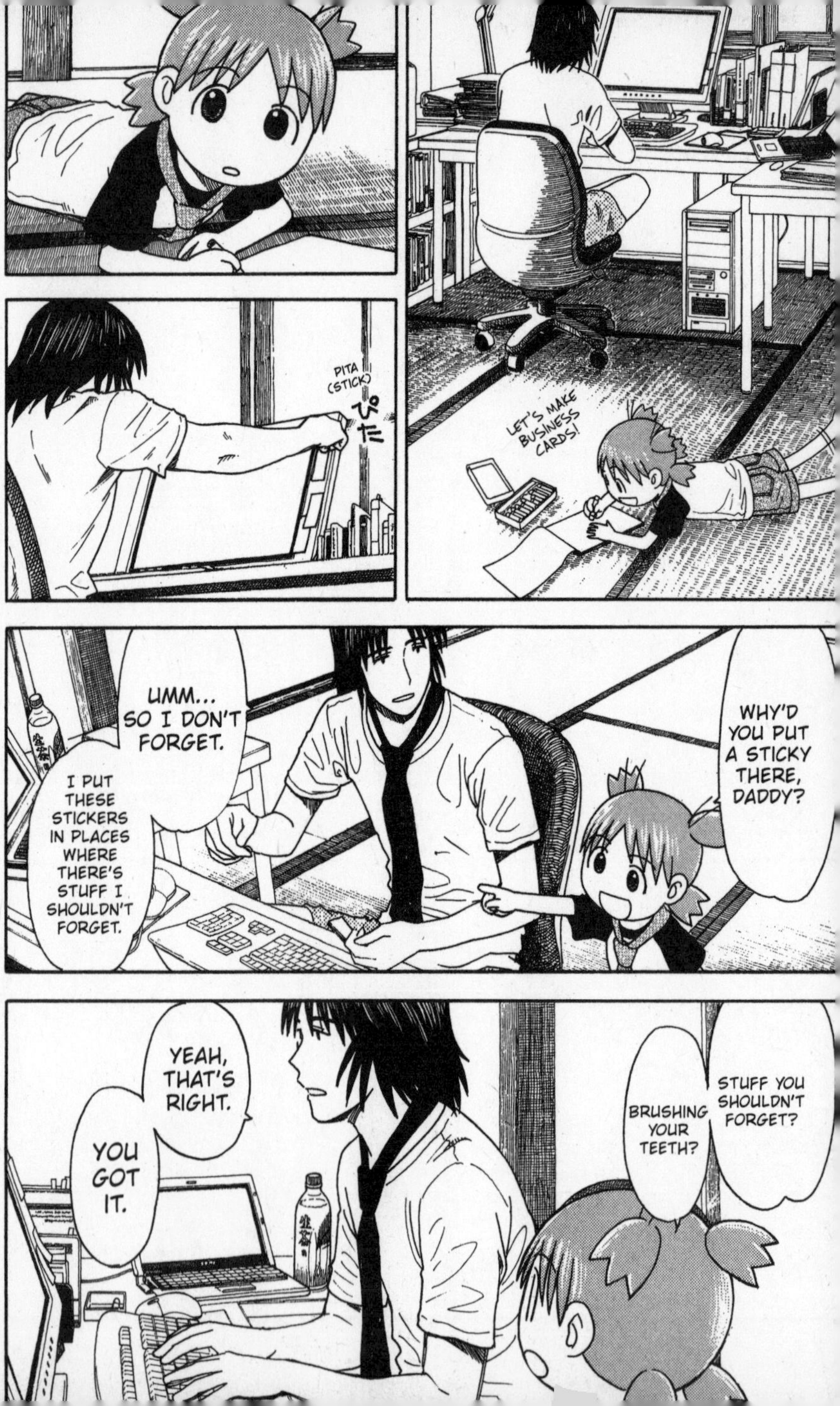
LET'S MAKE BUSINESS CARDS!
PITA (STICK)
ぴた
WHY'D YOU PUT A STICKY THERE, DADDY?
UMM... SO I DON'T FORGET.
I PUT THESE STICKERS IN PLACES WHERE THERE'S STUFF I SHOULDN'T FORGET.
STUFF YOU SHOULDN'T FORGET?
BRUSHING YOUR TEETH?
YEAH, THAT'S RIGHT.
YOU GOT IT.

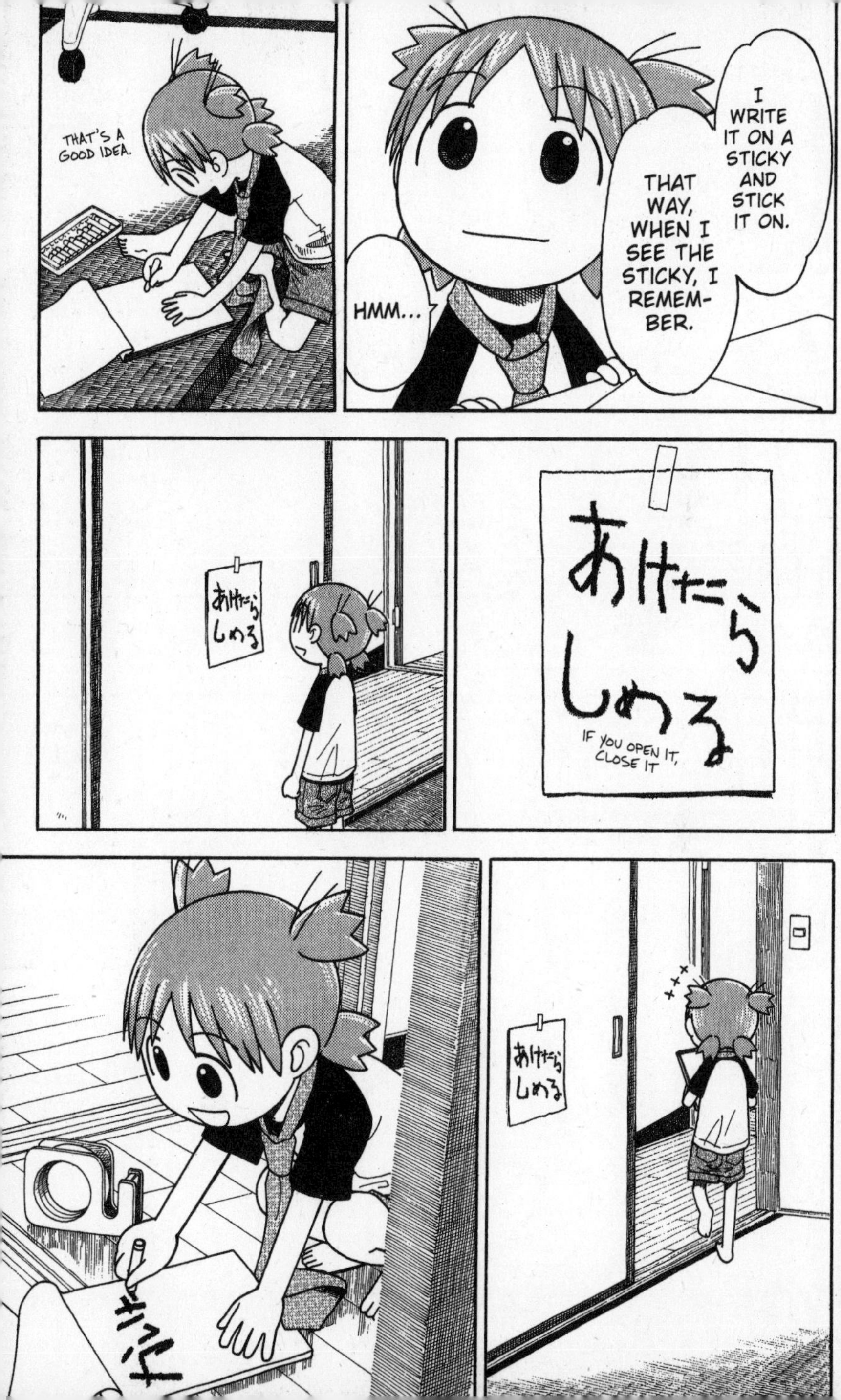
I WRITE IT ON A STICKY AND STICK IT ON.
THAT WAY, WHEN I SEE THE STICKY, I REMEMBER.
HMM...
THAT'S A GOOD IDEA.
あけたらしめる
IF YOU OPEN IT, CLOSE IT
あけたらしめる
あけたらしめる

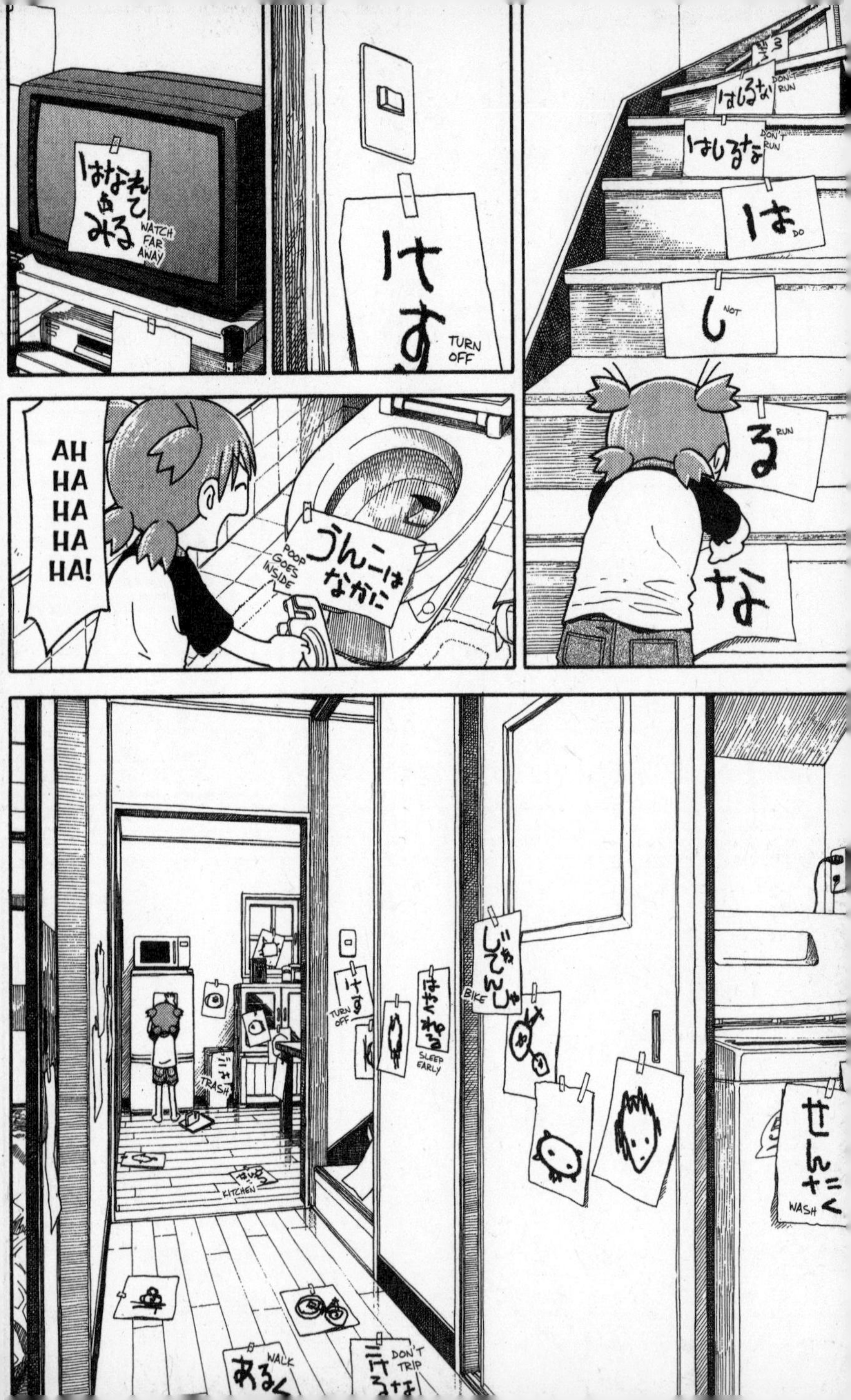
はしるな
DON'T RUN
はしるな
DON'T RUN
は
DO
し
NOT
る
RUN
な
けす
TURN OFF
はなれてみる
WATCH FAR AWAY
うんこはなかに
POOP GOES INSIDE
AH HA HA HA HA!
せんたく
WASH
じてんしゃ
BIKE
はやくねる
SLEEP EARLY
けす
TURN OFF
ごみ
TRASH
KITCHEN
ころぶな
DON'T TRIP
あるく
WALK

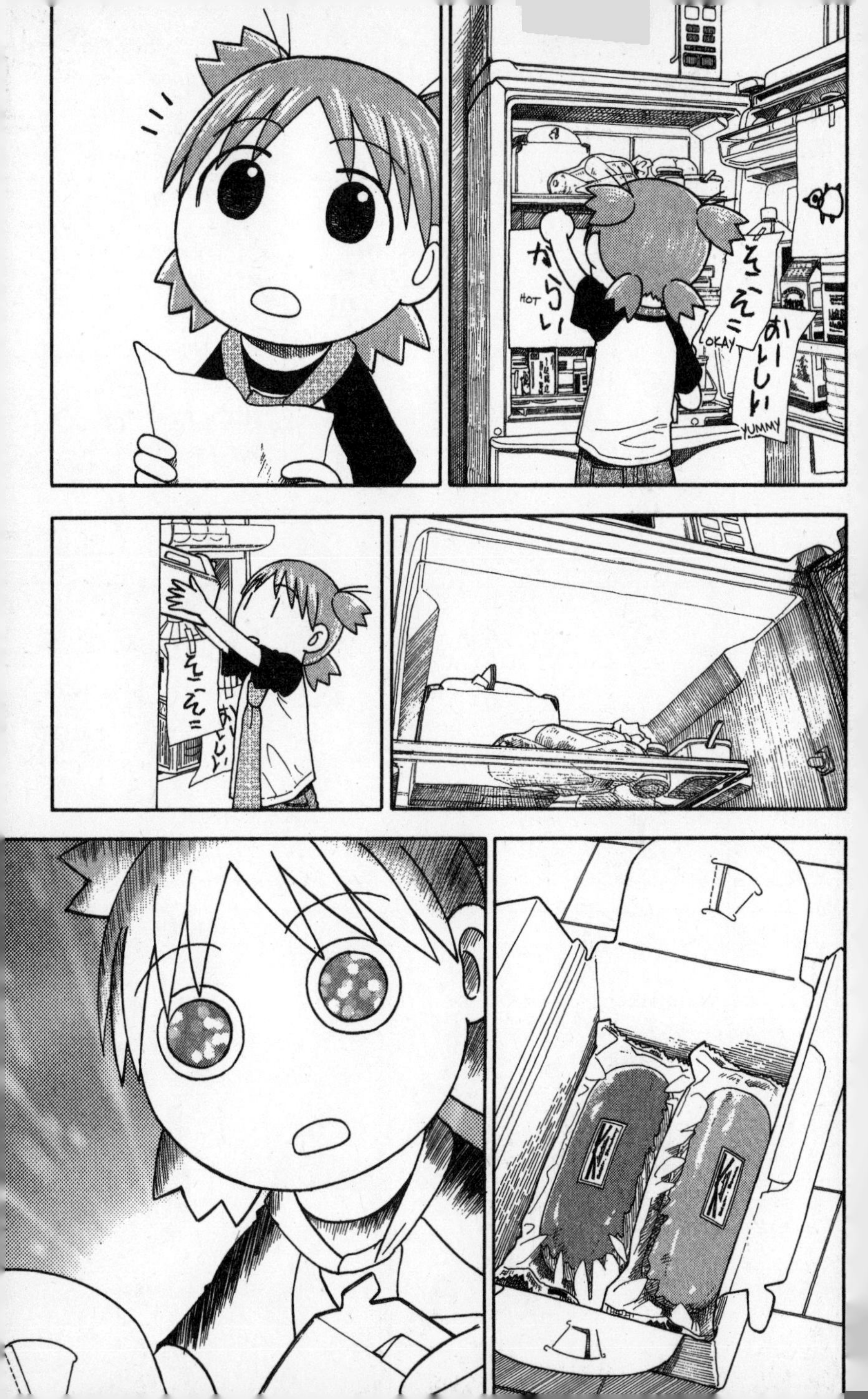

そこそこ
OKAY
おいしい
YUMMY
からい
HOT
そこそこ
おいしい

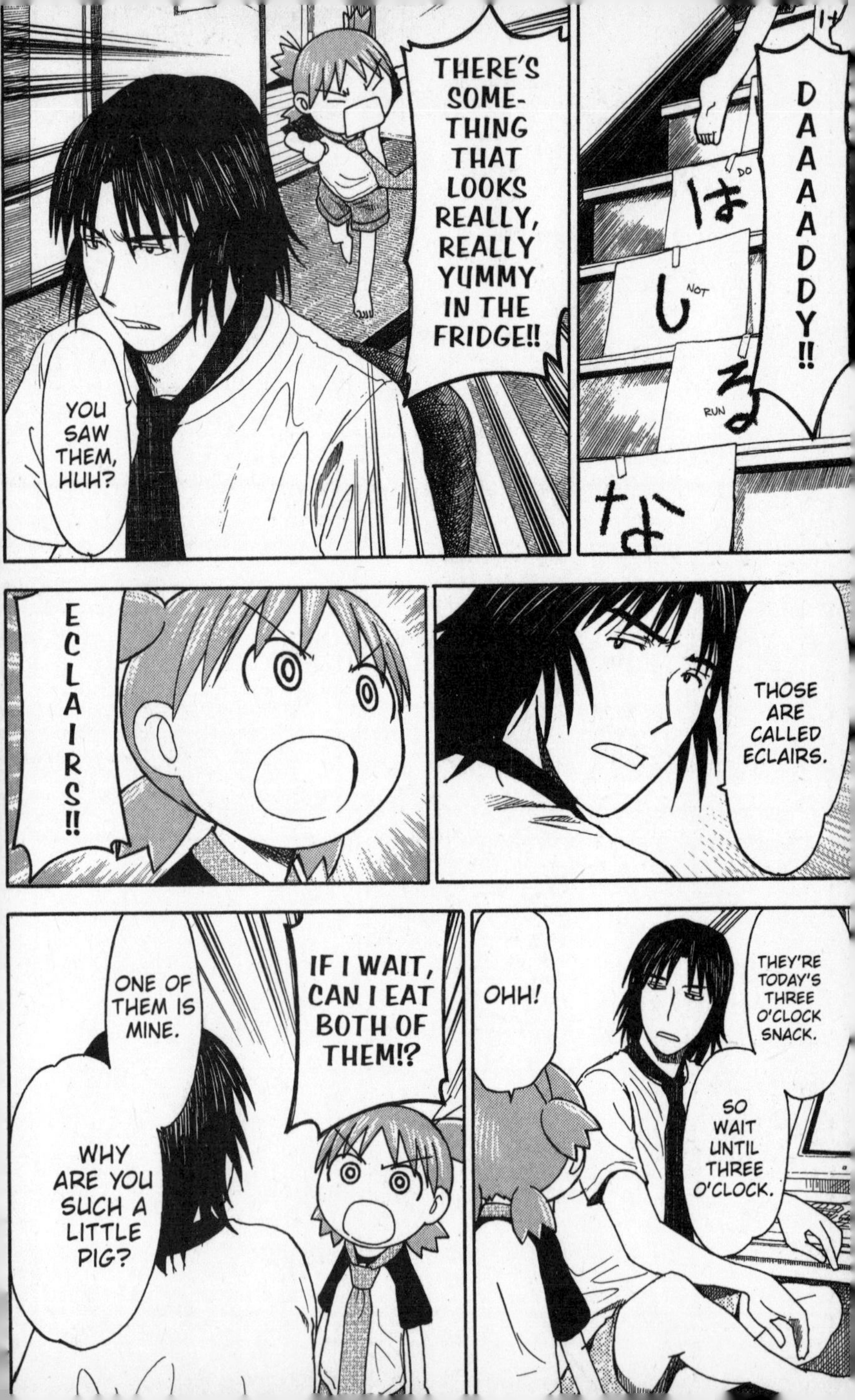
DAAAAADDY!!
は DO
し NOT
る RUN
な
THERE'S SOMETHING THAT LOOKS REALLY, REALLY YUMMY IN THE FRIDGE!!
YOU SAW THEM, HUH?
THOSE ARE CALLED ECLAIRS.
ECLAIRS!!
THEY'RE TODAY'S THREE O'CLOCK SNACK.
SO WAIT UNTIL THREE O'CLOCK.
OHH!
IF I WAIT, CAN I EAT BOTH OF THEM!?
ONE OF THEM IS MINE.
WHY ARE YOU SUCH A LITTLE PIG?

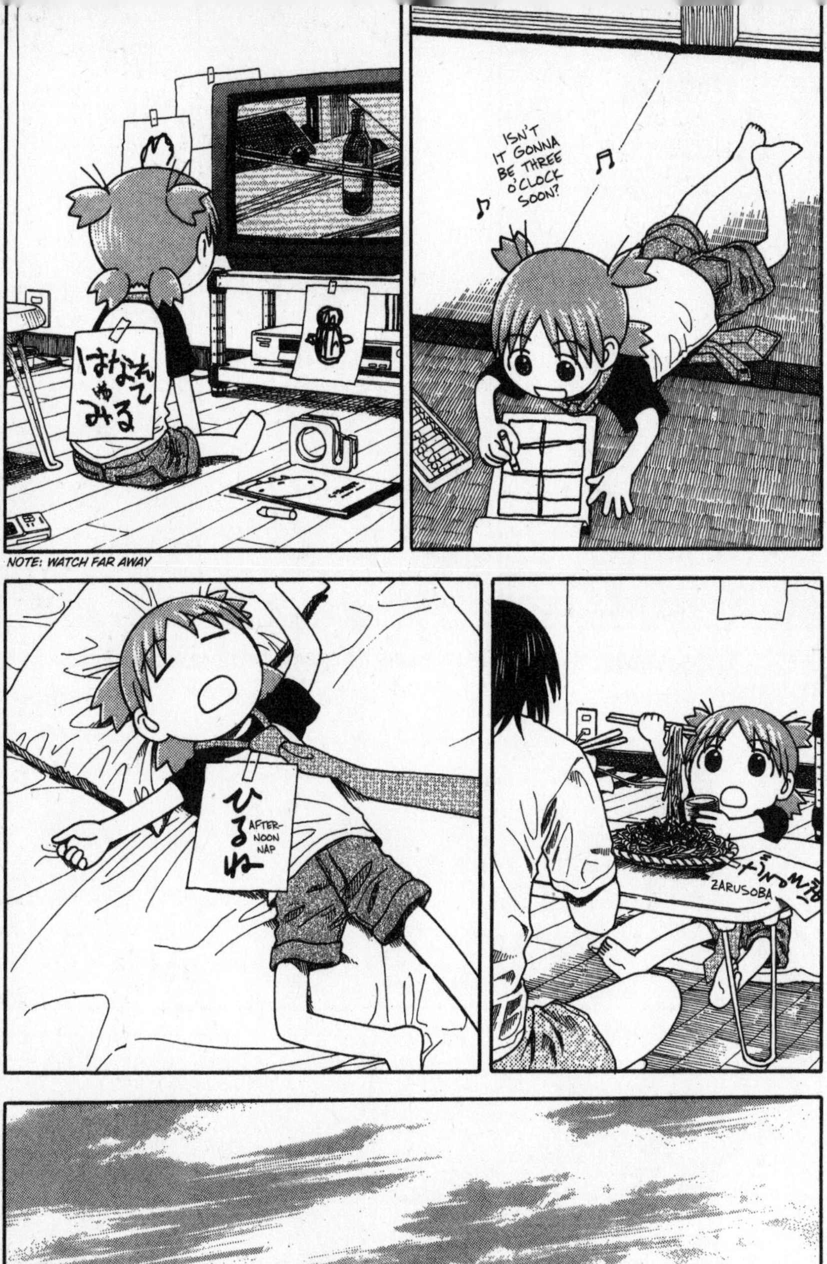
ISN'T IT GONNA BE THREE O'CLOCK SOON?
はなれてみる
NOTE: WATCH FAR AWAY
ZARUSOBA
ひるね
AFTERNOON NAP

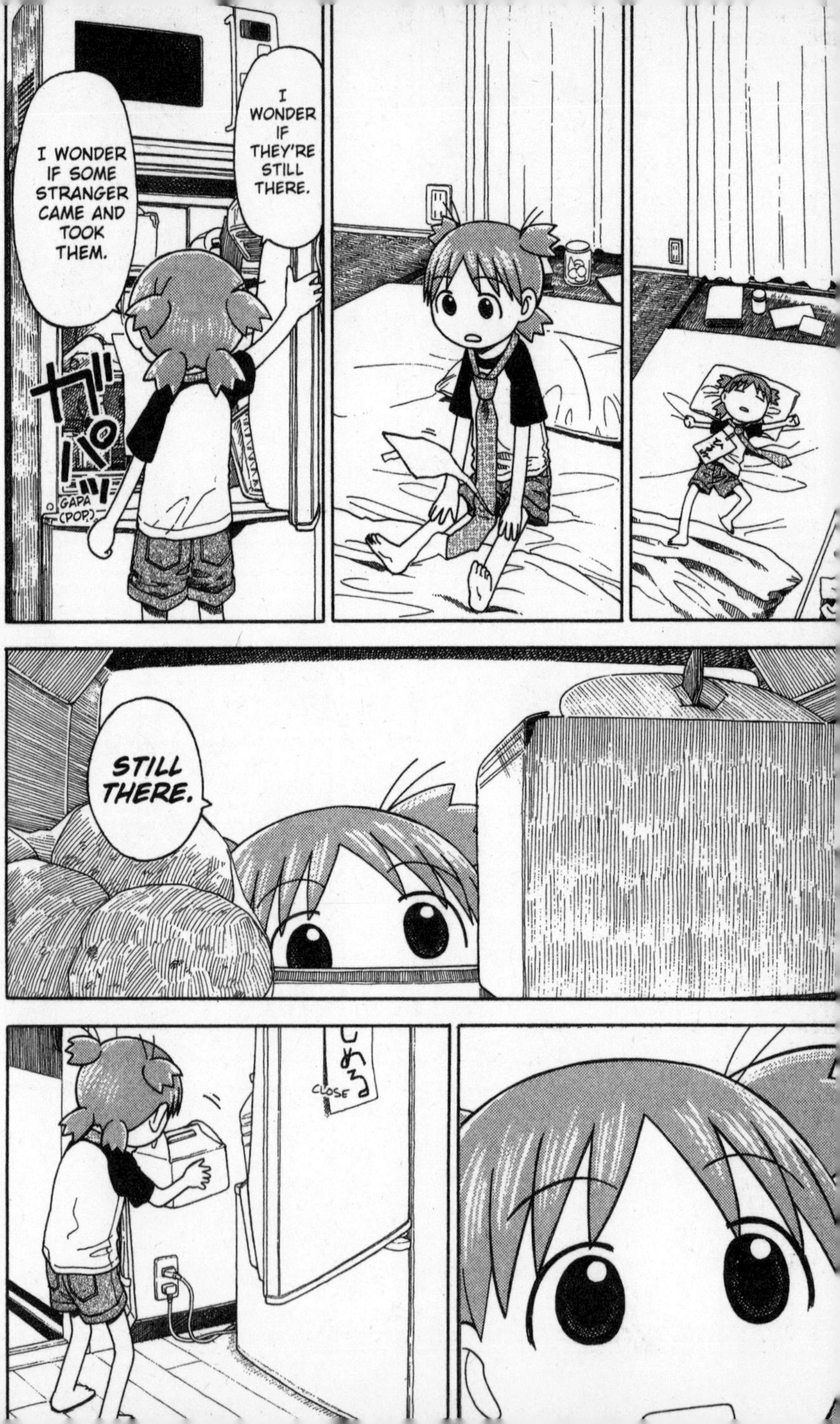
I WONDER IF THEY'RE STILL THERE.
I WONDER IF SOME STRANGER CAME AND TOOK THEM.
GAPA (POP)
STILL THERE.
CLOSE

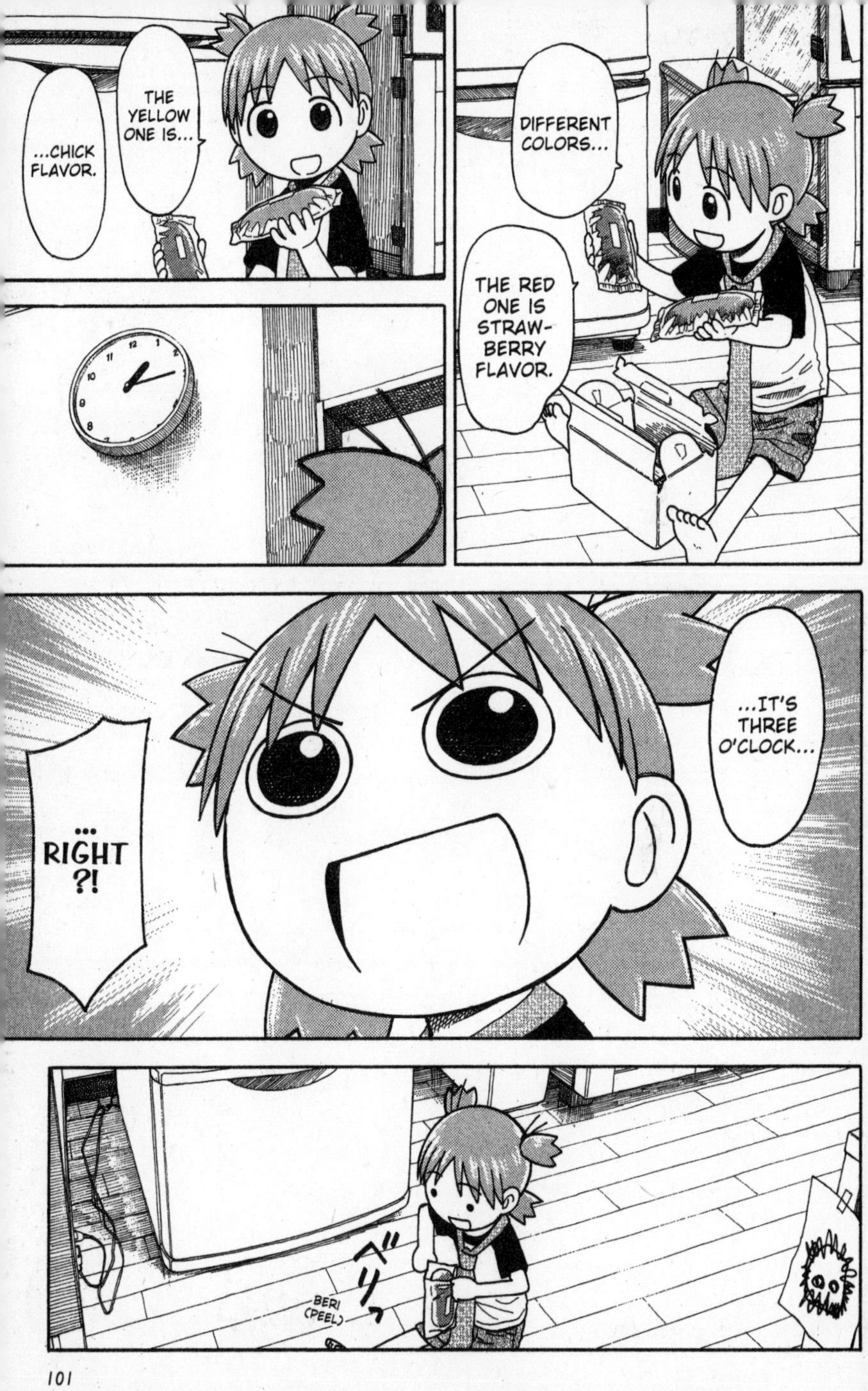
DIFFERENT COLORS...
THE RED ONE IS STRAWBERRY FLAVOR.
THE YELLOW ONE IS...
...CHICK FLAVOR.
...IT'S THREE O'CLOCK...
...RIGHT?!
べりっ
BERI (PEEL)

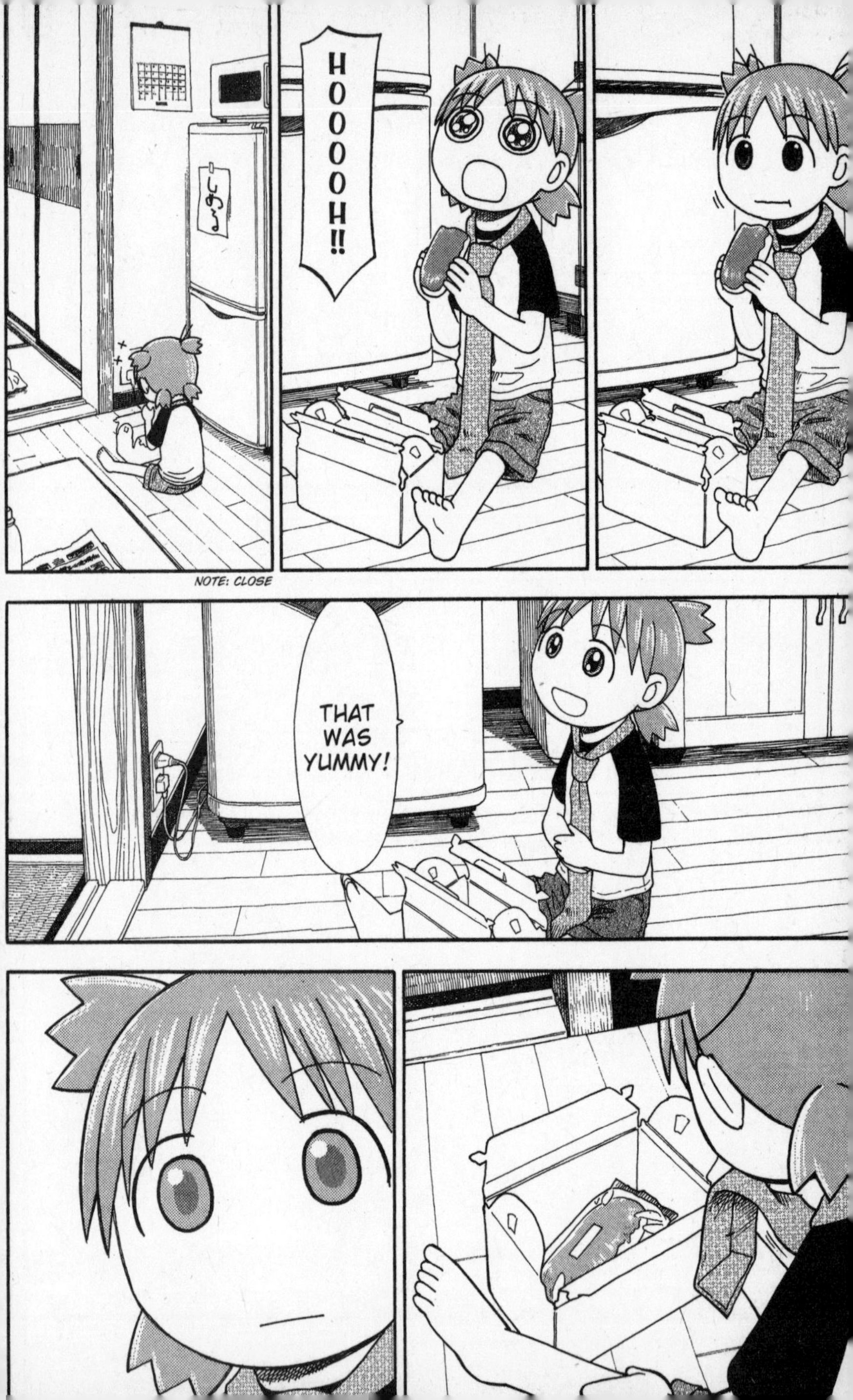
HOOOOOH!!
NOTE: CLOSE
THAT WAS YUMMY!

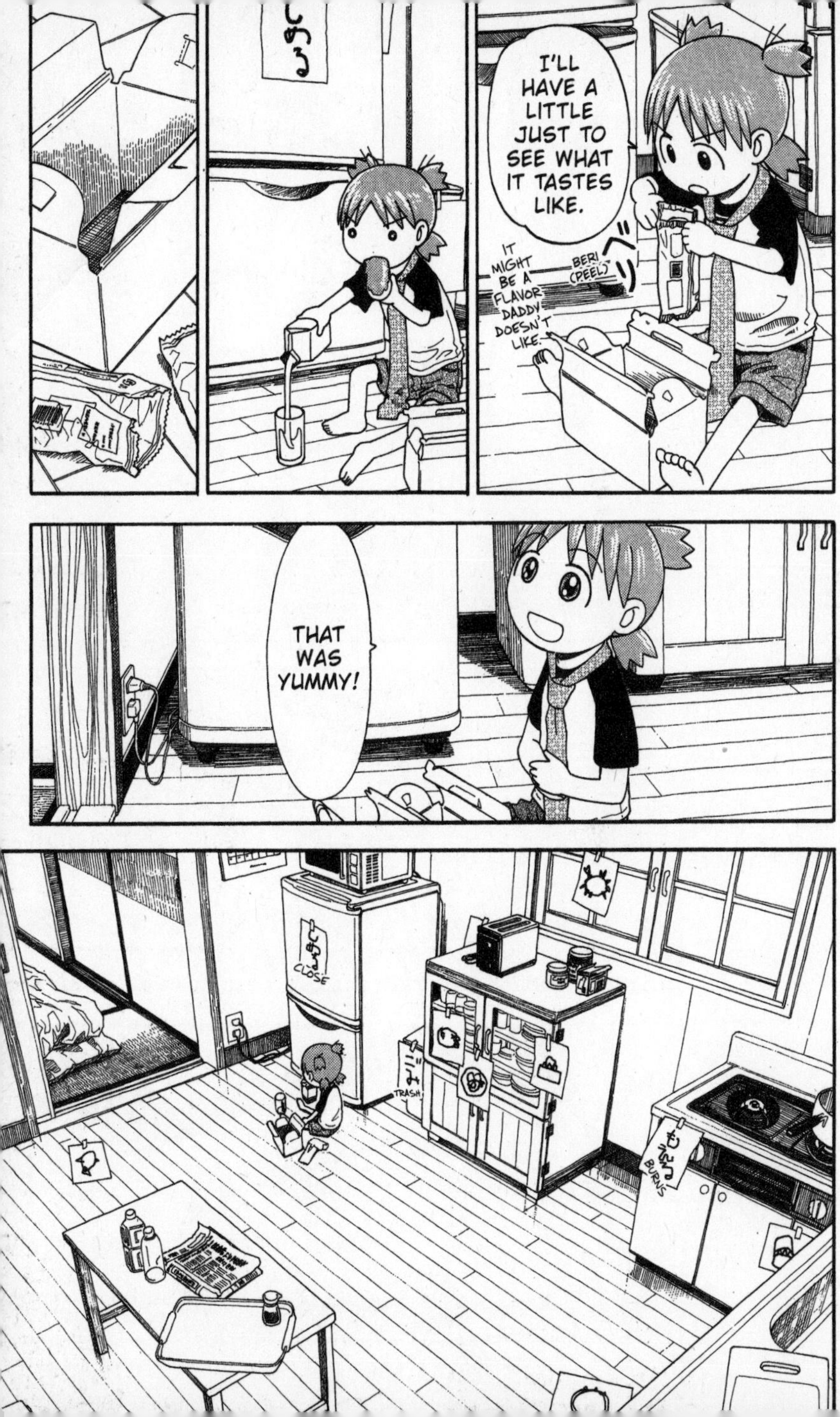
I'LL HAVE A LITTLE JUST TO SEE WHAT IT TASTES LIKE.
BERI (PEEL)
IT MIGHT BE A FLAVOR DADDY DOESN'T LIKE.
THAT WAS YUMMY!
CLOSE
TRASH
BURNS

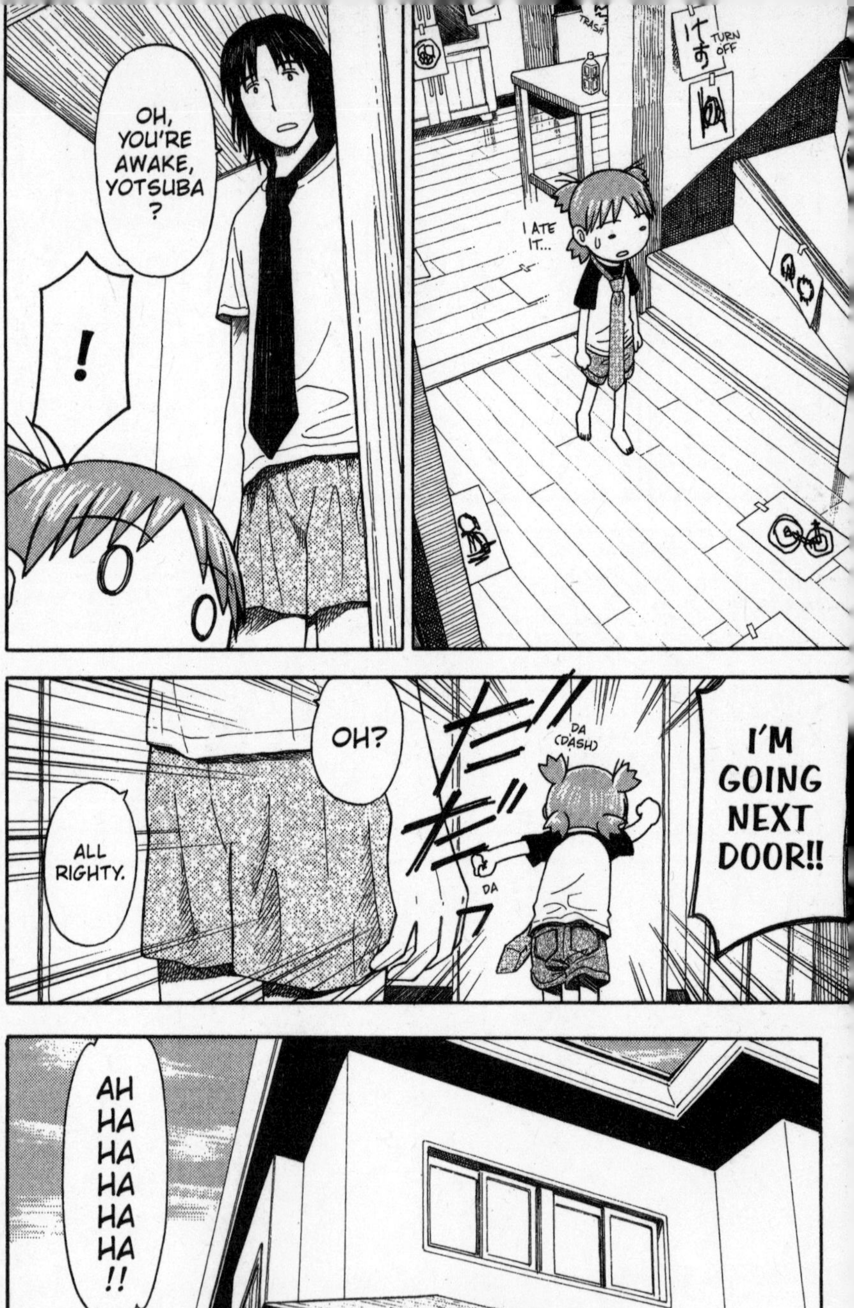

TRASH
けす
TURN OFF
I ATE IT...
OH, YOU'RE AWAKE, YOTSUBA?
!
I'M GOING NEXT DOOR!!
DA (DASH)
DA
OH?
ALL RIGHTY.
AH HA HA HA HA HA HA!!

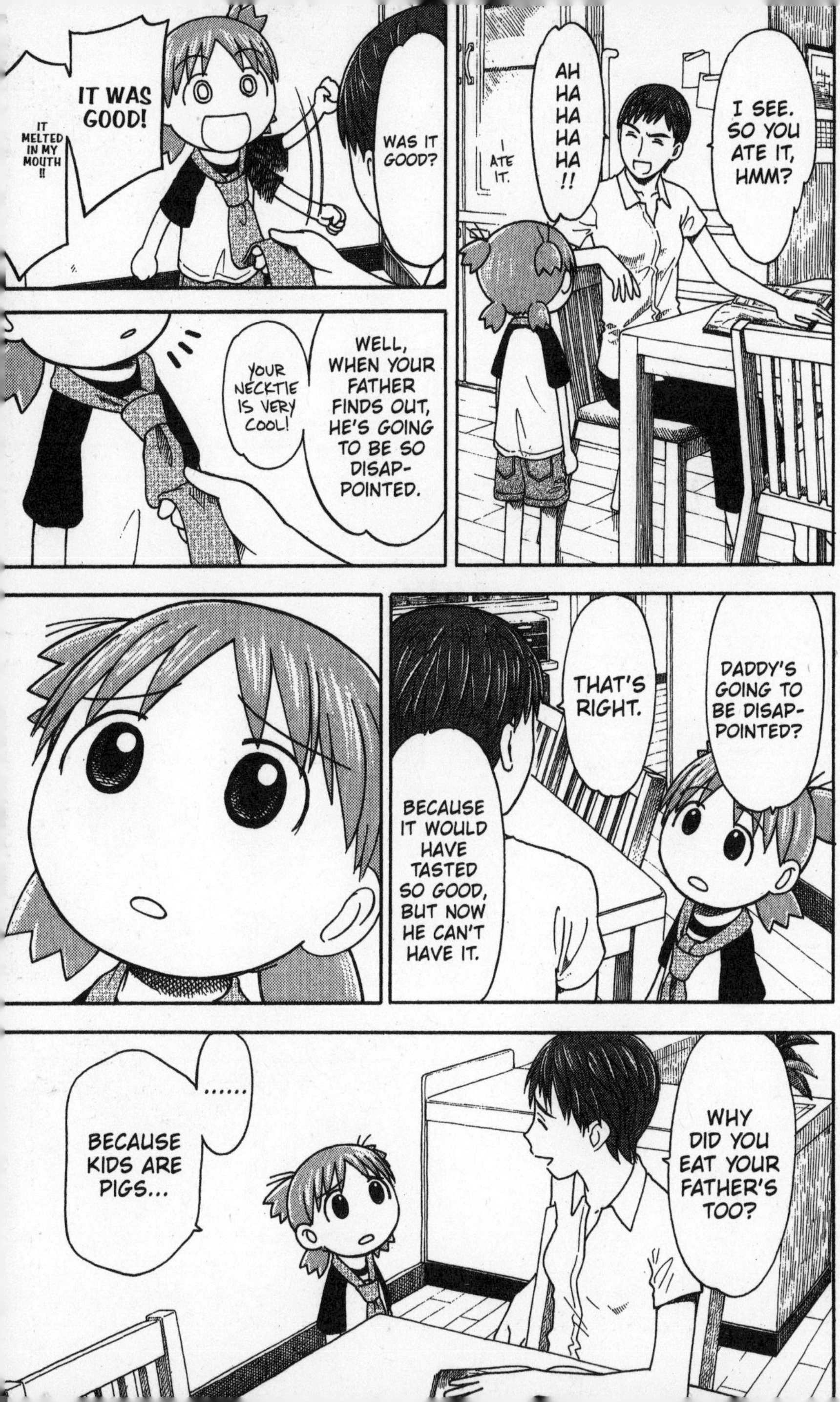
I SEE. SO YOU ATE IT, HMM?
AH HA HA HA HA HA!!
I ATE IT.
WAS IT GOOD?
IT WAS GOOD!
IT MELTED IN MY MOUTH!!
WELL, WHEN YOUR FATHER FINDS OUT, HE'S GOING TO BE SO DISAP-POINTED.
YOUR NECKTIE IS VERY COOL!
DADDY'S GOING TO BE DISAP-POINTED?
THAT'S RIGHT.
BECAUSE IT WOULD HAVE TASTED SO GOOD, BUT NOW HE CAN'T HAVE IT.
WHY DID YOU EAT YOUR FATHER'S TOO?
......
BECAUSE KIDS ARE PIGS...

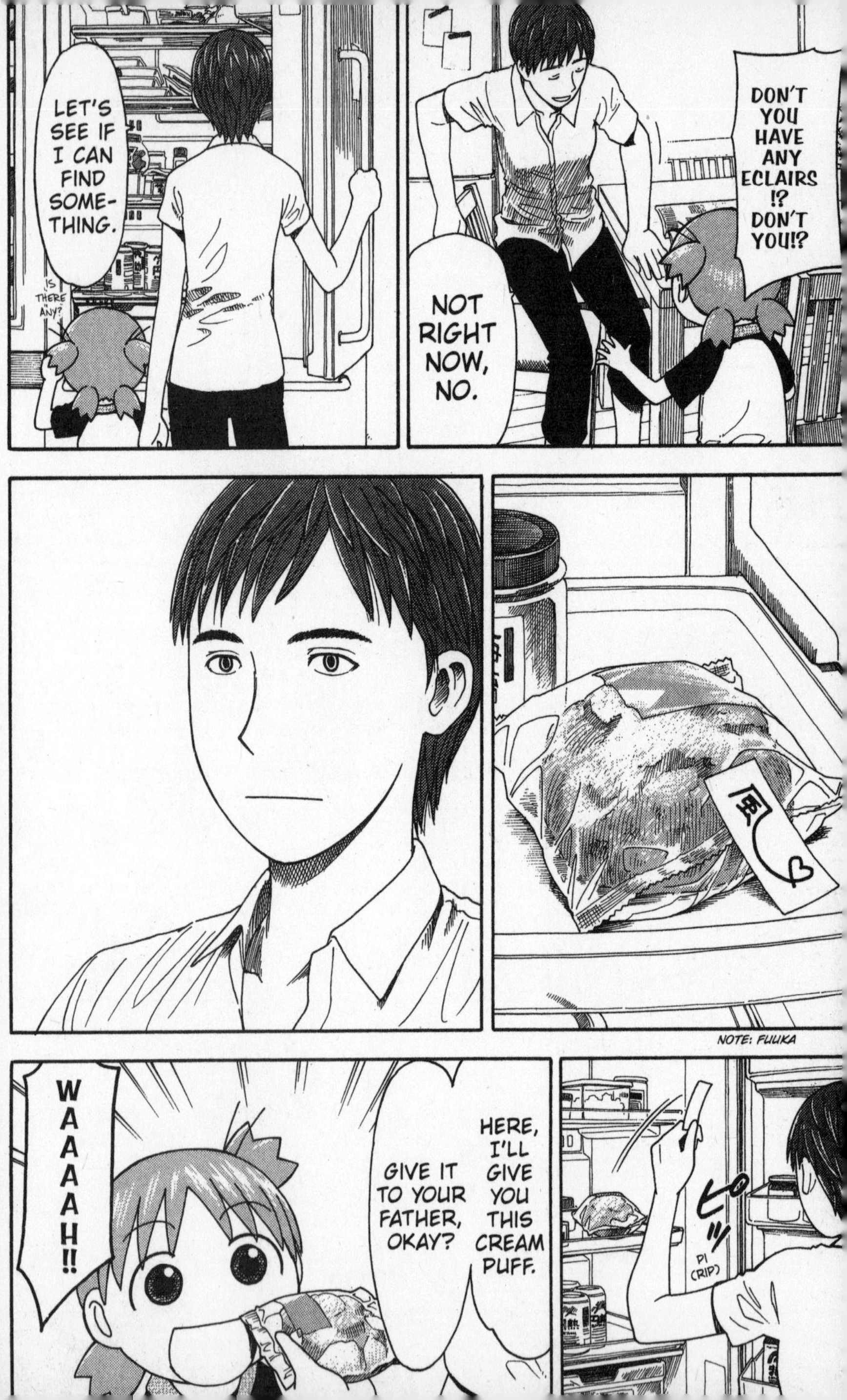

DON'T YOU HAVE ANY ECLAIRS!? DON'T YOU!?
NOT RIGHT NOW, NO.
LET'S SEE IF I CAN FIND SOME-THING.
IS THERE ANY?
風
NOTE: FUUKA
ピッ
PI (RIP)
HERE, I'LL GIVE YOU THIS CREAM PUFF.
GIVE IT TO YOUR FATHER, OKAY?
WAAAAAH!!

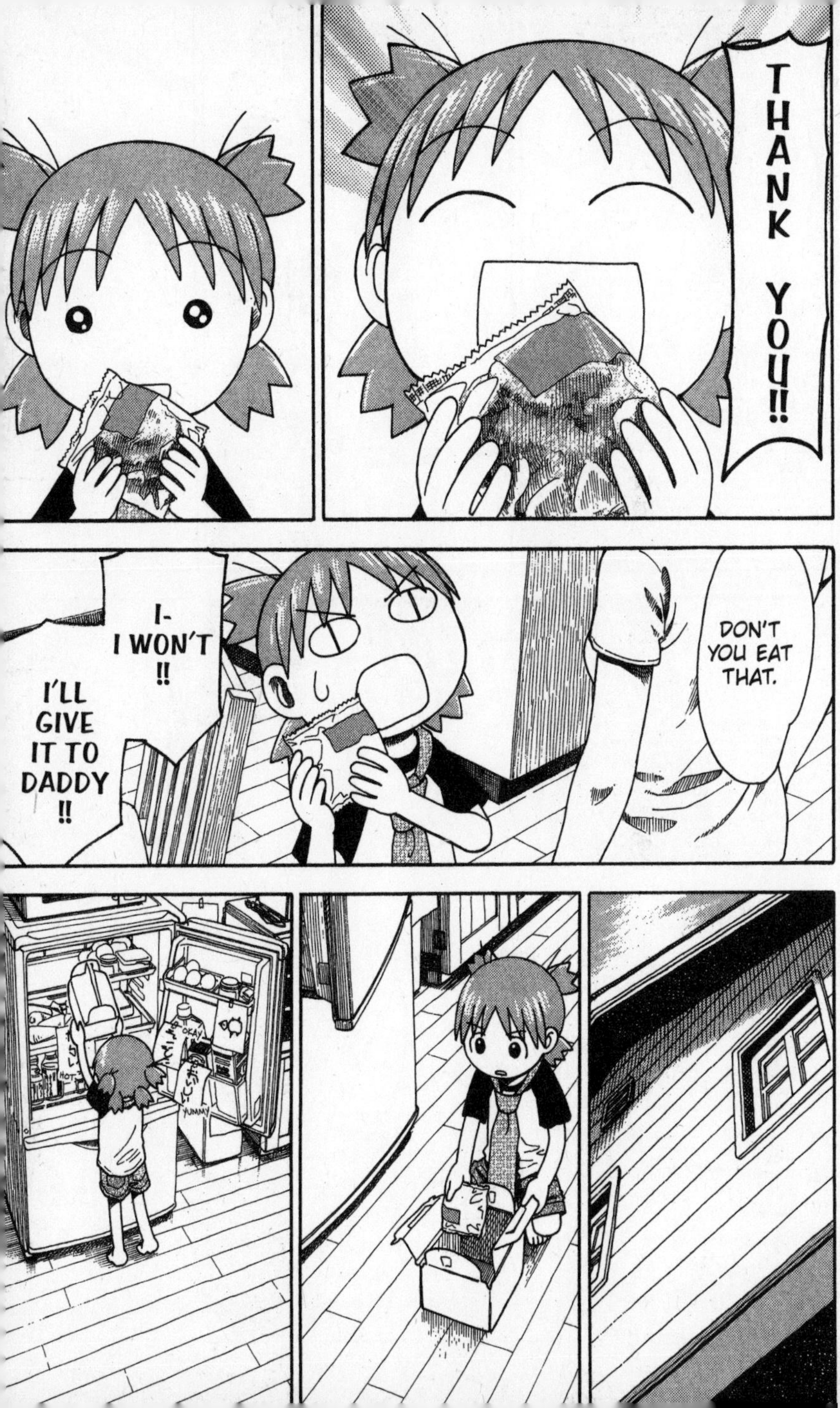
THANK YOU!!
DON'T YOU EAT THAT.
I- I WON'T!!
I'LL GIVE IT TO DADDY!!
OKAY
YUMMY
HOT

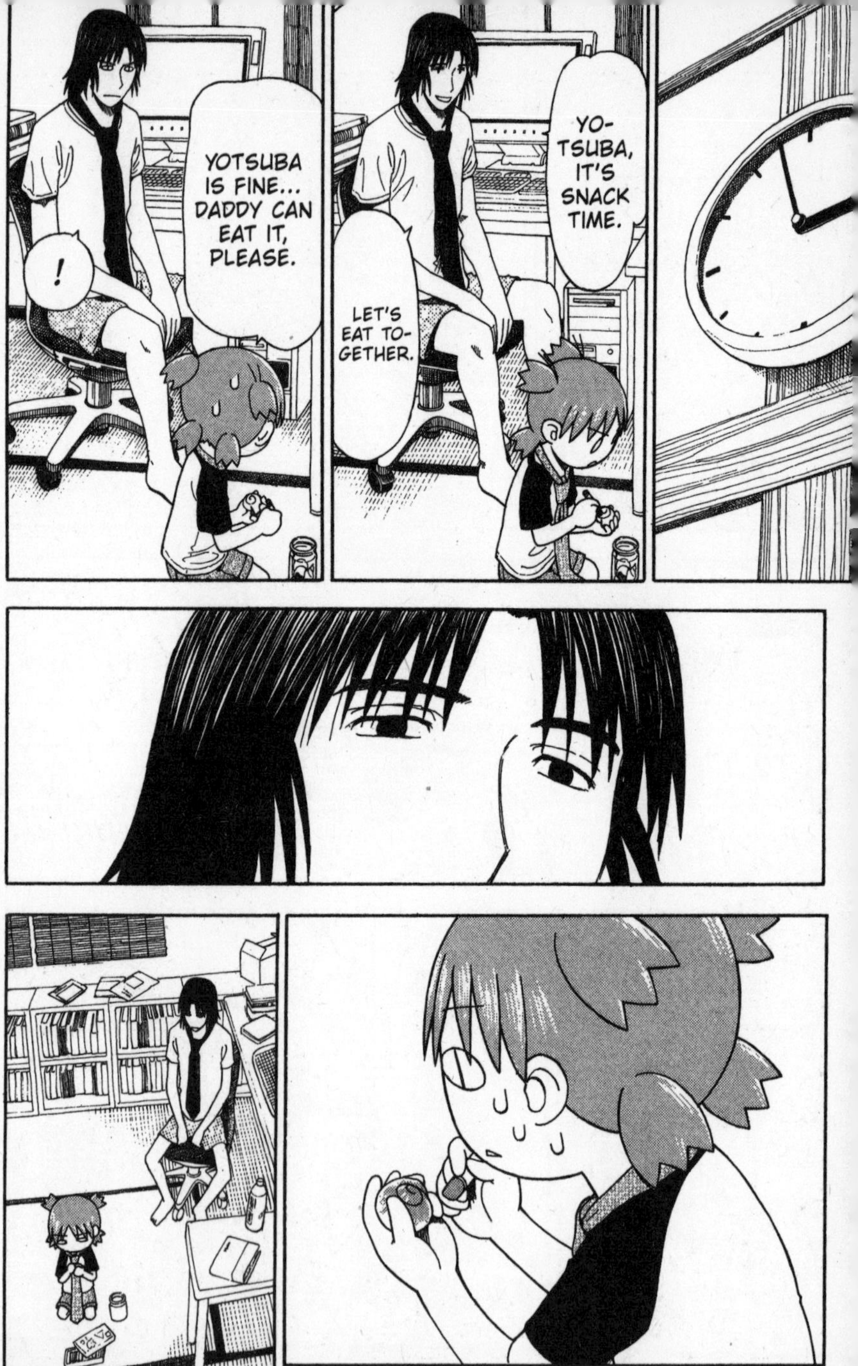
YO-TSUBA, IT'S SNACK TIME.
LET'S EAT TO-GETHER.
YOTSUBA IS FINE... DADDY CAN EAT IT, PLEASE.
!

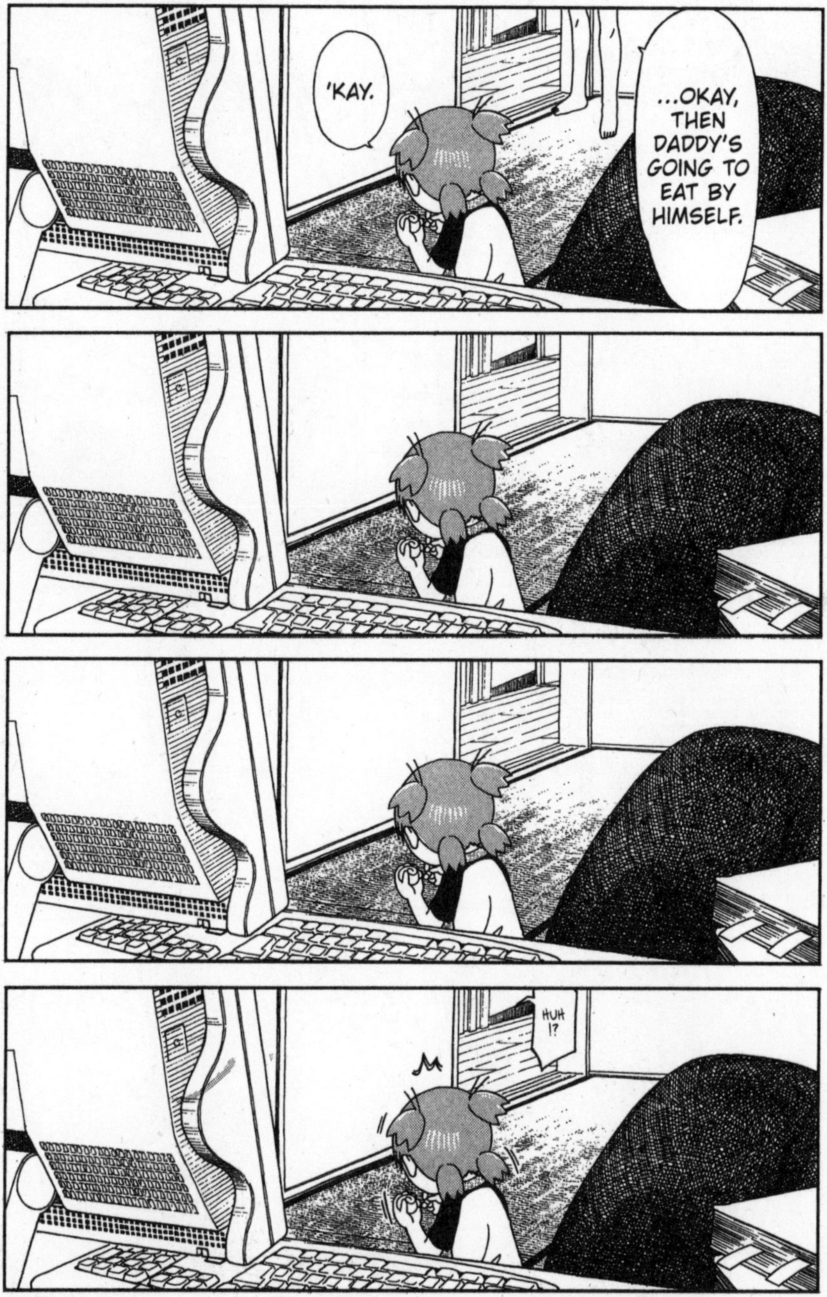
...OKAY, THEN DADDY'S GOING TO EAT BY HIMSELF.
'KAY.
HUH !?

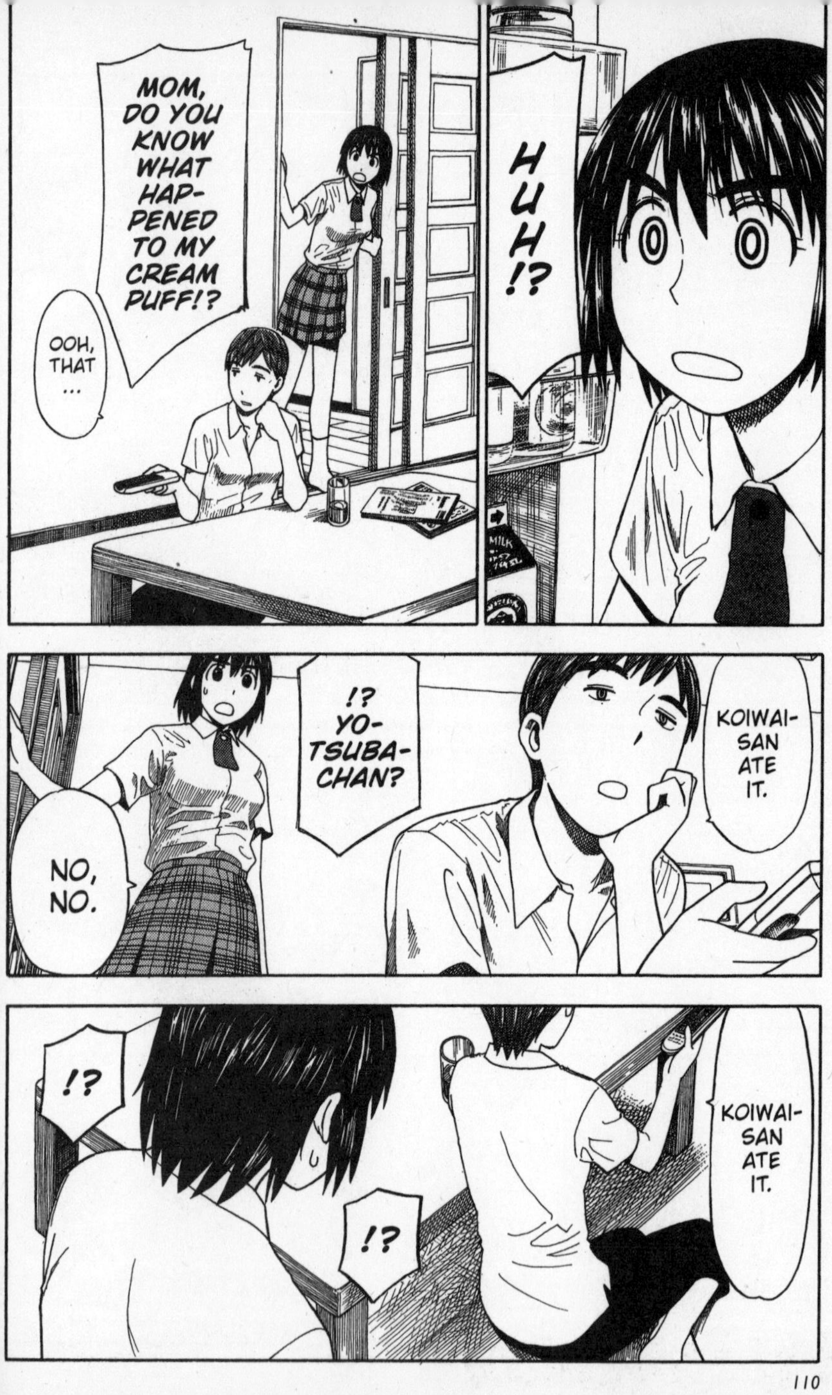
HUH!?
MOM, DO YOU KNOW WHAT HAP-PENED TO MY CREAM PUFF!?
OOH, THAT ...
KOIWAI-SAN ATE IT.
!? YO-TSUBA-CHAN?
NO, NO.
KOIWAI-SAN ATE IT.
!?
!?

YOTSUBA&!

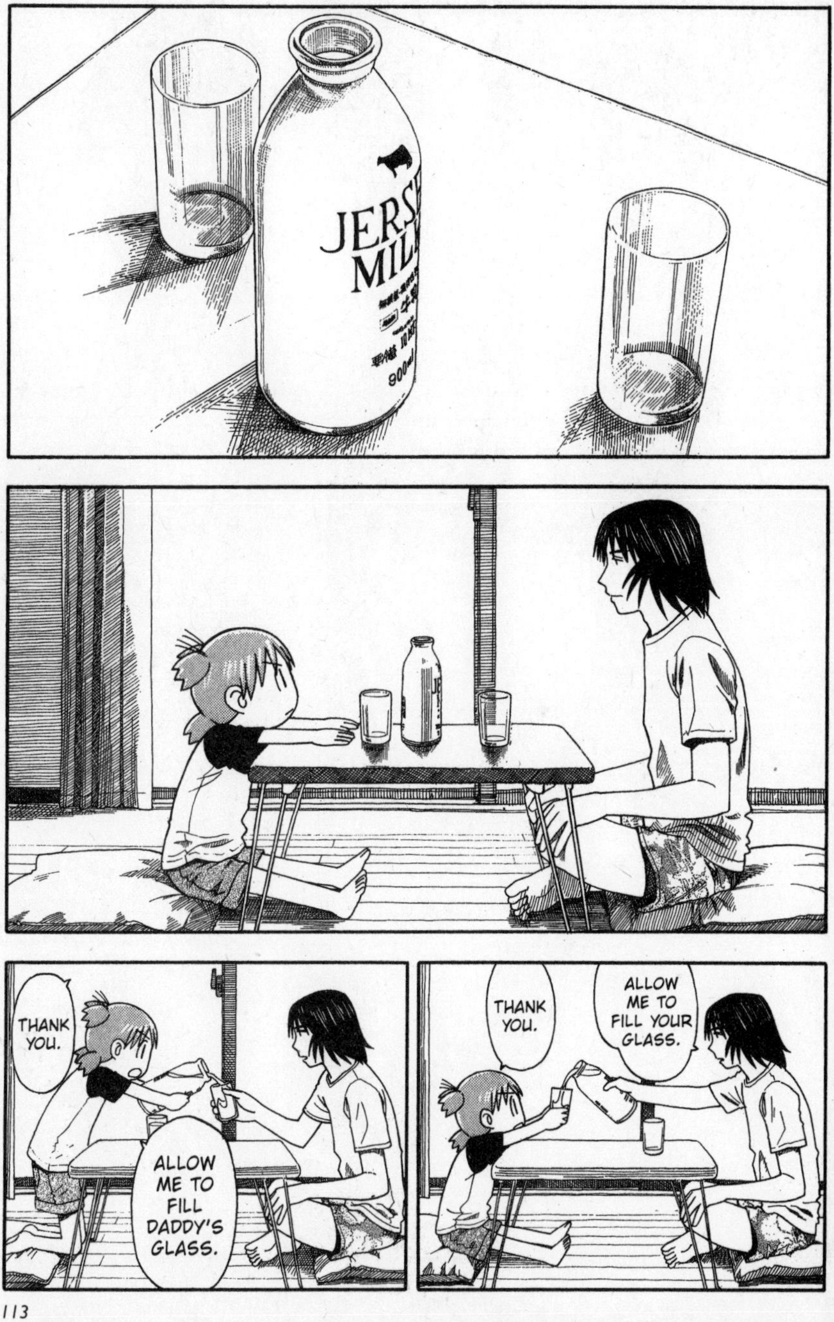
900ml
ALLOW ME TO FILL YOUR GLASS.
THANK YOU.
ALLOW ME TO FILL DADDY'S GLASS.
THANK YOU.

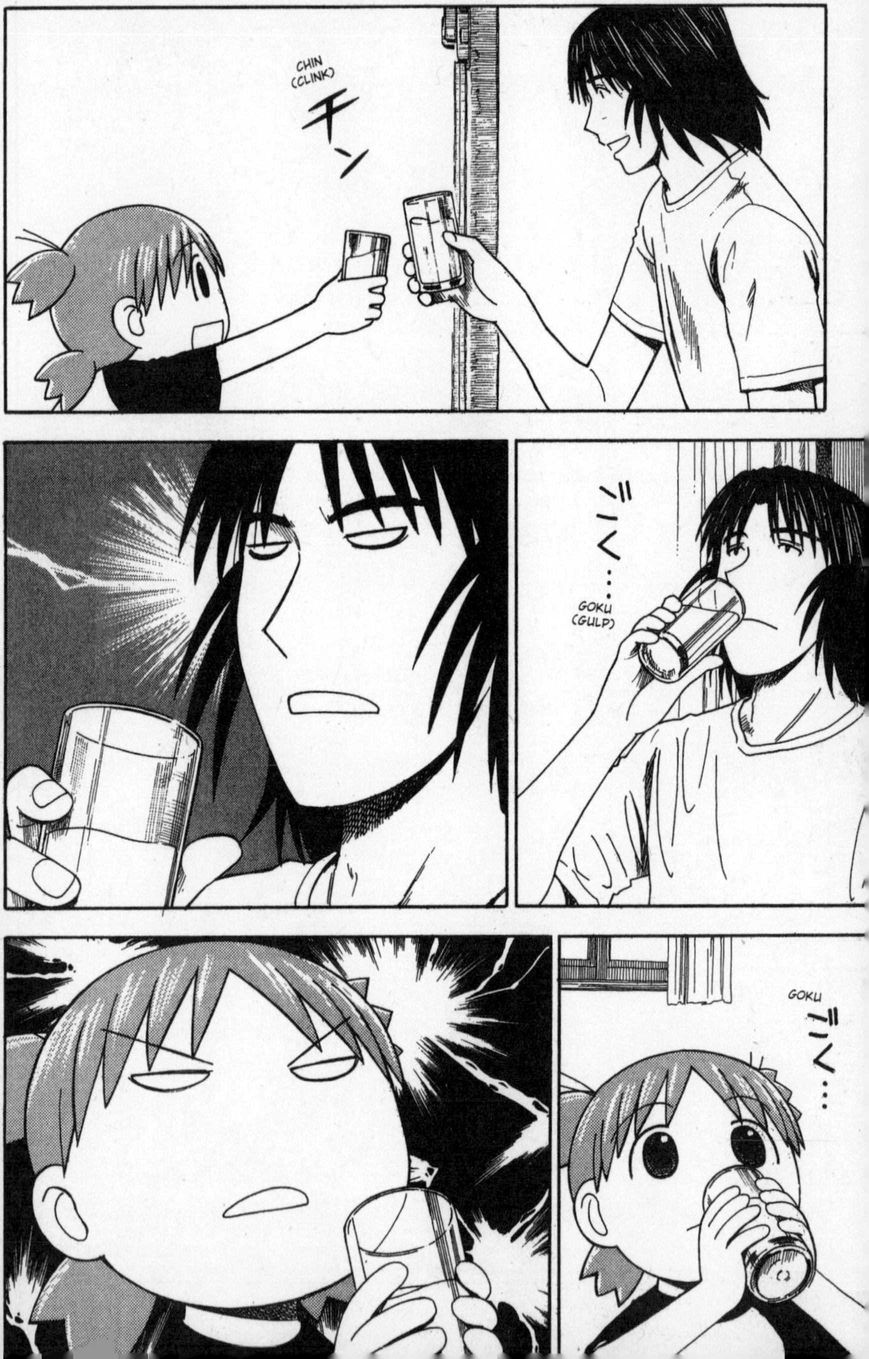

チン
CHIN (CLINK)
ゴく…
GOKU (GULP)
ゴく…
GOKU

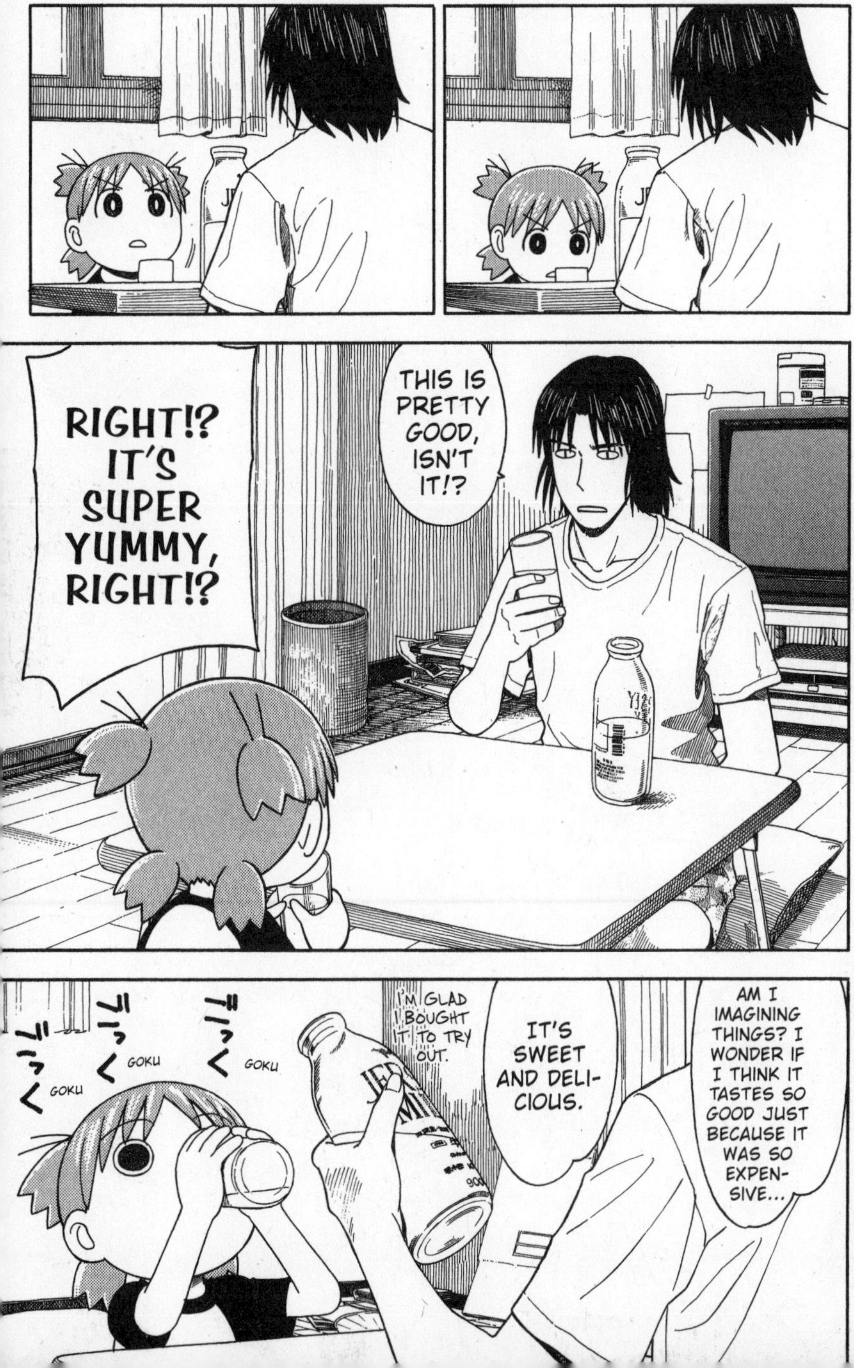
THIS IS PRETTY GOOD, ISN'T IT!?
RIGHT!? IT'S SUPER YUMMY, RIGHT!?
AM I IMAGINING THINGS? I WONDER IF I THINK IT TASTES SO GOOD JUST BECAUSE IT WAS SO EXPENSIVE...
IT'S SWEET AND DELICIOUS.
I'M GLAD I BOUGHT IT TO TRY OUT.
GOKU
GOKU
GOKU

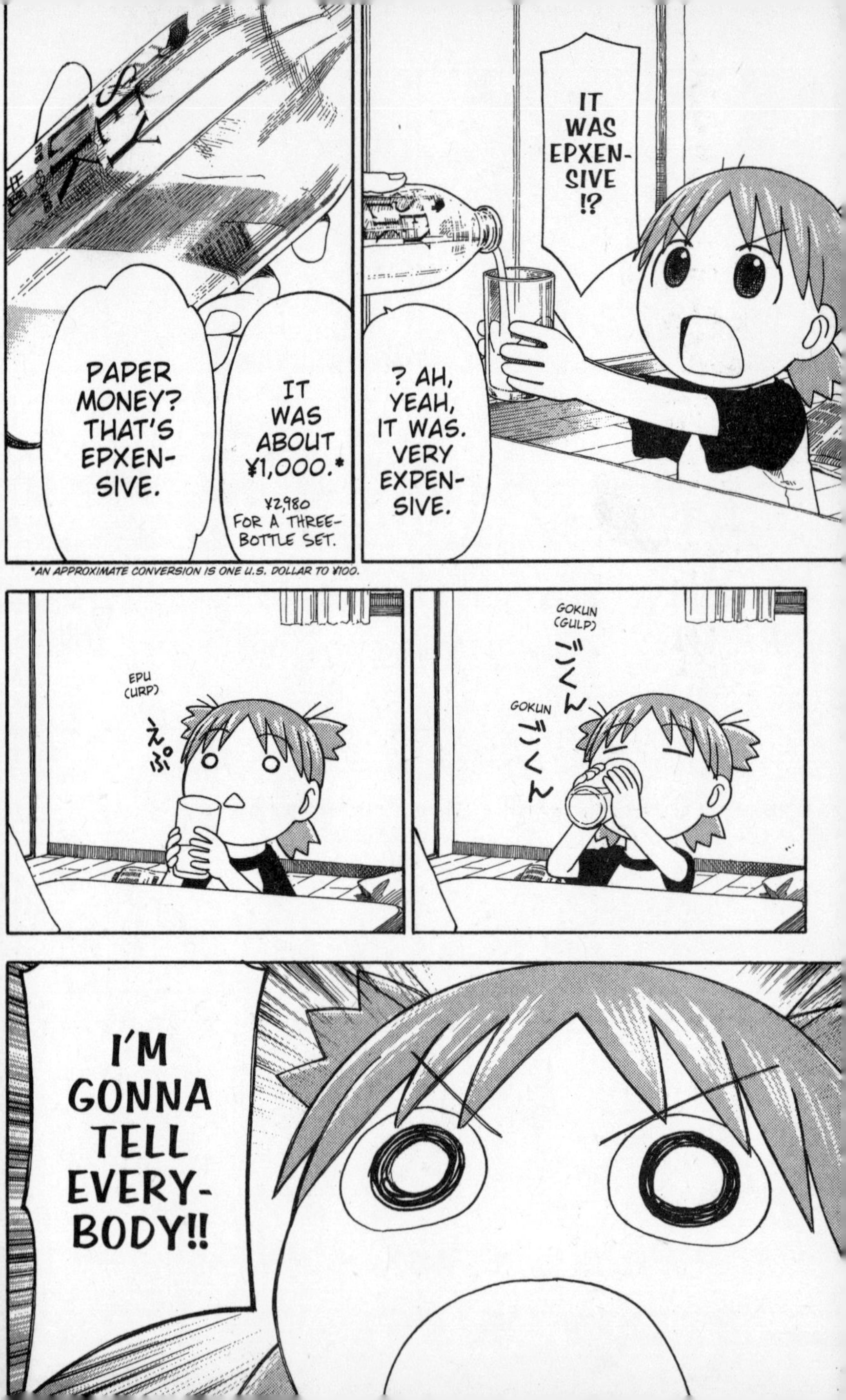
IT WAS EPXEN-SIVE !?
? AH, YEAH, IT WAS. VERY EXPEN-SIVE.
IT WAS ABOUT ¥1,000.*
¥2,980 FOR A THREE-BOTTLE SET.
PAPER MONEY? THAT'S EPXEN-SIVE.
*AN APPROXIMATE CONVERSION IS ONE U.S. DOLLAR TO ¥100.
GOKUN (GULP)
ごくん
GOKUN
ごくん
EPU (URP)
えぷ
I'M GONNA TELL EVERY-BODY!!

YOTSUBA& MILK!

#39

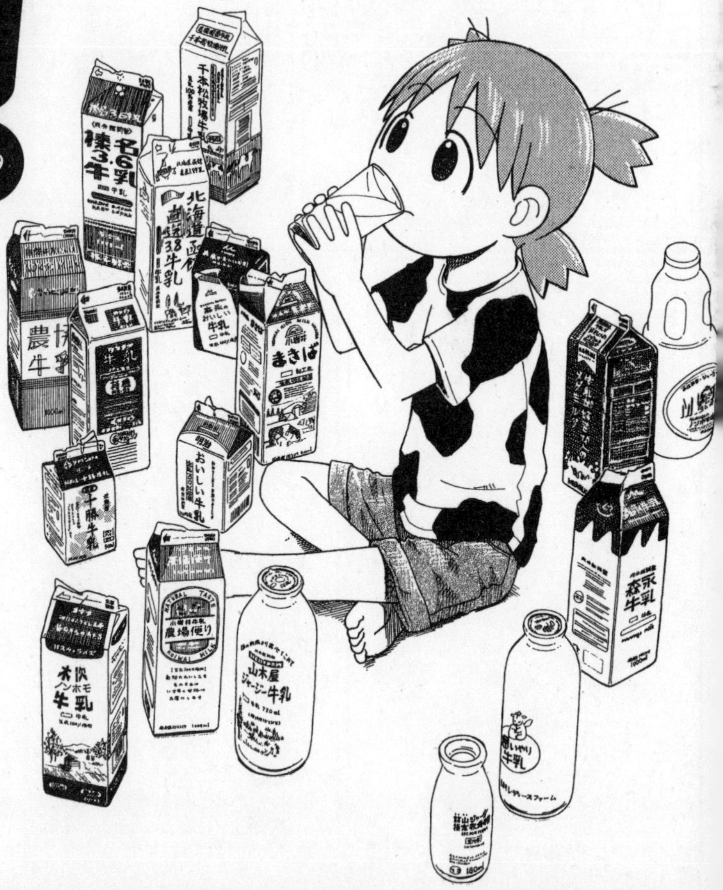

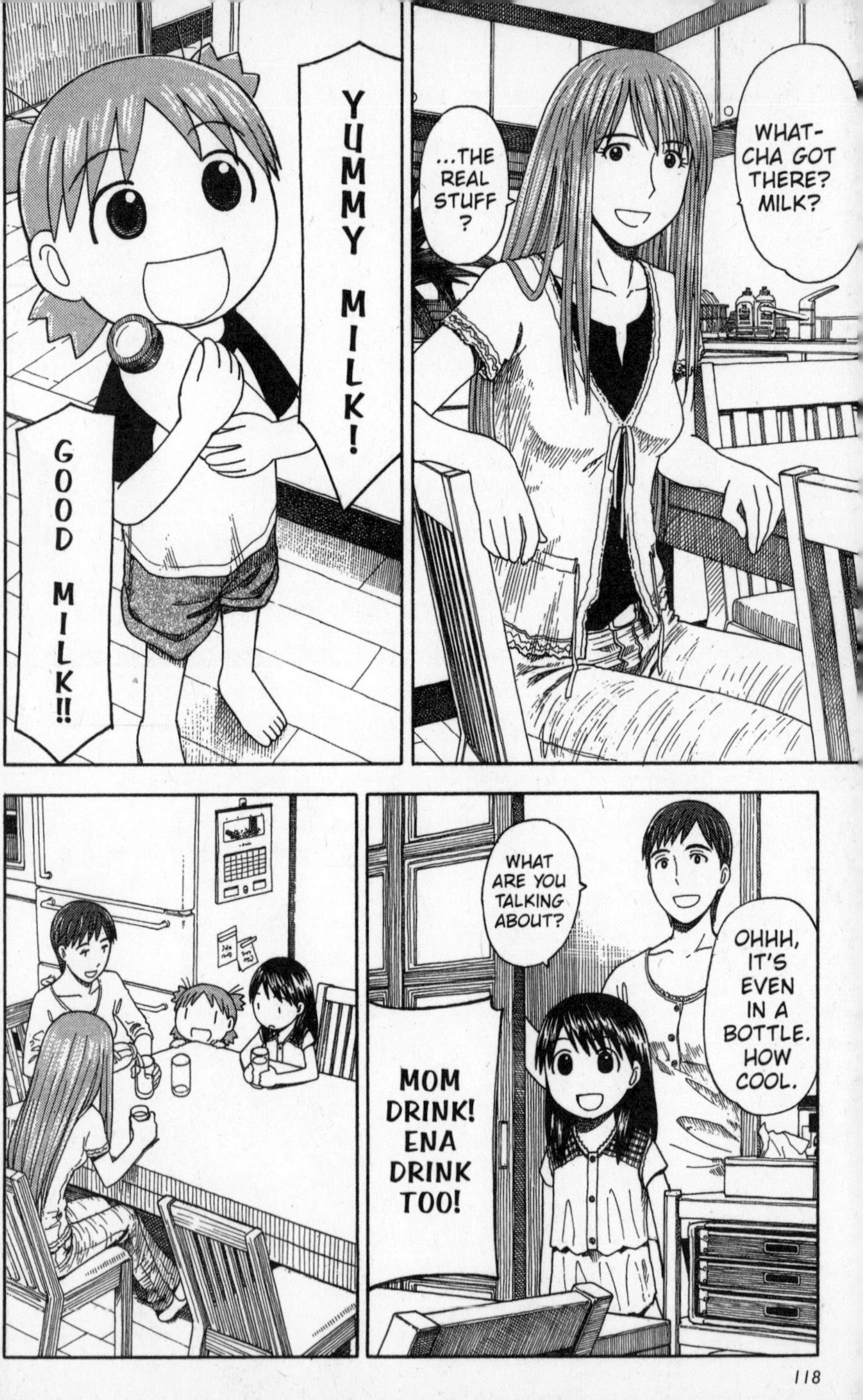
WHAT-CHA GOT THERE? MILK?
...THE REAL STUFF?
YUMMY MILK!
GOOD MILK!!
WHAT ARE YOU TALKING ABOUT?
OHHH, IT'S EVEN IN A BOTTLE. HOW COOL.
MOM DRINK! ENA DRINK TOO!

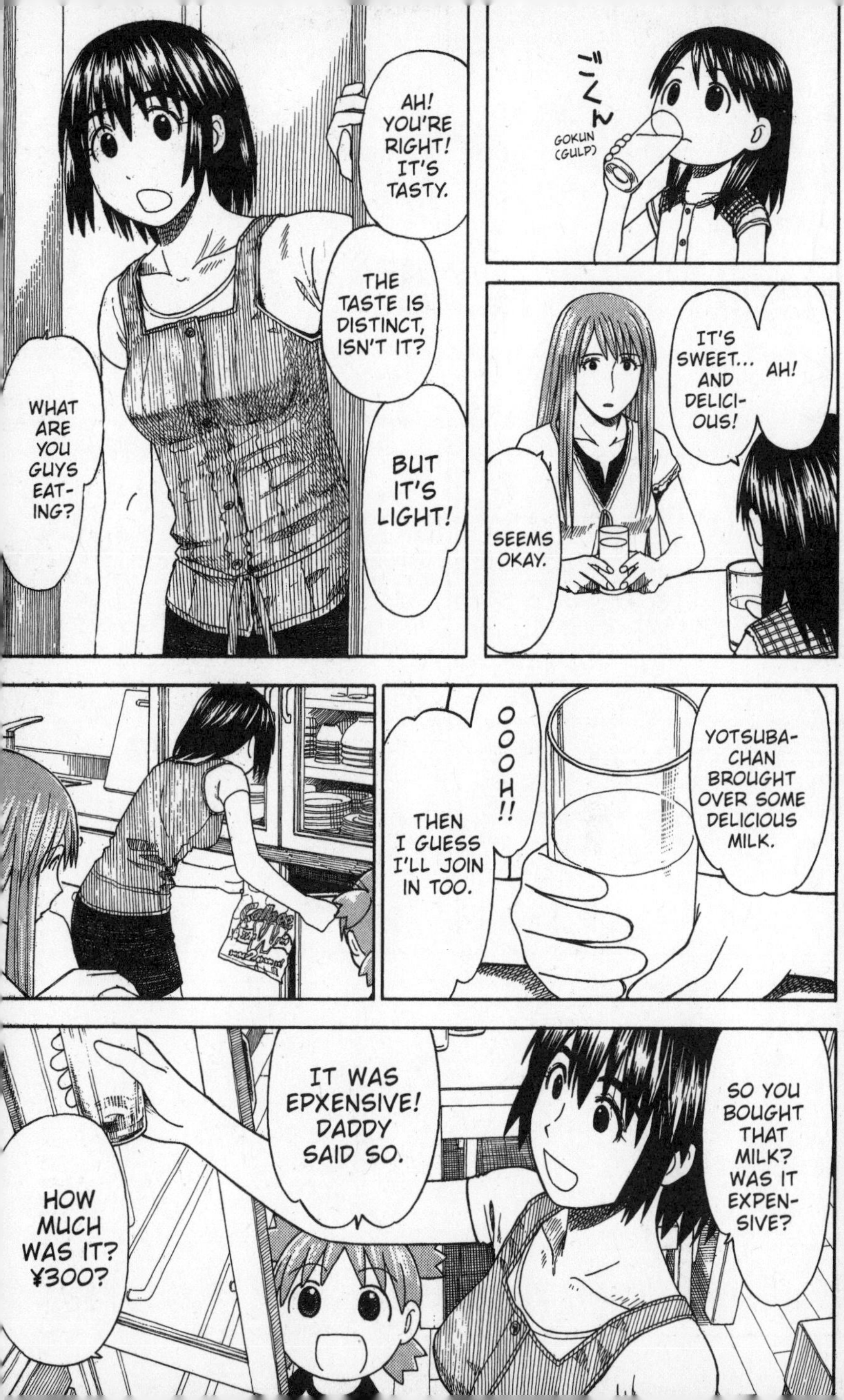
ごくん
GOKUN (GULP)
AH!
IT'S SWEET... AND DELICI-OUS!
SEEMS OKAY.
AH! YOU'RE RIGHT! IT'S TASTY.
THE TASTE IS DISTINCT, ISN'T IT?
BUT IT'S LIGHT!
WHAT ARE YOU GUYS EAT-ING?
YOTSUBA-CHAN BROUGHT OVER SOME DELICIOUS MILK.
OOOOH!!
THEN I GUESS I'LL JOIN IN TOO.
SO YOU BOUGHT THAT MILK? WAS IT EXPEN-SIVE?
IT WAS EPXENSIVE! DADDY SAID SO.
HOW MUCH WAS IT? ¥300?

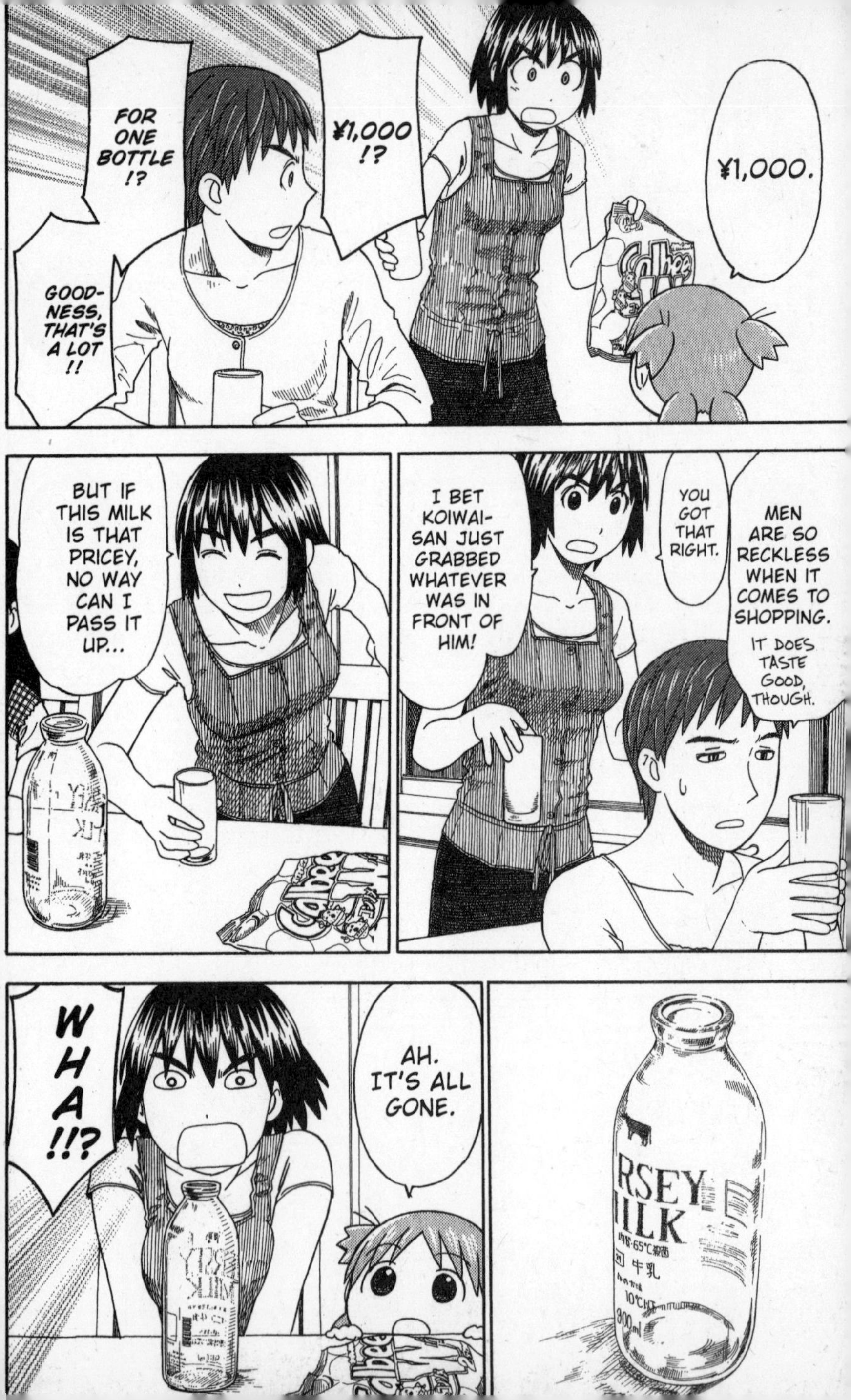
¥1,000.
¥1,000 !?
FOR ONE BOTTLE !?
GOOD-NESS, THAT'S A LOT !!
MEN ARE SO RECKLESS WHEN IT COMES TO SHOPPING.
IT DOES TASTE GOOD, THOUGH.
YOU GOT THAT RIGHT.
I BET KOIWAI-SAN JUST GRABBED WHATEVER WAS IN FRONT OF HIM!
BUT IF THIS MILK IS THAT PRICEY, NO WAY CAN I PASS IT UP...
RSEY
ILK
AH. IT'S ALL GONE.
WHA!!?

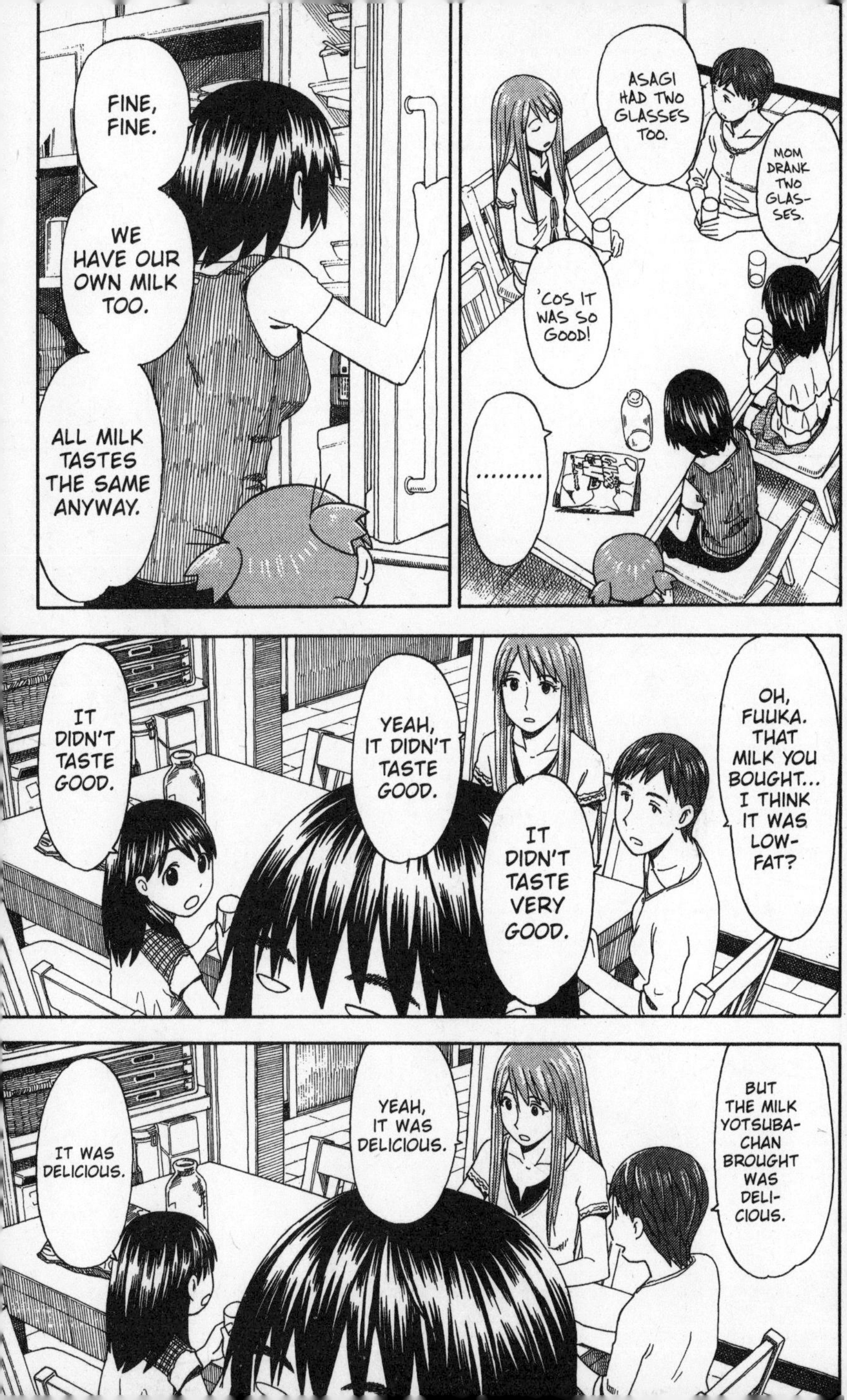
ASAGI HAD TWO GLASSES TOO.
MOM DRANK TWO GLAS-SES.
'COS IT WAS SO GOOD!
....
FINE, FINE.
WE HAVE OUR OWN MILK TOO.
ALL MILK TASTES THE SAME ANYWAY.
OH, FUUKA. THAT MILK YOU BOUGHT... I THINK IT WAS LOW-FAT?
IT DIDN'T TASTE VERY GOOD.
YEAH, IT DIDN'T TASTE GOOD.
IT DIDN'T TASTE GOOD.
BUT THE MILK YOTSUBA-CHAN BROUGHT WAS DELI-CIOUS.
YEAH, IT WAS DELICIOUS.
IT WAS DELICIOUS.

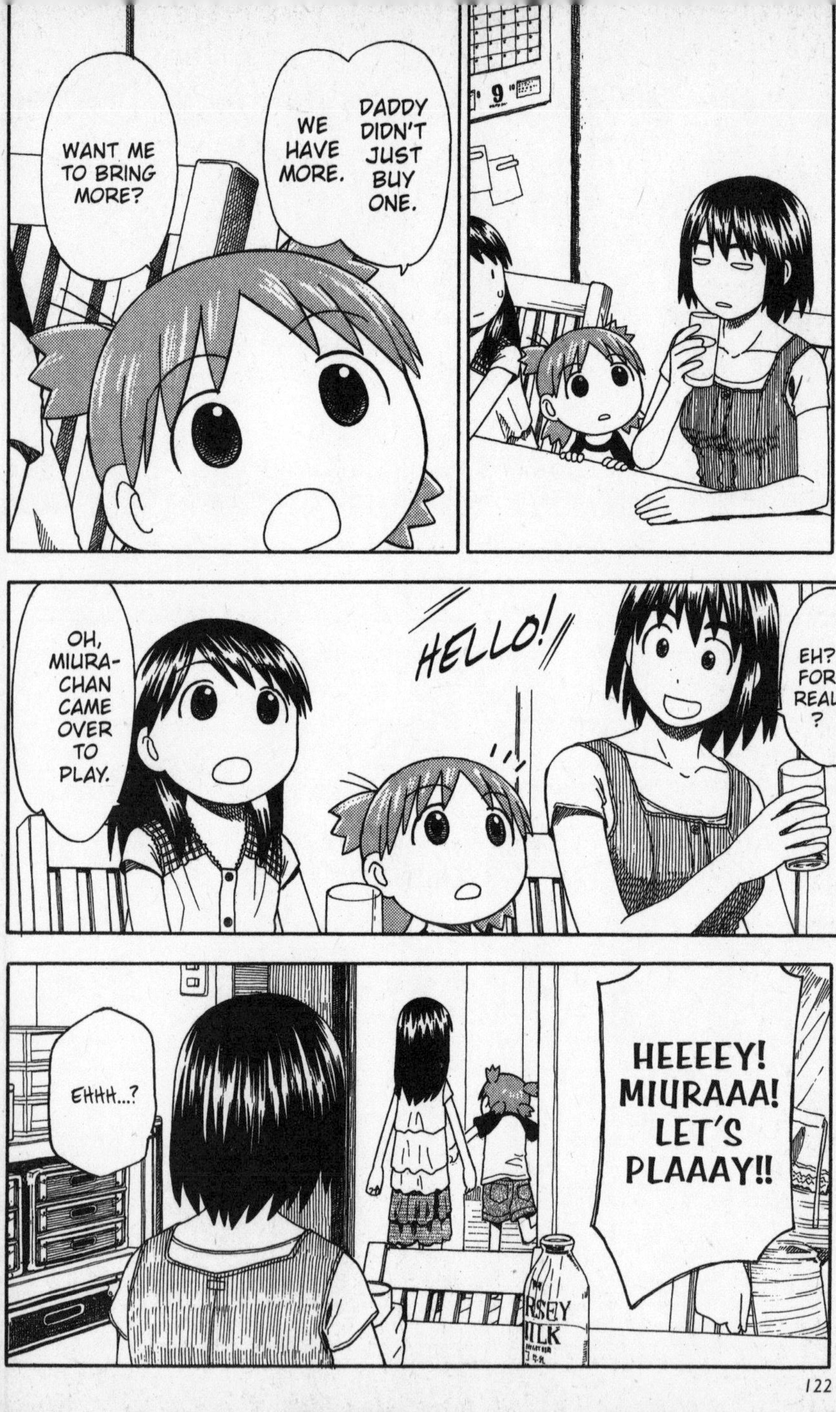
DADDY DIDN'T JUST BUY ONE.
WE HAVE MORE.
WANT ME TO BRING MORE?
EH? FOR REAL?
HELLO!
OH, MIURA-CHAN CAME OVER TO PLAY.
HEEEEY! MIURAAA! LET'S PLAAAY!!
EHHH...?

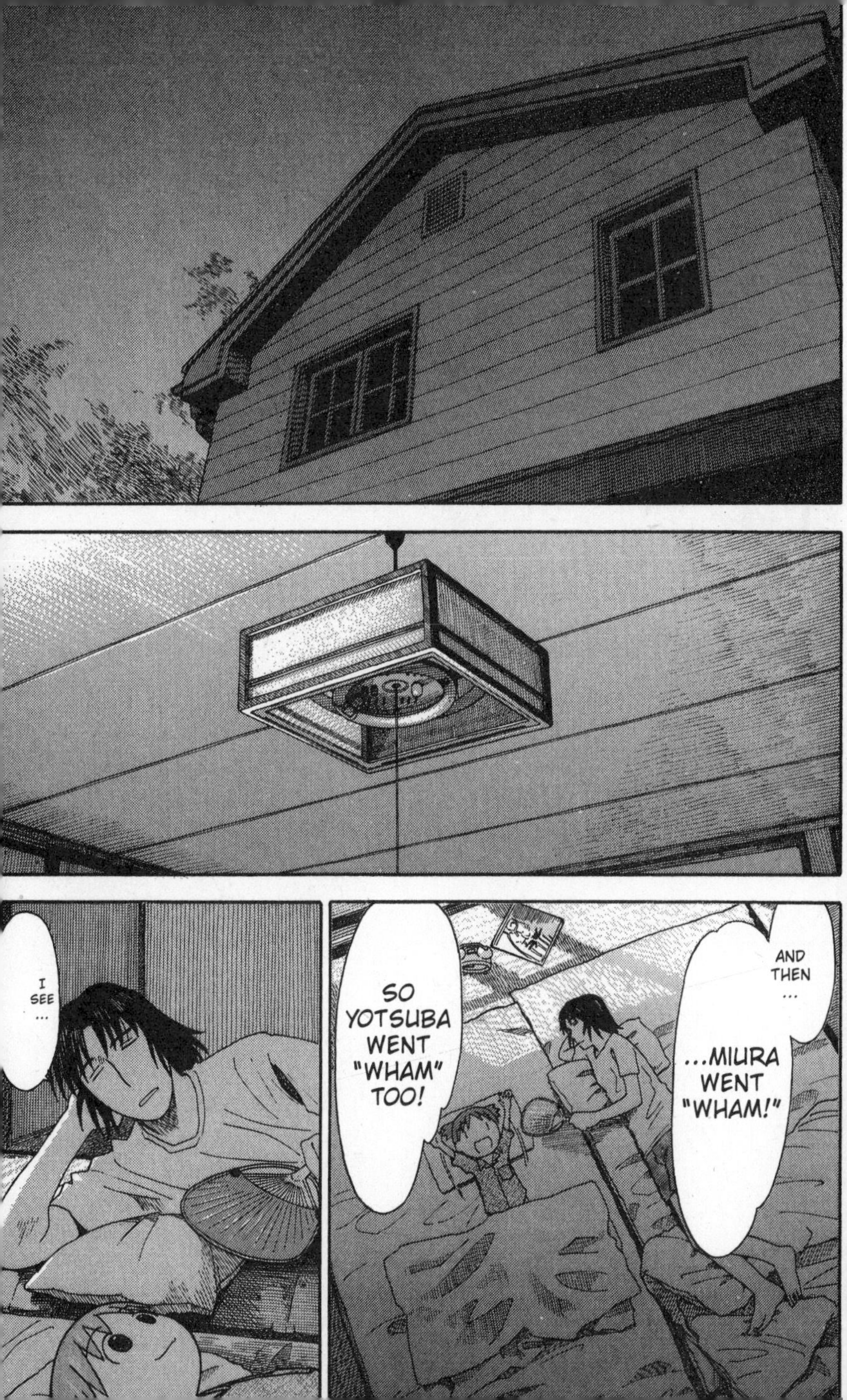
AND THEN ...
...MIURA WENT "WHAM!"
SO YOTSUBA WENT "WHAM" TOO!
I SEE ...

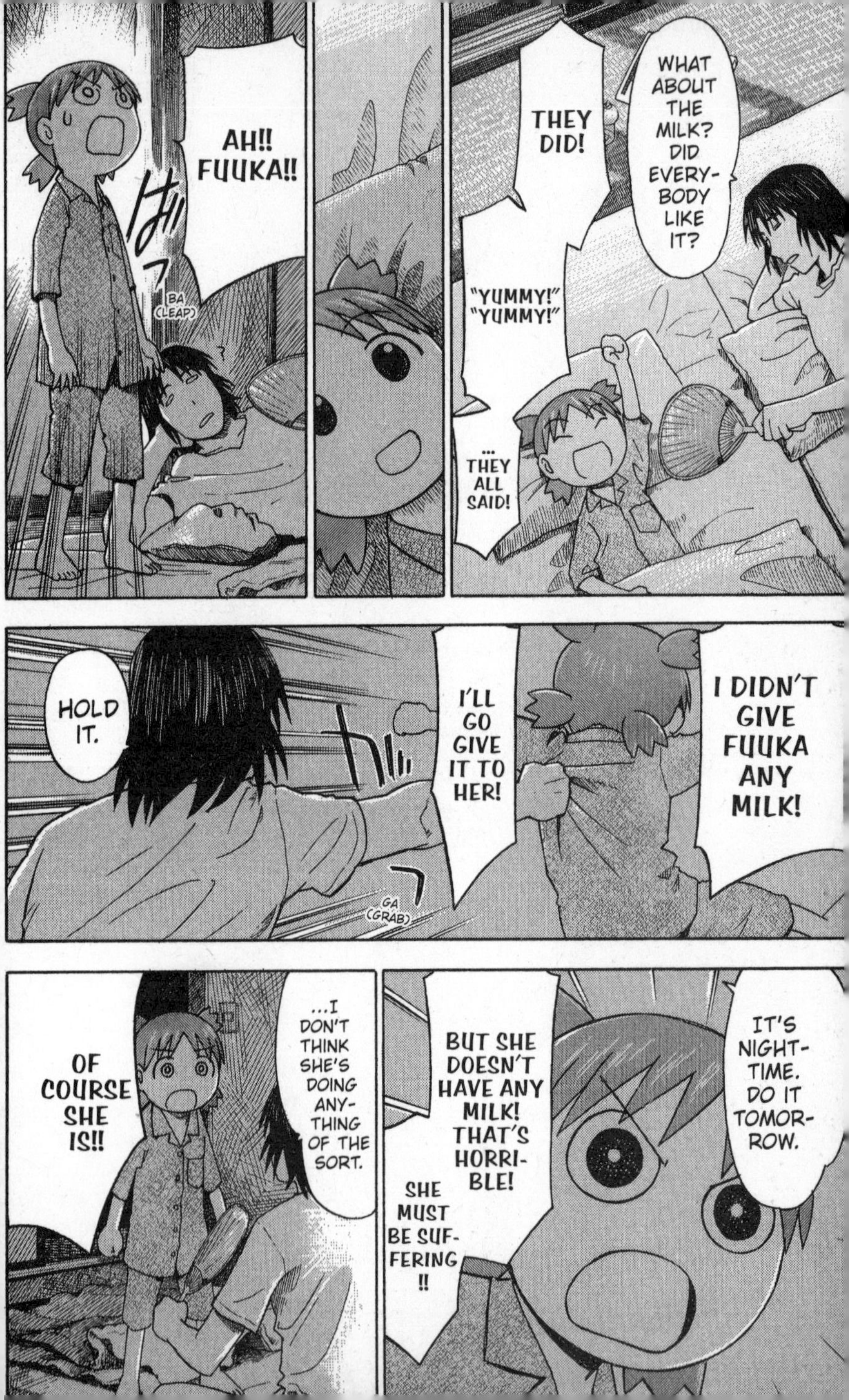
WHAT ABOUT THE MILK? DID EVERYBODY LIKE IT?
THEY DID!
"YUMMY!" "YUMMY!"
...THEY ALL SAID!
AH!! FUUKA!!
BA (LEAP)
I DIDN'T GIVE FUUKA ANY MILK!
I'LL GO GIVE IT TO HER!
HOLD IT.
GA (GRAB)
IT'S NIGHT-TIME. DO IT TOMORROW.
BUT SHE DOESN'T HAVE ANY MILK! THAT'S HORRIBLE!
SHE MUST BE SUFFERING!!
...I DON'T THINK SHE'S DOING ANYTHING OF THE SORT.
OF COURSE SHE IS!!

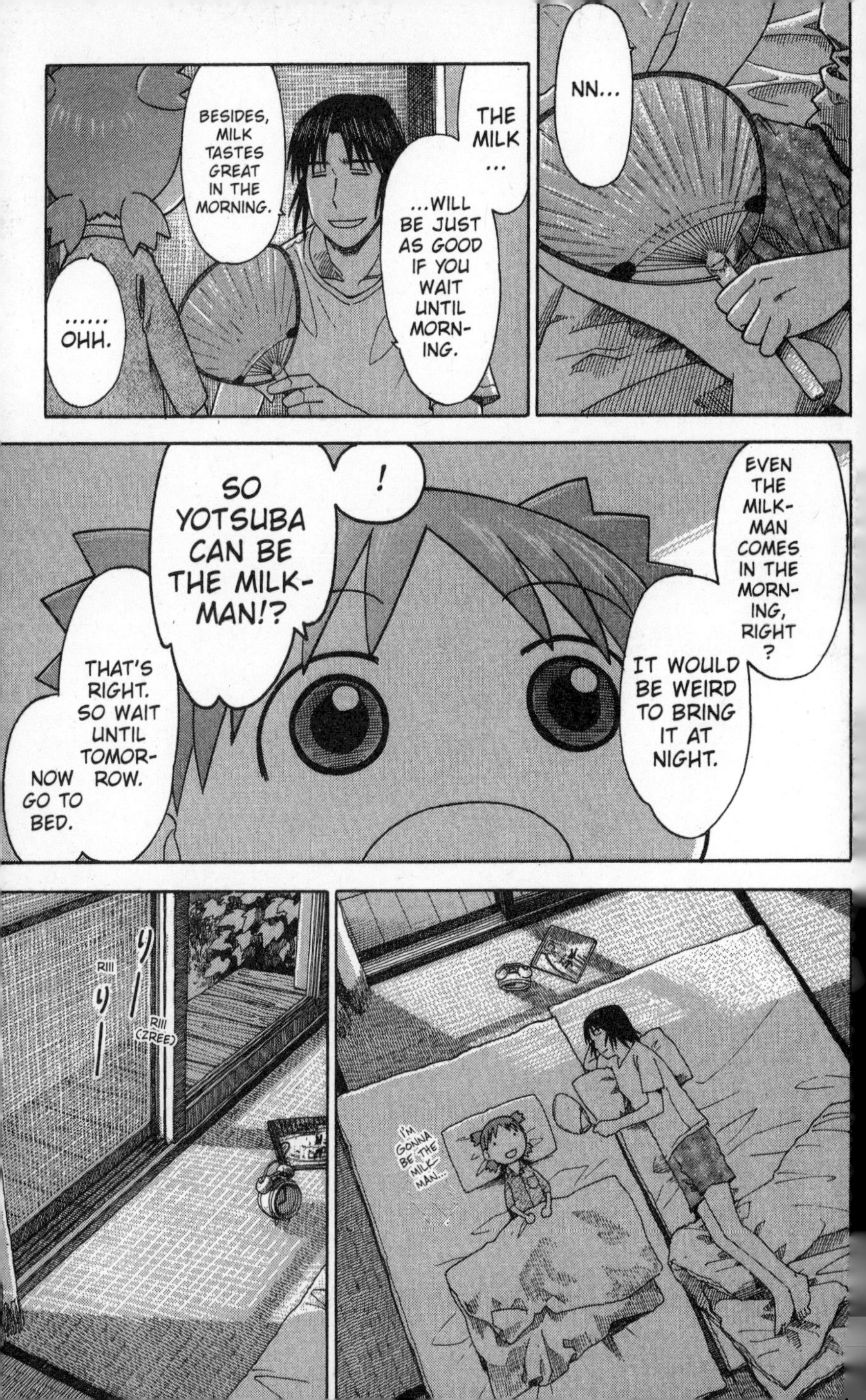
NN...
THE MILK ...
...WILL BE JUST AS GOOD IF YOU WAIT UNTIL MORNING.
BESIDES, MILK TASTES GREAT IN THE MORNING.
...... OHH.
EVEN THE MILKMAN COMES IN THE MORNING, RIGHT?
IT WOULD BE WEIRD TO BRING IT AT NIGHT.
!
SO YOTSUBA CAN BE THE MILKMAN!?
THAT'S RIGHT. SO WAIT UNTIL TOMORROW.
NOW GO TO BED.
I'M GONNA BE THE MILKMAN...
RIII
RIII (ZREE)

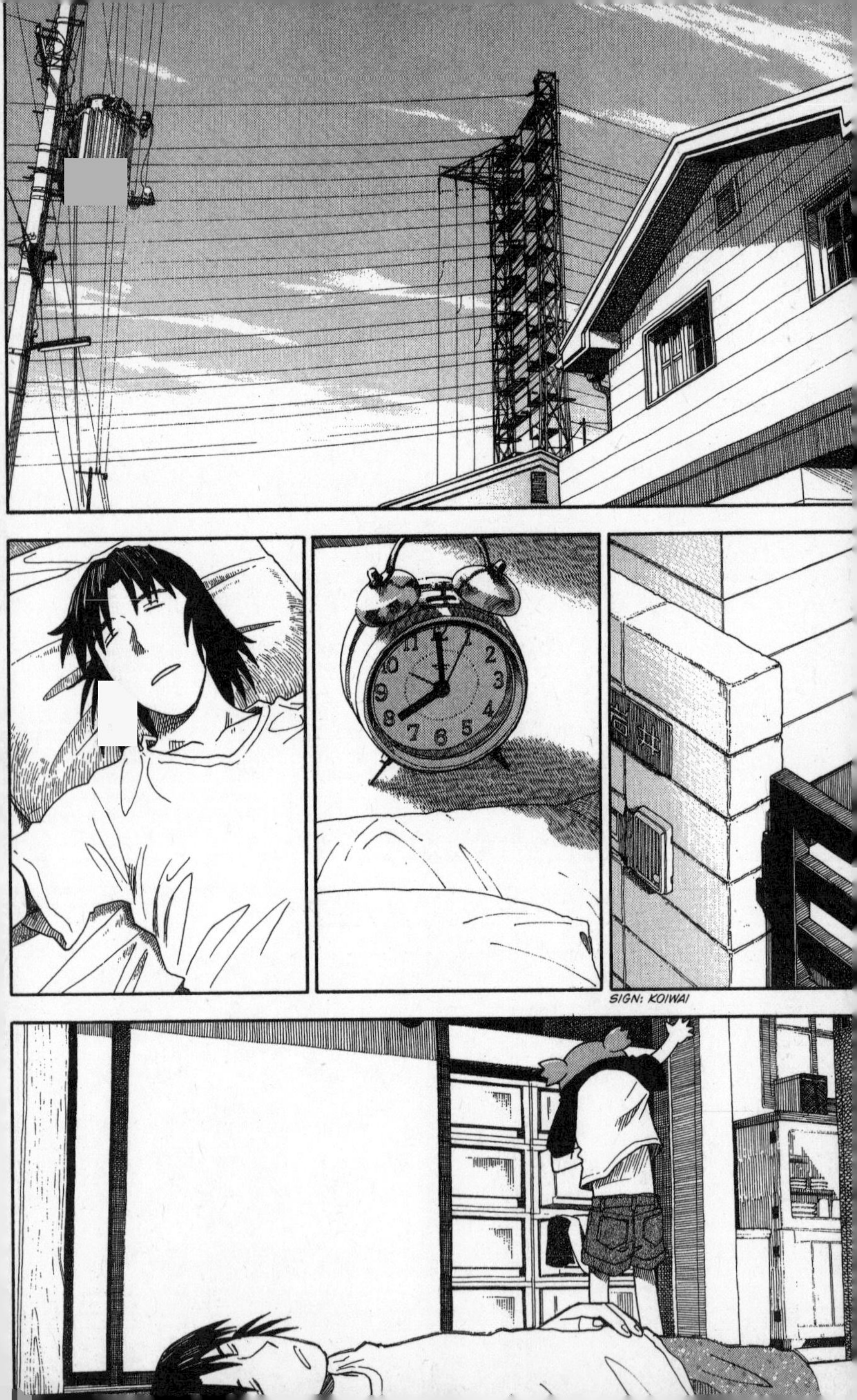
SIGN: KOIWAI

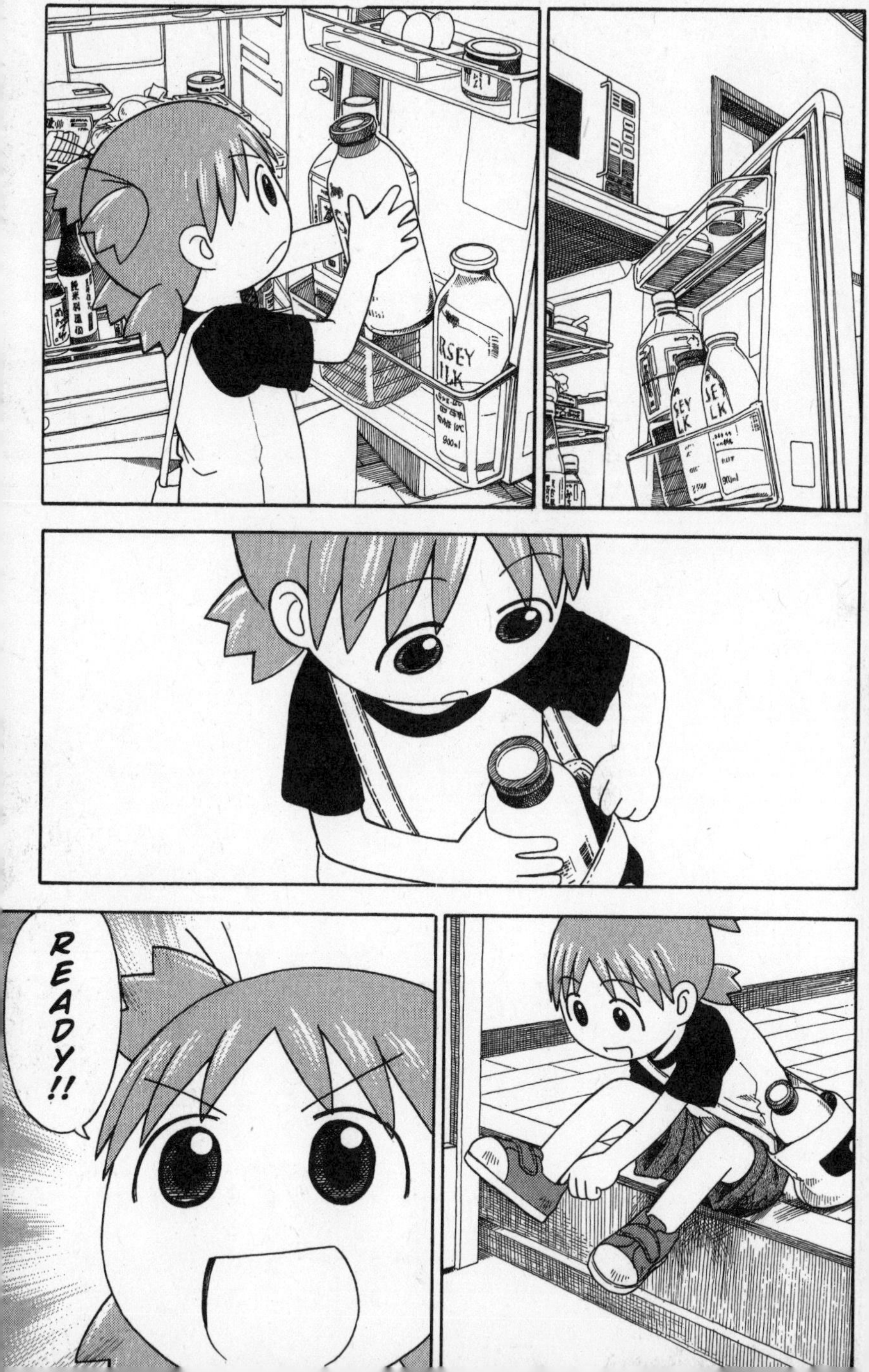
READY!!

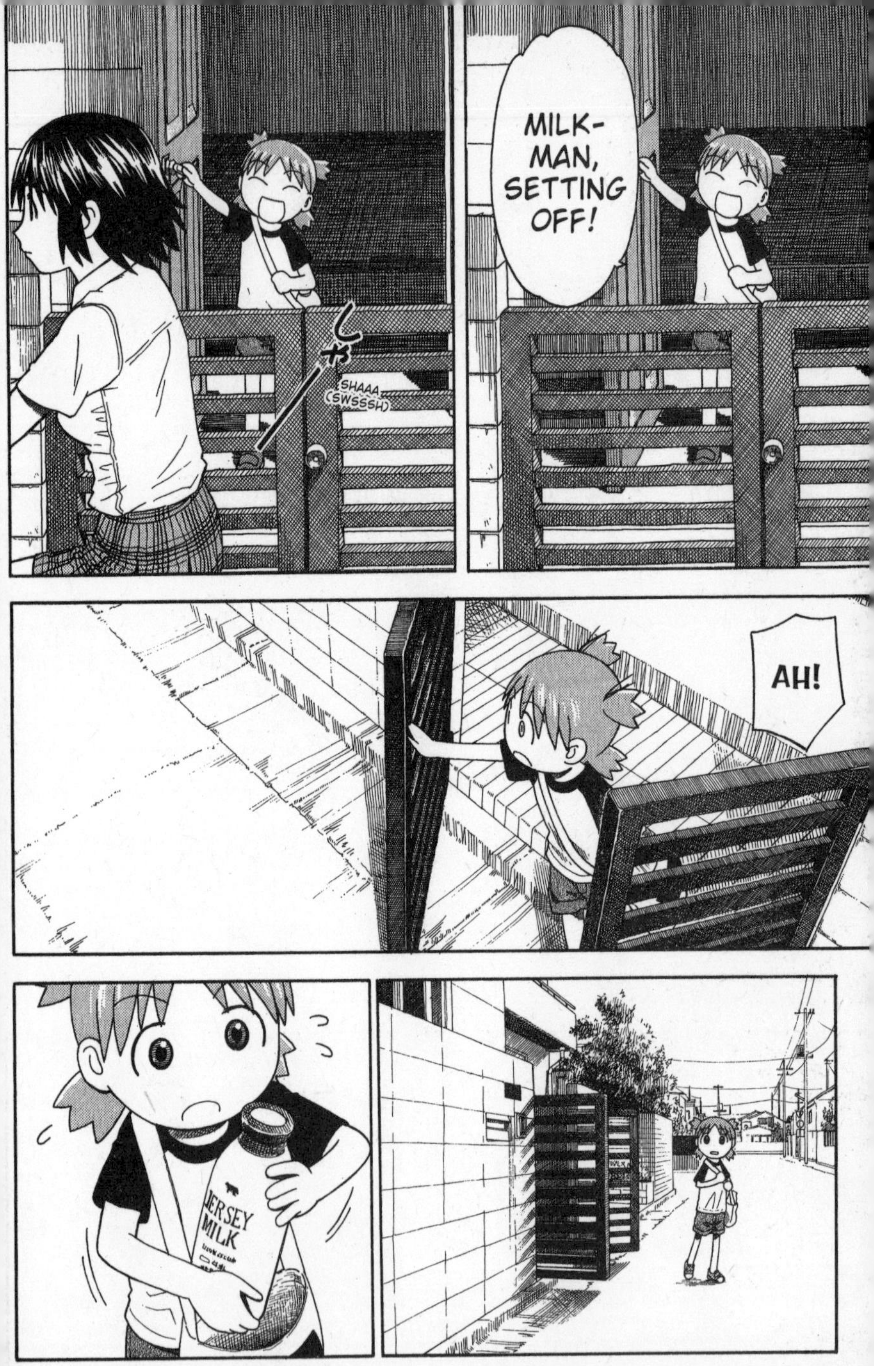
MILK-MAN, SETTING OFF!
SHAAA (SWSSSH)
AH!
JERSEY MILK

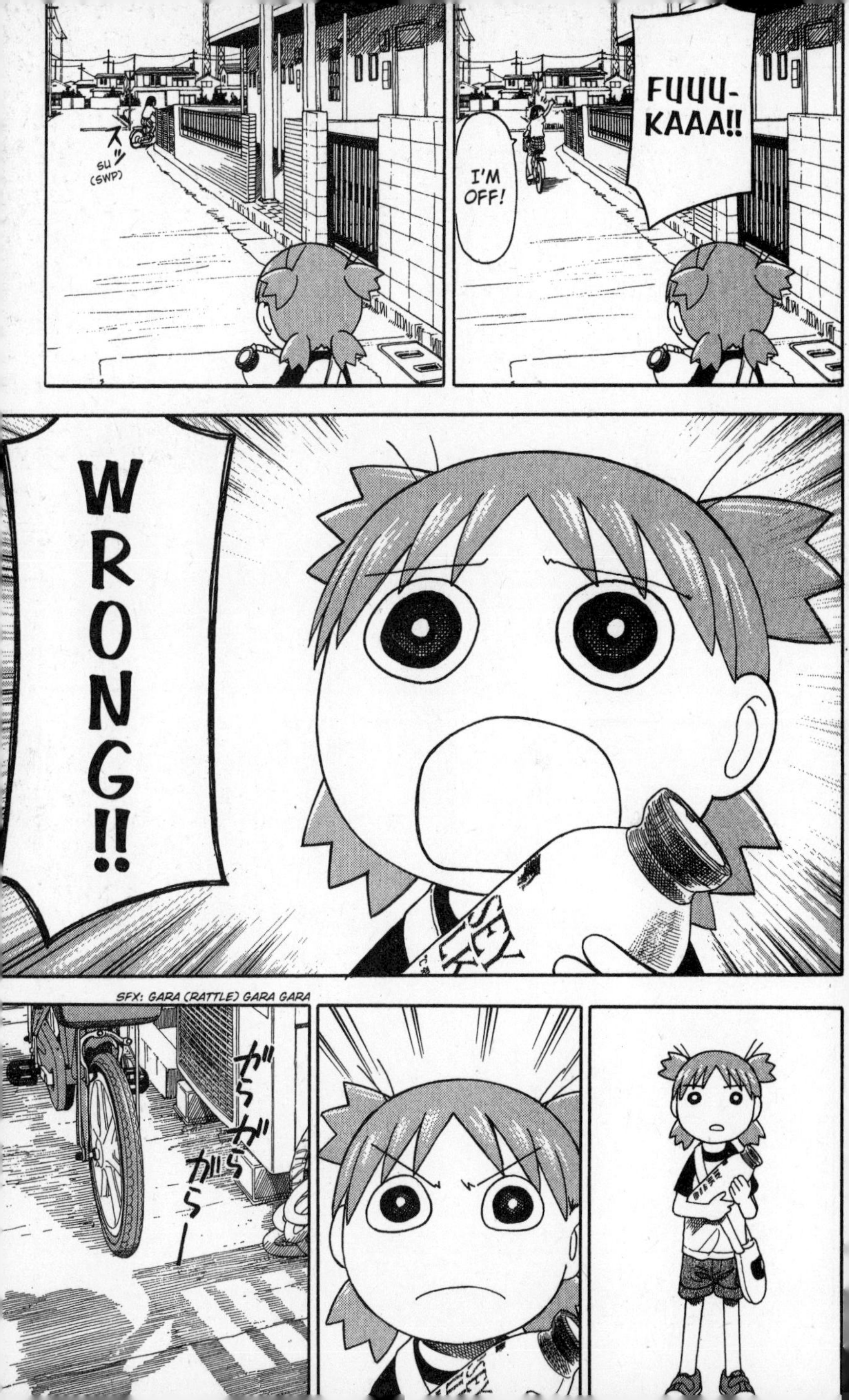
FUUU-KAAA!!
I'M OFF!
スッ
SU (SWP)
WRONG!!
SFX: GARA (RATTLE) GARA GARA
がらがらがらー

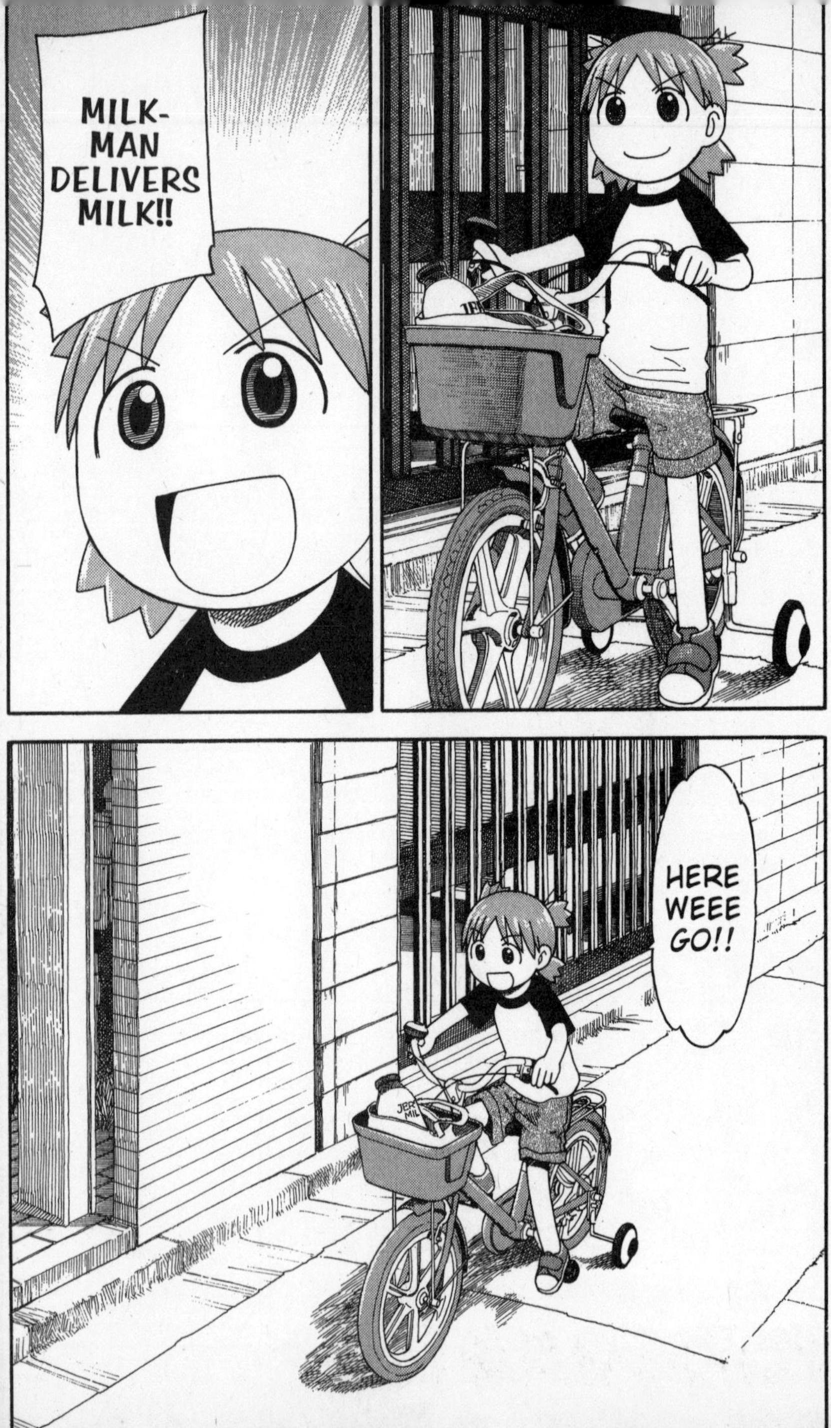
MILK-MAN DELIVERS MILK!!
HERE WEEE GO!!

YOTSUBA&!

!
SNORE

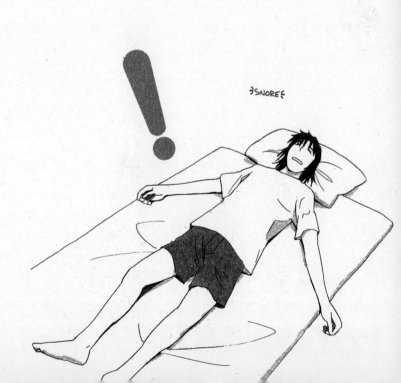

YOTSUBA& DELIVERING #40

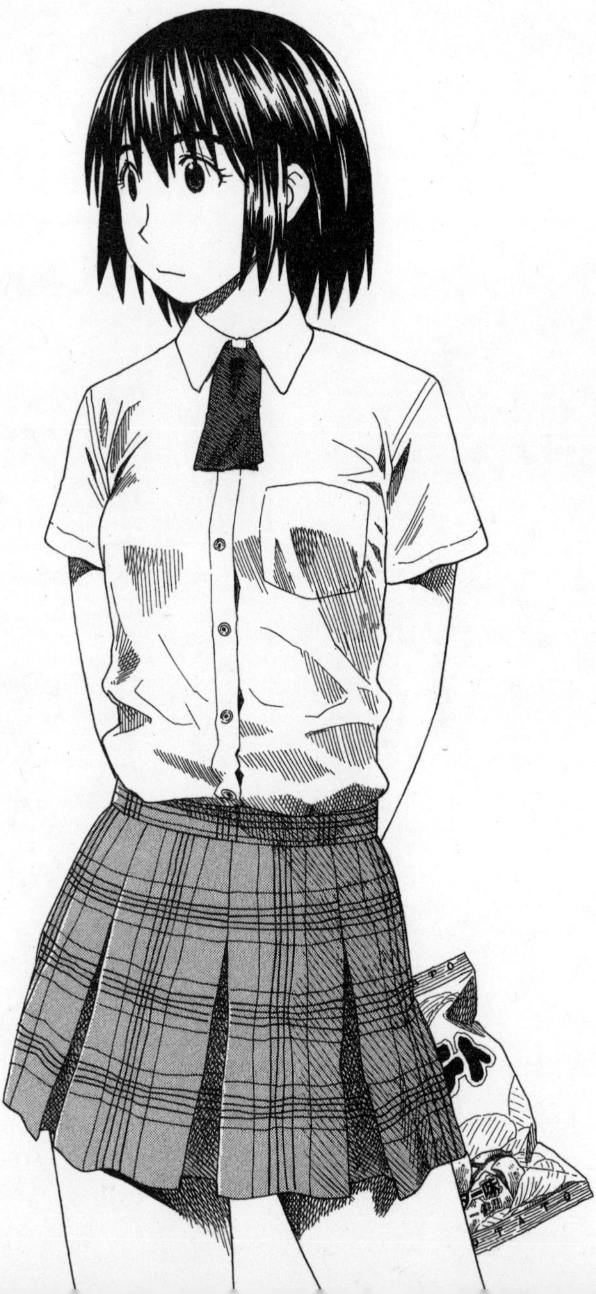

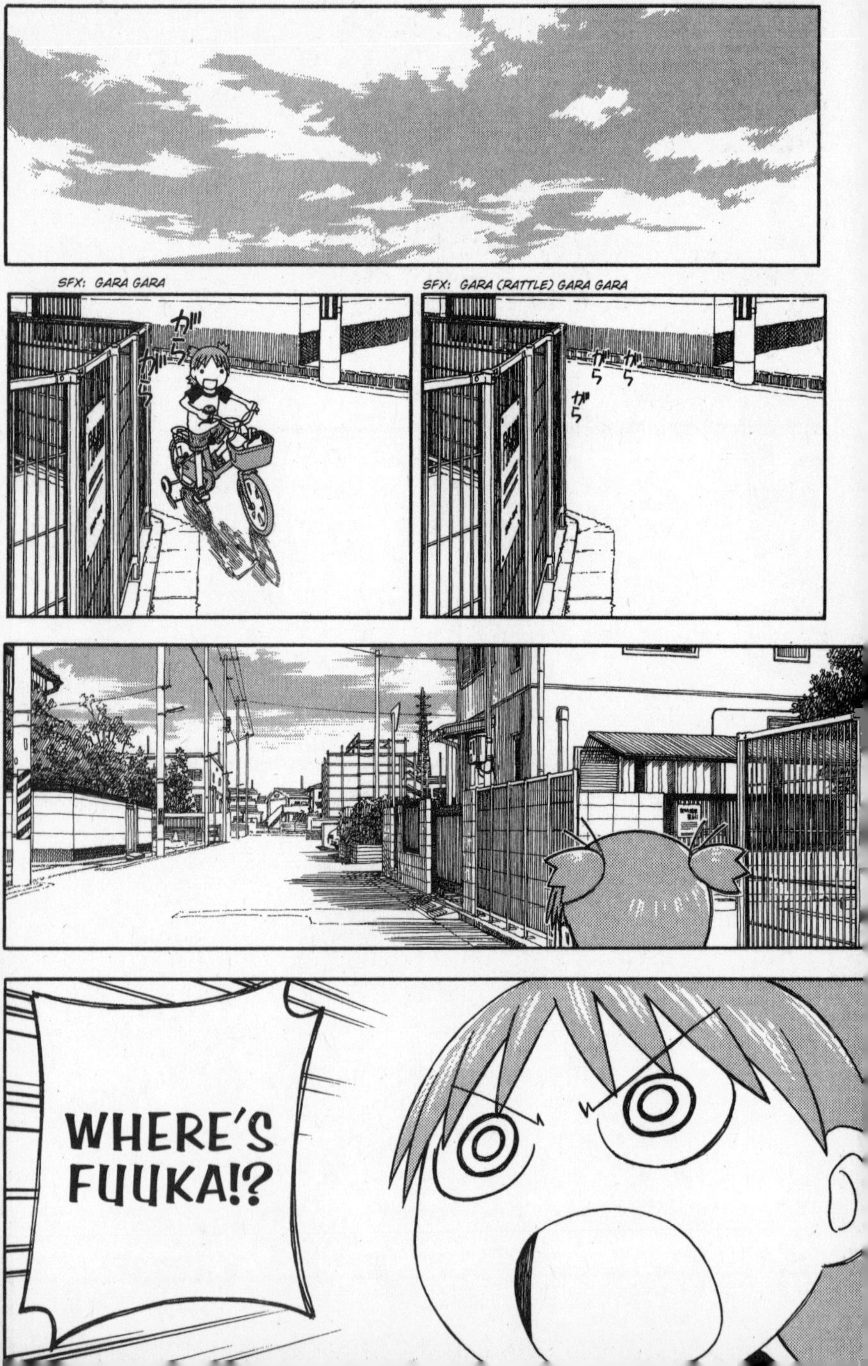

SFX: GARA (RATTLE) GARA GARA
がら がら がら
SFX: GARA GARA
がら がら
WHERE'S FUUKA!?

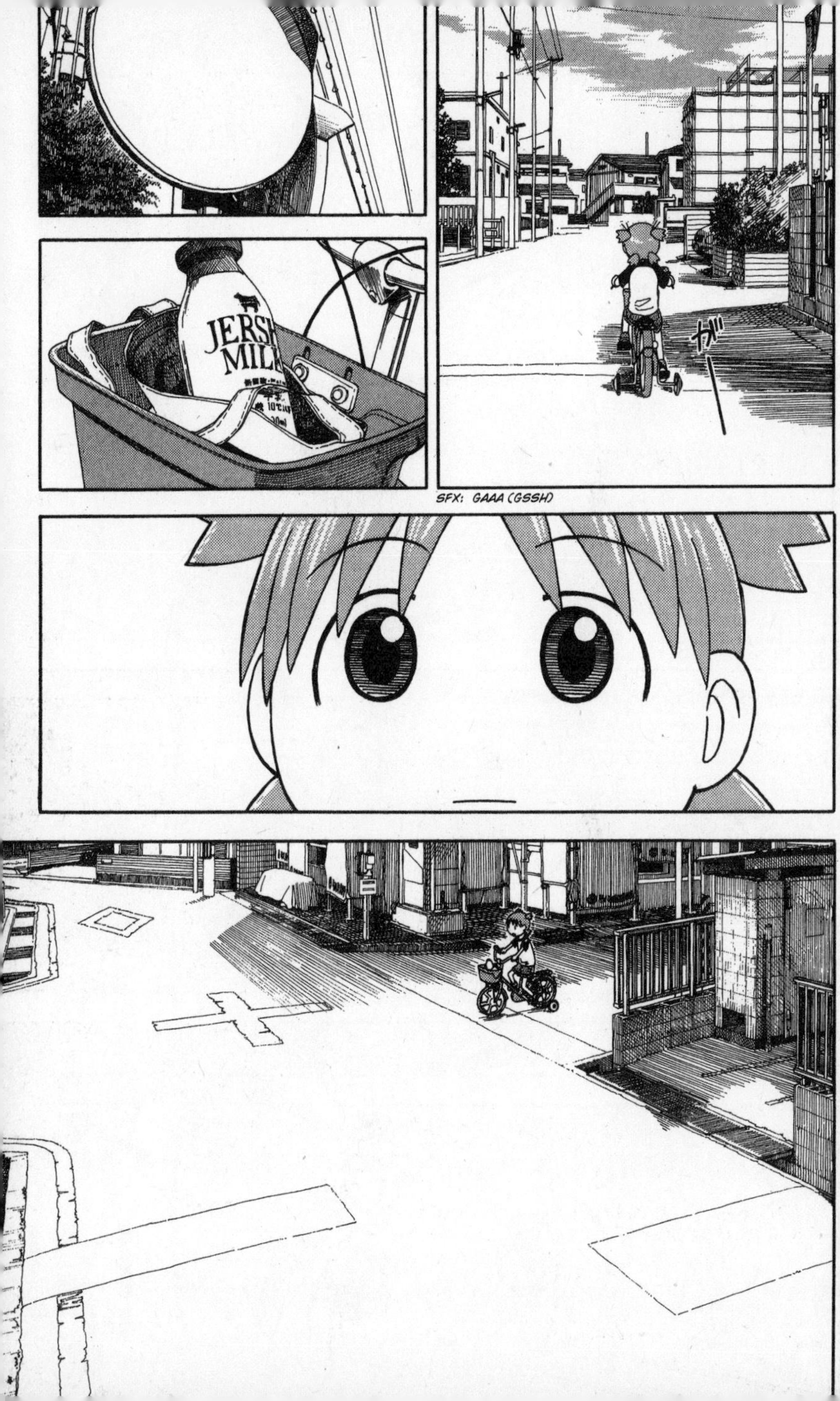
ガ
SFX: GAAA (GSSH)

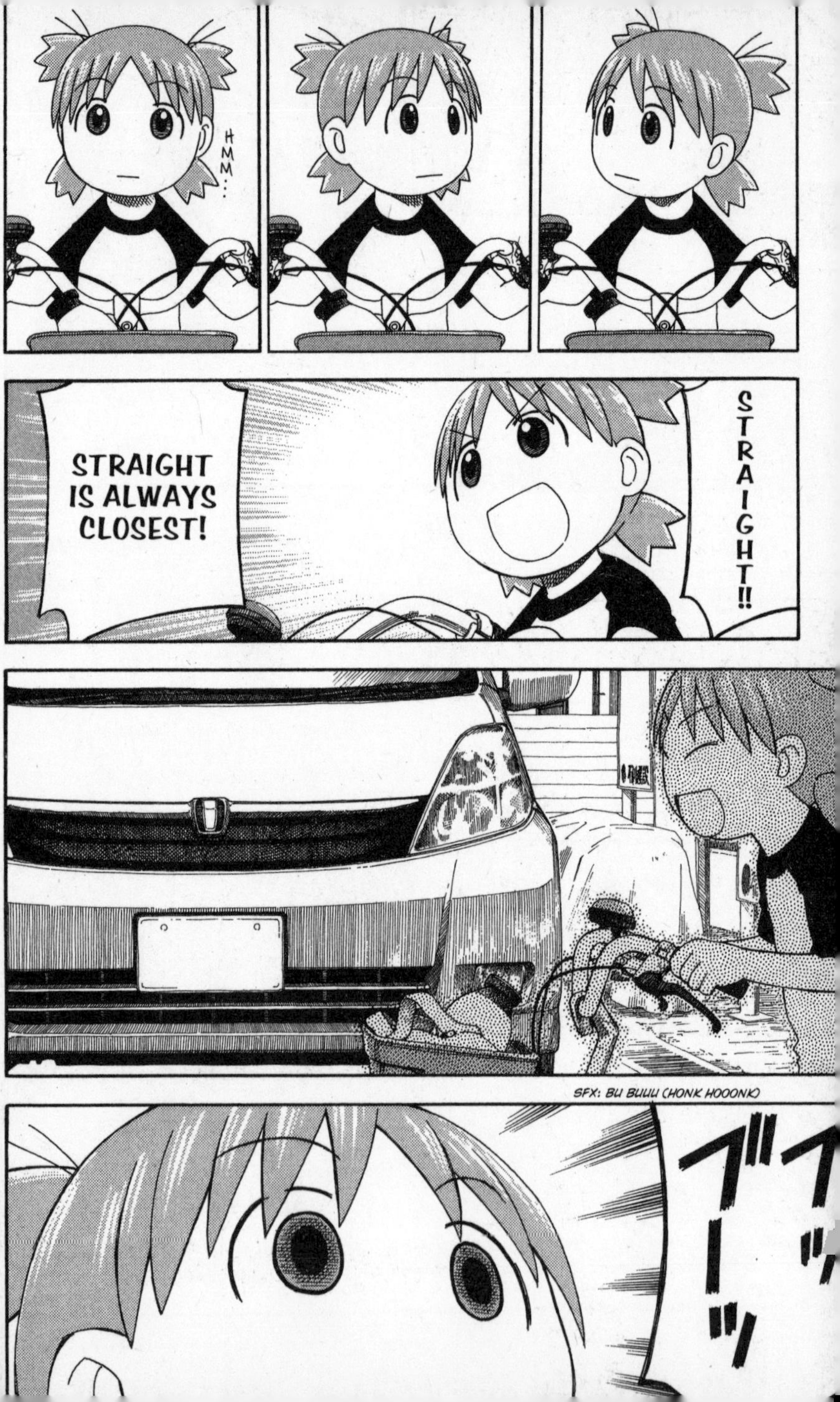
HMM...
STRAIGHT!!
STRAIGHT IS ALWAYS CLOSEST!
SFX: BU BUUU (HONK HOOONK)

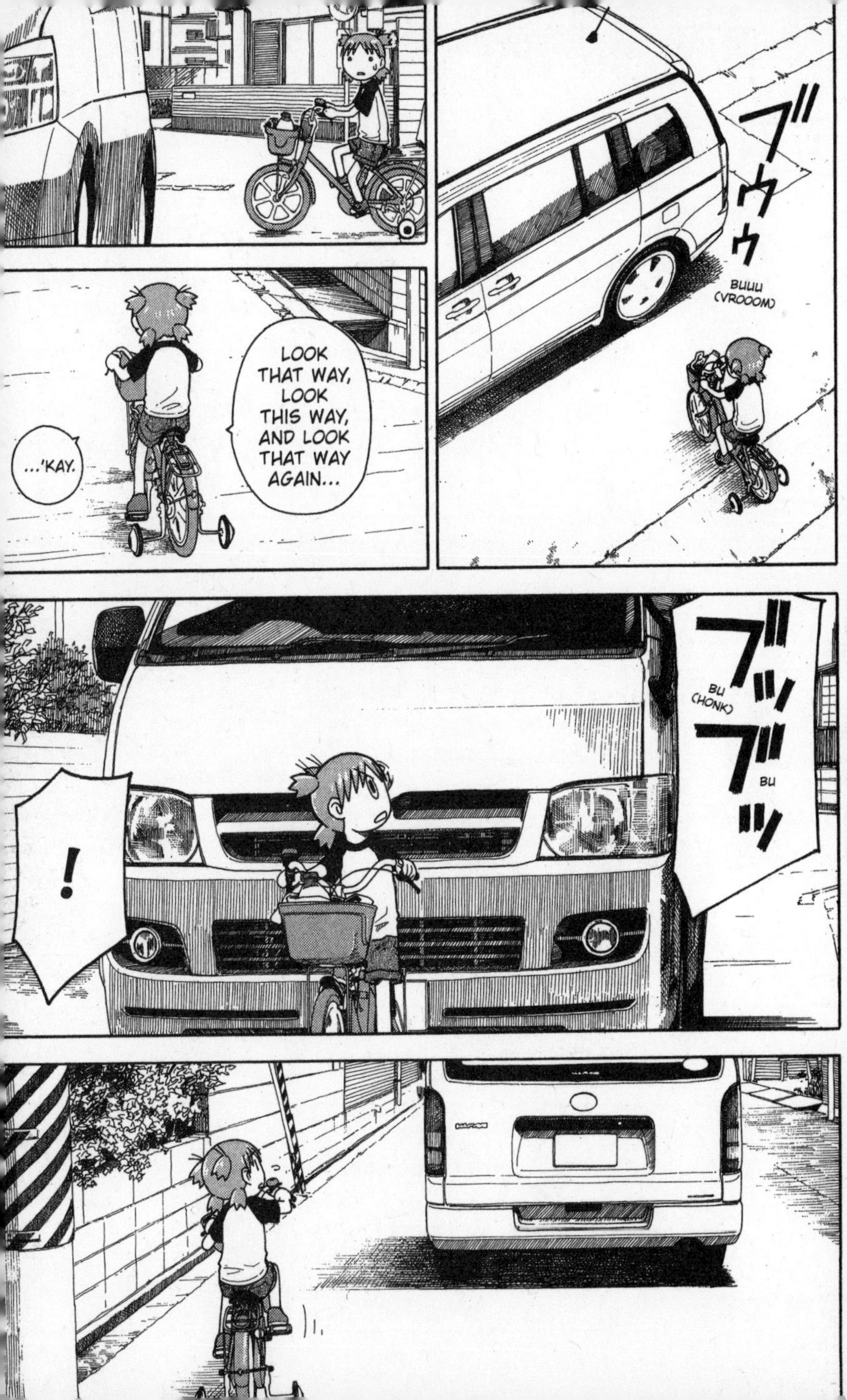
ブウウ
BUUU (VROOOM)
LOOK THAT WAY, LOOK THIS WAY, AND LOOK THAT WAY AGAIN...
...'KAY.
ブッブッ
BU (HONK)
BU
!

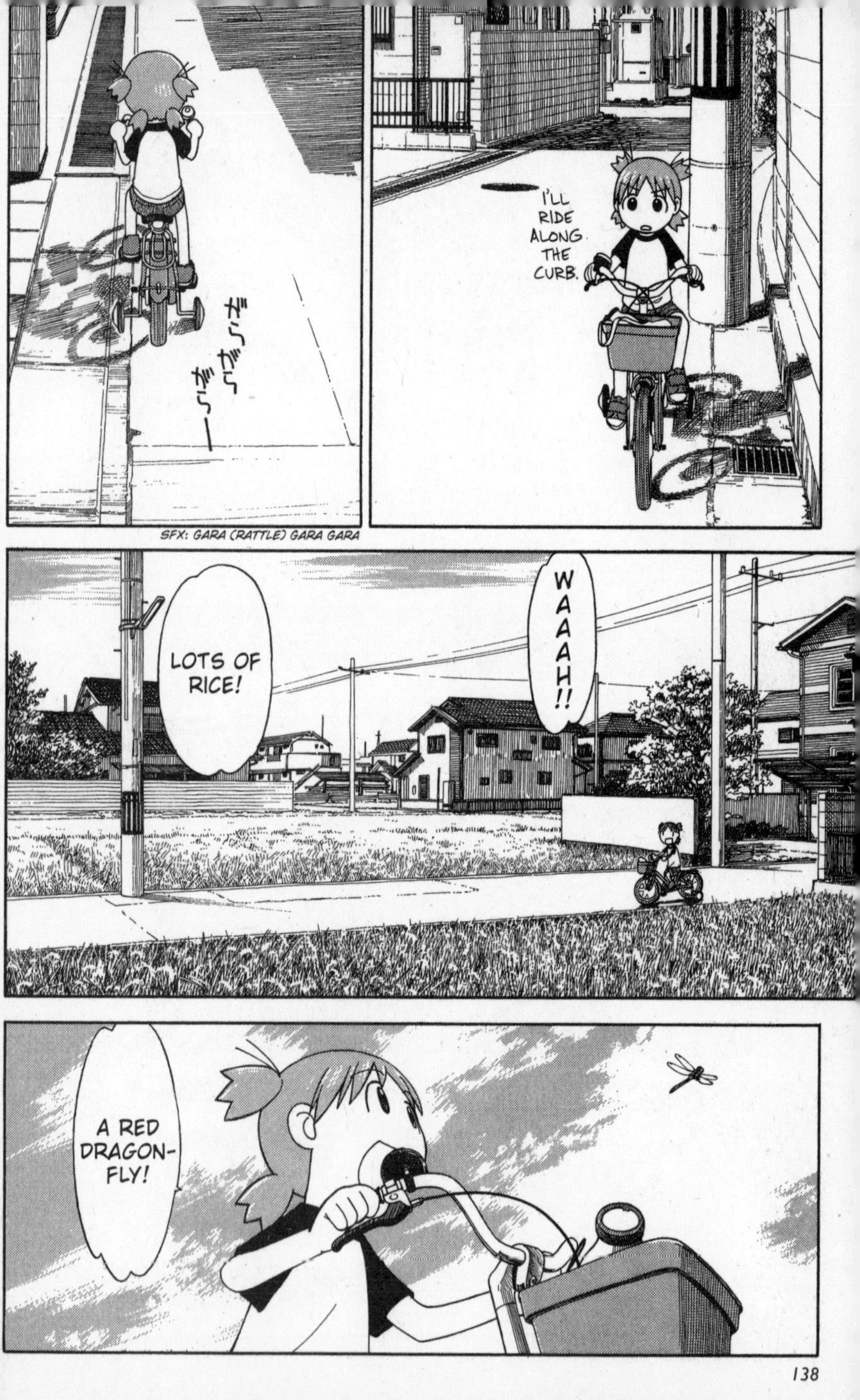
I'LL RIDE ALONG THE CURB.
がらがらがらー
SFX: GARA (RATTLE) GARA GARA
WAAAAH!!
LOTS OF RICE!
A RED DRAGON-FLY!

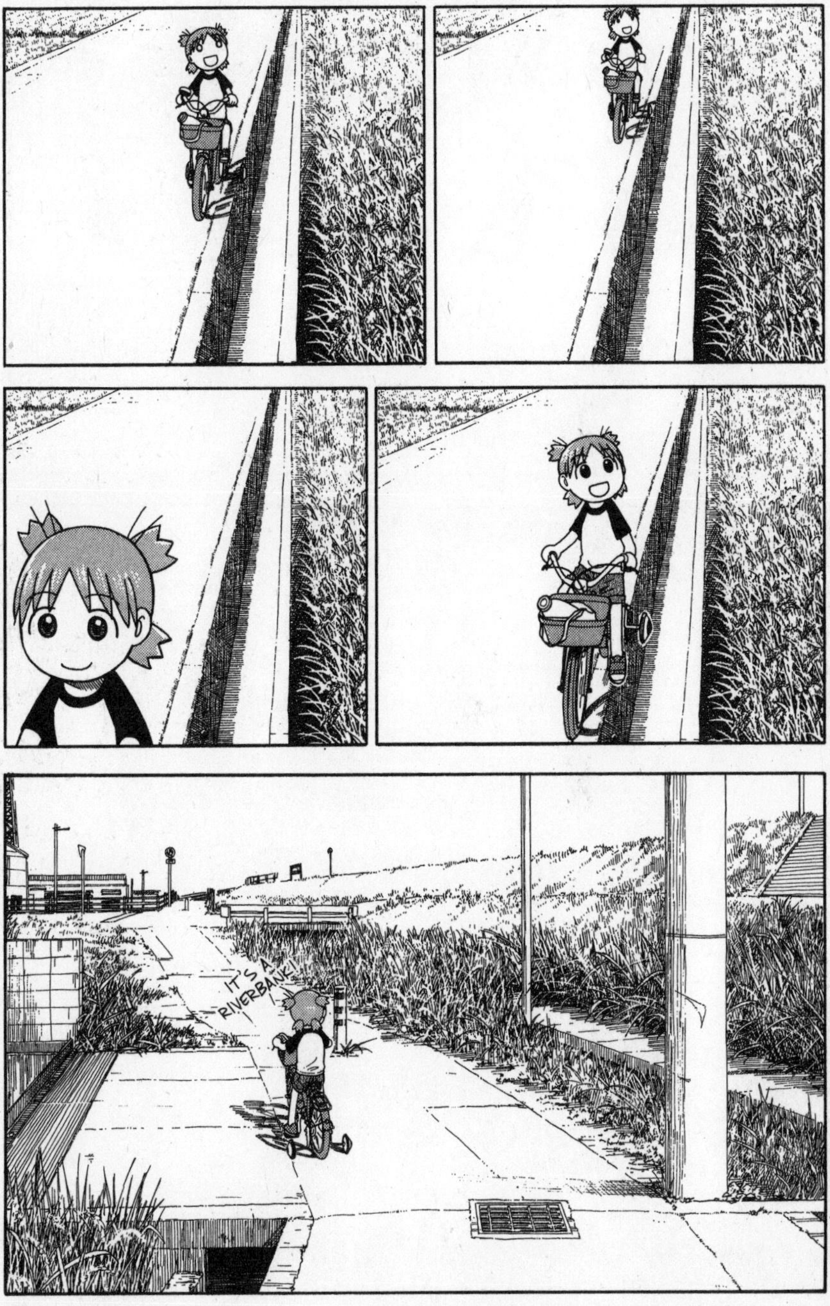
IT'S A RIVERBANK!

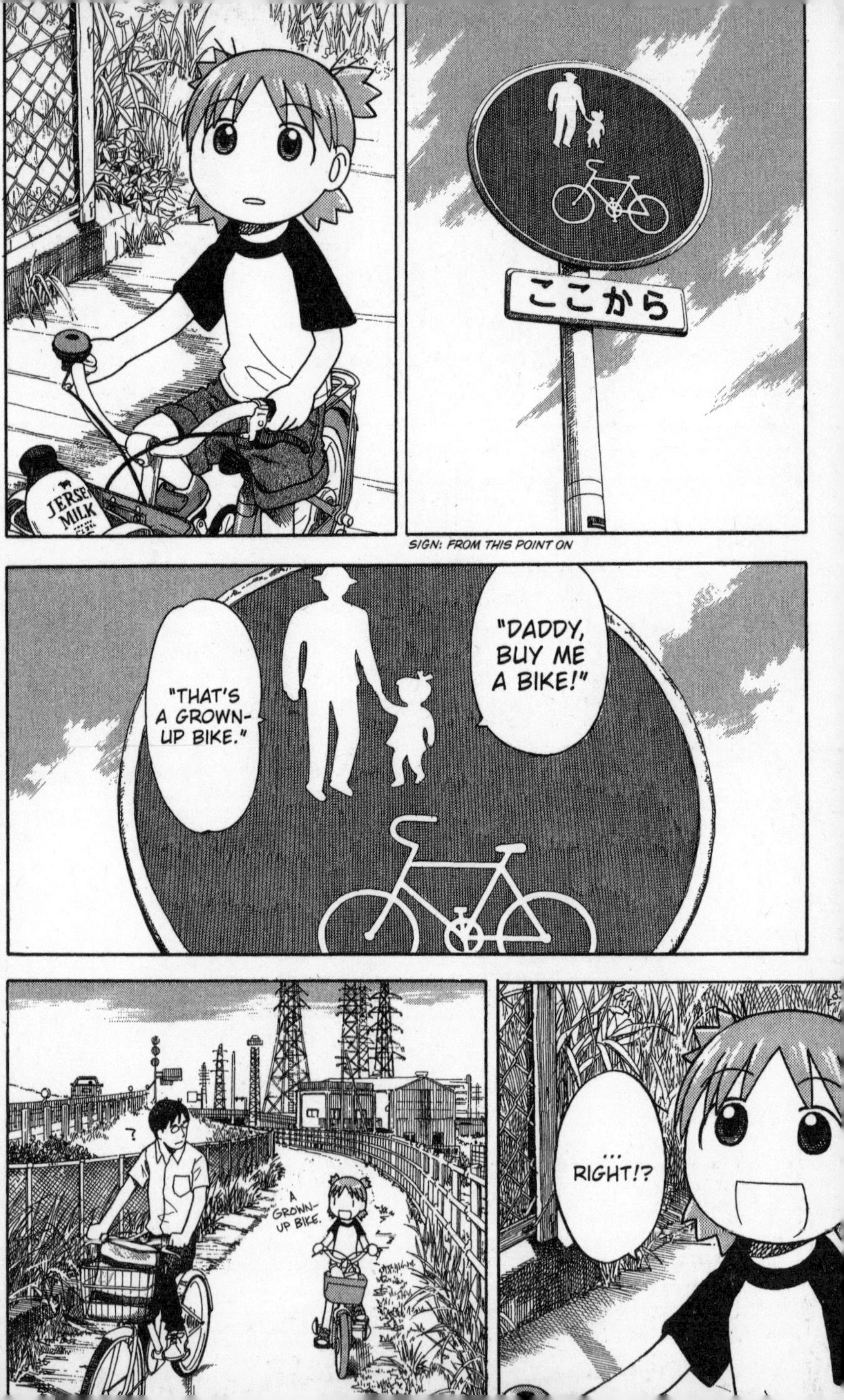
ここから
JERSE MILK
SIGN: FROM THIS POINT ON
"DADDY, BUY ME A BIKE!"
"THAT'S A GROWN-UP BIKE."
... RIGHT!?
?
A GROWN-UP BIKE.

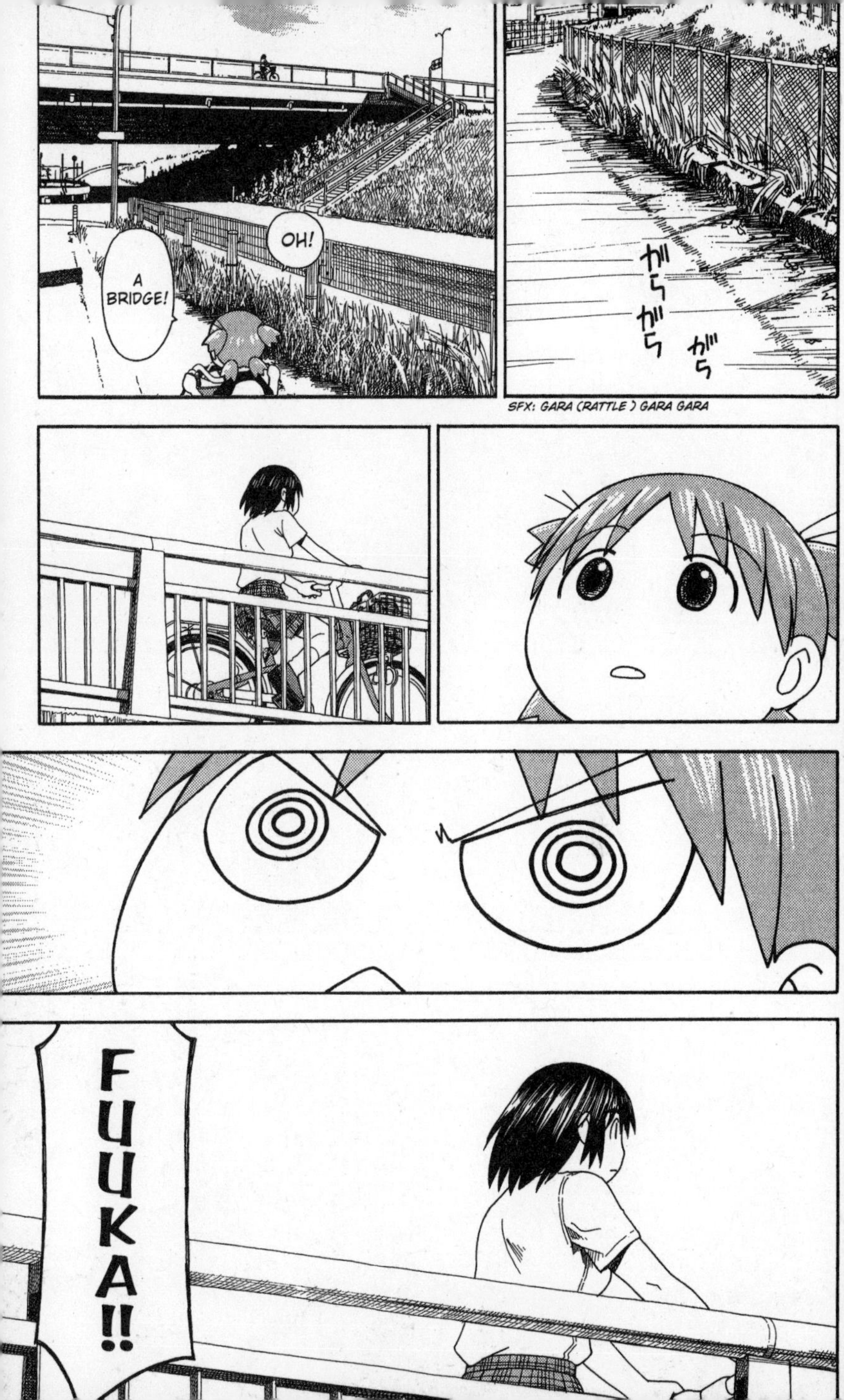
がらがら
がら
SFX: GARA (RATTLE) GARA GARA
OH!
A BRIDGE!
FUUKA!!

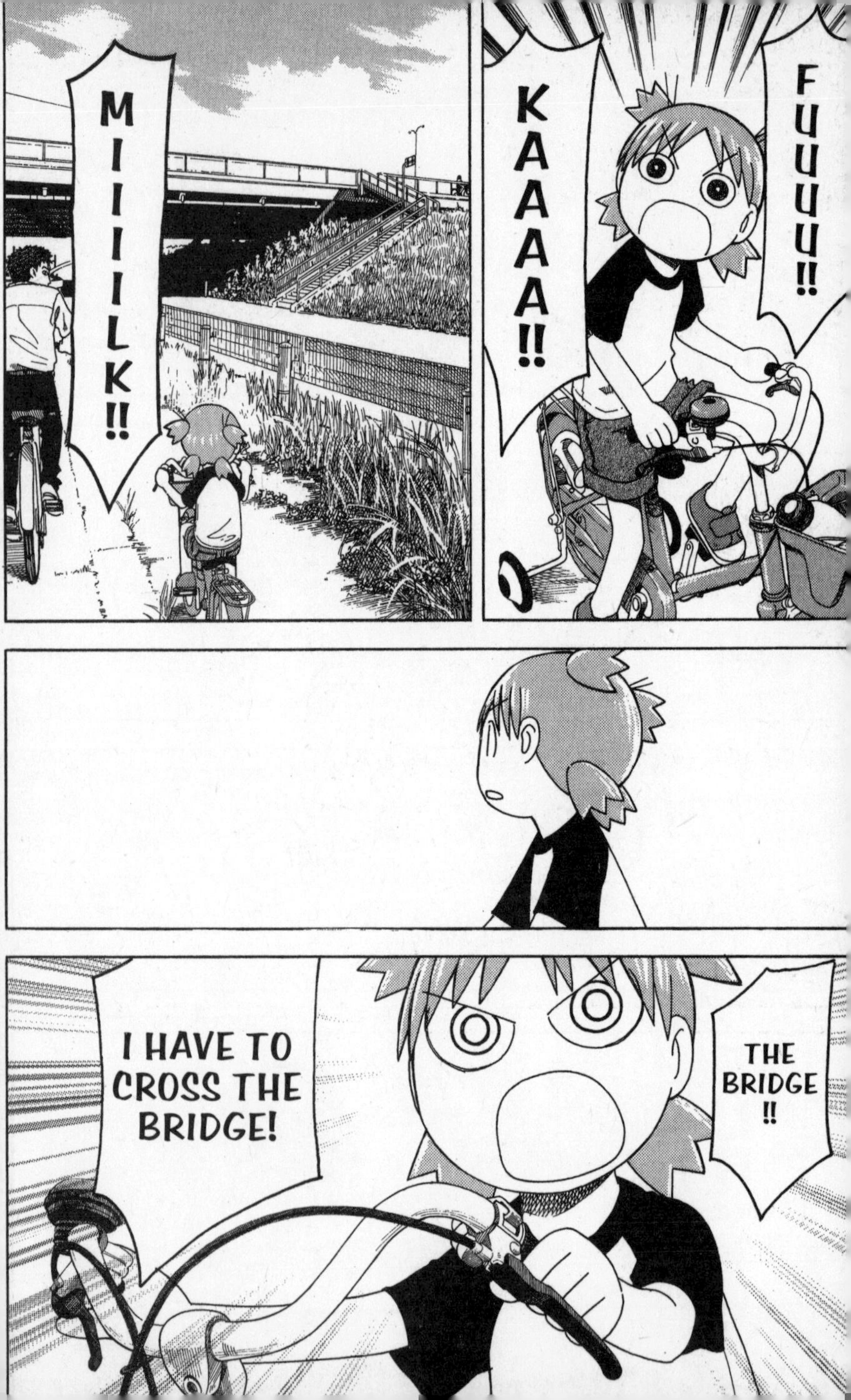
FUUUUU!!
KAAAA!!
MIIIILK!!
THE BRIDGE!!
I HAVE TO CROSS THE BRIDGE!

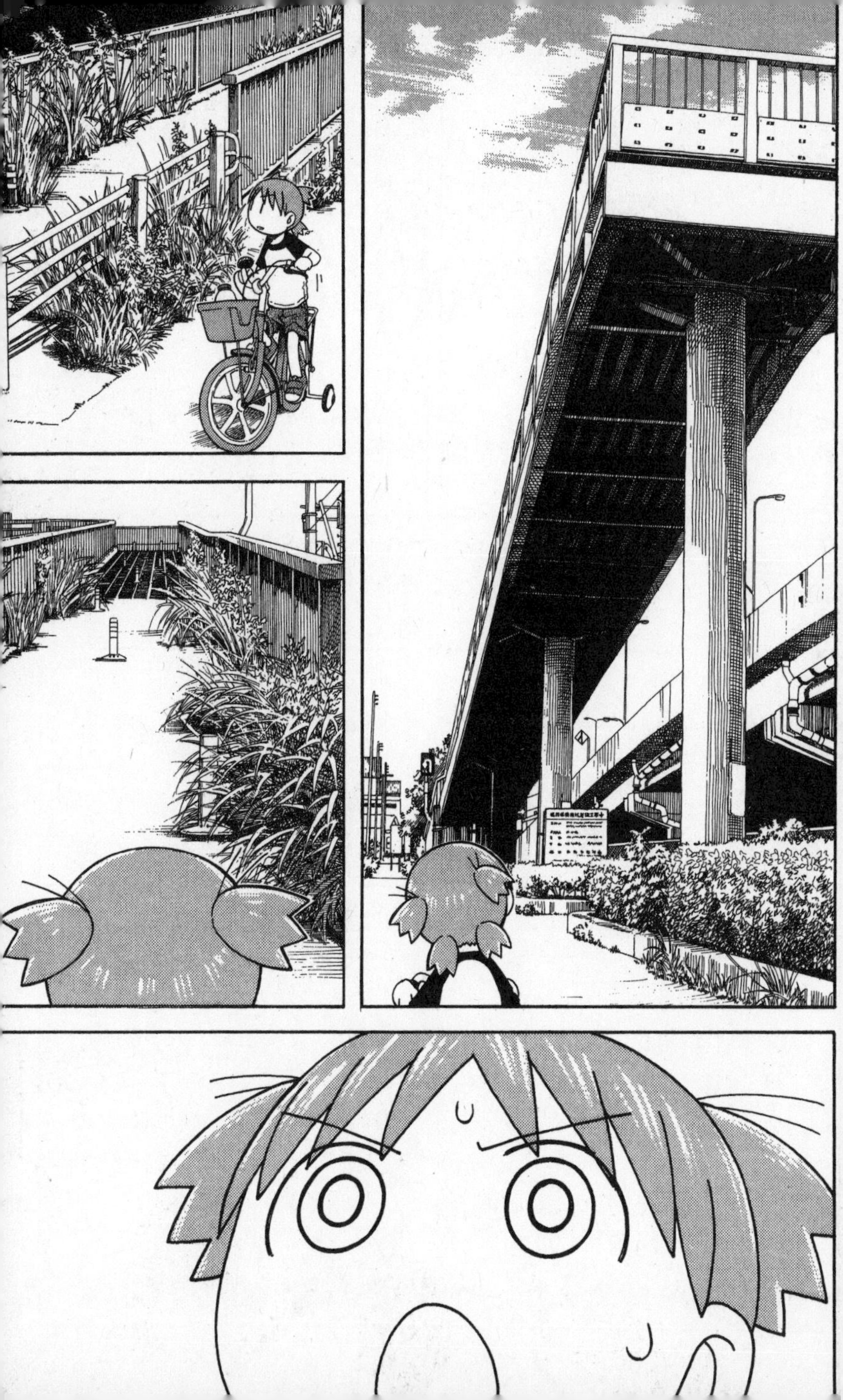

ONE!
TWO!
ONE!
UUUUGH
SOOO TIRED...

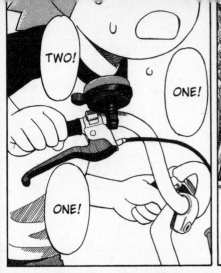

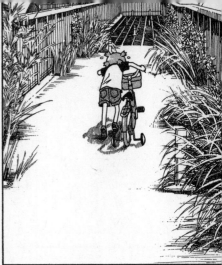

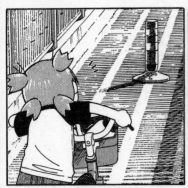

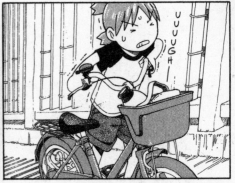

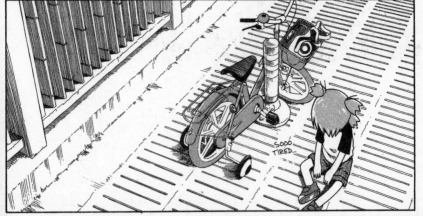

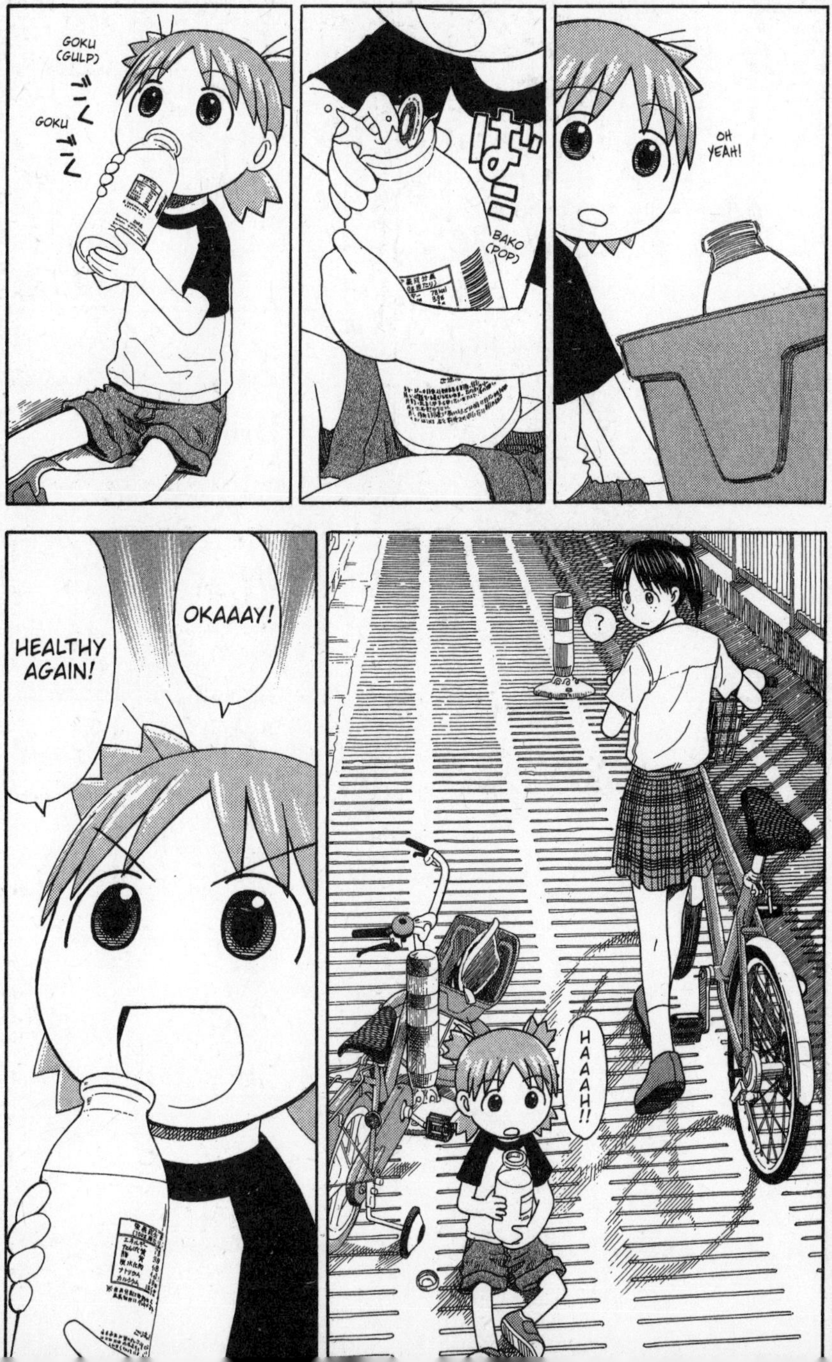
OH YEAH!
ぱこ
BAKO (POP)
GOKU (GULP)
GOKU
?
HAAAH!!
OKAAAY!
HEALTHY AGAIN!

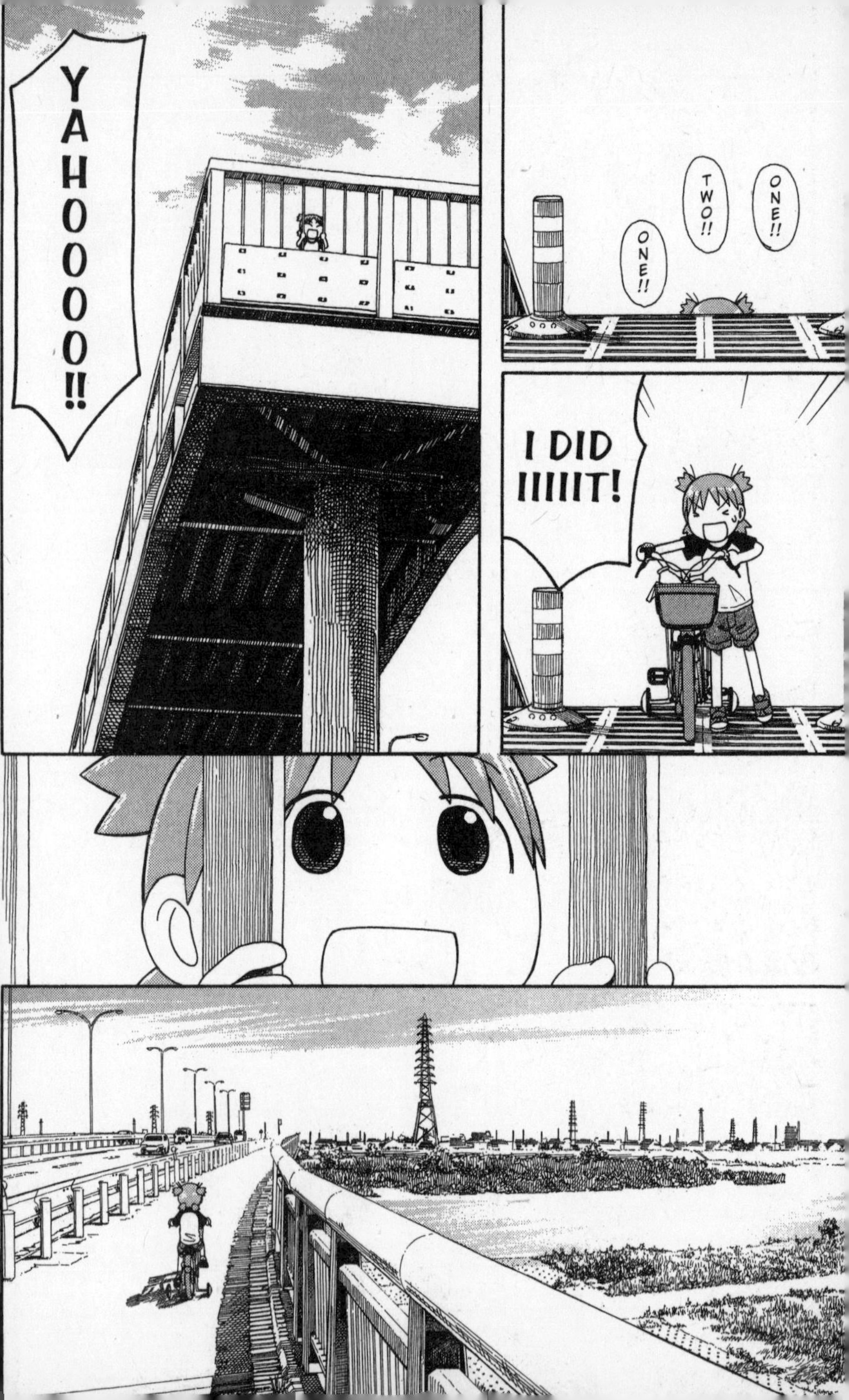
ONE!!
TWO!!
ONE!!
I DID IIIIIT!
YAHOOOOO!!

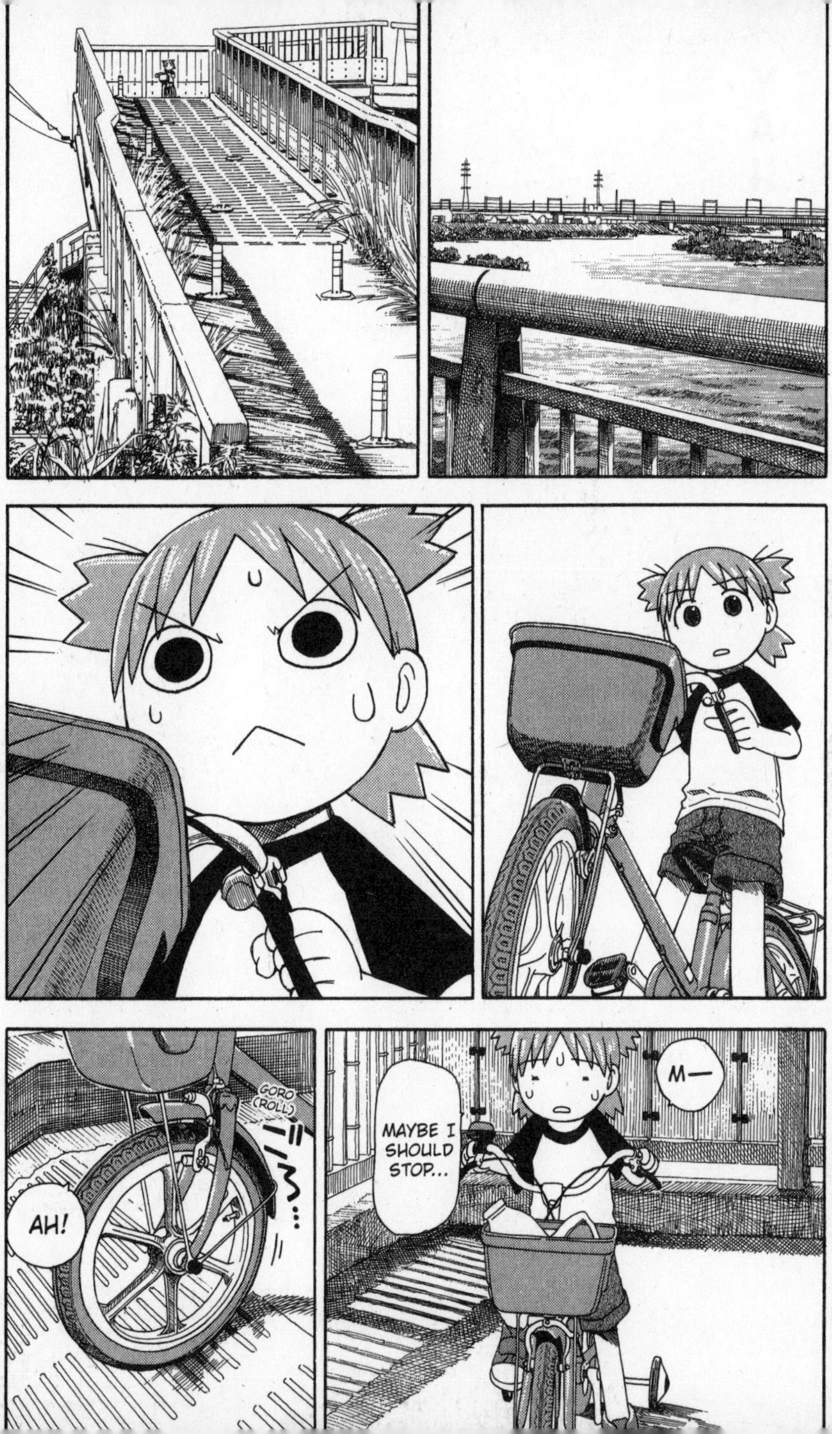
M—
MAYBE I SHOULD STOP...
GORO (ROLL)
AH!

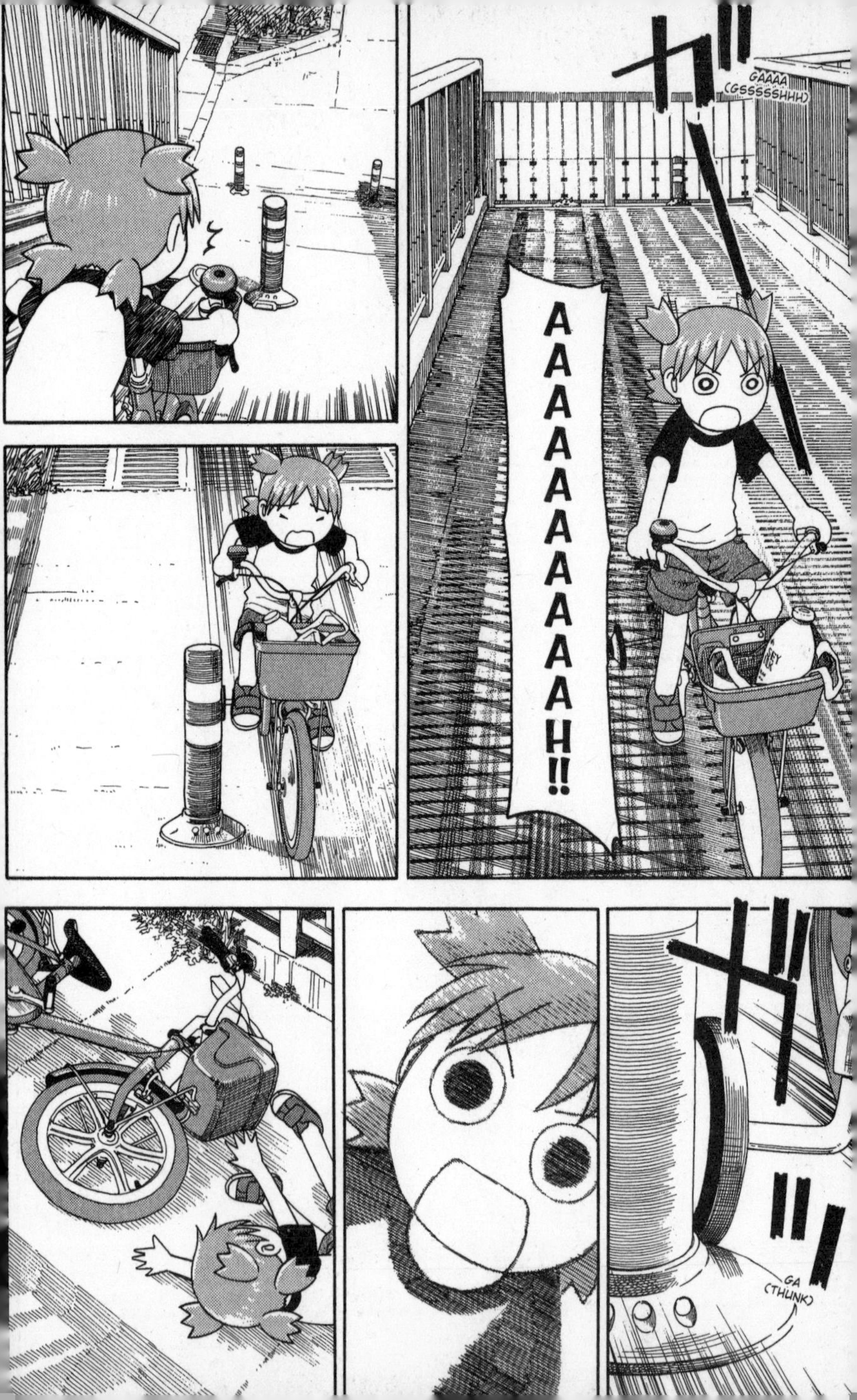
GAAAA
(GSSSSSHHH)
AAAAAAAAAAH!!
GA
(THUNK)

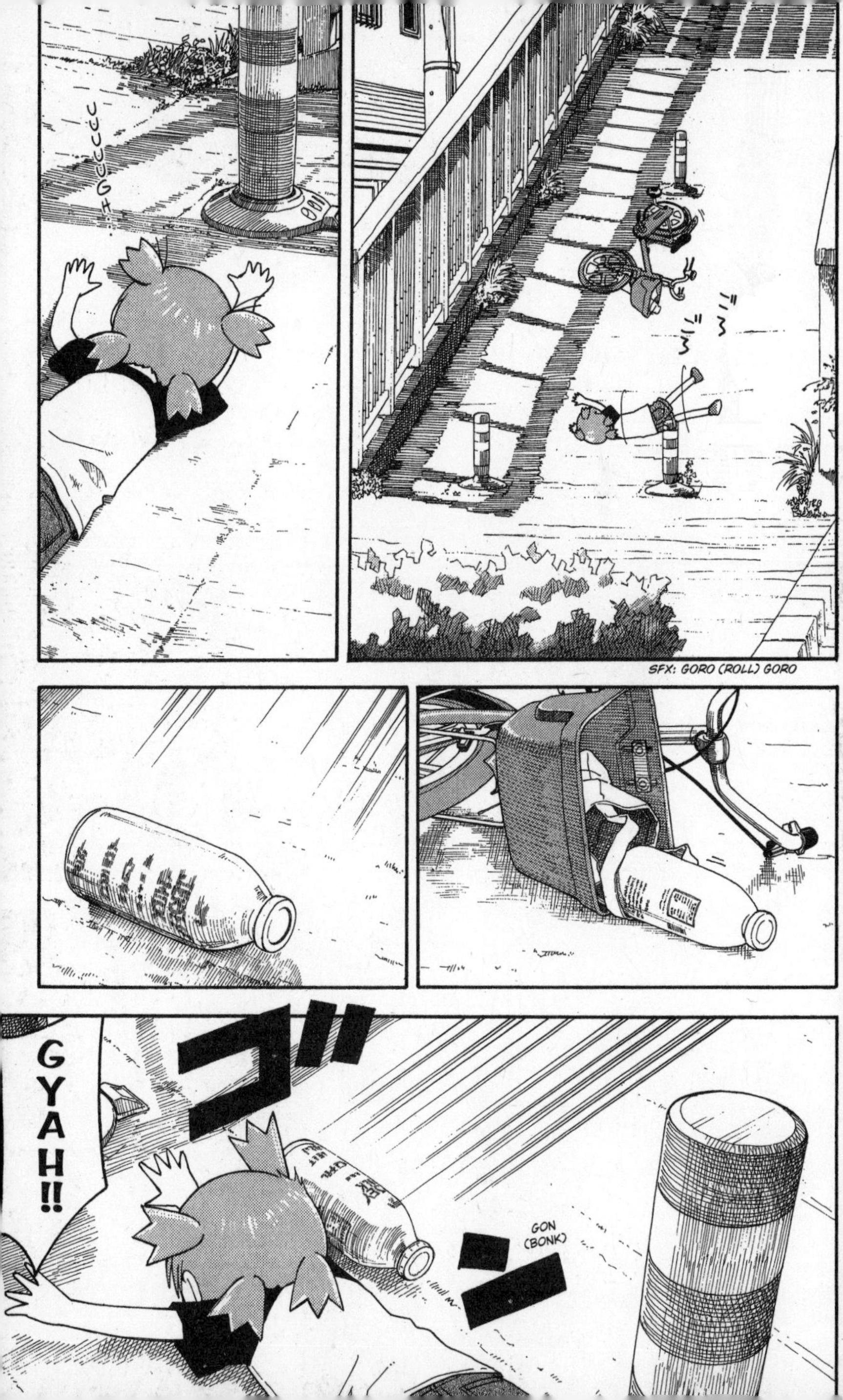
UUUUUGH...
SFX: GORO (ROLL) GORO
GYAH!!
ゴン
GON (BONK)

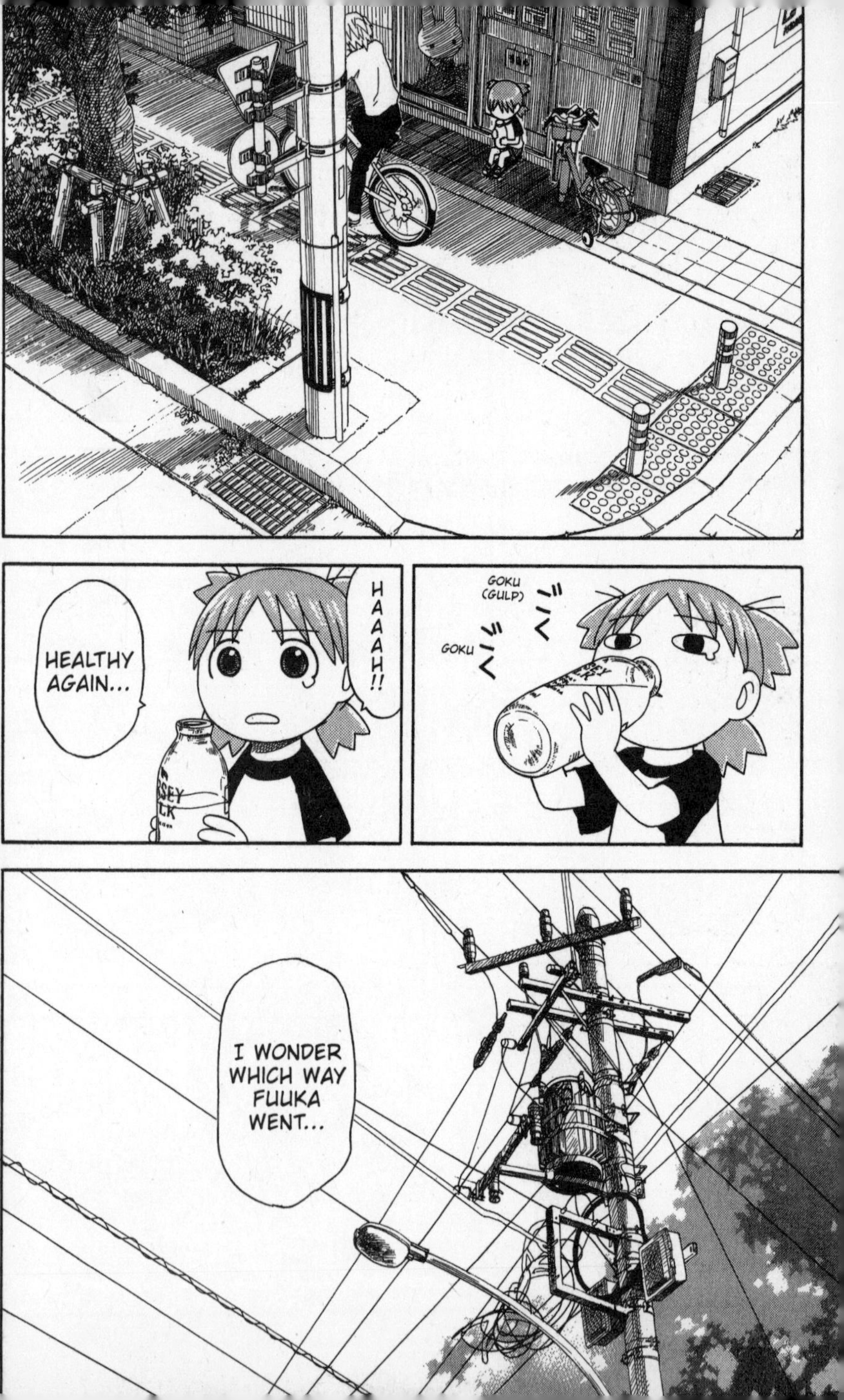
GOKU (GULP)
GOKU
HAAAAH!!
HEALTHY AGAIN...
I WONDER WHICH WAY FUUKA WENT...

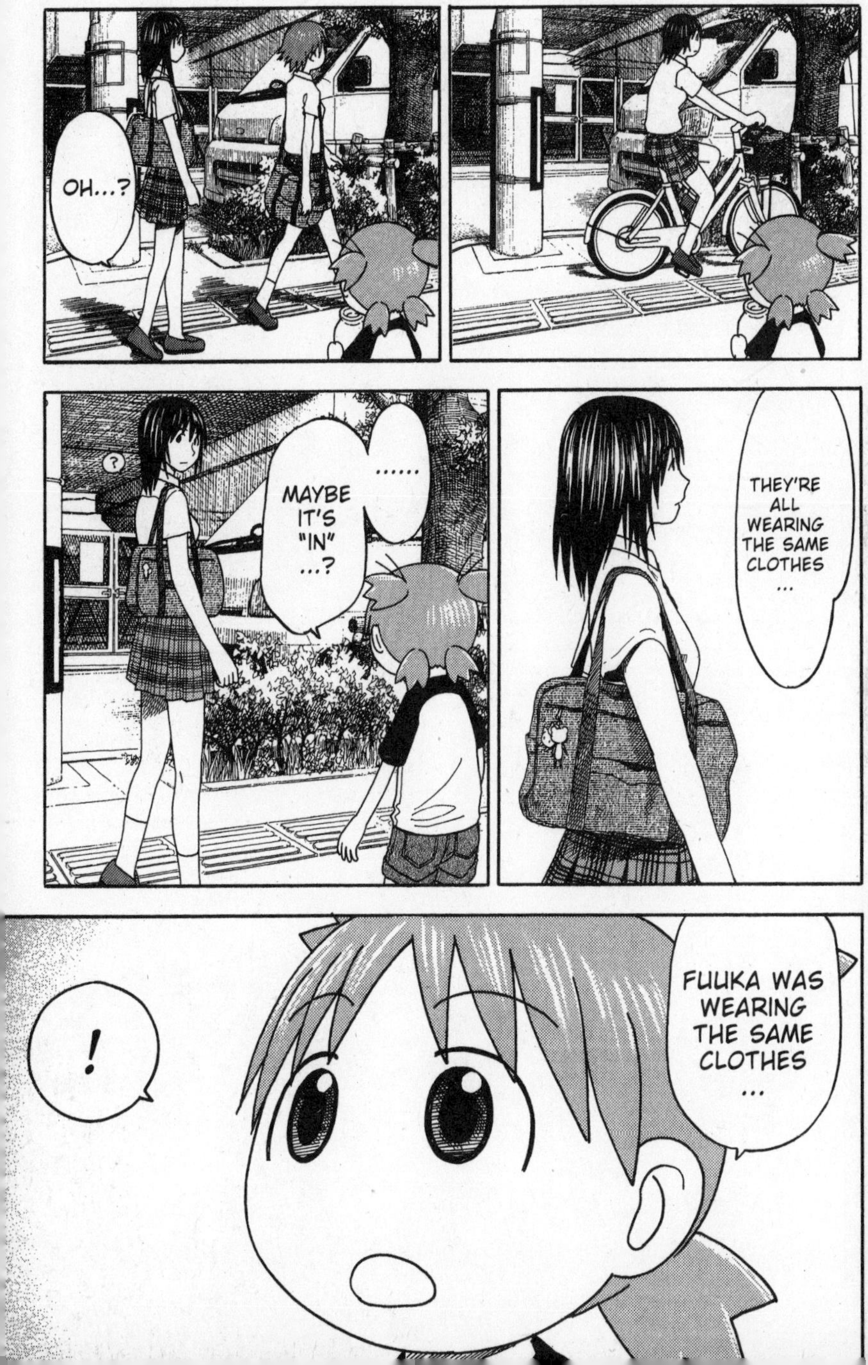
OH...?
THEY'RE ALL WEARING THE SAME CLOTHES ...
......
MAYBE IT'S "IN" ...?
FUUKA WAS WEARING THE SAME CLOTHES ...
!

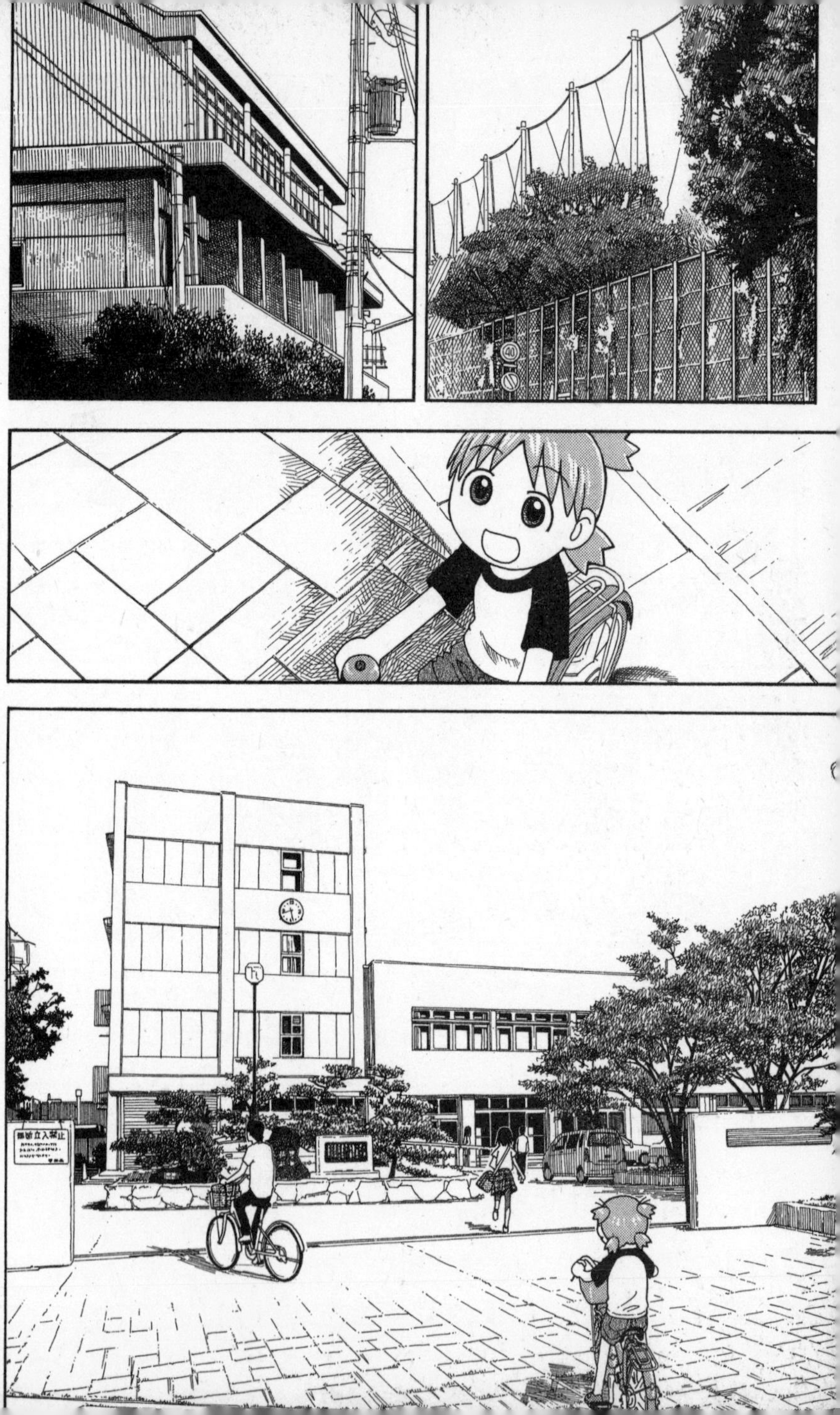
40

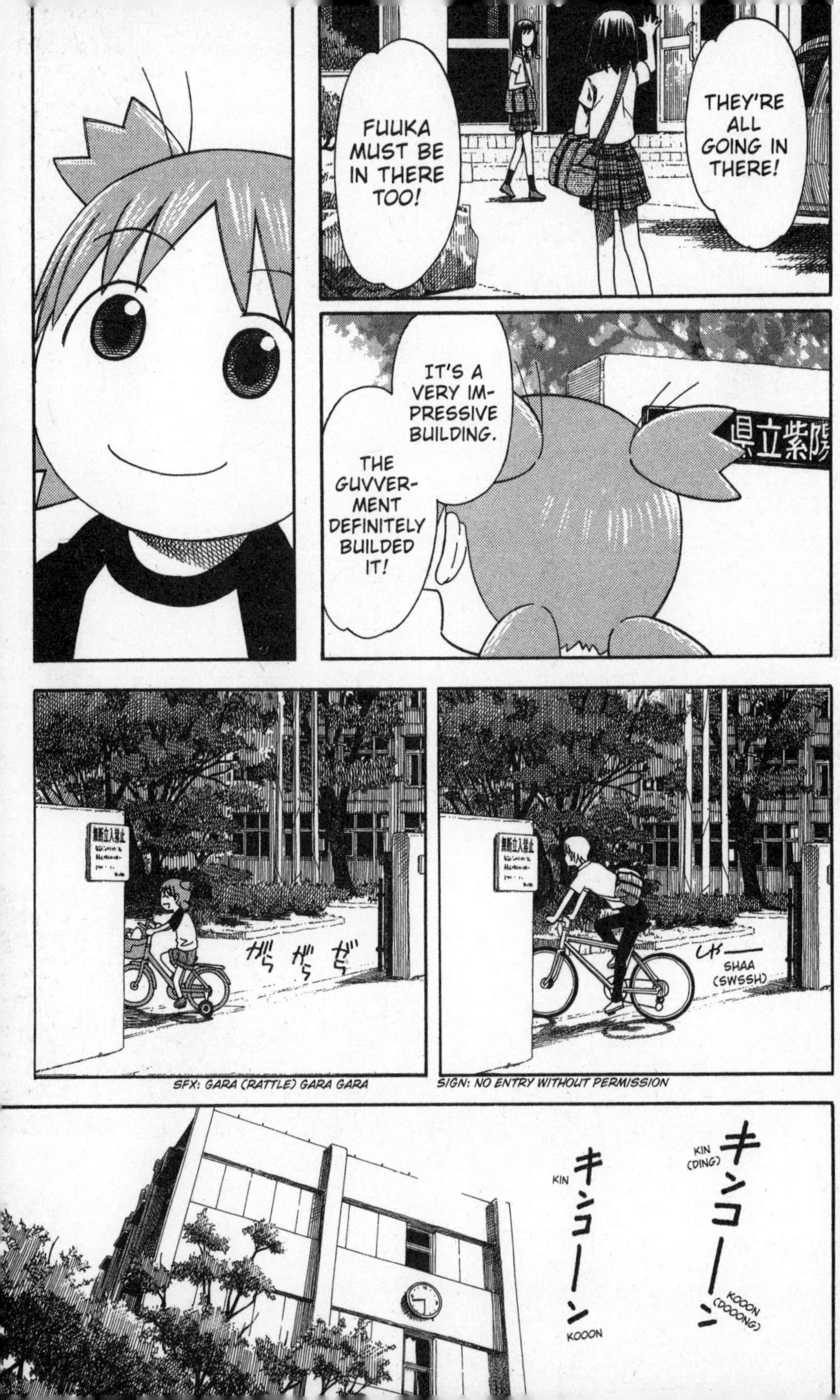
THEY'RE ALL GOING IN THERE!
FUUKA MUST BE IN THERE TOO!
IT'S A VERY IM-PRESSIVE BUILDING.
THE GUVVER-MENT DEFINITELY BUILDED IT!
しゃー SHAA (SWSSH)
SIGN: NO ENTRY WITHOUT PERMISSION
がら がら がら
SFX: GARA (RATTLE) GARA GARA
キンコーン KIN (DING) KOOON (DOOONG)
キンコーン KIN KOOON

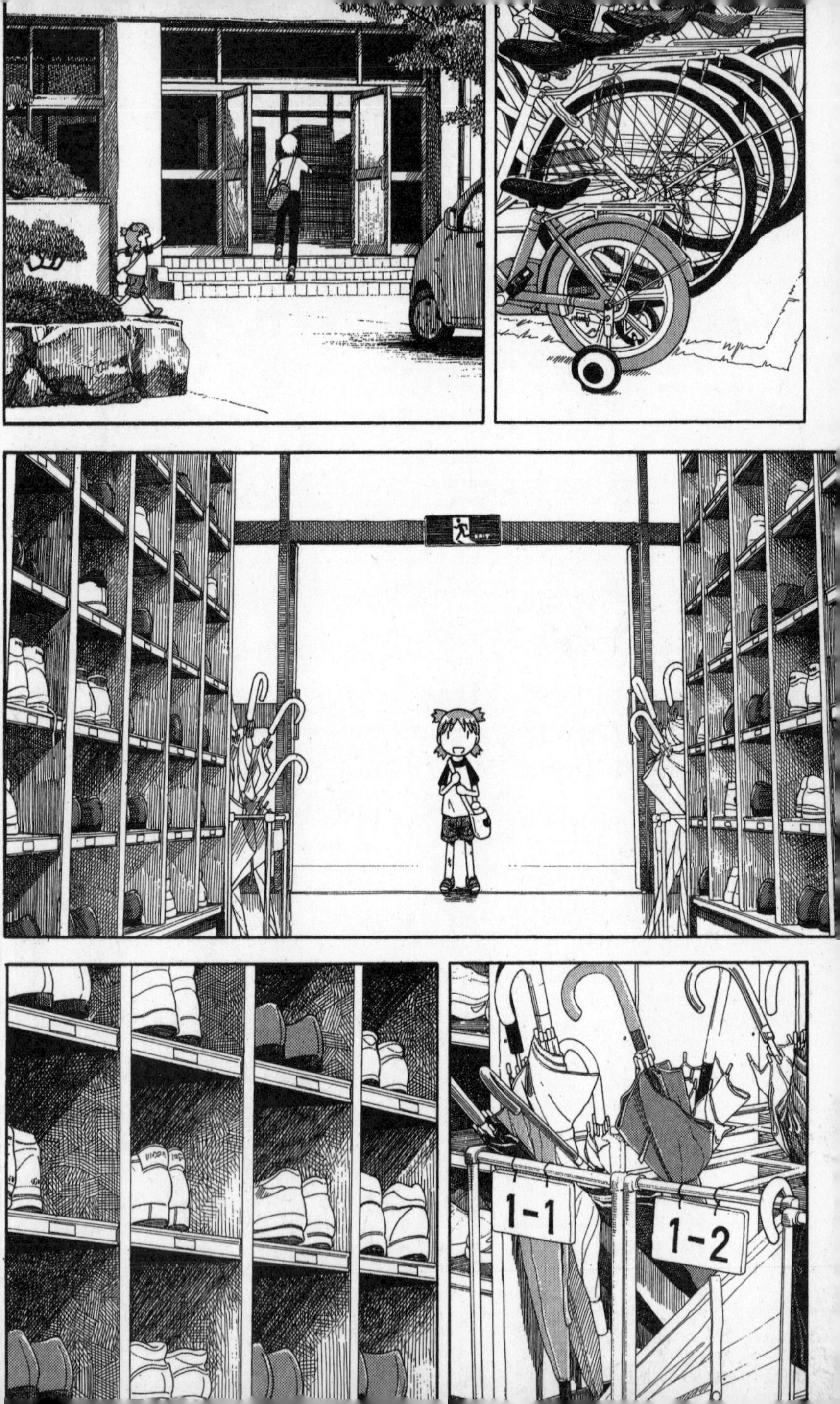
1-1
1-2

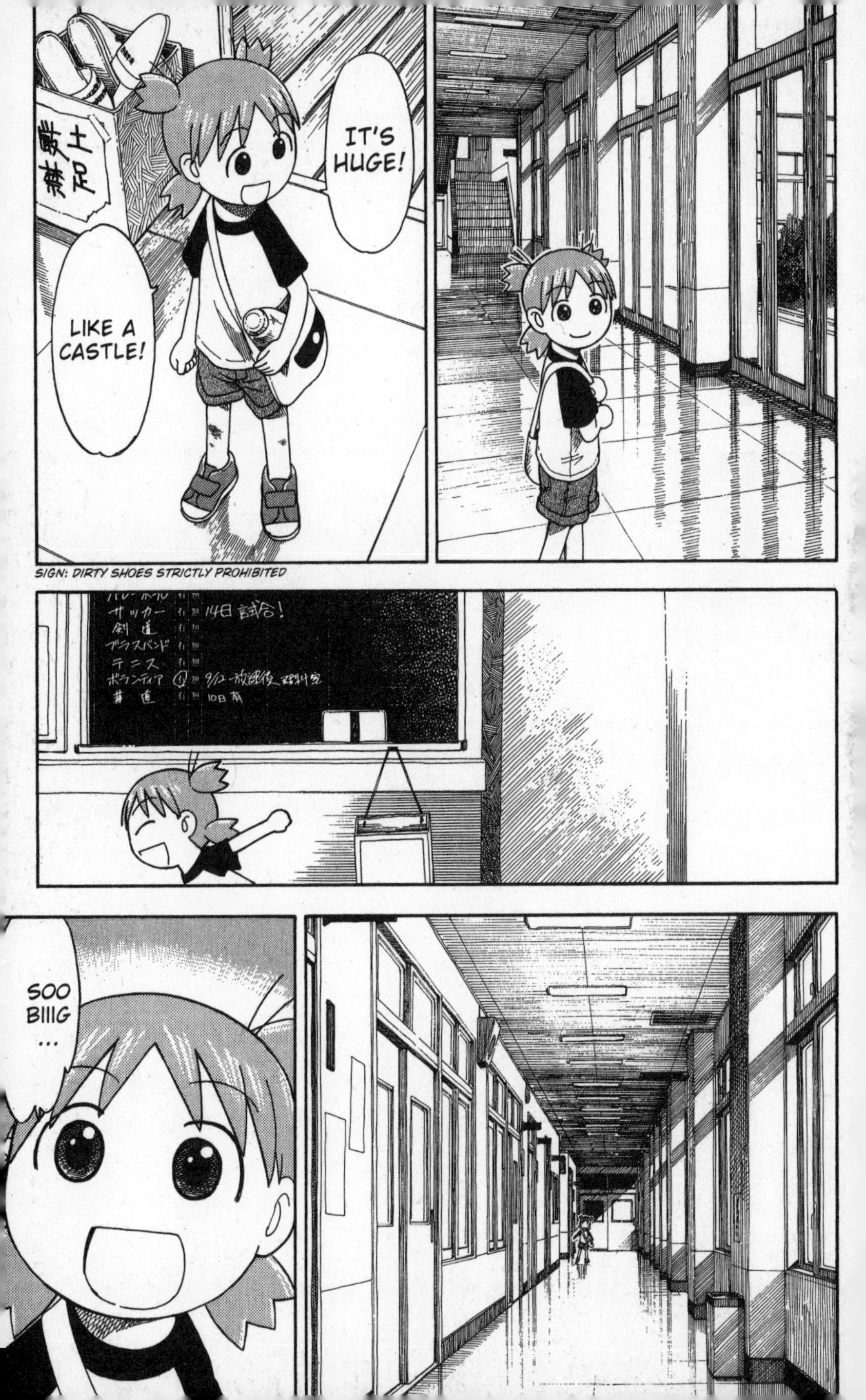

土足厳禁
IT'S HUGE!
LIKE A CASTLE!
SIGN: DIRTY SHOES STRICTLY PROHIBITED
サッカー
14日試合!
剣道
ブラスバンド
テニス
ボランティア
SOO BIIIG ...

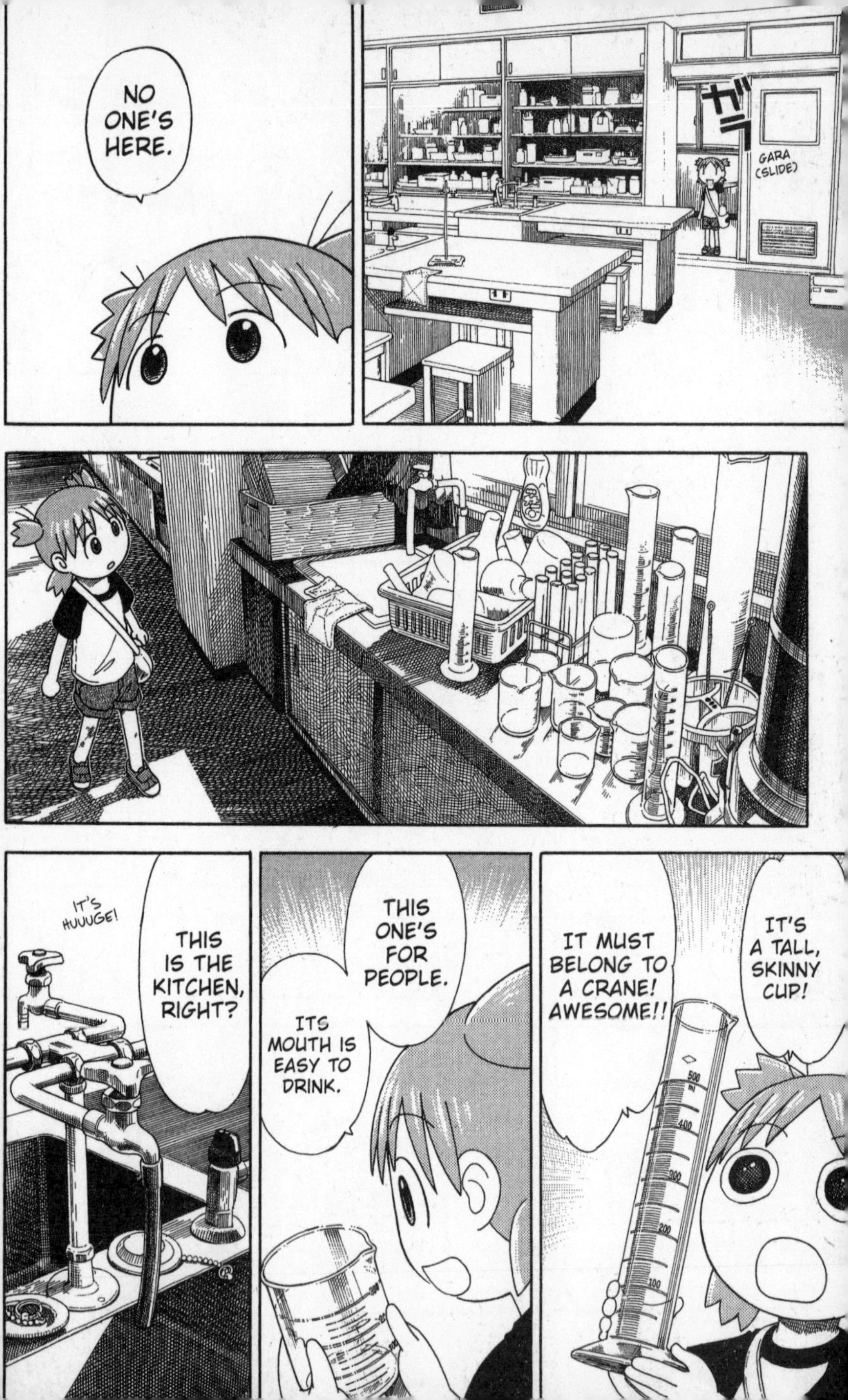
ガラ
GARA (SLIDE)
NO ONE'S HERE.
IT'S A TALL, SKINNY CUP!
IT MUST BELONG TO A CRANE! AWESOME!!
THIS ONE'S FOR PEOPLE.
ITS MOUTH IS EASY TO DRINK.
THIS IS THE KITCHEN, RIGHT?
IT'S HUUUGE!

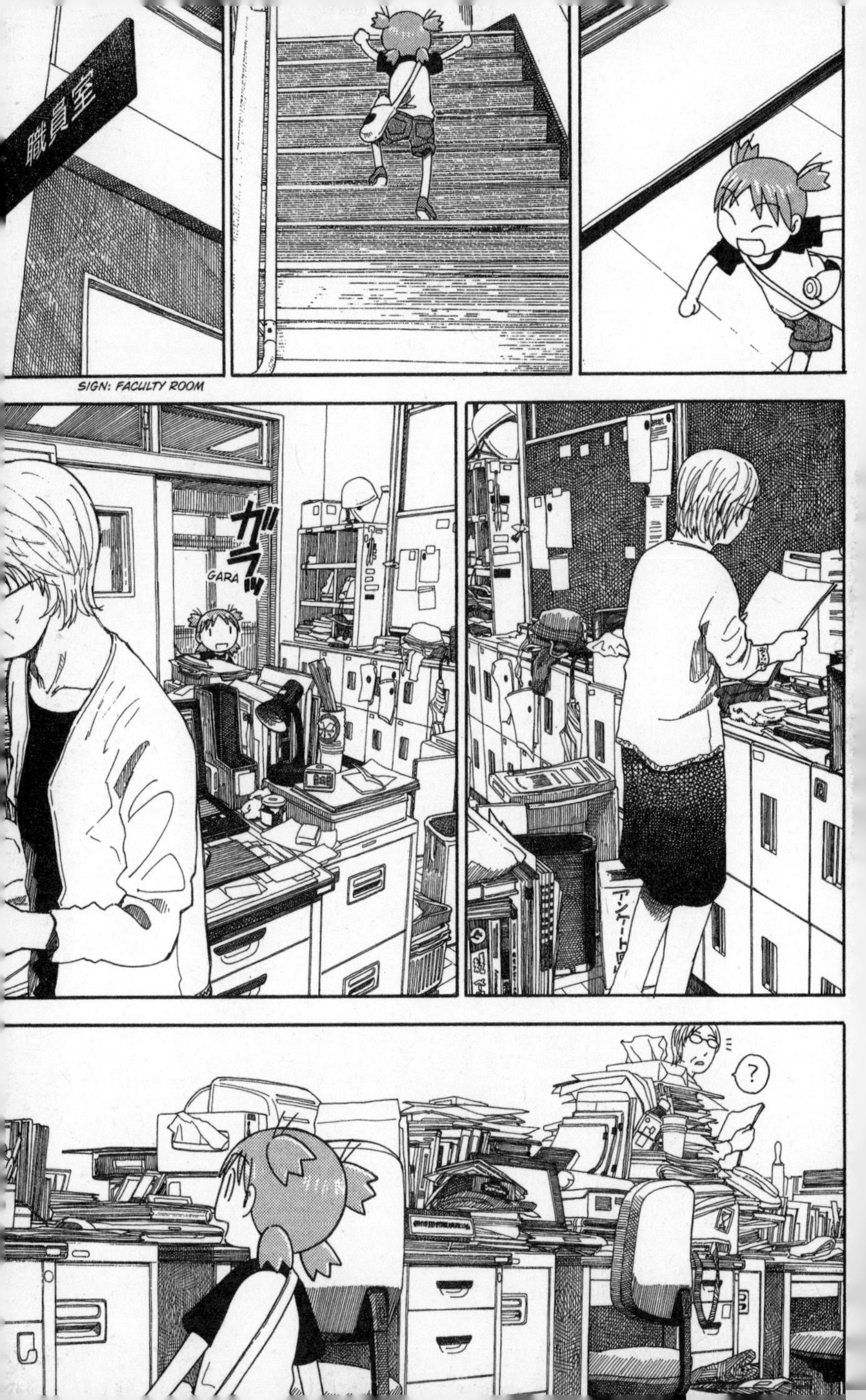
職員室
SIGN: FACULTY ROOM
ガラッ
GARA
?

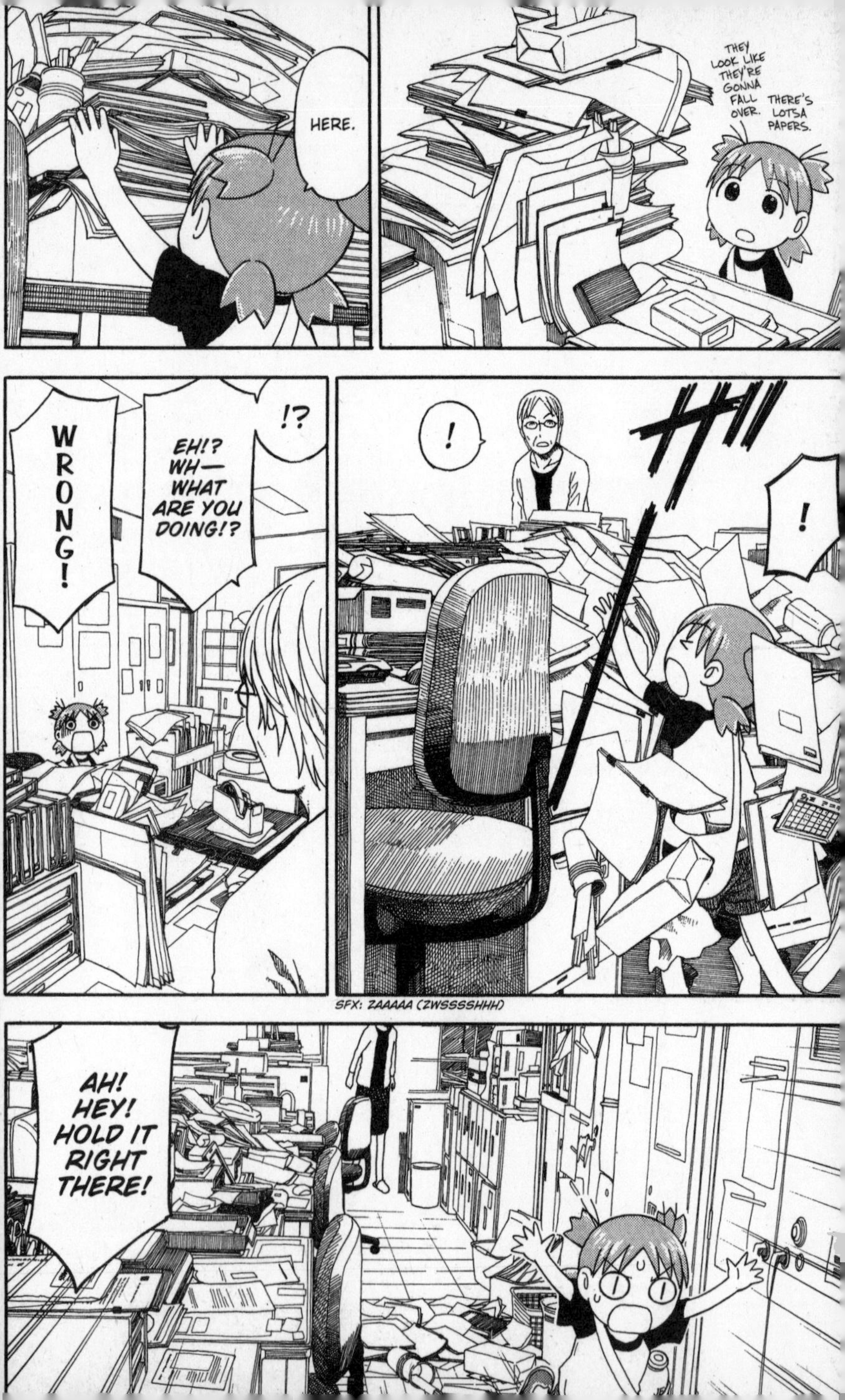
THERE'S LOTSA PAPERS.
THEY LOOK LIKE THEY'RE GONNA FALL OVER.
HERE.
!
!
!?
EH!? WH— WHAT ARE YOU DOING!?
WRONG!
SFX: ZAAAAA (ZWSSSSHHH)
AH! HEY! HOLD IT RIGHT THERE!

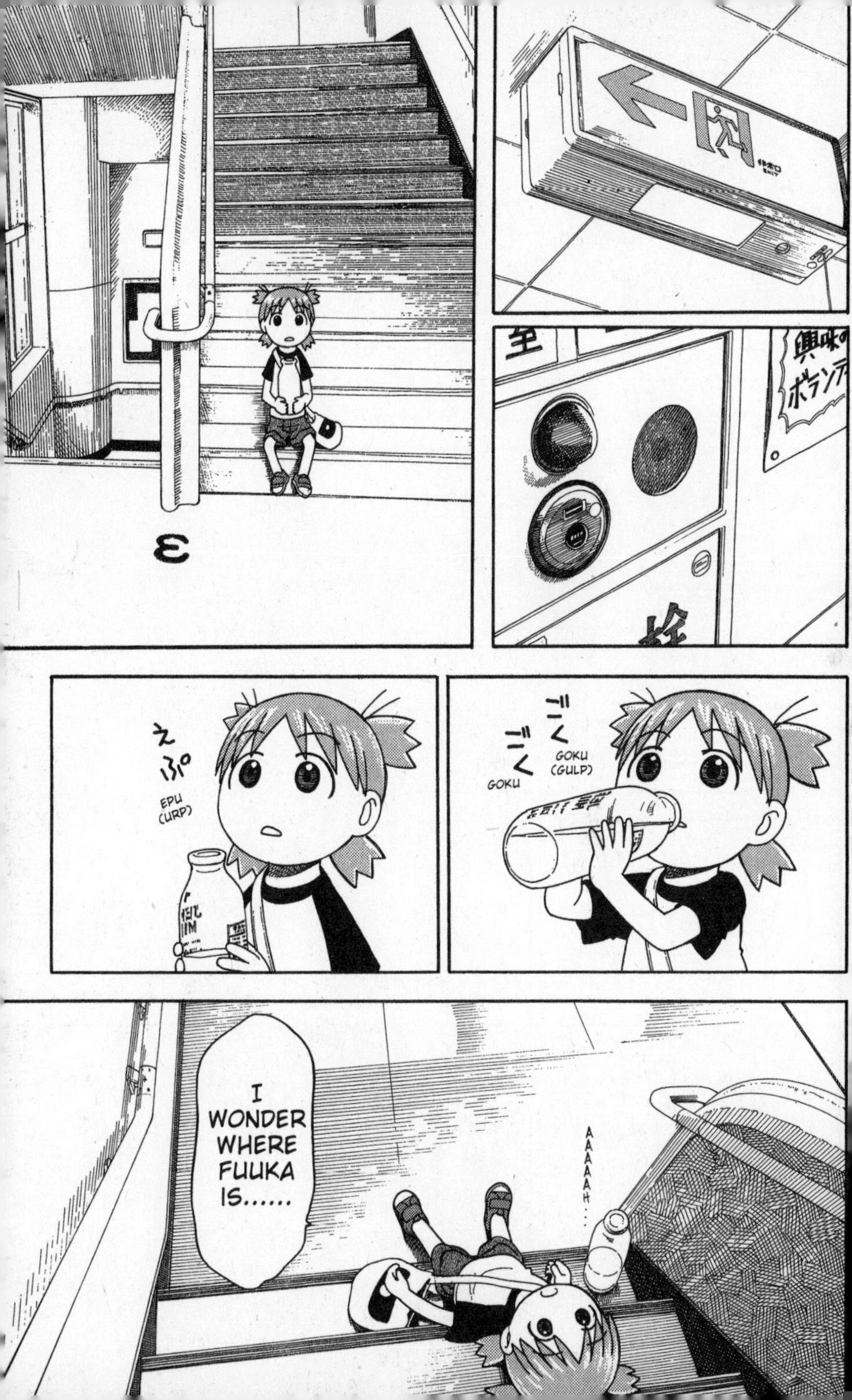

ごくごく
GOKU (GULP)
GOKU
えぷ
EPU (URP)
I WONDER WHERE FUUKA IS......
AAAAAH...

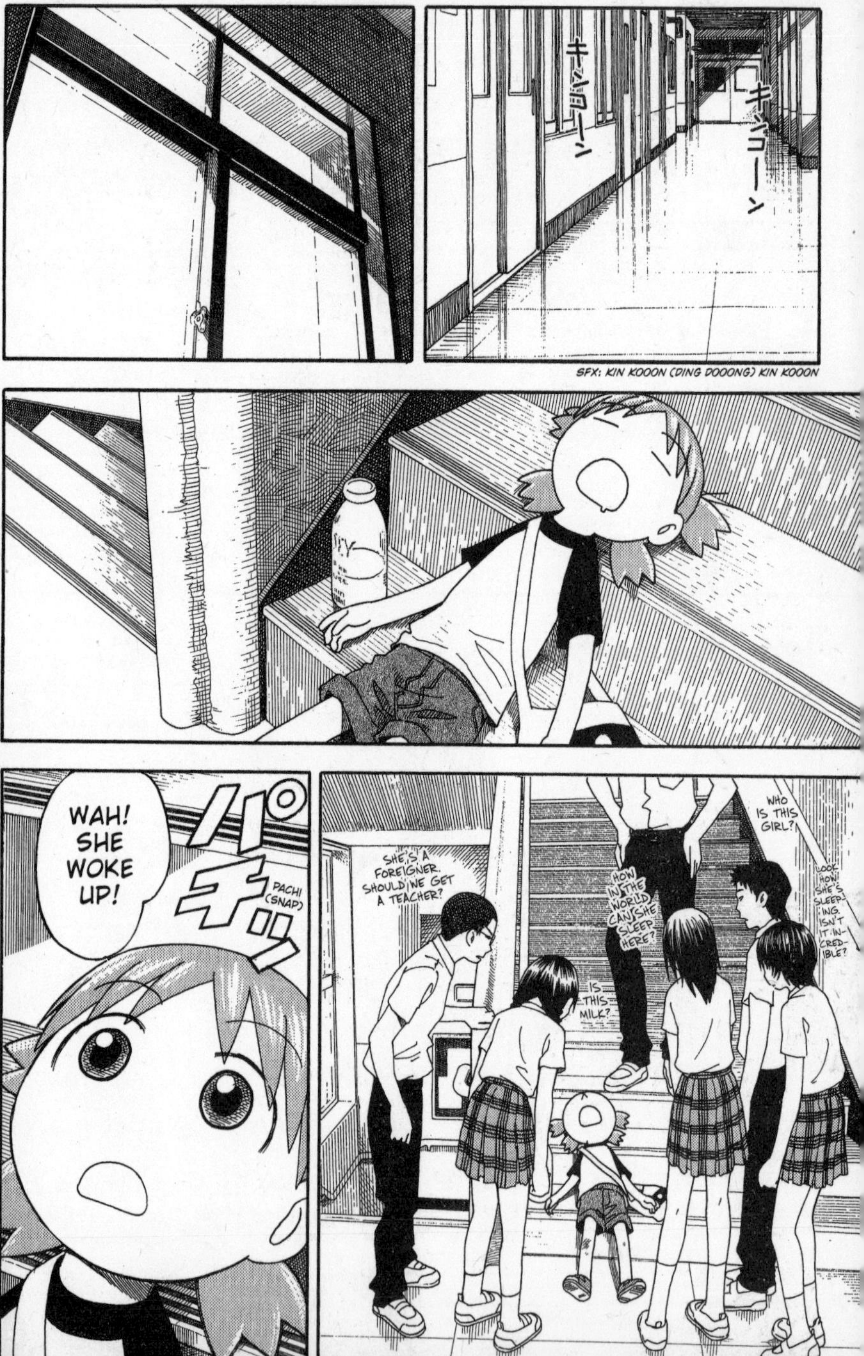
キンコーン
キンコーン
SFX: KIN KOOON (DING DOOONG) KIN KOOON
WHO IS THIS GIRL?
LOOK HOW SHE'S SLEEPING. ISN'T IT INCREDIBLE?
HOW IN THE WORLD CAN SHE SLEEP HERE?
SHE'S A FOREIGNER. SHOULD WE GET A TEACHER?
IS THIS MILK?
パチッ
PACHI (SNAP)
WAH! SHE WOKE UP!

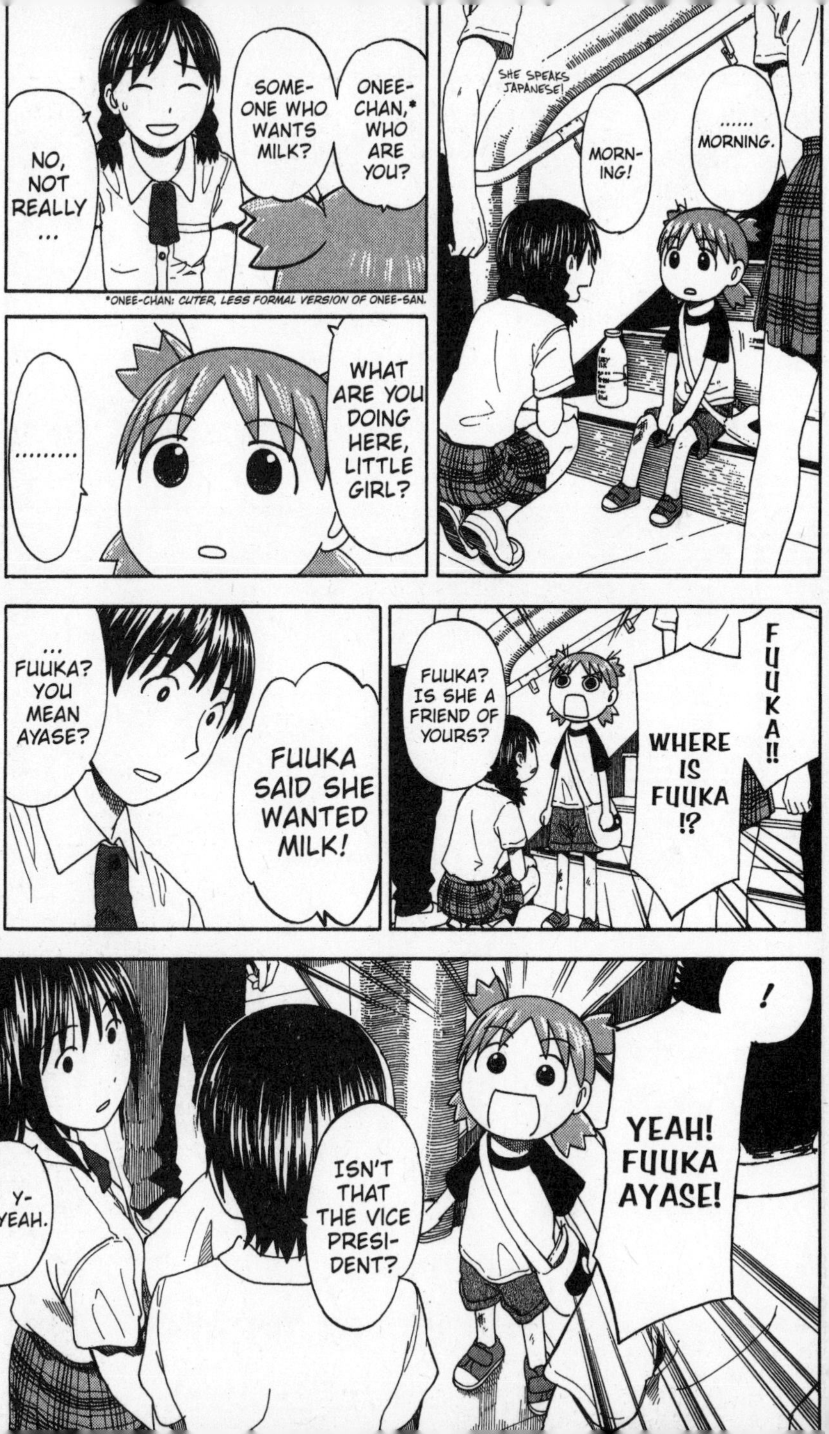

...... MORNING.
MORN-ING!
SHE SPEAKS JAPANESE!
ONEE-CHAN,* WHO ARE YOU?
SOME-ONE WHO WANTS MILK?
NO, NOT REALLY ...
*ONEE-CHAN: CUTER, LESS FORMAL VERSION OF ONEE-SAN.
WHAT ARE YOU DOING HERE, LITTLE GIRL?
....
FUUKA!!
WHERE IS FUUKA!?
FUUKA? IS SHE A FRIEND OF YOURS?
FUUKA SAID SHE WANTED MILK!
... FUUKA? YOU MEAN AYASE?
!
YEAH! FUUKA AYASE!
ISN'T THAT THE VICE PRESIDENT?
Y-YEAH.

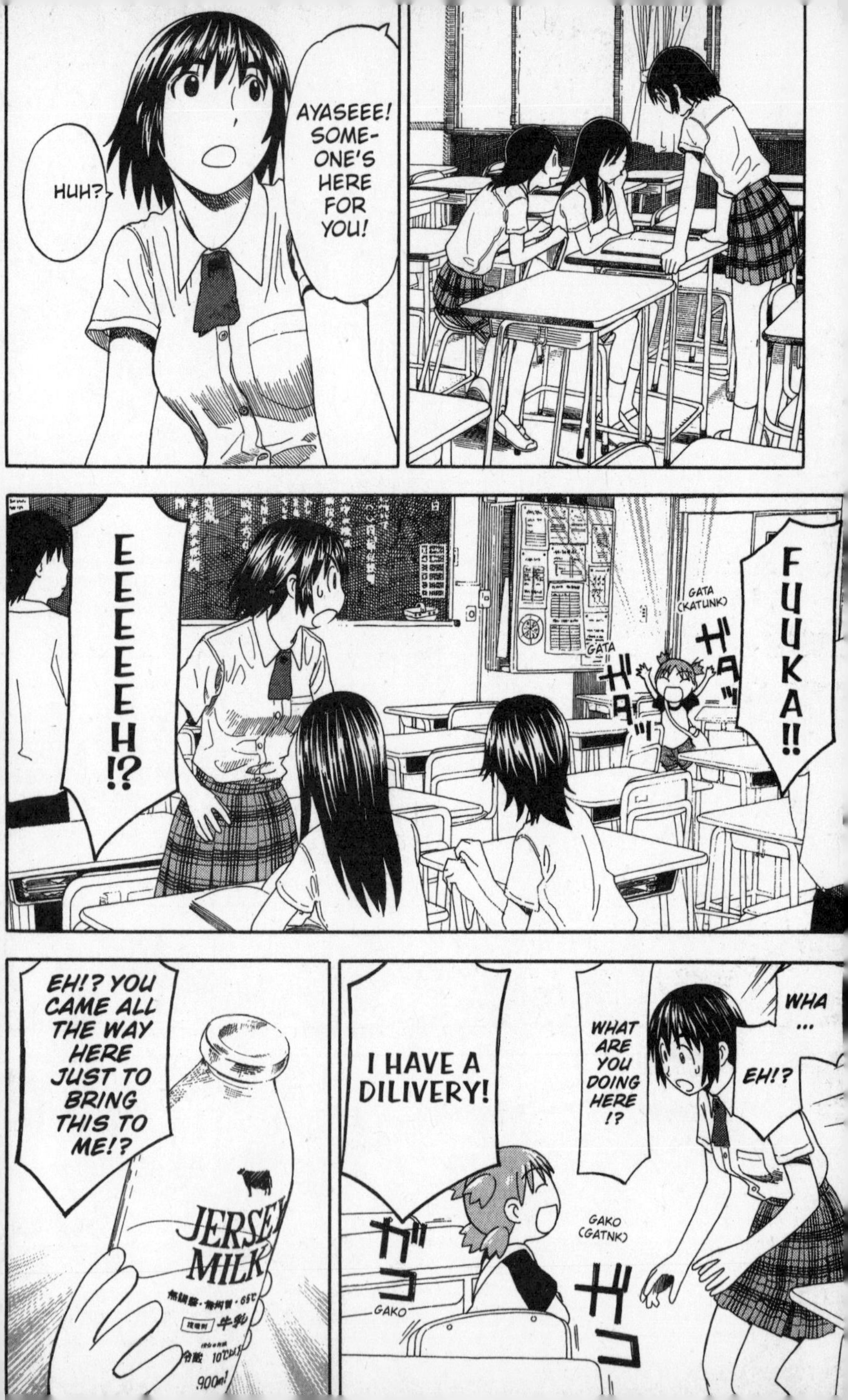
AYASEEE! SOMEONE'S HERE FOR YOU!
HUH?
FUUKA!!
GATA (KATUNK)
ガタッ
GATA
ガタッ
EEEEEEH!?
WHA ... EH!?
WHAT ARE YOU DOING HERE!?
I HAVE A DILIVERY!
GAKO (GATNK)
ガコ
ガコ
GAKO
EH!? YOU CAME ALL THE WAY HERE JUST TO BRING THIS TO ME!?
JERSE
MILK
900ml

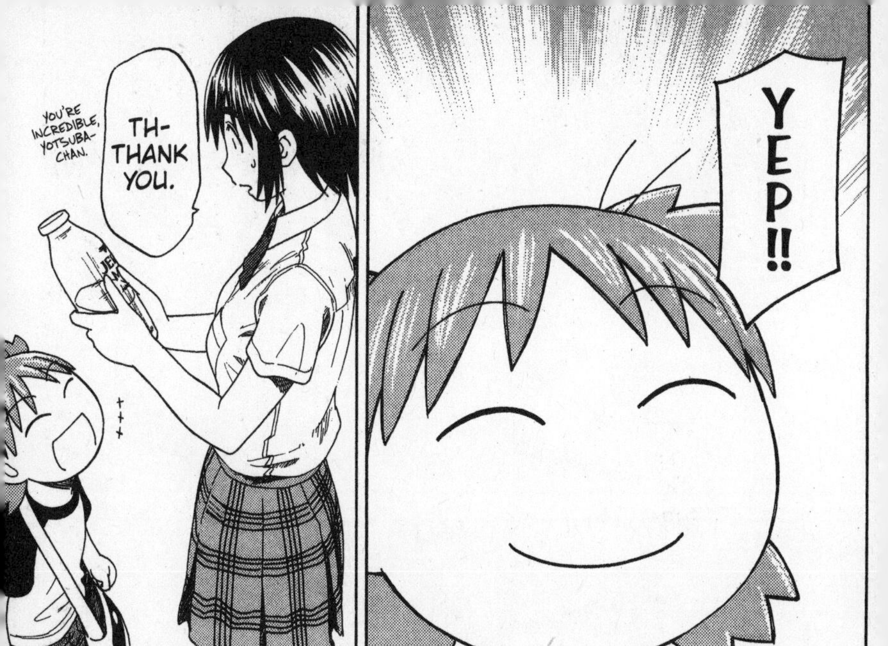
YEP!!
TH-THANK YOU.
YOU'RE INCREDIBLE, YOTSUBA-CHAN.
STAMP HERE* PLEASE.
EH!? STAMP!?

*IN JAPAN, PEOPLE USE STAMPS TO "SIGN" THEIR NAMES ON OFFICIAL DOCUMENTS. SO YOTSUBA IS IMITATING A REAL JAPANESE DELIVERYMAN BY ASKING FOR A STAMP OF RECEIPT.

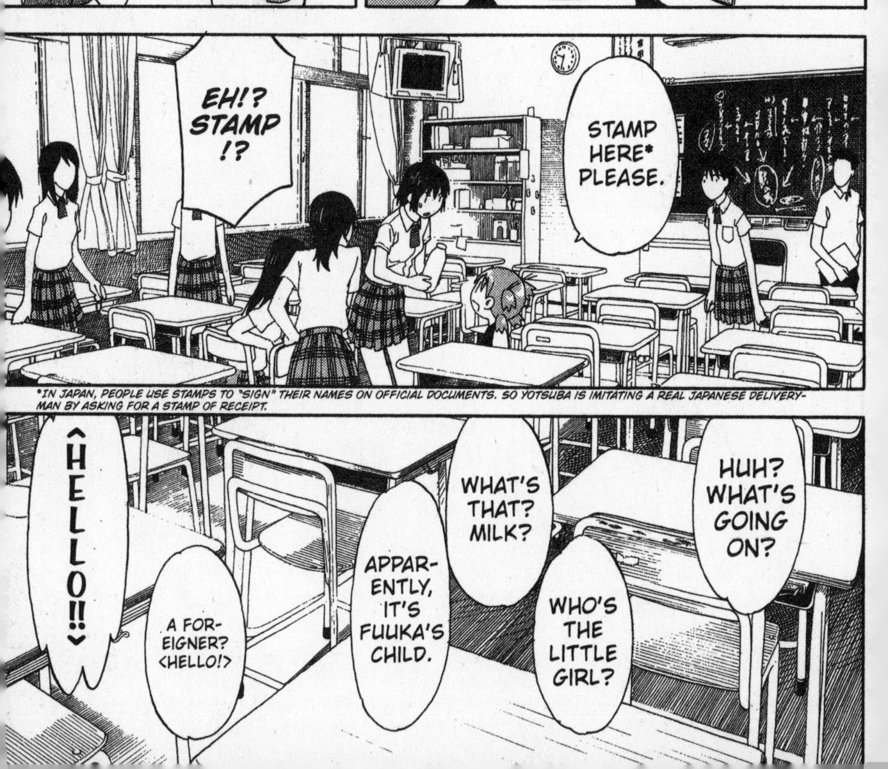
HUH? WHAT'S GOING ON?
WHO'S THE LITTLE GIRL?
WHAT'S THAT? MILK?
APPARENTLY, IT'S FUUKA'S CHILD.
A FOREIGNER? <HELLO!>
<HELLO!!>

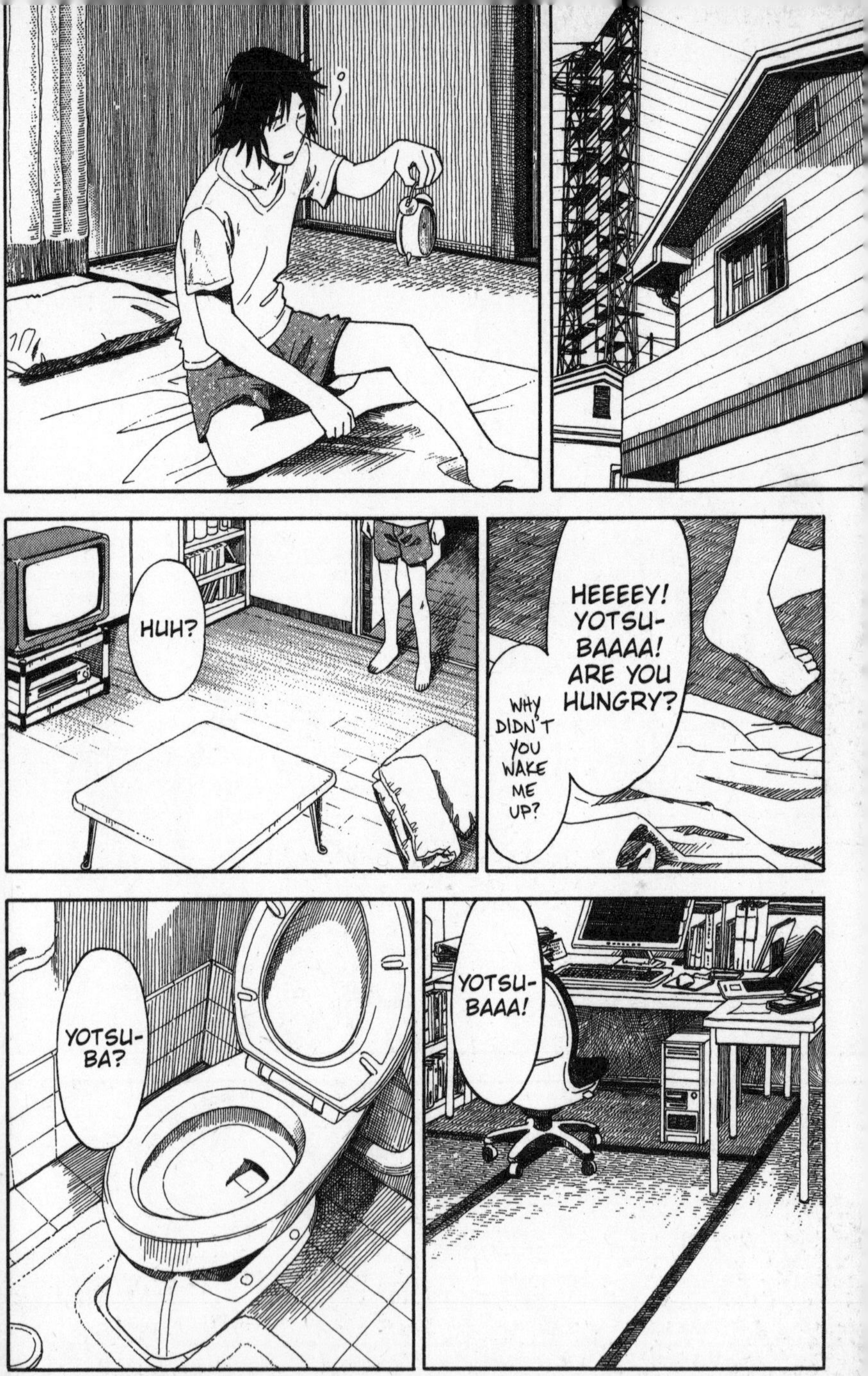
HEEEEY! YOTSU-BAAAA! ARE YOU HUNGRY?
WHY DIDN'T YOU WAKE ME UP?
HUH?
YOTSU-BAAA!
YOTSU-BA?

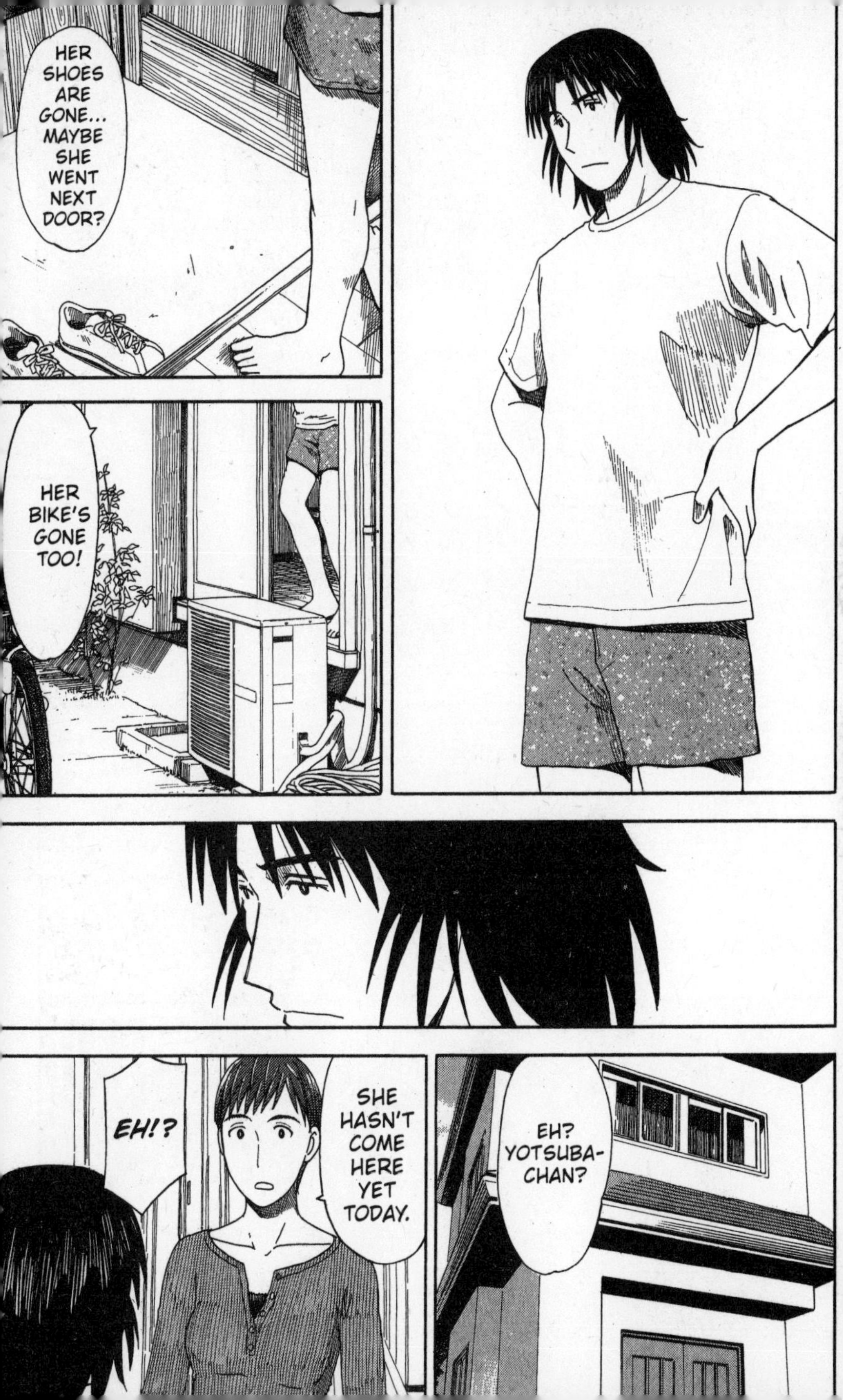
HER SHOES ARE GONE... MAYBE SHE WENT NEXT DOOR?
HER BIKE'S GONE TOO!
EH? YOTSUBA-CHAN?
SHE HASN'T COME HERE YET TODAY.
EH!?

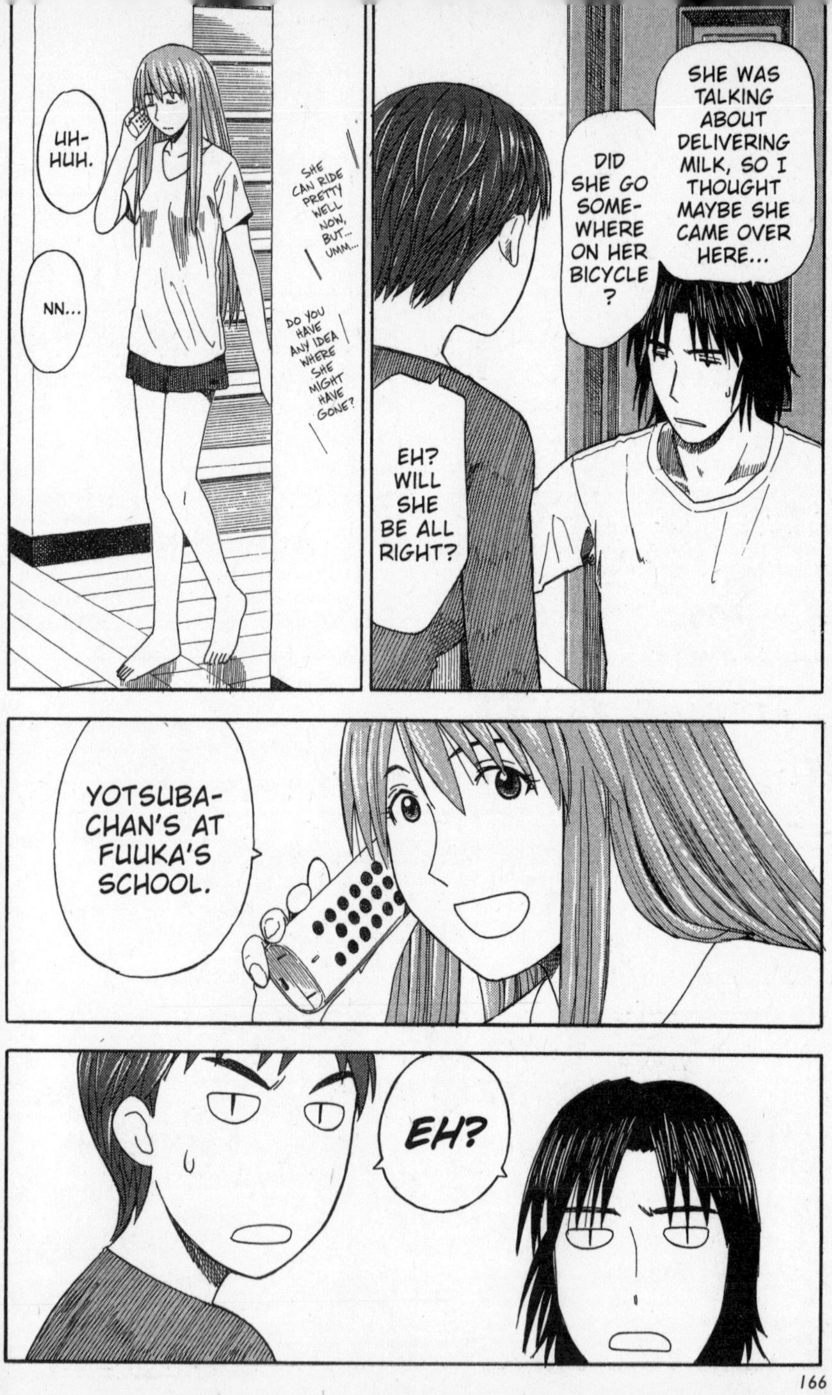
SHE WAS TALKING ABOUT DELIVERING MILK, SO I THOUGHT MAYBE SHE CAME OVER HERE...
DID SHE GO SOME-WHERE ON HER BICYCLE?
EH? WILL SHE BE ALL RIGHT?
SHE CAN RIDE PRETTY WELL NOW, BUT... UMM...
DO YOU HAVE ANY IDEA WHERE SHE MIGHT HAVE GONE?
UH-HUH.
NN...
YOTSUBA-CHAN'S AT FUUKA'S SCHOOL.
EH?

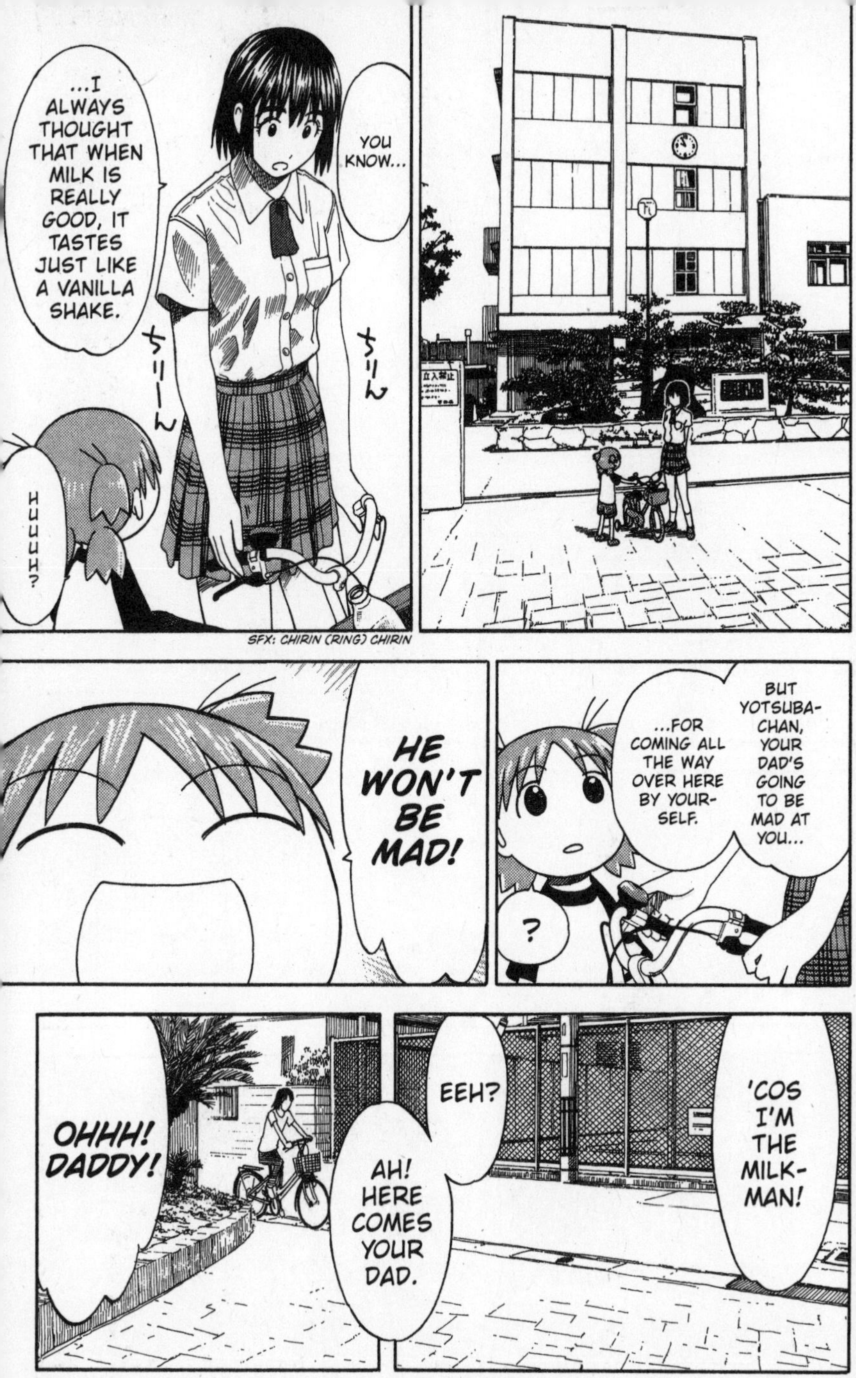
YOU KNOW...
ちりん
...I ALWAYS THOUGHT THAT WHEN MILK IS REALLY GOOD, IT TASTES JUST LIKE A VANILLA SHAKE.
ちりーん
HUUUUH?
SFX: CHIRIN (RING) CHIRIN
BUT YOTSUBA-CHAN, YOUR DAD'S GOING TO BE MAD AT YOU...
...FOR COMING ALL THE WAY OVER HERE BY YOURSELF.
?
HE WON'T BE MAD!
'COS I'M THE MILK-MAN!
EEH?
AH! HERE COMES YOUR DAD.
OHHH! DADDY!

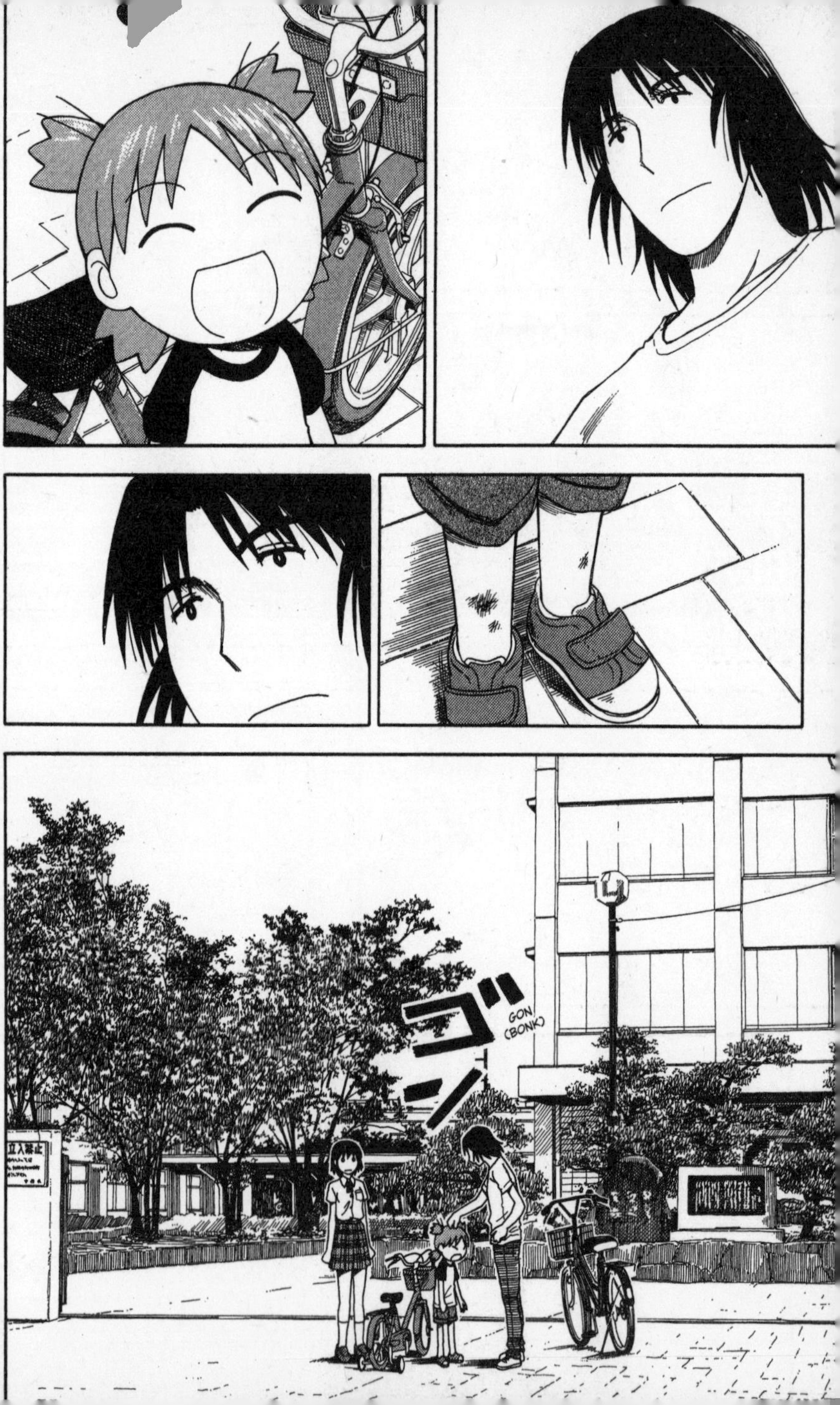
ゴン
GON
(BONK)

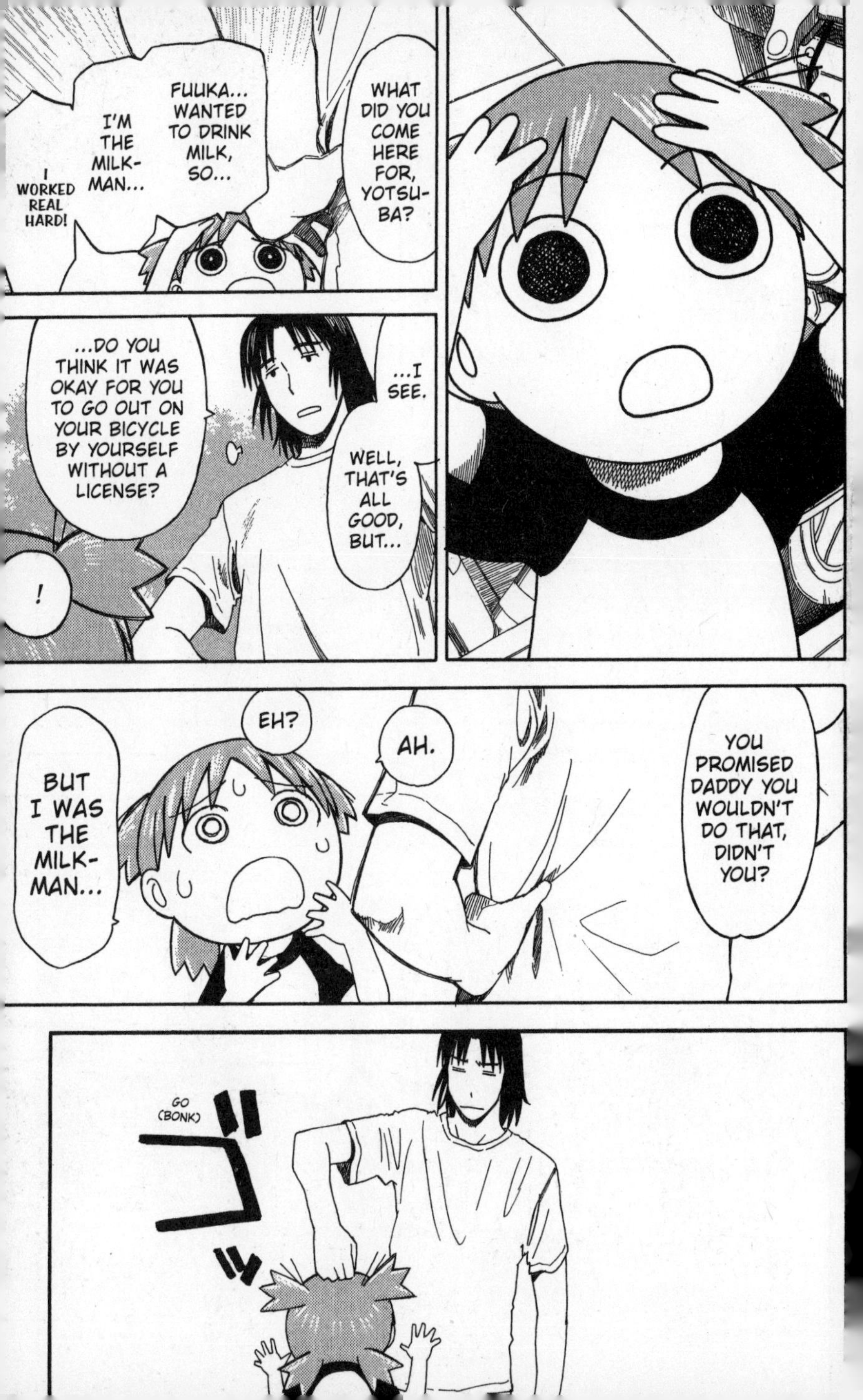
WHAT DID YOU COME HERE FOR, YOTSUBA?
FUUKA... WANTED TO DRINK MILK, SO...
I'M THE MILK-MAN...
I WORKED REAL HARD!
...I SEE.
WELL, THAT'S ALL GOOD, BUT...
...DO YOU THINK IT WAS OKAY FOR YOU TO GO OUT ON YOUR BICYCLE BY YOURSELF WITHOUT A LICENSE?
!
YOU PROMISED DADDY YOU WOULDN'T DO THAT, DIDN'T YOU?
AH.
EH?
BUT I WAS THE MILK-MAN...
GO (BONK)

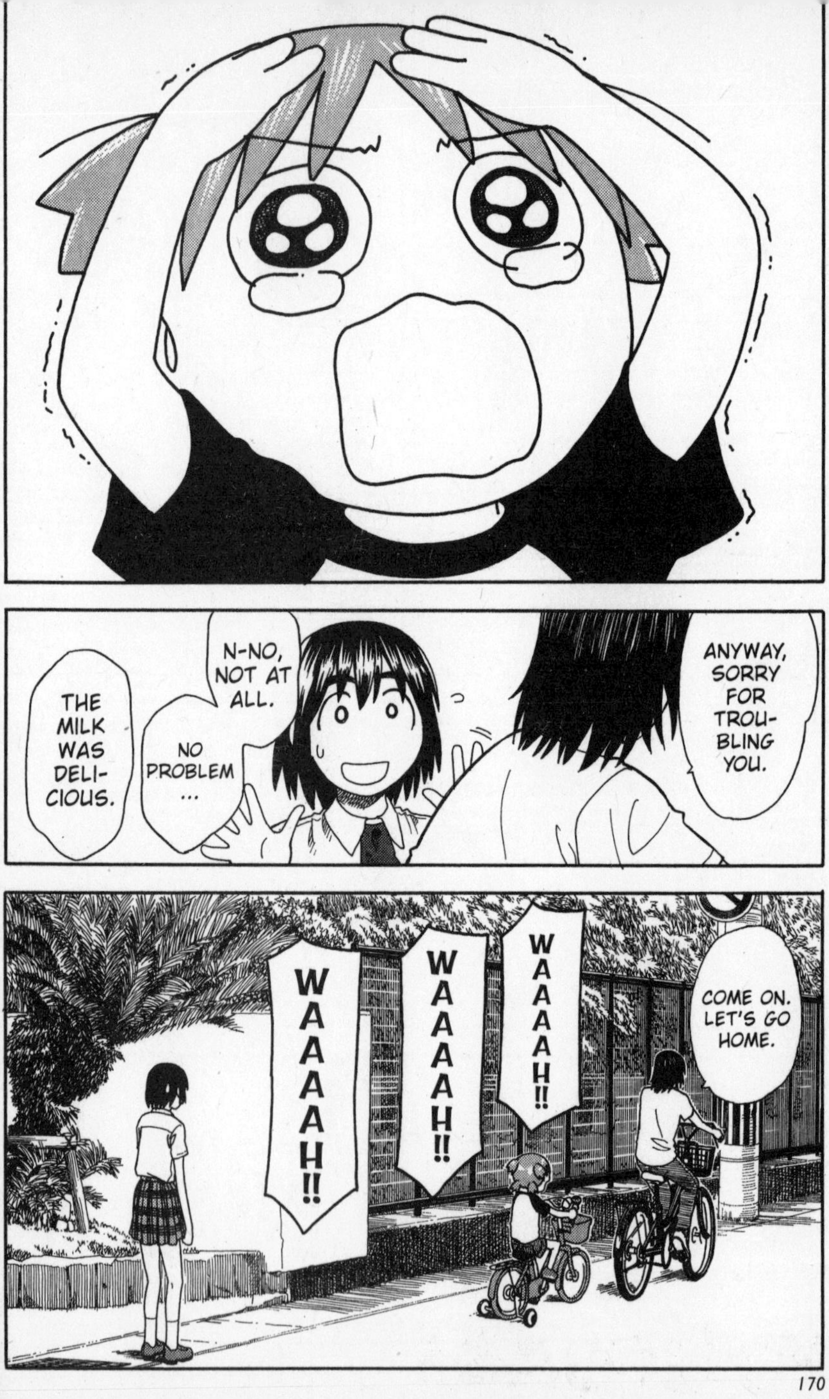

ANYWAY, SORRY FOR TROU-BLING YOU.
N-NO, NOT AT ALL.
NO PROBLEM ...
THE MILK WAS DELI-CIOUS.
COME ON. LET'S GO HOME.
WAAAAAH!!
WAAAAAH!!
WAAAAAH!!

YOTSUBA&!

*TATAMI: WOVEN RICE STRAW MATS TRADITIONALLY USED AS FLOORING IN JAPAN.

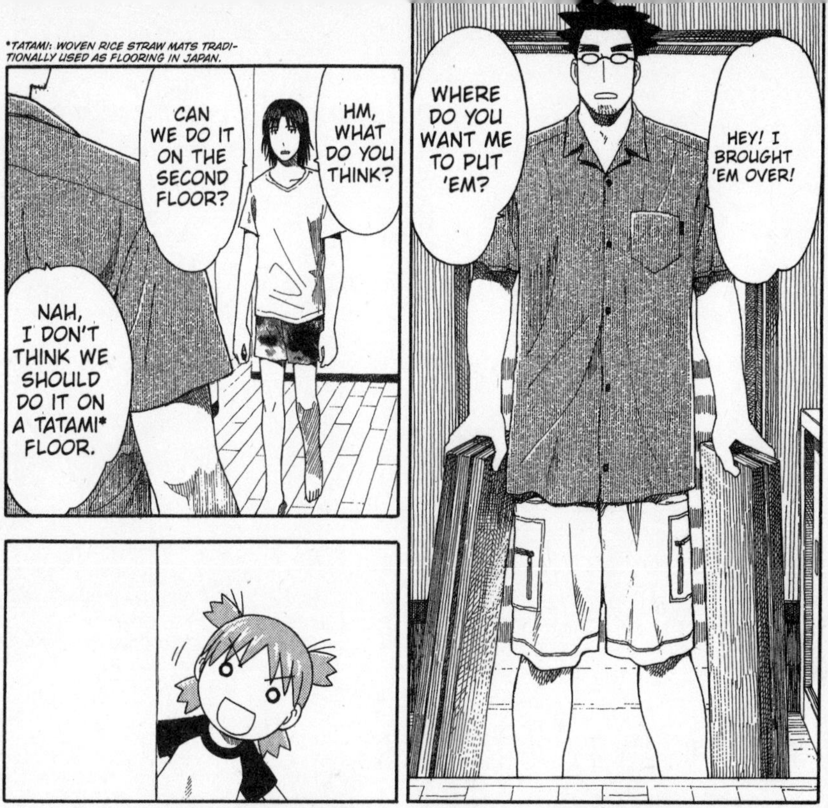
HEY! I BROUGHT 'EM OVER!
WHERE DO YOU WANT ME TO PUT 'EM?
HM, WHAT DO YOU THINK?
CAN WE DO IT ON THE SECOND FLOOR?
NAH, I DON'T THINK WE SHOULD DO IT ON A TATAMI* FLOOR.

SFX: DA (THUD) DA DA DA

CARD: 1 2 3 4BA ("4BA" CAN BE READ AS "YOTSUBA") KOIWAIA

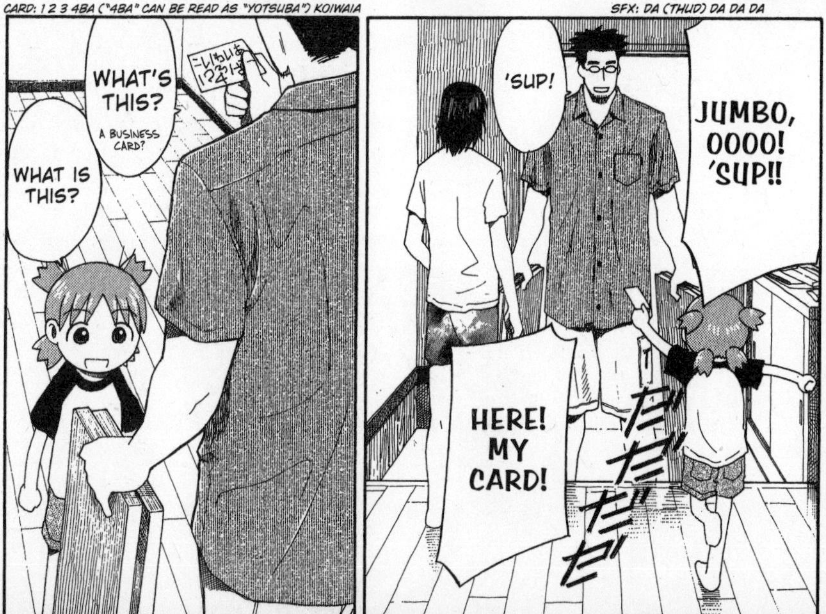
JUMBO, OOOO! 'SUP!!
'SUP!
HERE! MY CARD!
だだだだ
WHAT'S THIS?
A BUSINESS CARD?
WHAT IS THIS?

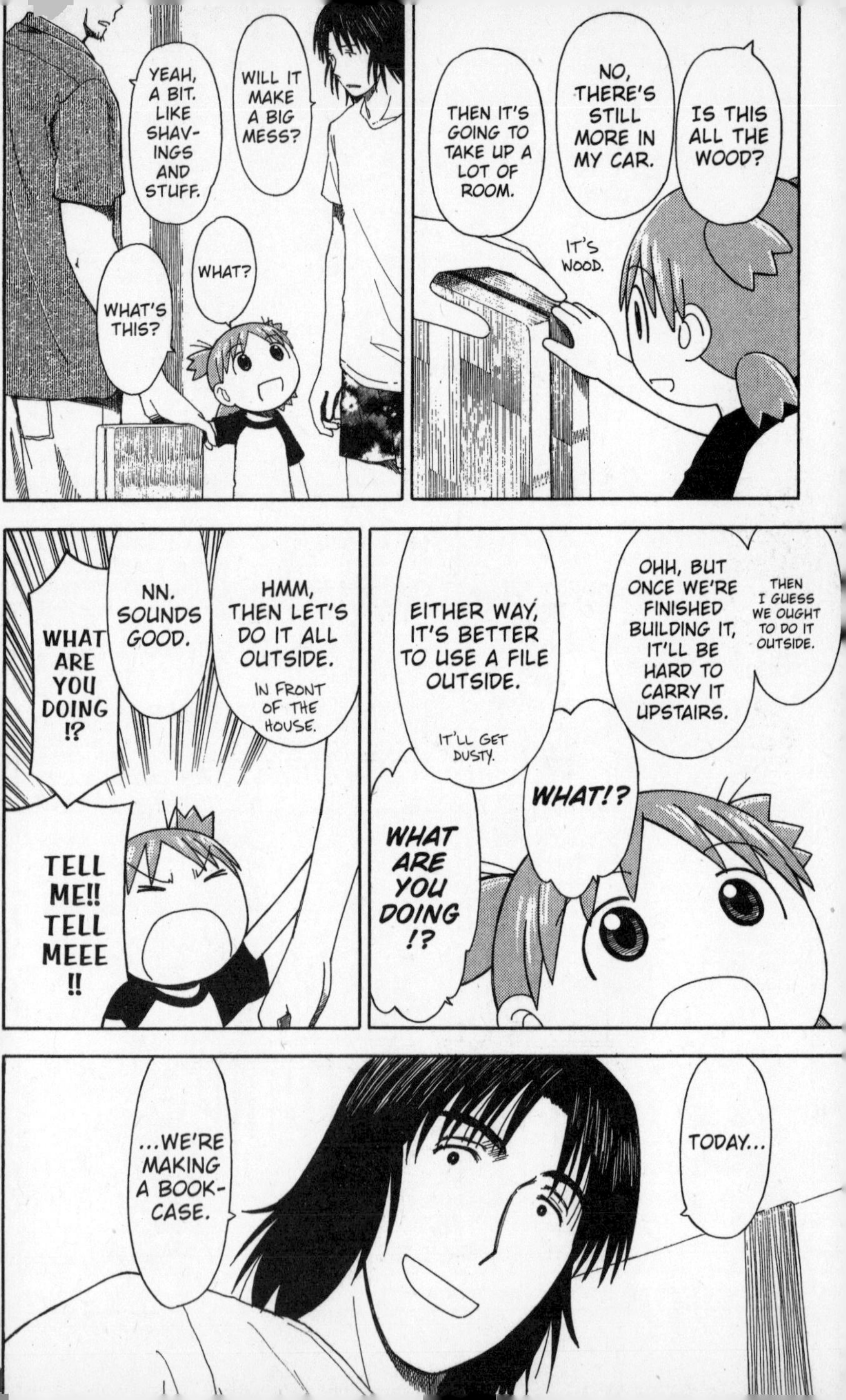
IS THIS ALL THE WOOD?
NO, THERE'S STILL MORE IN MY CAR.
THEN IT'S GOING TO TAKE UP A LOT OF ROOM.
IT'S WOOD.
WILL IT MAKE A BIG MESS?
YEAH, A BIT. LIKE SHAV-INGS AND STUFF.
WHAT?
WHAT'S THIS?
THEN I GUESS WE OUGHT TO DO IT OUTSIDE.
OHH, BUT ONCE WE'RE FINISHED BUILDING IT, IT'LL BE HARD TO CARRY IT UPSTAIRS.
EITHER WAY, IT'S BETTER TO USE A FILE OUTSIDE.
IT'LL GET DUSTY.
WHAT!?
WHAT ARE YOU DOING!?
HMM, THEN LET'S DO IT ALL OUTSIDE.
IN FRONT OF THE HOUSE.
NN. SOUNDS GOOD.
WHAT ARE YOU DOING!?
TELL ME!! TELL MEEE!!
TODAY...
...WE'RE MAKING A BOOK-CASE.

YOTSUBA& THE BOOKCASE

#41

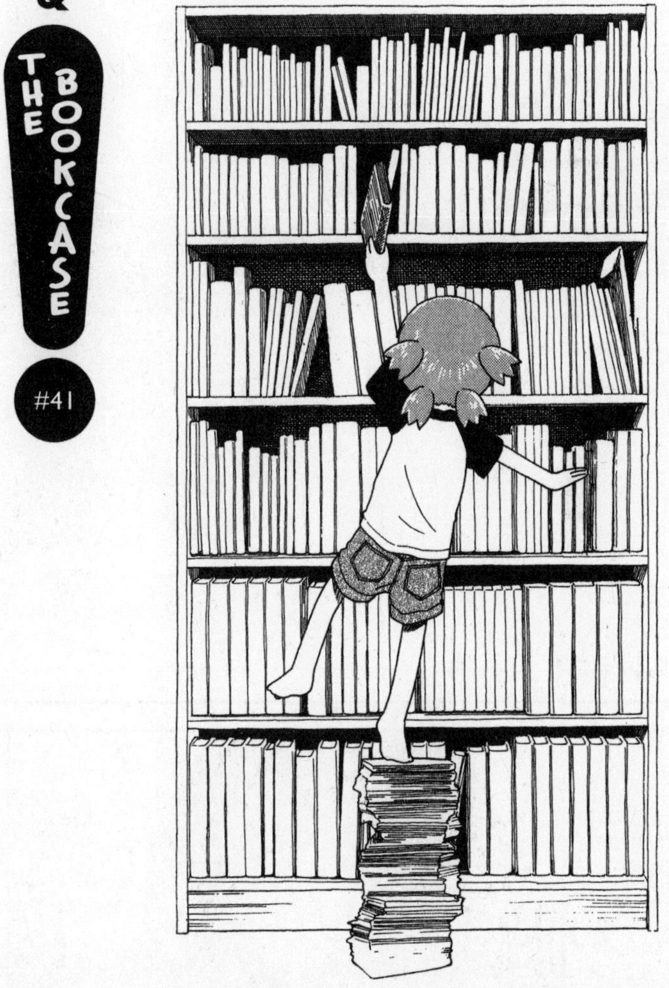

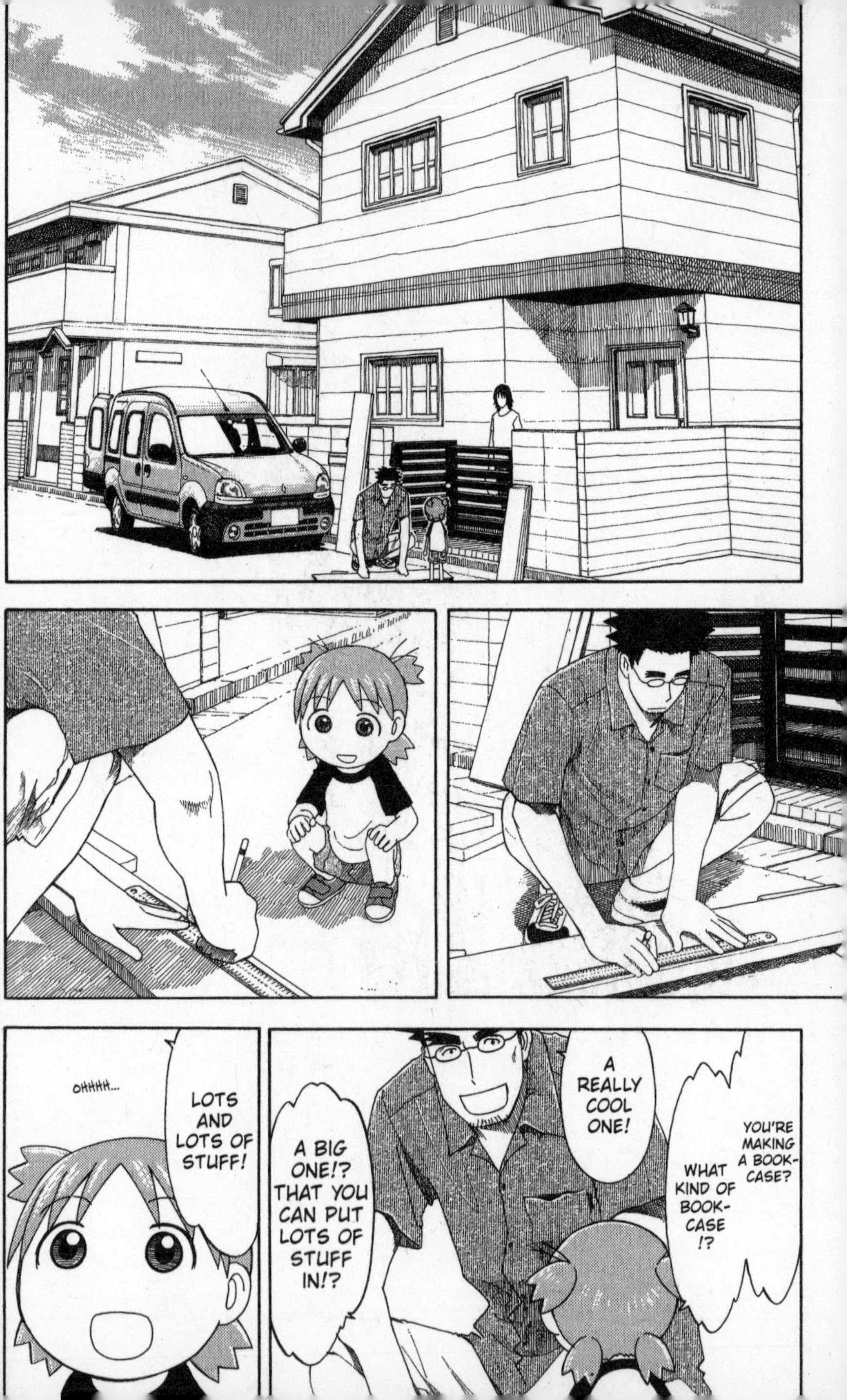
YOU'RE MAKING A BOOK-CASE?
WHAT KIND OF BOOK-CASE!?
A REALLY COOL ONE!
A BIG ONE!? THAT YOU CAN PUT LOTS OF STUFF IN!?
LOTS AND LOTS OF STUFF!
OHHHH...

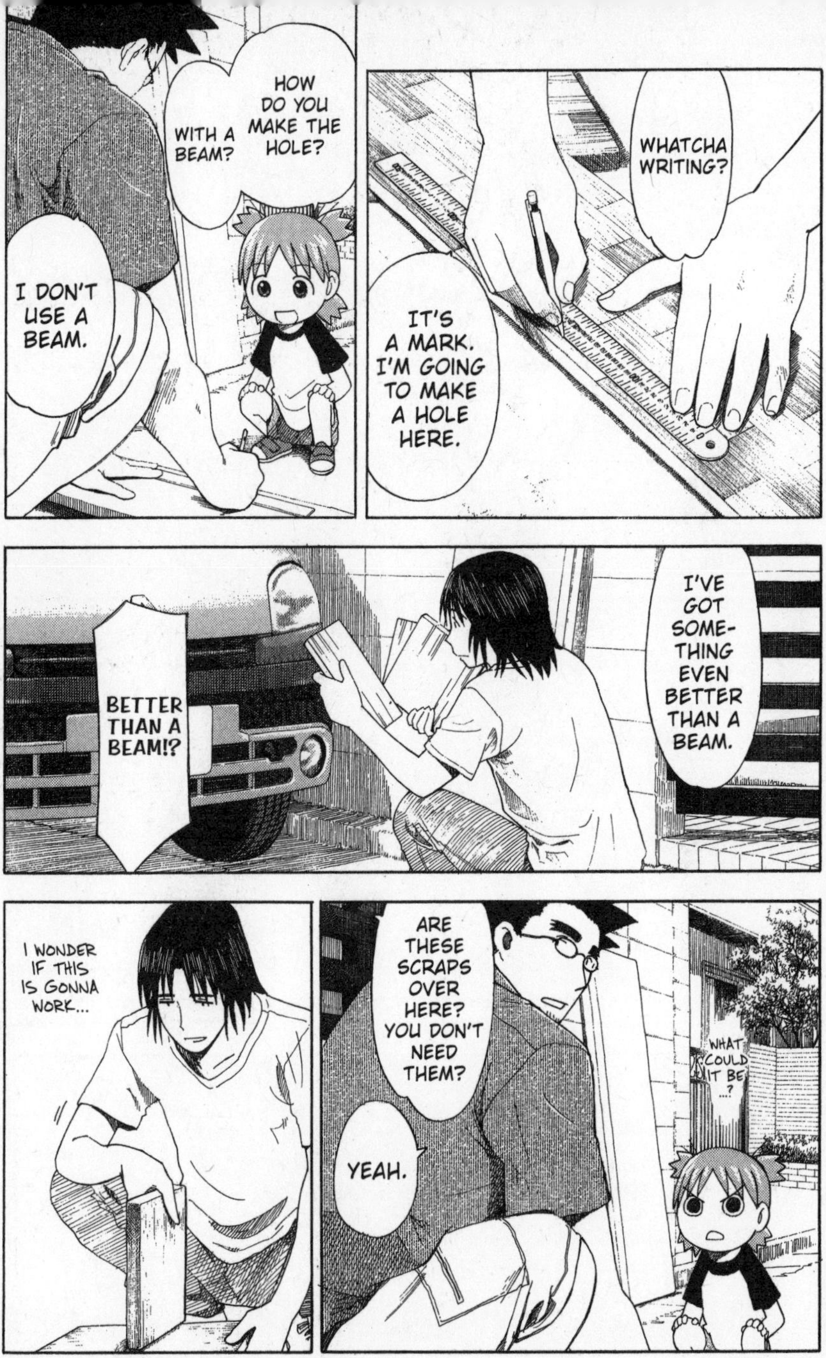

WHATCHA WRITING?
IT'S A MARK. I'M GOING TO MAKE A HOLE HERE.
HOW DO YOU MAKE THE HOLE?
WITH A BEAM?
I DON'T USE A BEAM.
I'VE GOT SOMETHING EVEN BETTER THAN A BEAM.
BETTER THAN A BEAM!?
ARE THESE SCRAPS OVER HERE? YOU DON'T NEED THEM?
YEAH.
WHAT COULD IT BE ...?
I WONDER IF THIS IS GONNA WORK...

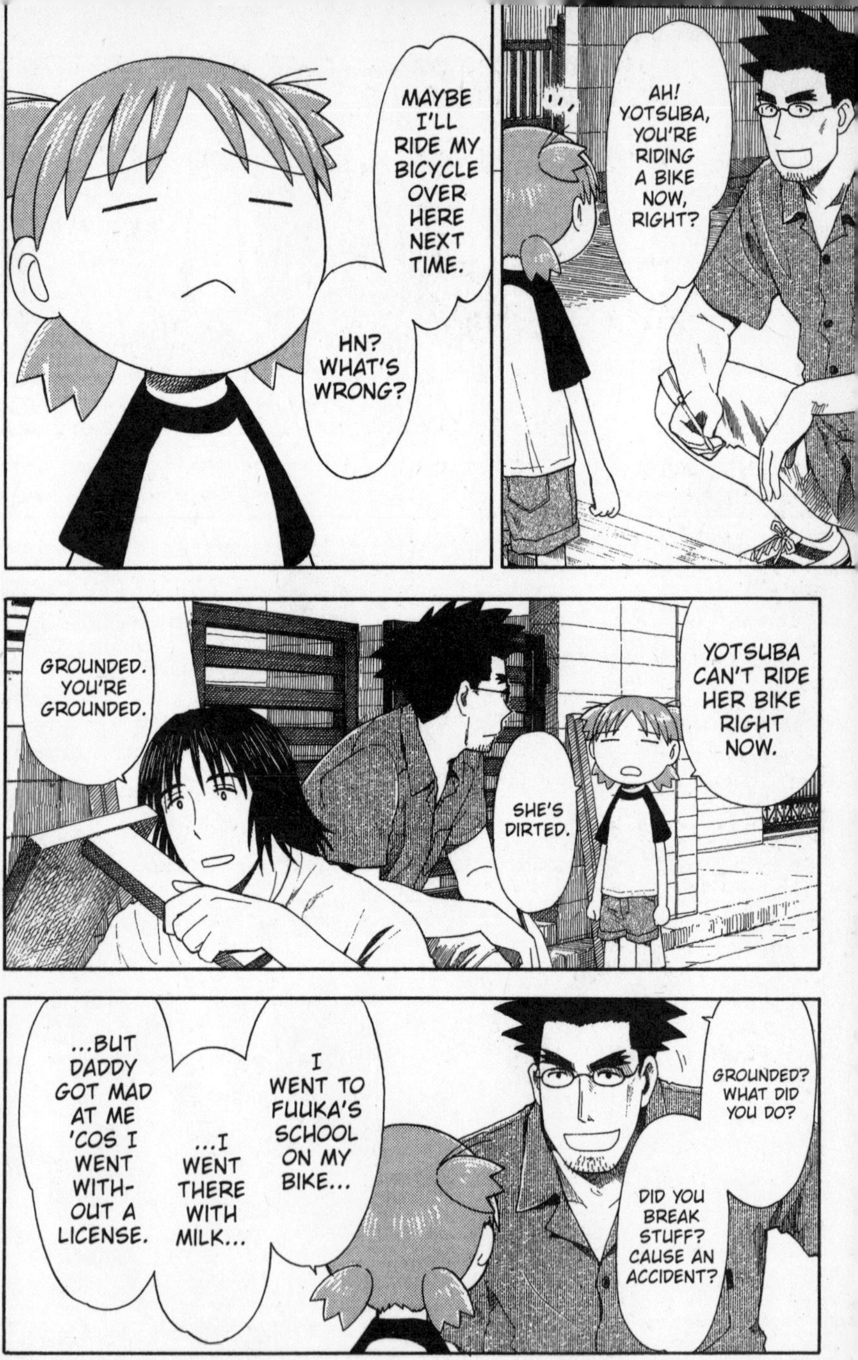
AH! YOTSUBA, YOU'RE RIDING A BIKE NOW, RIGHT?
MAYBE I'LL RIDE MY BICYCLE OVER HERE NEXT TIME.
HN? WHAT'S WRONG?
YOTSUBA CAN'T RIDE HER BIKE RIGHT NOW.
SHE'S DIRTED.
GROUNDED. YOU'RE GROUNDED.
GROUNDED? WHAT DID YOU DO?
DID YOU BREAK STUFF? CAUSE AN ACCIDENT?
I WENT TO FUUKA'S SCHOOL ON MY BIKE...
...I WENT THERE WITH MILK...
...BUT DADDY GOT MAD AT ME 'COS I WENT WITH-OUT A LICENSE.

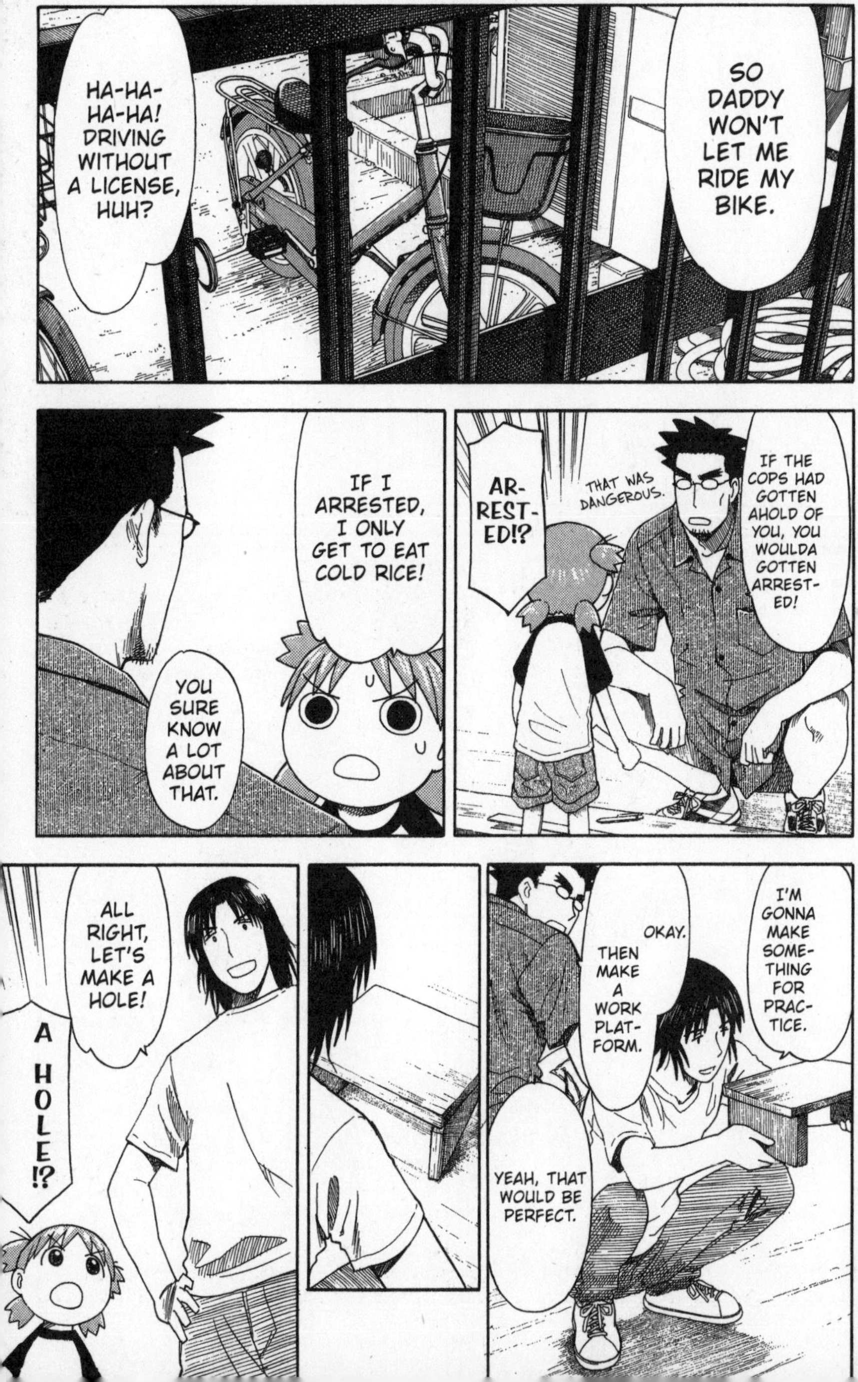
SO DADDY WON'T LET ME RIDE MY BIKE.
HA-HA-HA-HA! DRIVING WITHOUT A LICENSE, HUH?
IF THE COPS HAD GOTTEN AHOLD OF YOU, YOU WOULDA GOTTEN ARREST-ED!
THAT WAS DANGEROUS.
AR-REST-ED!?
IF I ARRESTED, I ONLY GET TO EAT COLD RICE!
YOU SURE KNOW A LOT ABOUT THAT.
I'M GONNA MAKE SOME-THING FOR PRAC-TICE.
OKAY.
THEN MAKE A WORK PLAT-FORM.
YEAH, THAT WOULD BE PERFECT.
ALL RIGHT, LET'S MAKE A HOLE!
A HOLE!?

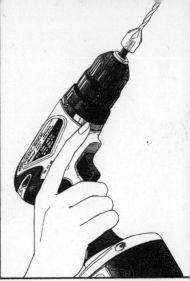

OHHHH!!

WHAT'S THAT!? IT'S COOL!!

A DRILL !?

THIS IS A DRILL.

HERE I GO! WATCH THIS.

SFX: NIIIII (VWEEEEEEN)

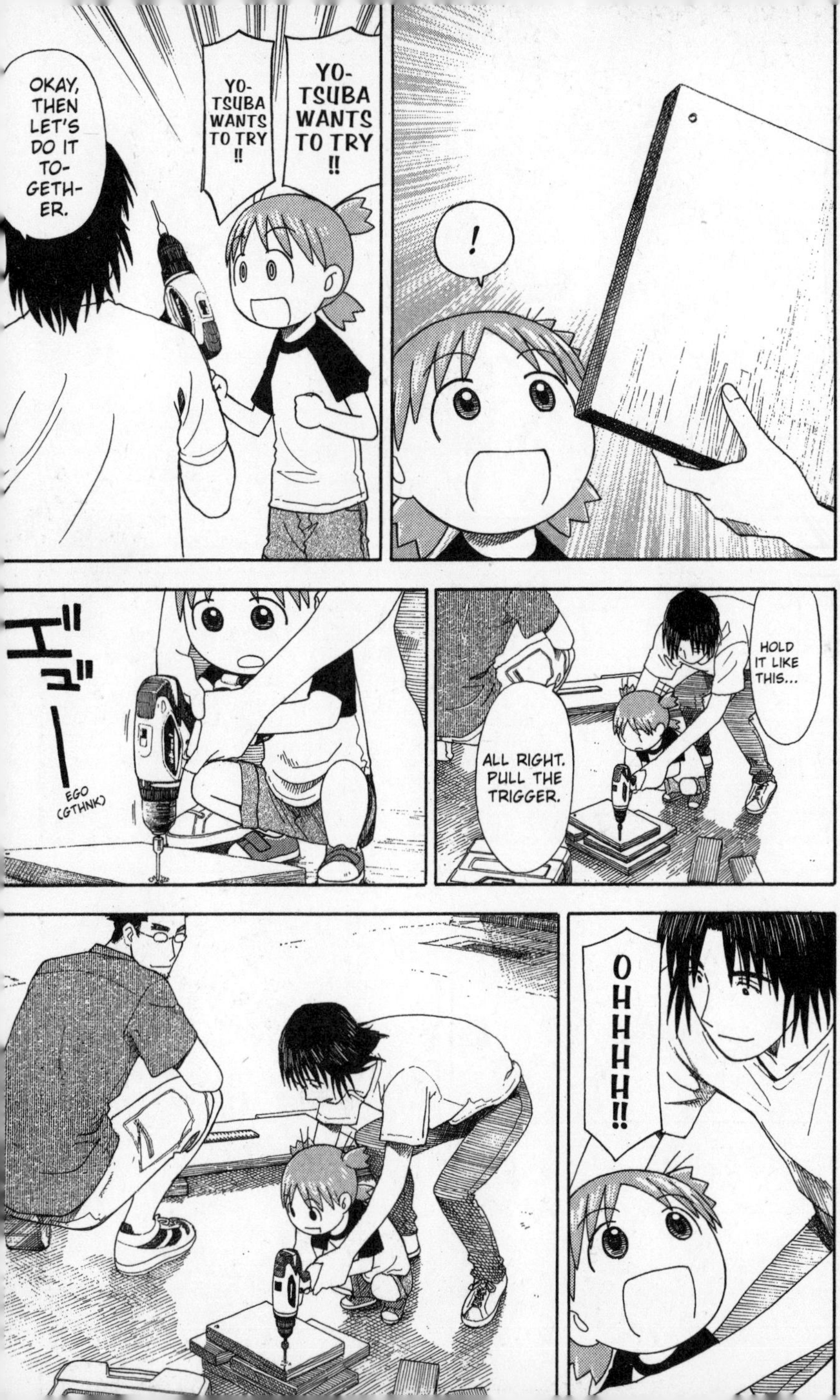
!
YO-TSUBA WANTS TO TRY!!
YO-TSUBA WANTS TO TRY!!
OKAY, THEN LET'S DO IT TO-GETH-ER.
HOLD IT LIKE THIS...
ALL RIGHT. PULL THE TRIGGER.
ギュー
EGO (GTHNK)
OHHHHH!!

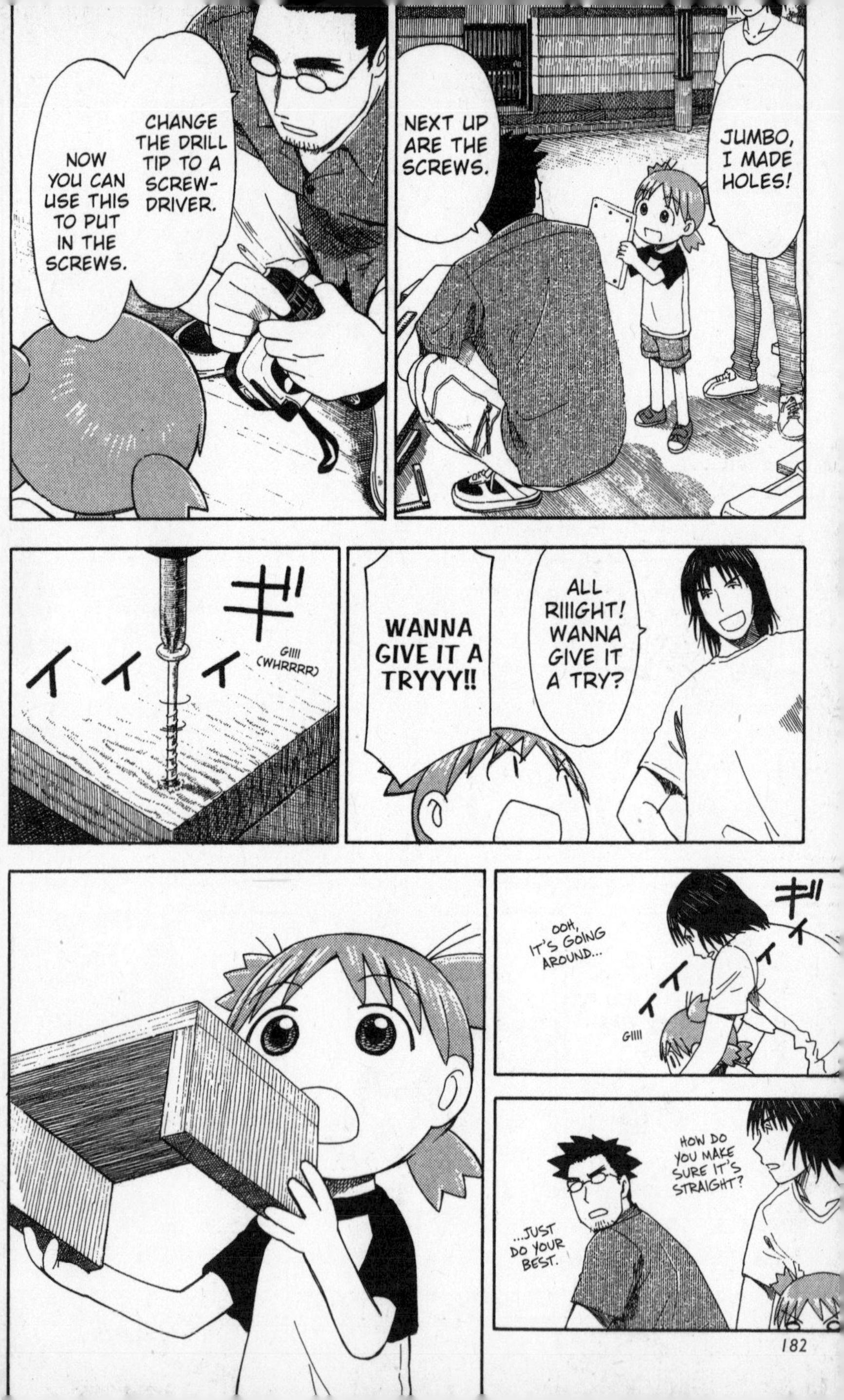
JUMBO, I MADE HOLES!
NEXT UP ARE THE SCREWS.
CHANGE THE DRILL TIP TO A SCREW-DRIVER.
NOW YOU CAN USE THIS TO PUT IN THE SCREWS.
ALL RIIIGHT! WANNA GIVE IT A TRY?
WANNA GIVE IT A TRYYY!!
ギイイイ
GIIII (WHRRRR)
ギイイイ
OOH, IT'S GOING AROUND...
GIIII
HOW DO YOU MAKE SURE IT'S STRAIGHT?
...JUST DO YOUR BEST.

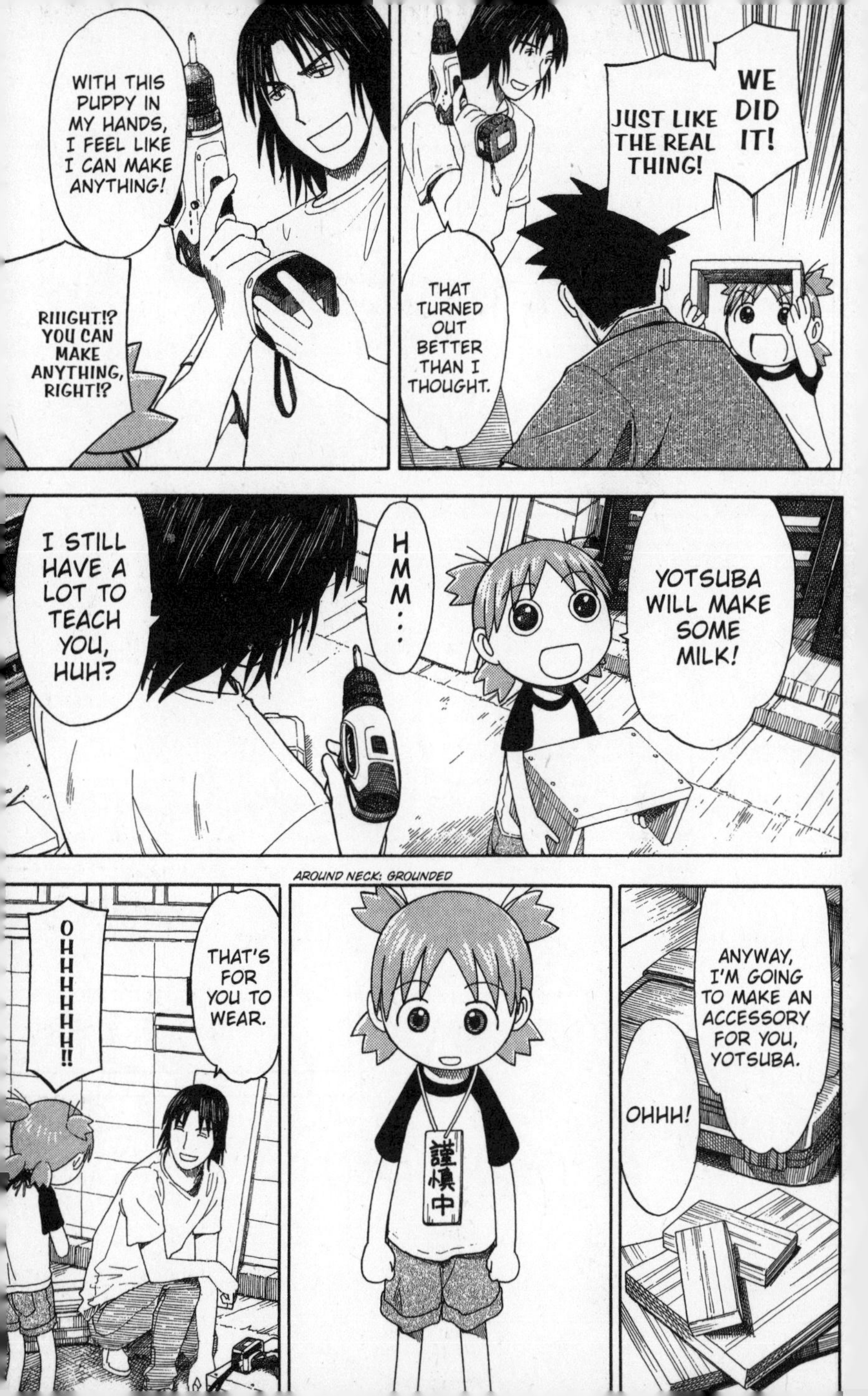
WE DID IT!
JUST LIKE THE REAL THING!
THAT TURNED OUT BETTER THAN I THOUGHT.
WITH THIS PUPPY IN MY HANDS, I FEEL LIKE I CAN MAKE ANYTHING!
RIIIGHT!? YOU CAN MAKE ANYTHING, RIGHT!?
YOTSUBA WILL MAKE SOME MILK!
HMM...
I STILL HAVE A LOT TO TEACH YOU, HUH?
ANYWAY, I'M GOING TO MAKE AN ACCESSORY FOR YOU, YOTSUBA.
OHHH!
AROUND NECK: GROUNDED
謹慎中
THAT'S FOR YOU TO WEAR.
OHHHHHH!!

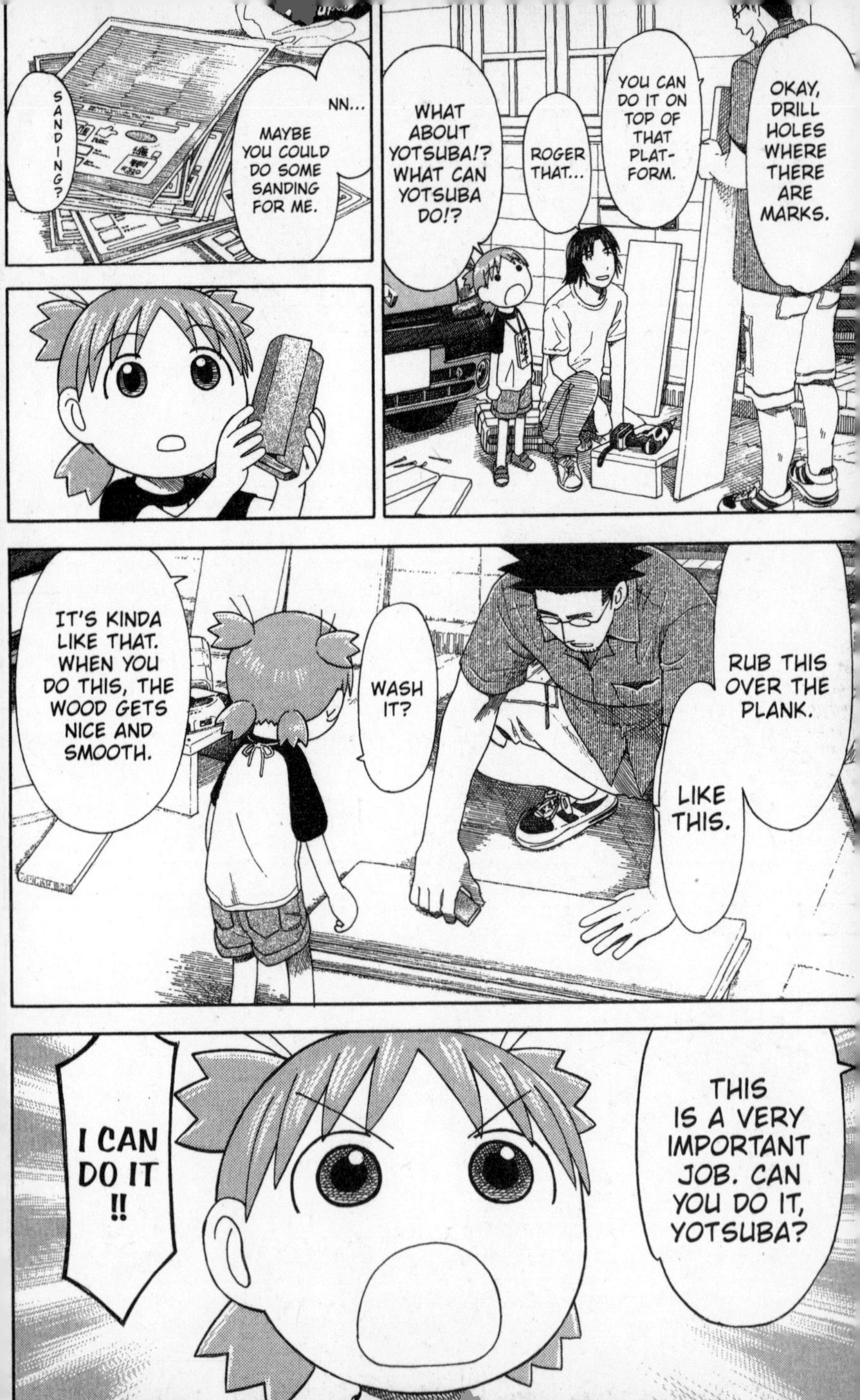
OKAY, DRILL HOLES WHERE THERE ARE MARKS.
YOU CAN DO IT ON TOP OF THAT PLATFORM.
ROGER THAT...
WHAT ABOUT YOTSUBA!? WHAT CAN YOTSUBA DO!?
NN...
MAYBE YOU COULD DO SOME SANDING FOR ME.
SANDING?
RUB THIS OVER THE PLANK.
LIKE THIS.
WASH IT?
IT'S KINDA LIKE THAT. WHEN YOU DO THIS, THE WOOD GETS NICE AND SMOOTH.
THIS IS A VERY IMPORTANT JOB. CAN YOU DO IT, YOTSUBA?
I CAN DO IT !!

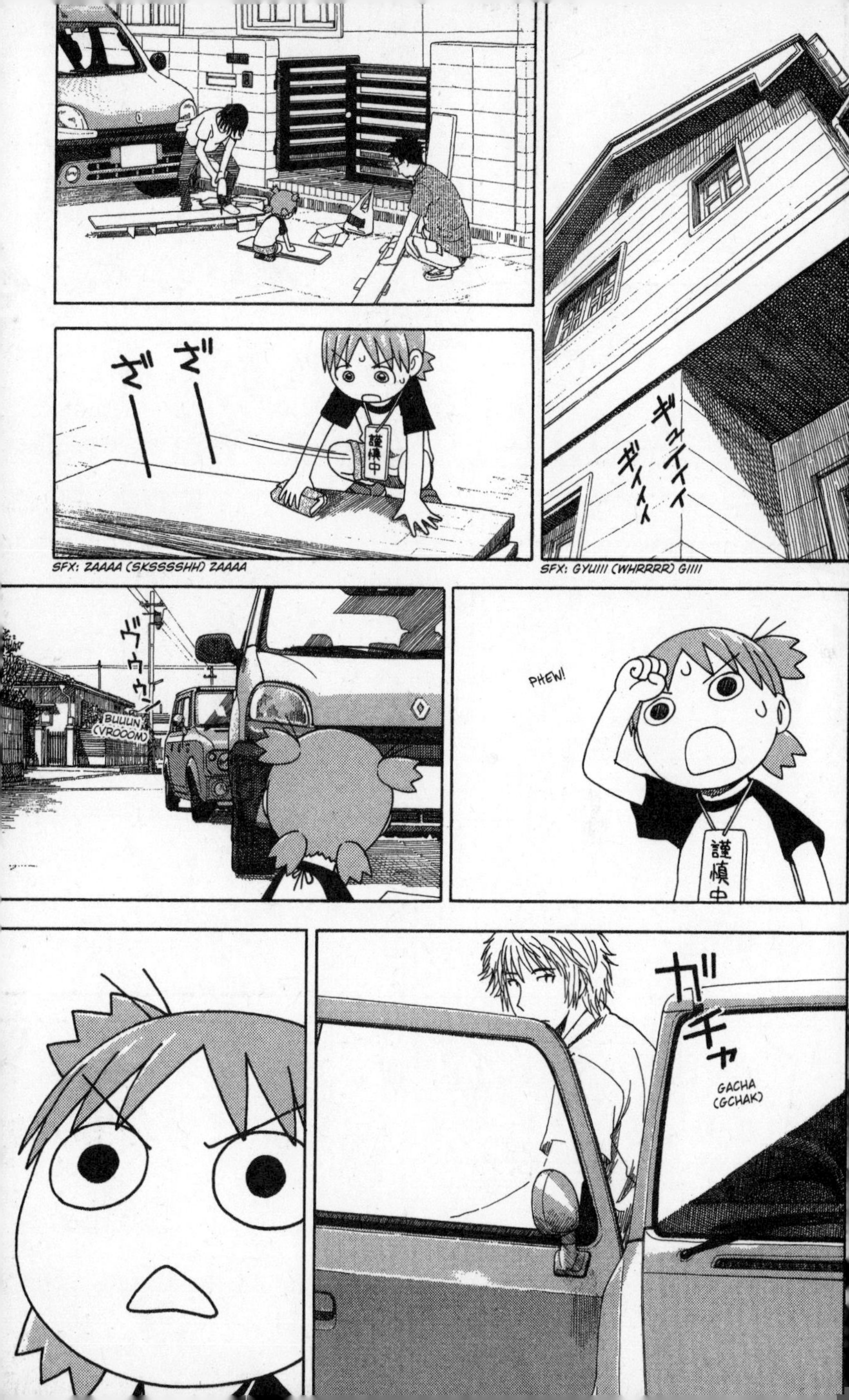
ギュイイ ギイイ
SFX: GYUIII (WHRRRR) GIIII
ざー ざー
謹慎中
SFX: ZAAAA (SKSSSSHH) ZAAAA
PHEW!
謹慎中
ヴウゥウン
BUUUN (VROOOM)
ガチャ
GACHA (GCHAK)

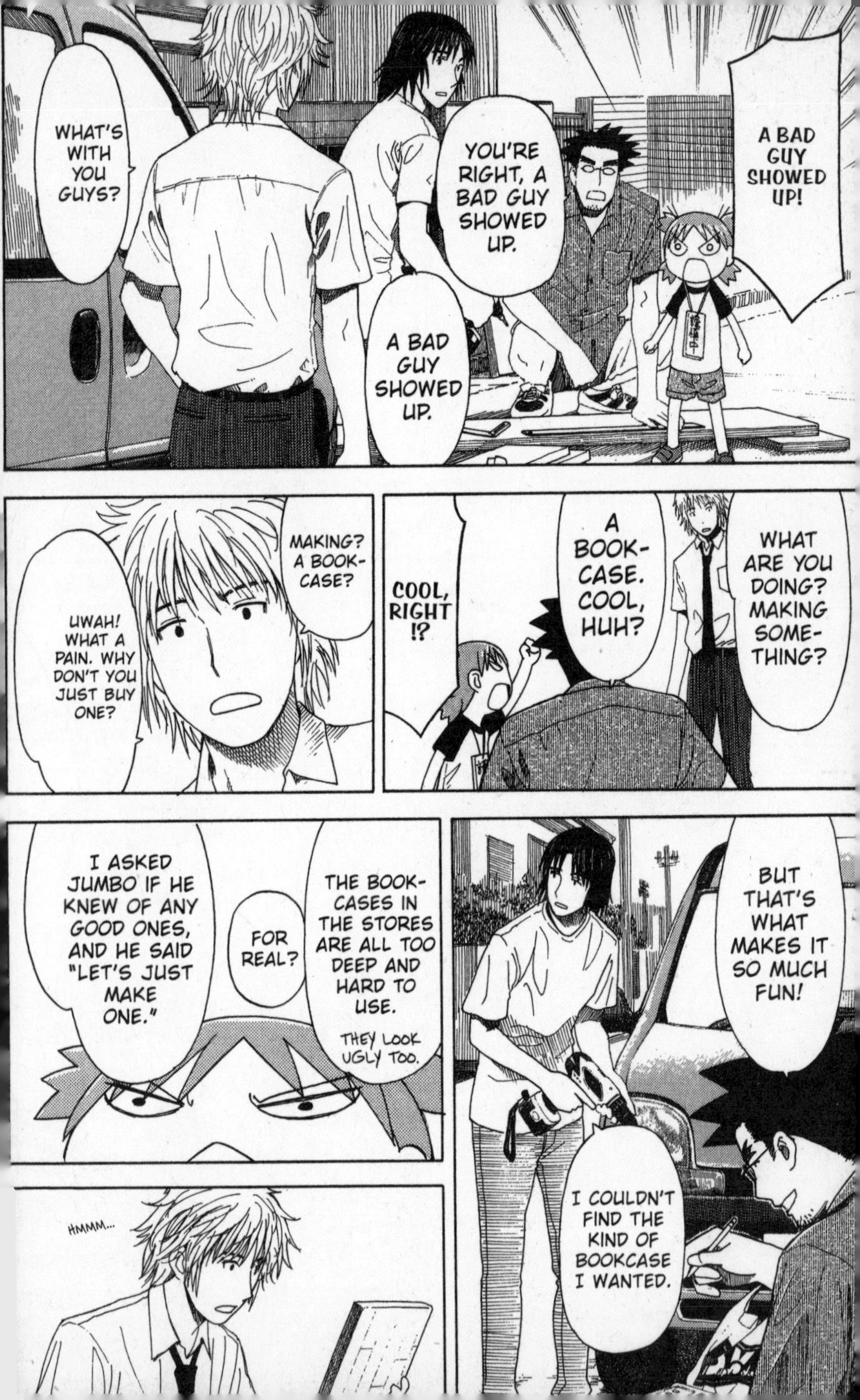
A BAD GUY SHOWED UP!
YOU'RE RIGHT, A BAD GUY SHOWED UP.
A BAD GUY SHOWED UP.
WHAT'S WITH YOU GUYS?
WHAT ARE YOU DOING? MAKING SOMETHING?
A BOOK-CASE. COOL, HUH?
COOL, RIGHT!?
MAKING? A BOOK-CASE?
UWAH! WHAT A PAIN. WHY DON'T YOU JUST BUY ONE?
BUT THAT'S WHAT MAKES IT SO MUCH FUN!
I COULDN'T FIND THE KIND OF BOOKCASE I WANTED.
THE BOOK-CASES IN THE STORES ARE ALL TOO DEEP AND HARD TO USE.
THEY LOOK UGLY TOO.
FOR REAL?
I ASKED JUMBO IF HE KNEW OF ANY GOOD ONES, AND HE SAID "LET'S JUST MAKE ONE."
HMMM...

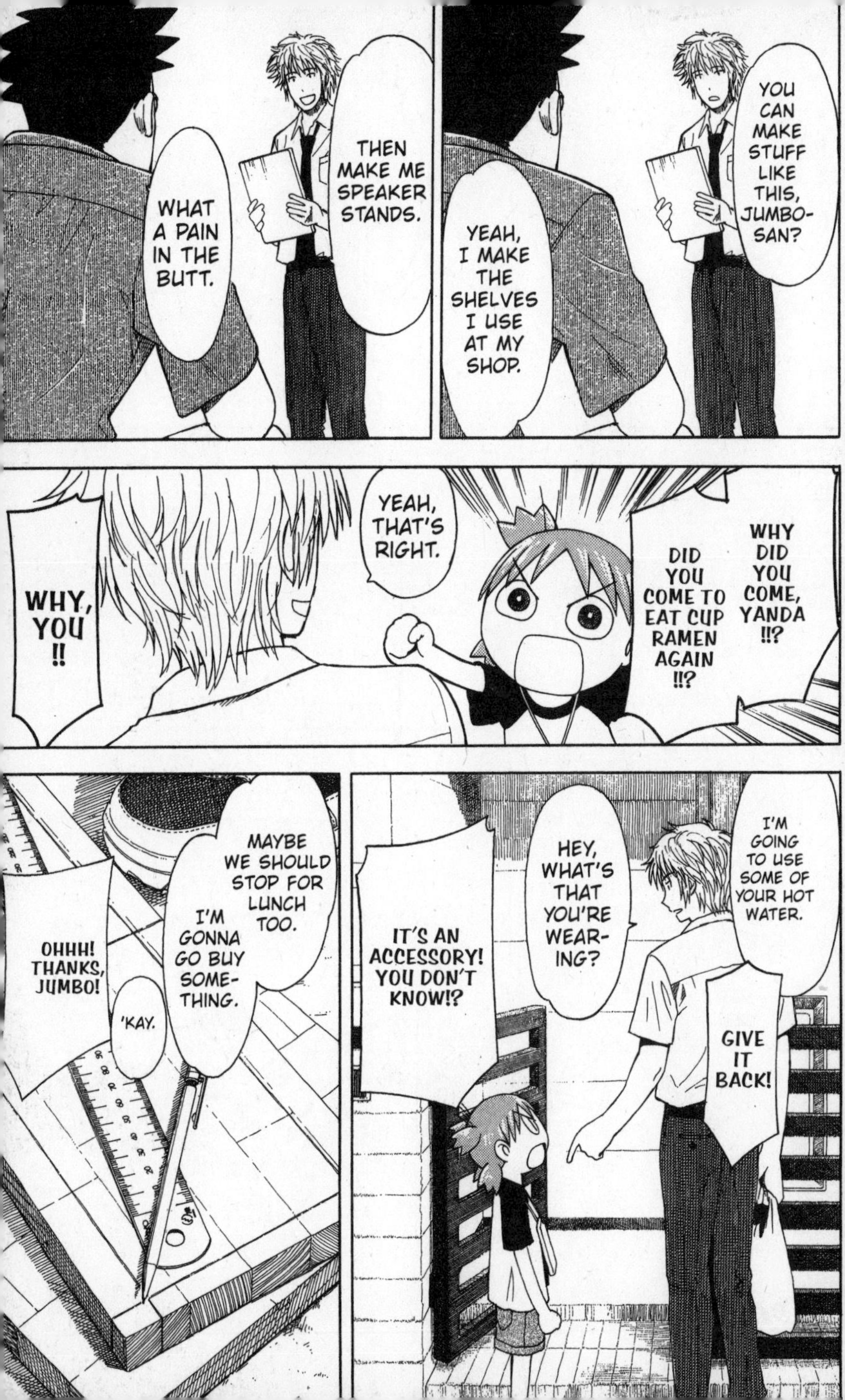
YOU CAN MAKE STUFF LIKE THIS, JUMBO-SAN?
YEAH, I MAKE THE SHELVES I USE AT MY SHOP.
THEN MAKE ME SPEAKER STANDS.
WHAT A PAIN IN THE BUTT.
WHY DID YOU COME, YANDA!!?
DID YOU COME TO EAT CUP RAMEN AGAIN!!?
YEAH, THAT'S RIGHT.
WHY, YOU!!
I'M GOING TO USE SOME OF YOUR HOT WATER.
HEY, WHAT'S THAT YOU'RE WEARING?
GIVE IT BACK!
IT'S AN ACCESSORY! YOU DON'T KNOW!?
MAYBE WE SHOULD STOP FOR LUNCH TOO.
I'M GONNA GO BUY SOMETHING.
'KAY.
OHHH! THANKS, JUMBO!

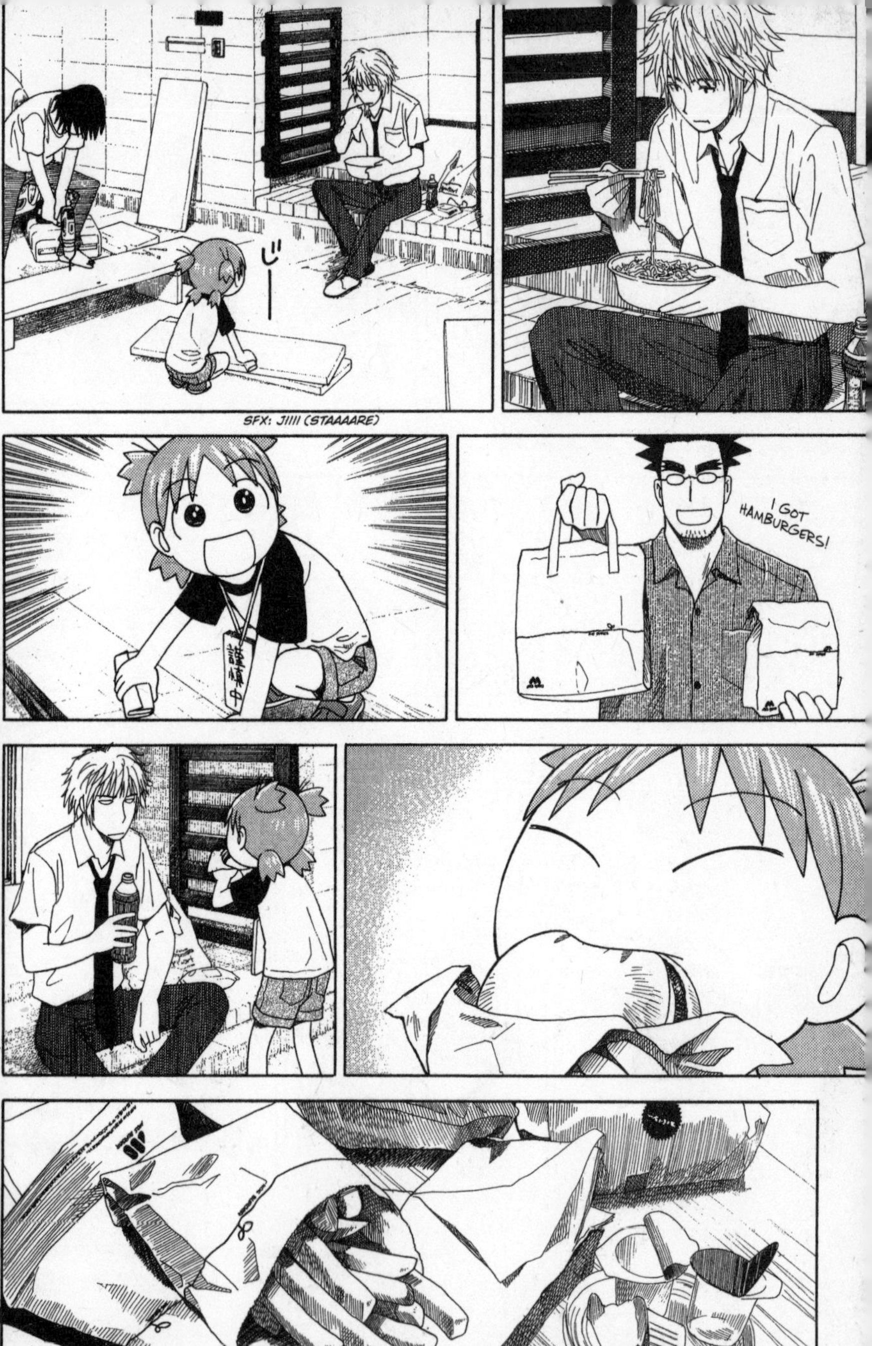
じー
SFX: JIIII (STAAAARE)
I GOT HAMBURGERS!
謹慎中

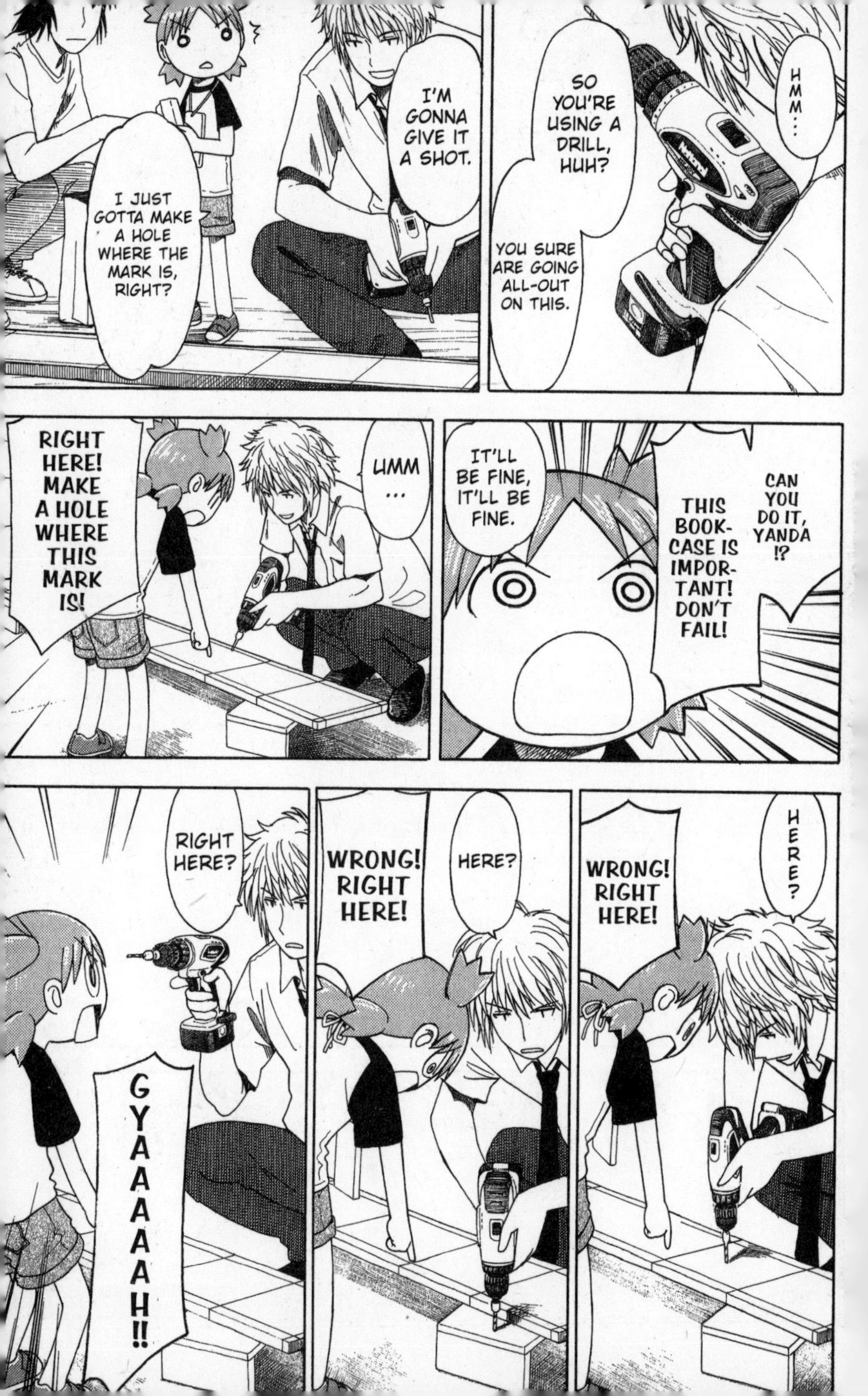
HMM...
SO YOU'RE USING A DRILL, HUH?
YOU SURE ARE GOING ALL-OUT ON THIS.
I'M GONNA GIVE IT A SHOT.
I JUST GOTTA MAKE A HOLE WHERE THE MARK IS, RIGHT?
CAN YOU DO IT, YANDA!?
THIS BOOKCASE IS IMPORTANT! DON'T FAIL!
IT'LL BE FINE, IT'LL BE FINE.
UMM...
RIGHT HERE! MAKE A HOLE WHERE THIS MARK IS!
HERE?
WRONG! RIGHT HERE!
HERE?
WRONG! RIGHT HERE!
RIGHT HERE?
GYAAAAAH!!

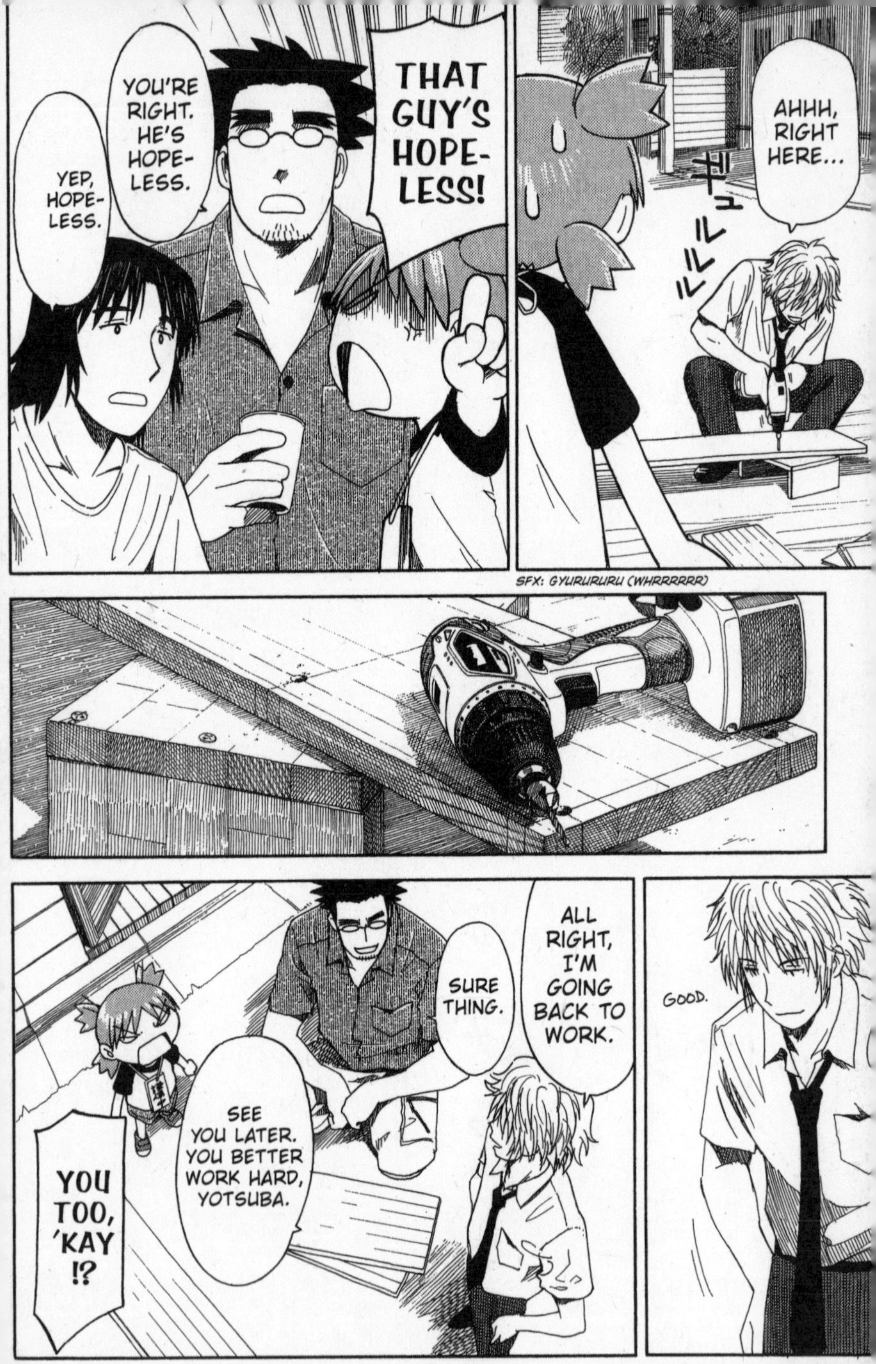
AHHH, RIGHT HERE...
SFX: GYURURURU (WHRRRRRR)
THAT GUY'S HOPE-LESS!
YOU'RE RIGHT. HE'S HOPE-LESS.
YEP, HOPE-LESS.
GOOD.
ALL RIGHT, I'M GOING BACK TO WORK.
SURE THING.
SEE YOU LATER. YOU BETTER WORK HARD, YOTSUBA.
YOU TOO, 'KAY!?

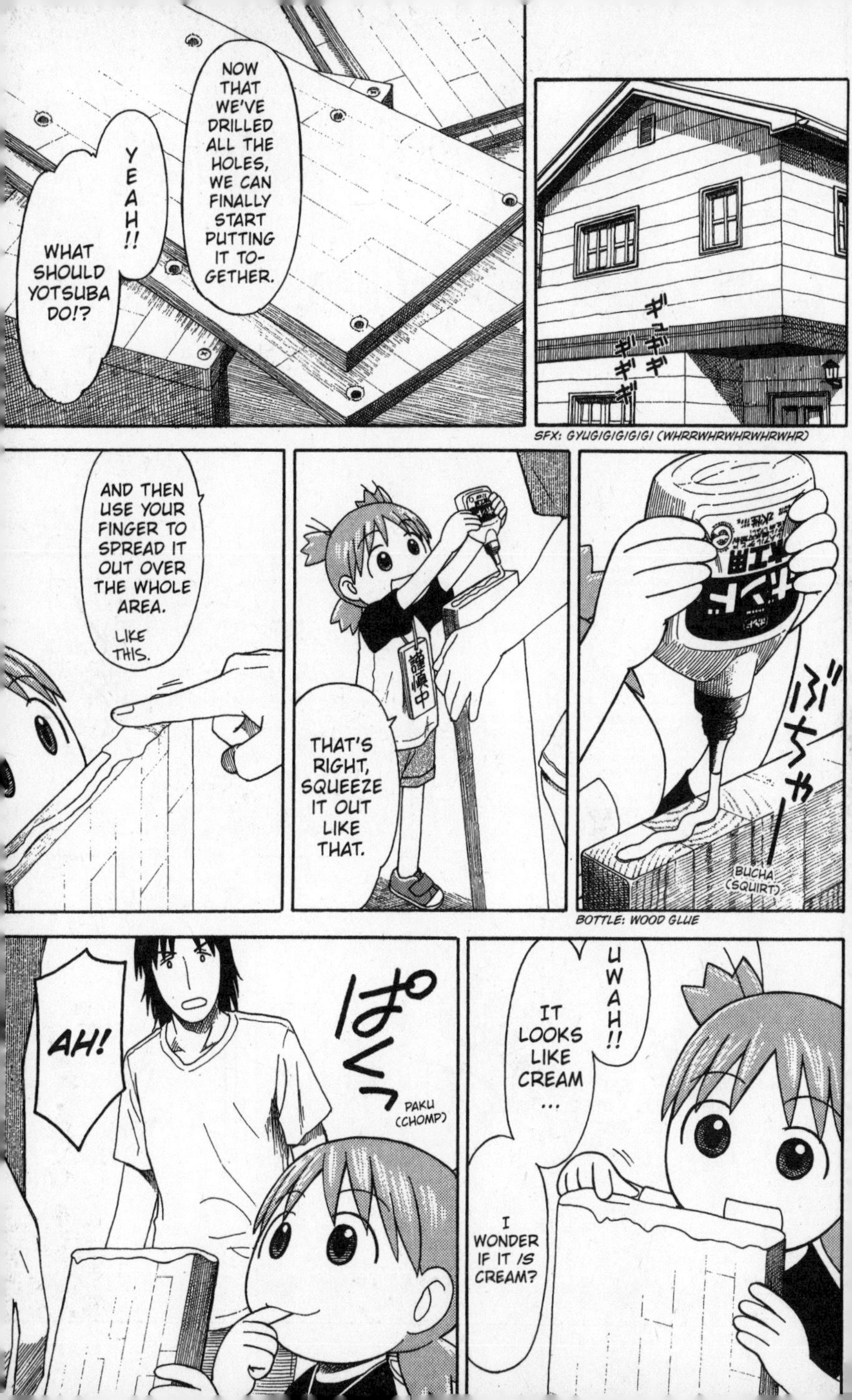
SFX: GYUGIGIGIGIGI (WHRRWHRWHRWHRWHR)
NOW THAT WE'VE DRILLED ALL THE HOLES, WE CAN FINALLY START PUTTING IT TO-GETHER.
YEAH!!
WHAT SHOULD YOTSUBA DO!?
BUCHA (SQUIRT)
BOTTLE: WOOD GLUE
THAT'S RIGHT, SQUEEZE IT OUT LIKE THAT.
AND THEN USE YOUR FINGER TO SPREAD IT OUT OVER THE WHOLE AREA.
LIKE THIS.
UWAH!!
IT LOOKS LIKE CREAM...
I WONDER IF IT IS CREAM?
PAKU (CHOMP)
AH!

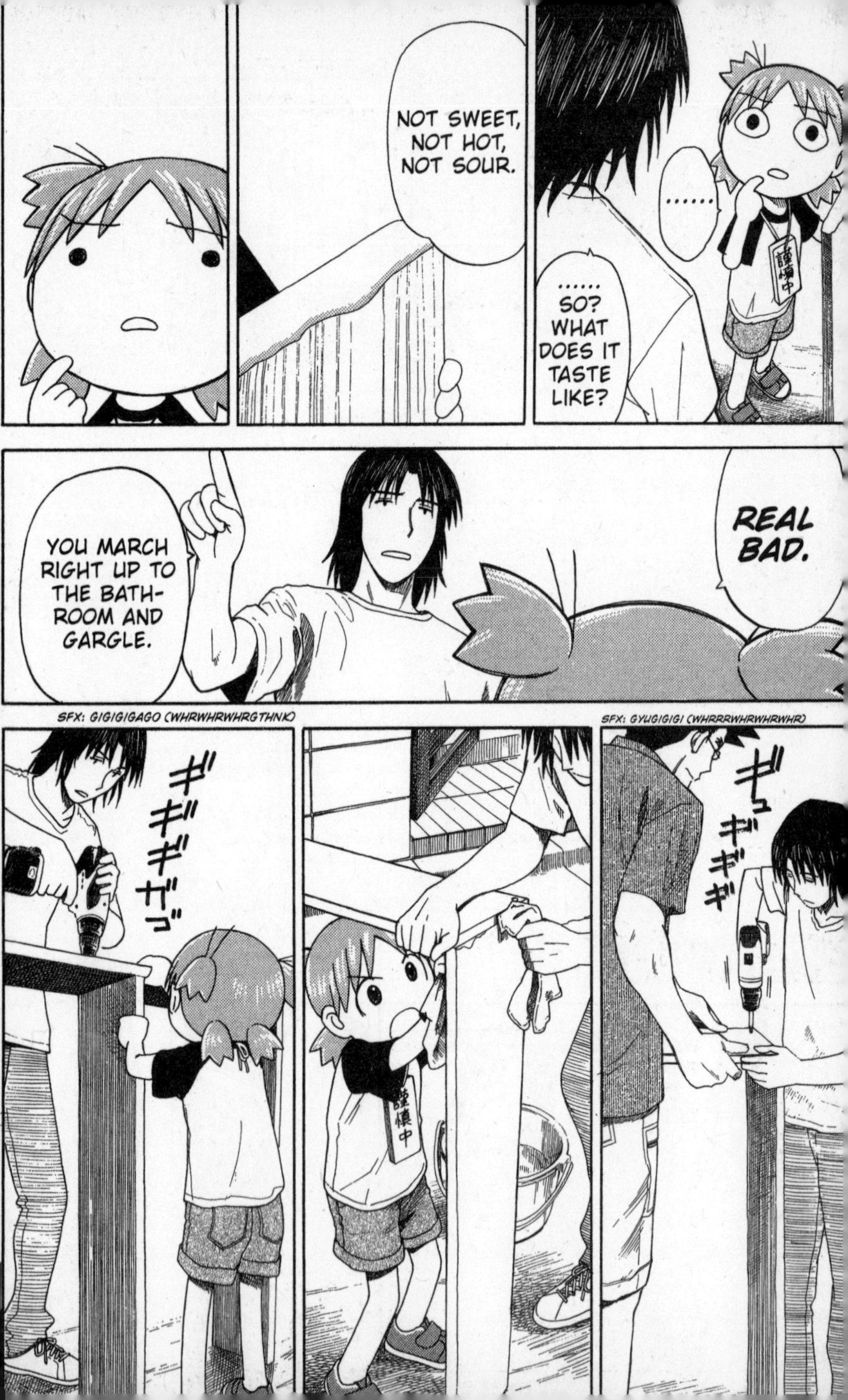
......
謹慎中
......
SO? WHAT DOES IT TASTE LIKE?
NOT SWEET, NOT HOT, NOT SOUR.
REAL BAD.
YOU MARCH RIGHT UP TO THE BATH-ROOM AND GARGLE.
SFX: GYUGIGIGI (WHRRRWHRWHRWHR)
ギュギギギ
謹慎中
SFX: GIGIGIGAGO (WHRWHRWHRGTHNK)
ギギギガゴ

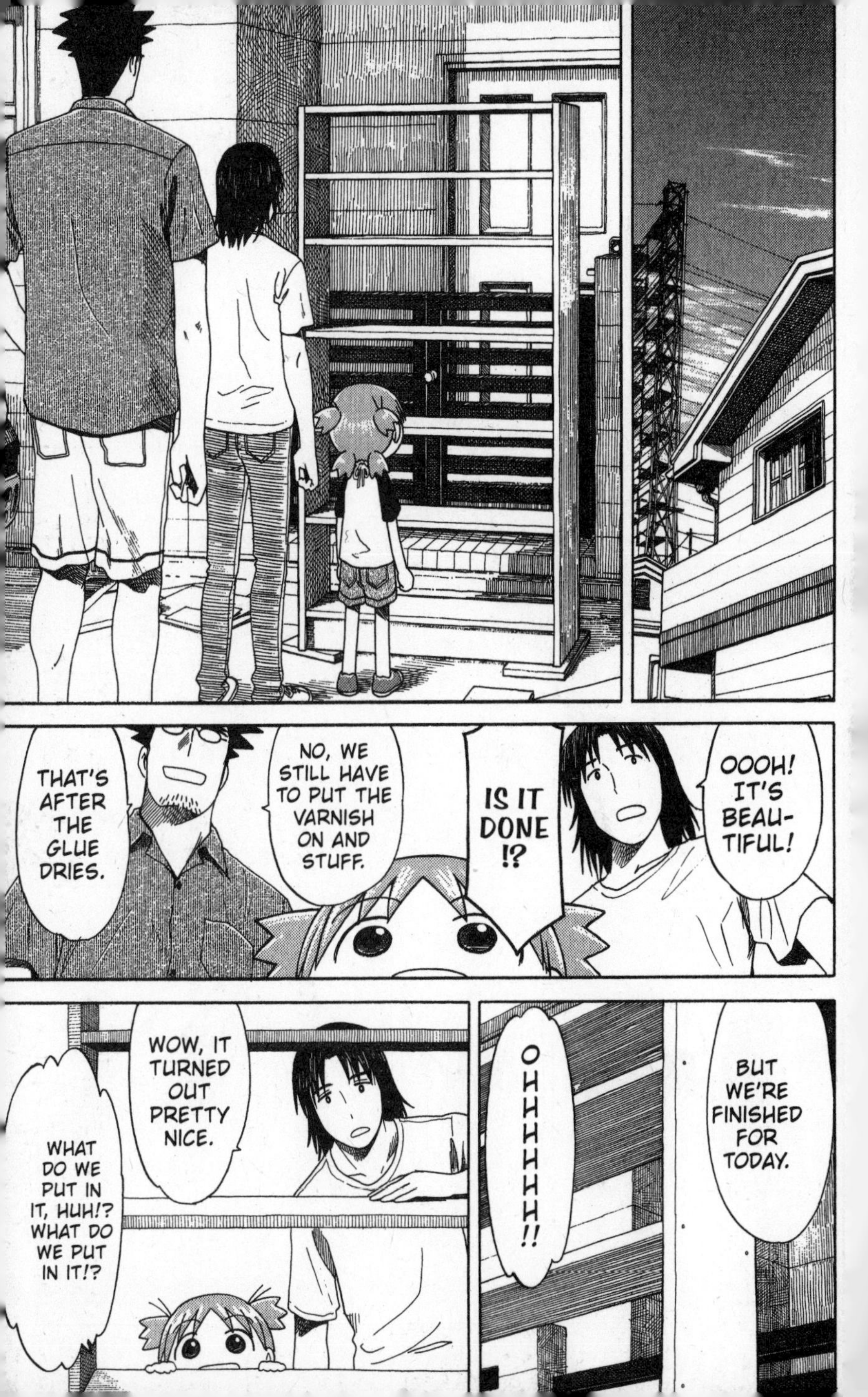
OOOH! IT'S BEAU-TIFUL!
IS IT DONE!?
NO, WE STILL HAVE TO PUT THE VARNISH ON AND STUFF.
THAT'S AFTER THE GLUE DRIES.
BUT WE'RE FINISHED FOR TODAY.
OHHHHHH!!
WOW, IT TURNED OUT PRETTY NICE.
WHAT DO WE PUT IN IT, HUH!? WHAT DO WE PUT IN IT!?

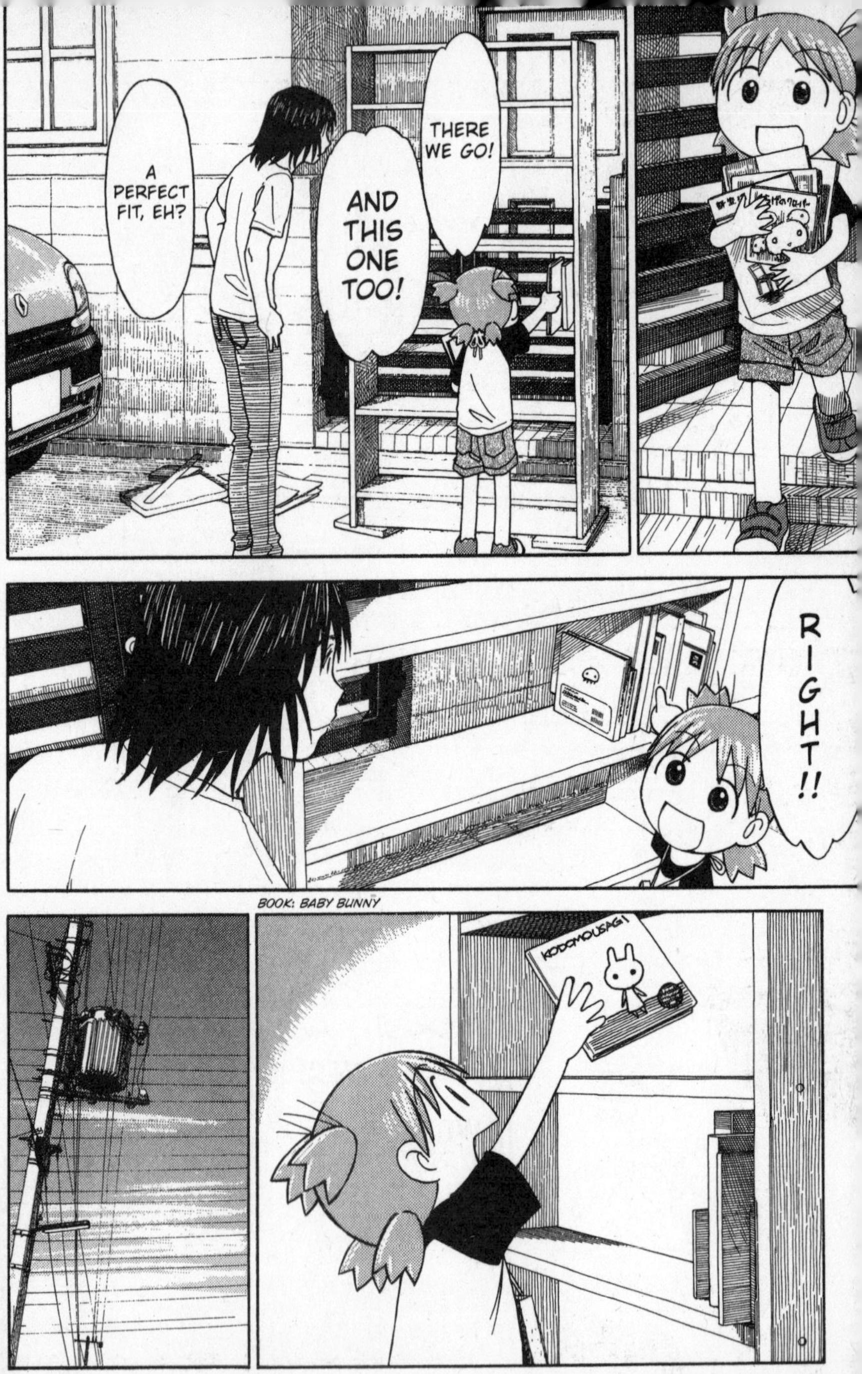
THERE WE GO!
AND THIS ONE TOO!
A PERFECT FIT, EH?
RIGHT!!
BOOK: BABY BUNNY
KODOMOUSAGI

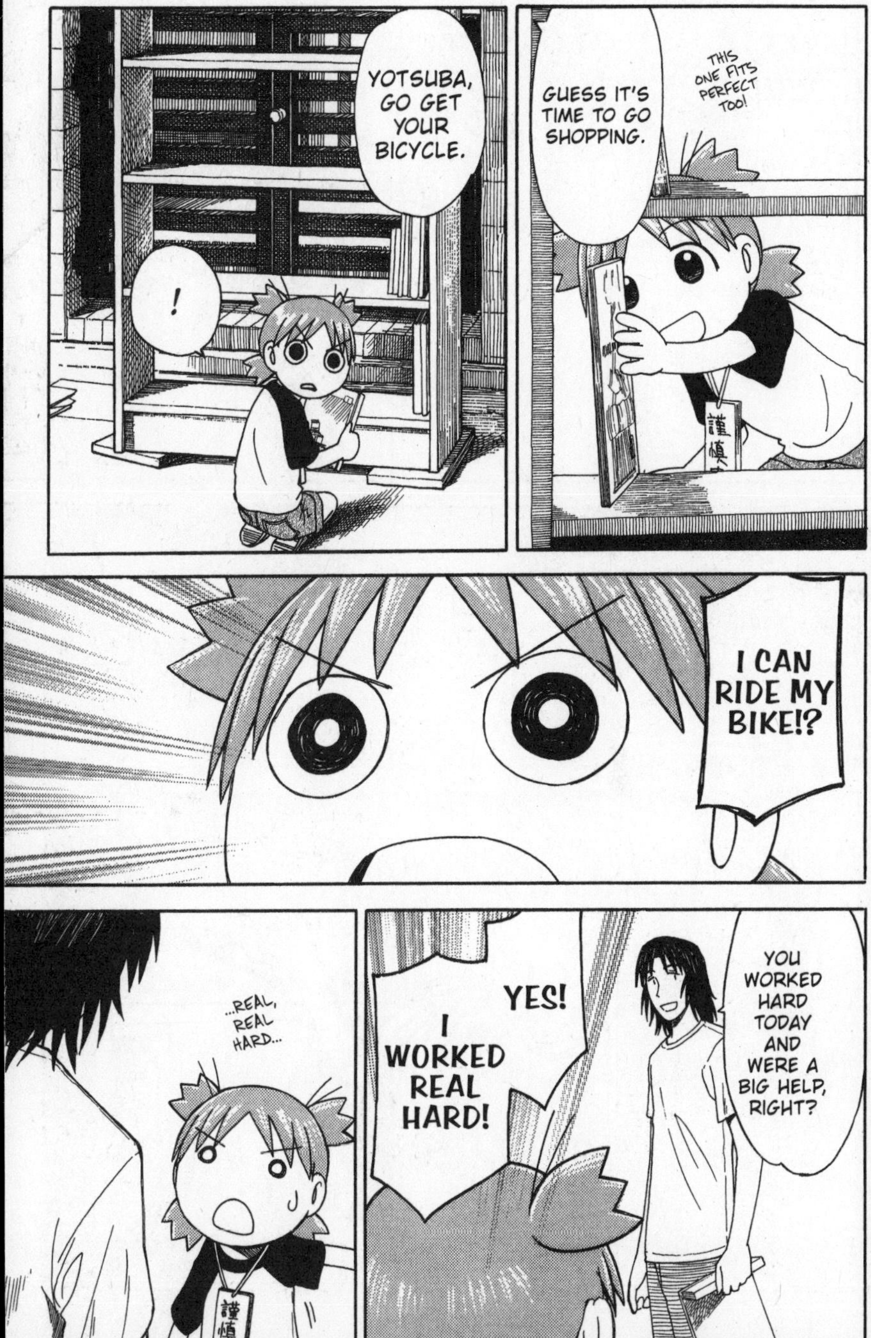
GUESS IT'S TIME TO GO SHOPPING.
THIS ONE FITS PERFECT TOO!
YOTSUBA, GO GET YOUR BICYCLE.
!
I CAN RIDE MY BIKE!?
YOU WORKED HARD TODAY AND WERE A BIG HELP, RIGHT?
YES!
I WORKED REAL HARD!
...REAL, REAL HARD...
謹慎中

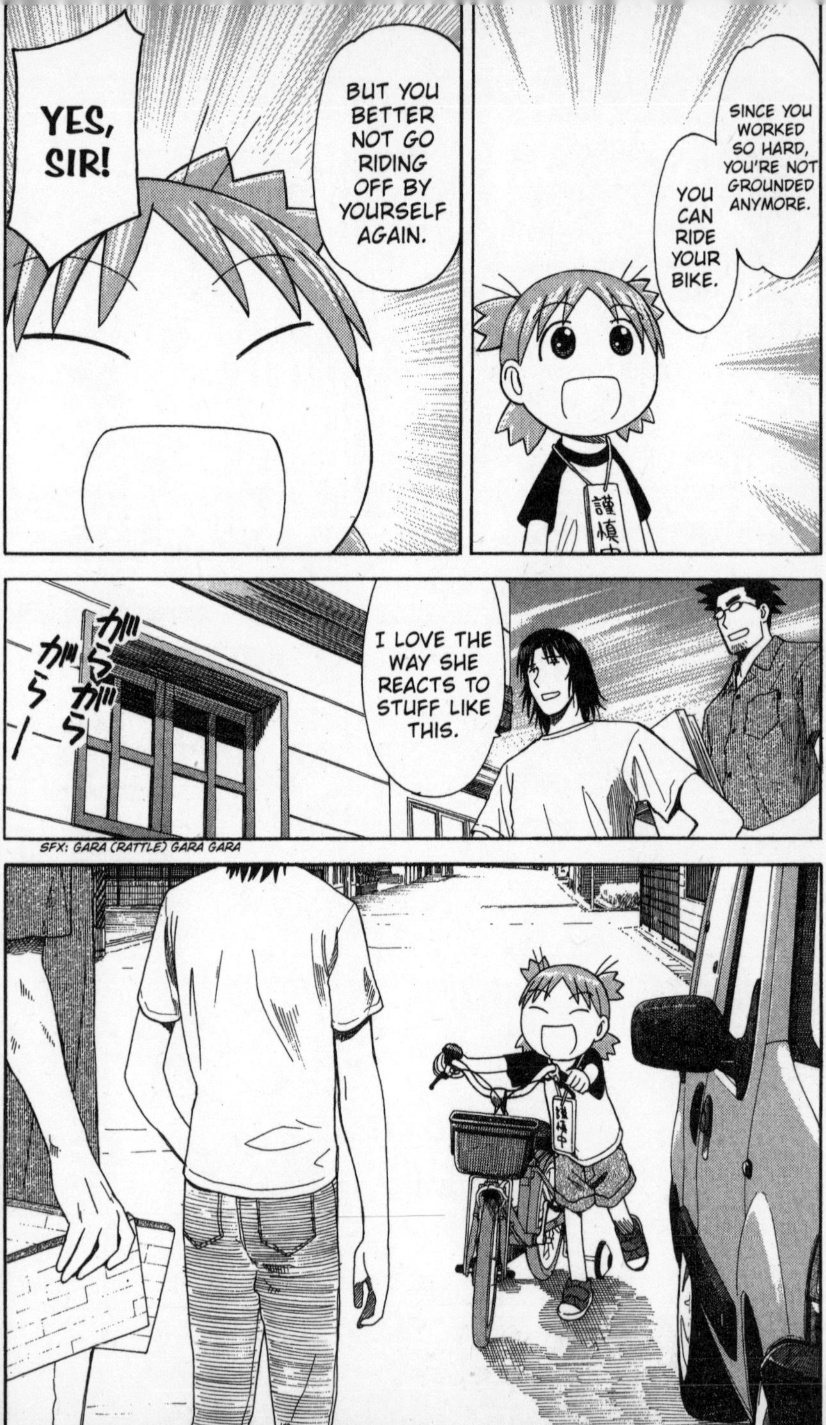
SINCE YOU WORKED SO HARD, YOU'RE NOT GROUNDED ANYMORE.
YOU CAN RIDE YOUR BIKE.
BUT YOU BETTER NOT GO RIDING OFF BY YOURSELF AGAIN.
YES, SIR!
がらがらがら～！
I LOVE THE WAY SHE REACTS TO STUFF LIKE THIS.
SFX: GARA (RATTLE) GARA GARA

YOTSUBA&!

YOTSUBA&!

7

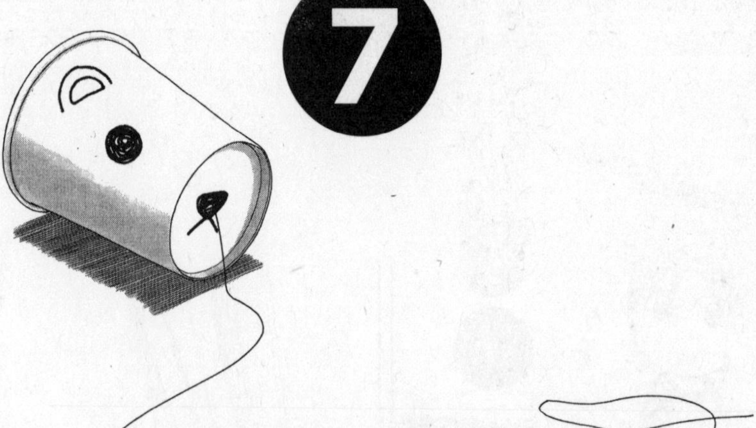

PREVIEW

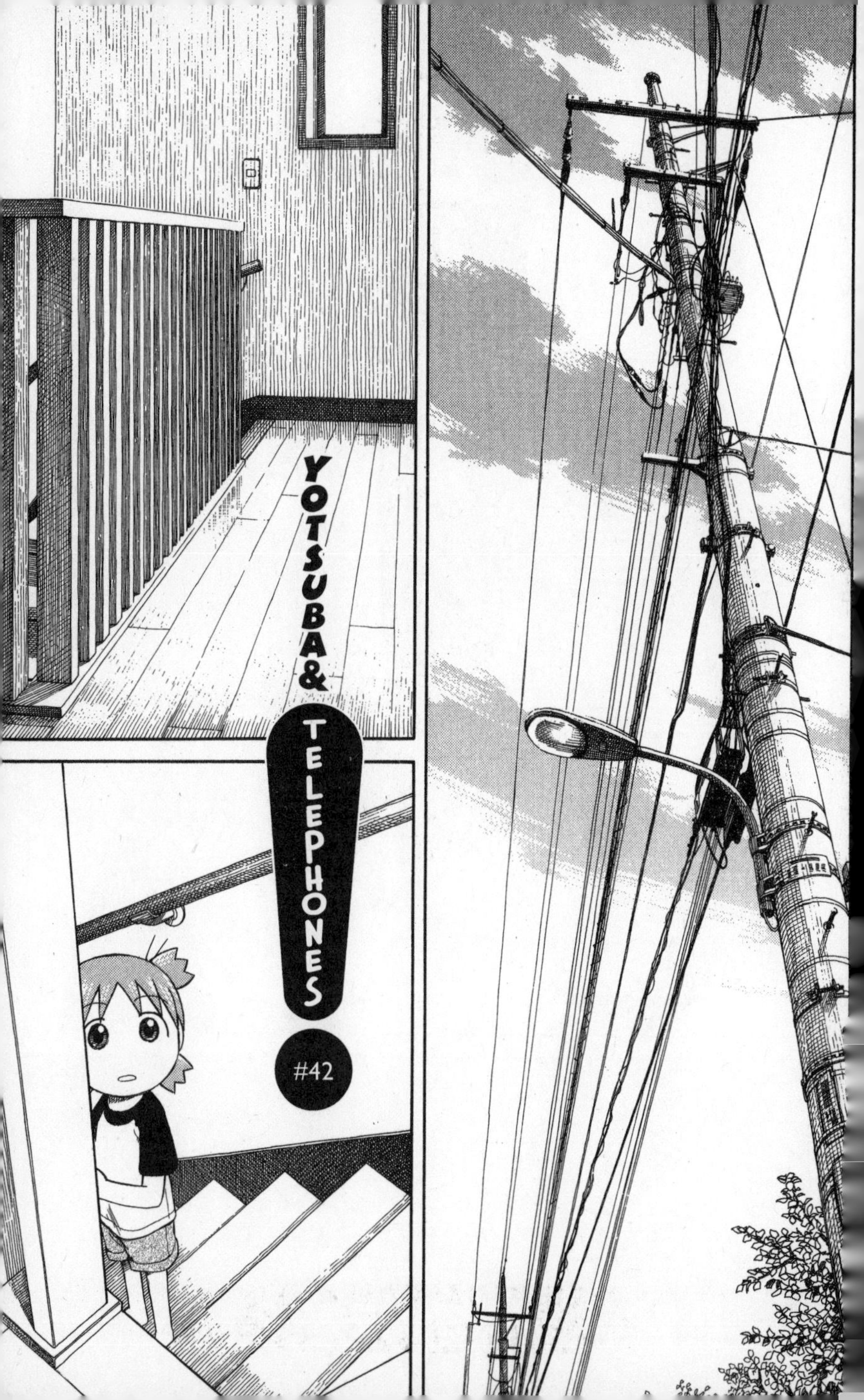
YOTSUBA&
TELEPHONES!
#42

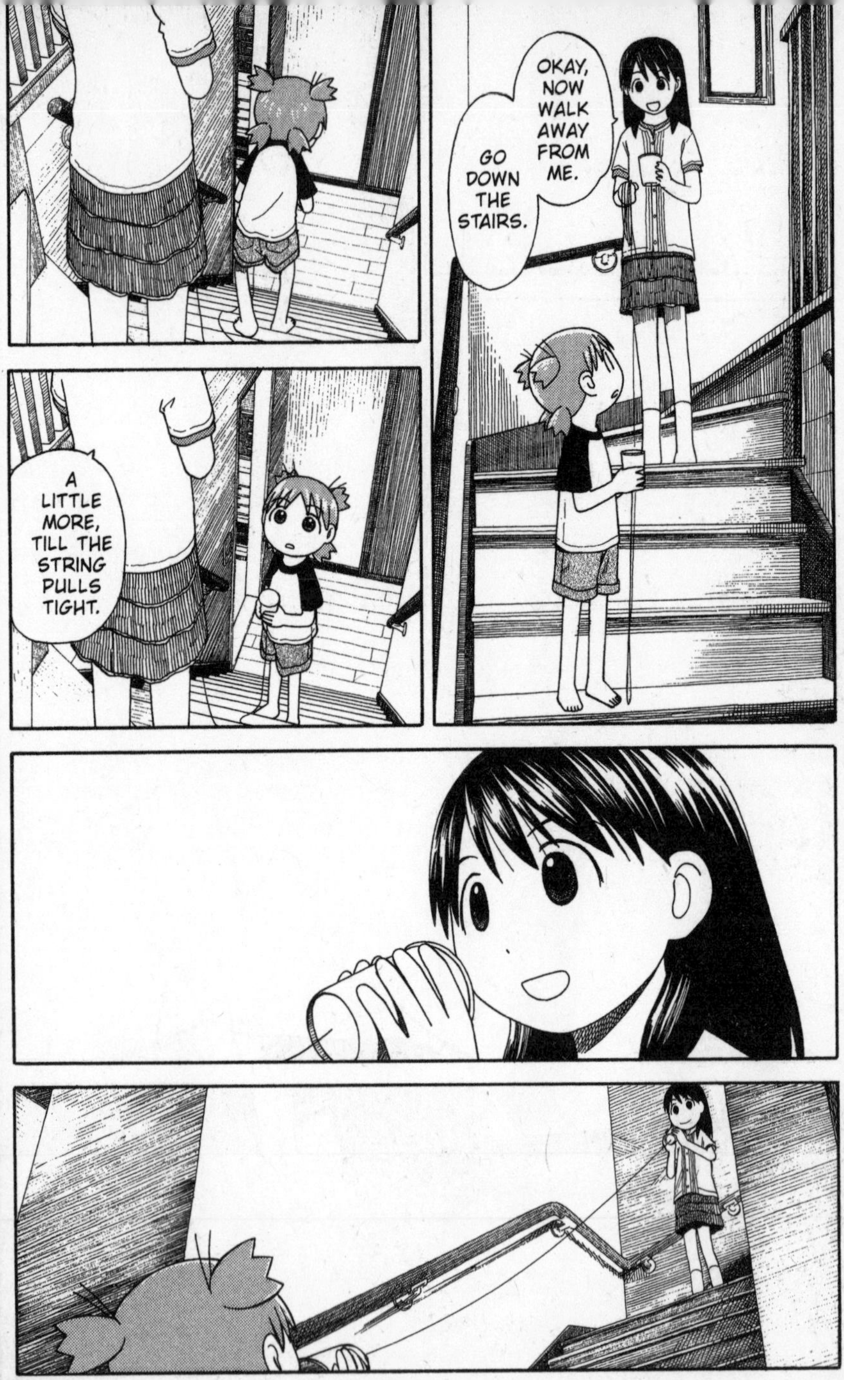
OKAY, NOW WALK AWAY FROM ME.
GO DOWN THE STAIRS.
A LITTLE MORE, TILL THE STRING PULLS TIGHT.

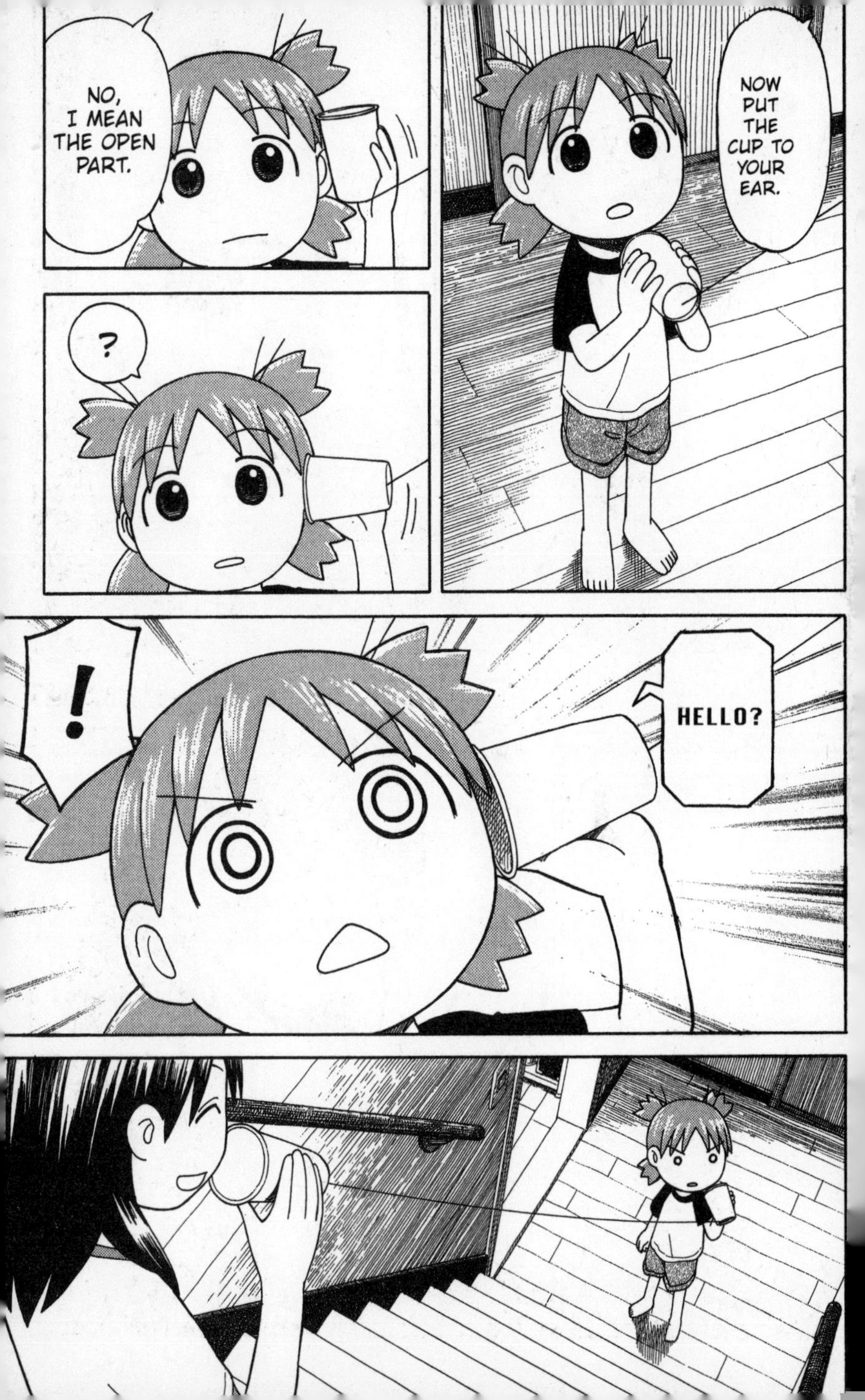
NOW PUT THE CUP TO YOUR EAR.
NO, I MEAN THE OPEN PART.
?
HELLO?
!

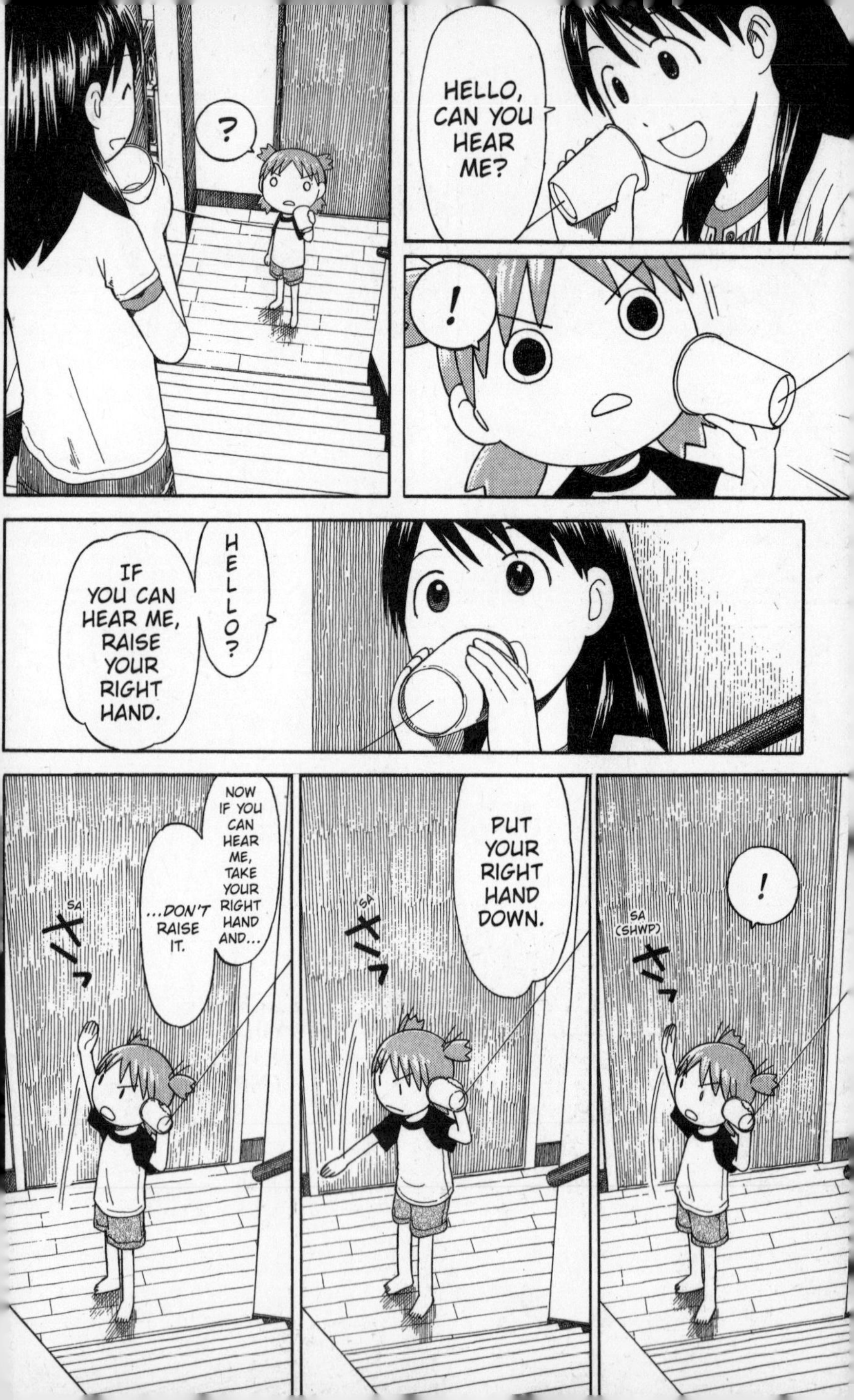
HELLO, CAN YOU HEAR ME?
!
?
HELLO?
IF YOU CAN HEAR ME, RAISE YOUR RIGHT HAND.
!
SA (SHWP)
PUT YOUR RIGHT HAND DOWN.
SA
NOW IF YOU CAN HEAR ME, TAKE YOUR RIGHT HAND AND...
...DON'T RAISE IT.
SA

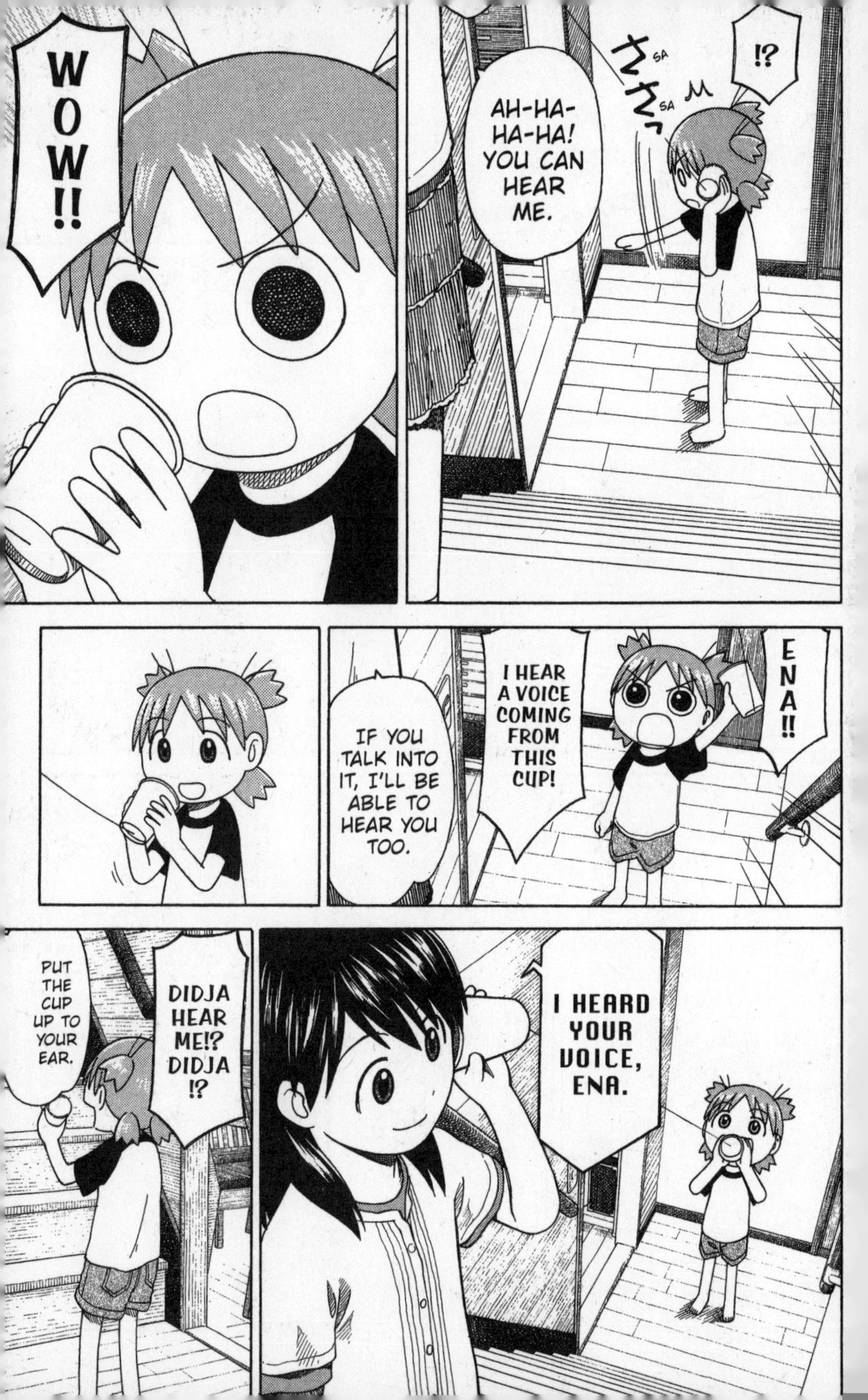
!?
さ SA さ SA
AH-HA-HA-HA! YOU CAN HEAR ME.
WOW!!
ENA!!
I HEAR A VOICE COMING FROM THIS CUP!
IF YOU TALK INTO IT, I'LL BE ABLE TO HEAR YOU TOO.
I HEARD YOUR VOICE, ENA.
DIDJA HEAR ME!? DIDJA!?
PUT THE CUP UP TO YOUR EAR.

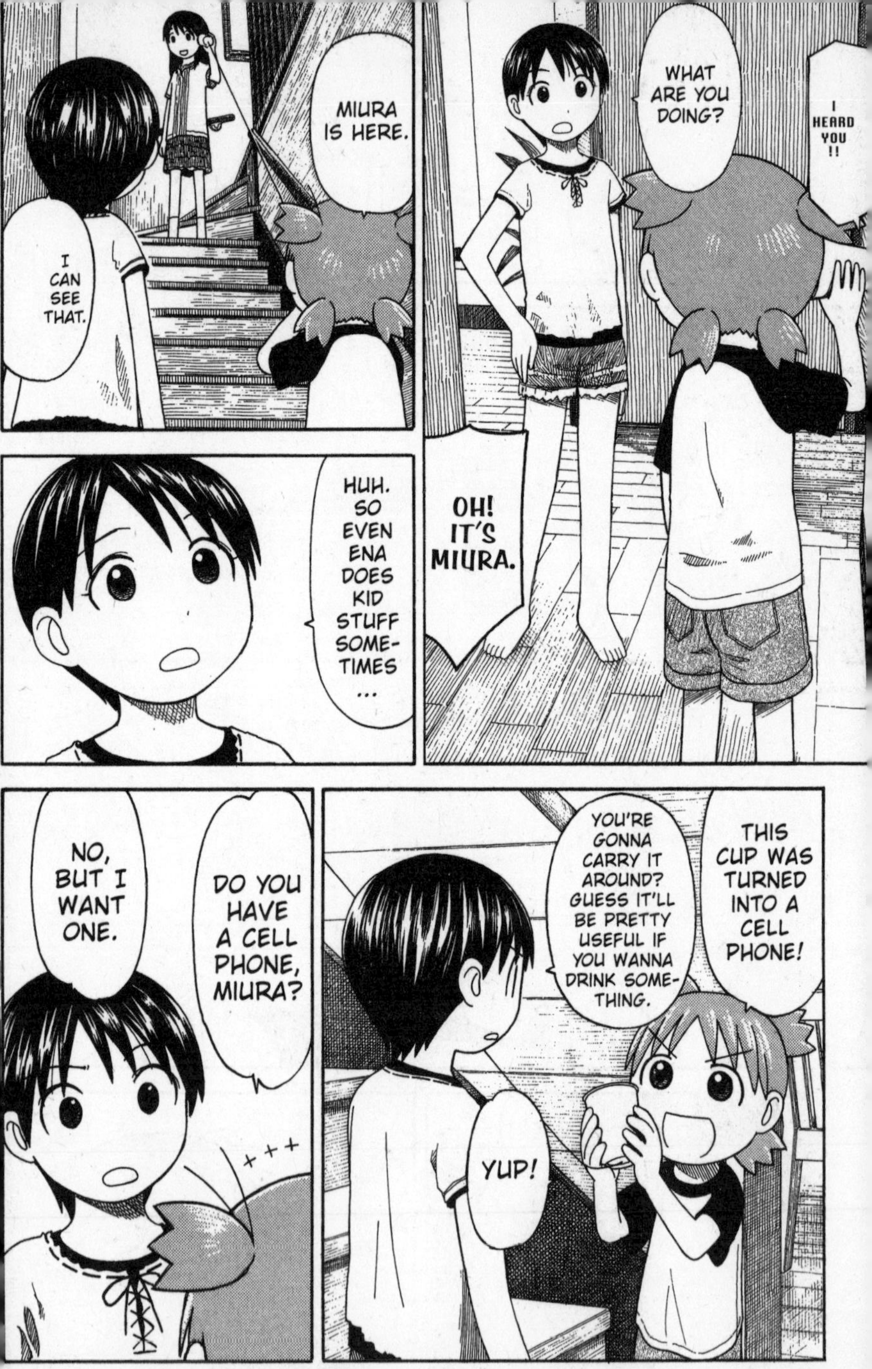
WHAT ARE YOU DOING?
I HEARD YOU !!
OH! IT'S MIURA.
MIURA IS HERE.
I CAN SEE THAT.
HUH. SO EVEN ENA DOES KID STUFF SOME-TIMES...
THIS CUP WAS TURNED INTO A CELL PHONE!
YOU'RE GONNA CARRY IT AROUND? GUESS IT'LL BE PRETTY USEFUL IF YOU WANNA DRINK SOME-THING.
YUP!
DO YOU HAVE A CELL PHONE, MIURA?
NO, BUT I WANT ONE.

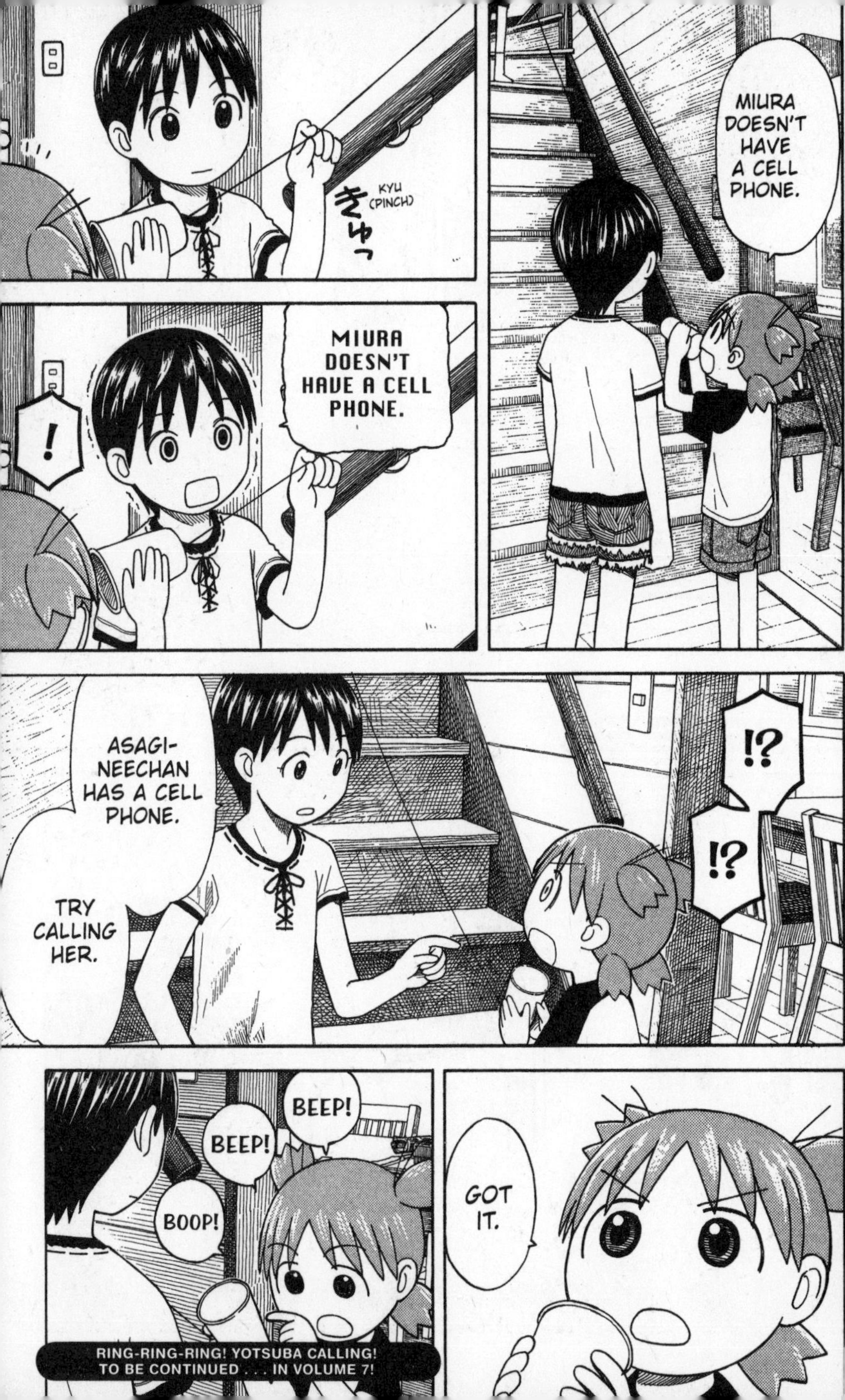
MIURA DOESN'T HAVE A CELL PHONE.
きゅっ
KYU (PINCH)
MIURA DOESN'T HAVE A CELL PHONE.
!
!?
!?
ASAGI-NEECHAN HAS A CELL PHONE.
TRY CALLING HER.
GOT IT.
BEEP!
BEEP!
BOOP!
RING-RING-RING! YOTSUBA CALLING! TO BE CONTINUED . . . IN VOLUME 7!

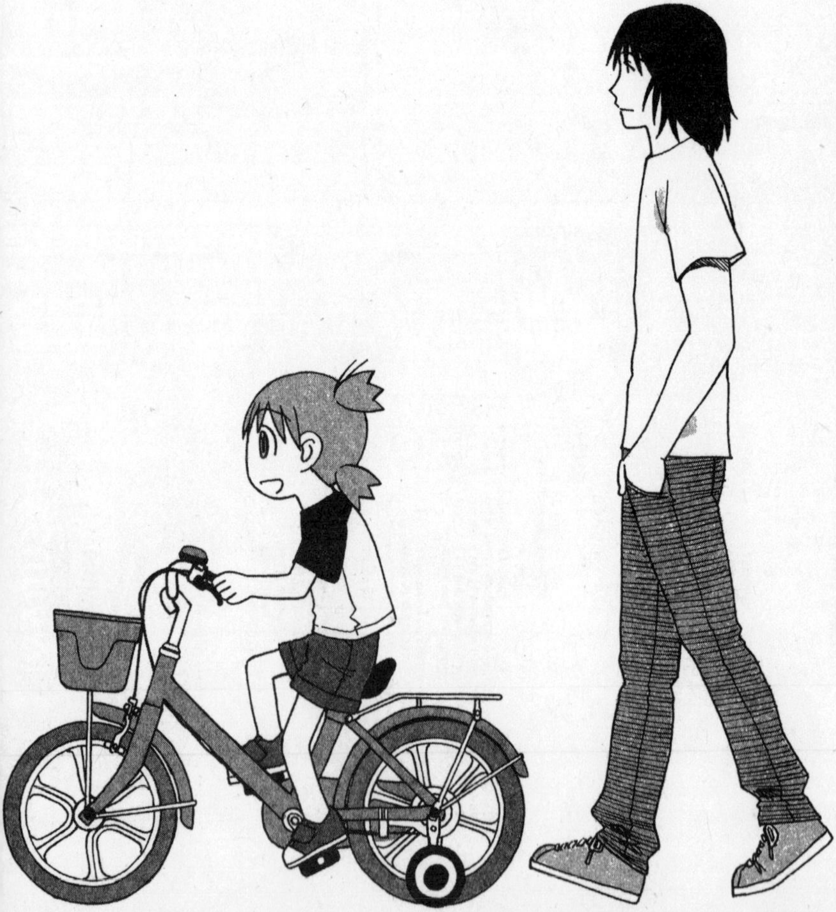

YOTSUBA&!

6

KIYOHIKO AZUMA

Translation: Amy Forsyth

Lettering: Terri Delgado

YOTSUBA&! Vol. 6

© KIYOHIKO AZUMA / YOTUBA SUTAZIO 2006

Edited by ASCII MEDIA WORKS

First published in Japan in 2006 by KADOKAWA CORPORATION, Tokyo.

English translation rights arranged with KADOKAWA CORPORATION, Tokyo, through Tuttle-Mori Agency, Inc., Tokyo.

English translation © 2009 by Yen Press, LLC

Yen Press

1290 Avenue of the Americas

New York, NY 10104

Visit us at yenpress.com

facebook.com/yenpress

twitter.com/yenpress

yenpress.tumblr.com

instagram.com/yenpress

First Yen Press Edition: September 2009

Yen Press is an imprint of Yen Press, LLC.

The Yen Press name and logo are trademarks of Yen Press, LLC.

The publisher is not responsible for websites (or their content) that are not owned by the publisher.

ISBN: 978-0-316-07324-0

20 19 18 17 16 15 14

WOR

Printed in the United States of America

YOTSUBA&!

ENJOY EVERYTHING.

TO BE CONTINUED!